# SCIENTIFIC INNOVATION, PHILOSOPHY, AND PUBLIC POLICY

# SCIENTIFIC INNOVATION, PHILOSOPHY, AND PUBLIC POLICY

*Edited by*

**Ellen Frankel Paul, Fred D. Miller, Jr., and Jeffrey Paul**

Published by the Press Syndicate of the University of Cambridge
The Pitt Building, Trumpington Street, Cambridge CB2 1RP, England
40 West 20th Street, New York, NY 10011, USA
10 Stamford Road, Oakleigh, Melbourne, Victoria 3166, Australia



First published 1996

Printed in the United States of America

*Library of Congress Cataloging-in-Publication Data*

Scientific Innovation, Philosophy, and Public Policy / edited by Ellen Frankel Paul,
Fred D. Miller, Jr., and Jeffrey Paul. p. cm.
Includes bibliographical references and index.
ISBN 0-521-58994-0
1. Medical policy—United States. 2. Science and state—United States.
3. Technology and state—United States. I. Paul, Ellen Frankel. II. Miller,
Fred Dycus, 1944- . III. Paul, Jeffrey.
RA395.A3S415 1996
338.97306-dc20 96-7838
CIP
ISBN 0-521-58994-0 paperback

The essays in this book have also been published,
without introduction and index, in the semiannual journal
*Social Philosophy & Policy*, Volume 13, Number 2,
which is available by subscription.

# CONTENTS

# INTRODUCTION

Recent and ongoing developments in science and technology—such as the prevention and treatment of disease through genetics and the development of increasingly sophisticated computer systems with wide-ranging applications—hold out the promise of vastly improving the quality of human life, but they can also raise serious ethical, legal, and public-policy questions. What direction should scientific inquiry take, and what moral principles should guide it? To what extent and in what ways should governments use public policy to encourage, support, influence, or inhibit scientific and technological research? And when governments do become involved, how can we prevent politics from exercising an inappropriate influence on the course of research?

The thirteen essays in this volume address these questions and related issues from a variety of perspectives. Some explore the implications of genetic engineering, discussing the role of government in funding research in this area and in regulating the uses of the medical technologies which may emerge from it. Some examine the propriety of using genetics to enhance human abilities and ask whether we need to be concerned about the inequalities that may result from such uses. Other essays discuss the need for laws protecting the intellectual property of scientific researchers, attempting to determine whether, on balance, patents promote progress by providing financial incentives or inhibit it by restricting research in areas where there is a danger of liability for patent infringement. Still other essays explore the reliability and safety of computer systems used in decision making, the ability of computer communications technologies to enhance privacy, or the possibility of creating intelligent computer systems which may be held morally responsible for their actions.

The first group of essays deals with recent advances in genetic technology. In "The Human Genome Project: Research Tactics and Economic Strategies," Alexander Rosenberg analyzes the motives behind the U.S. Human Genome Project (HGP) currently being funded by the National Institutes of Health, and attempts to assess the project's value. The announced objective of the HGP, he notes, is to sequence the entire three billion base pairs of the human genome; but this objective seems to be of doubtful scientific interest, given the present state of our functional knowledge of the genome. Transcribing the entire sequence will not tell us what the interesting regions of the genome are or what we can do once we have identified them; moreover, it is possible to discover genes which lead to abnormalities—and thus to identify promising areas of research—without knowing the entire sequence. Why, then, have members of the molecular-biology community been eager to pursue the sequencing project, and how have they been able to convince the government to support the HGP? Rosenberg argues that molecular biologists are actually interested not in the sequence itself, but in the various spin-offs and technological breakthroughs that will no doubt emerge from the project: research methods, computer programs, pieces of machinery for automated sequencing, and so on. The cost of obtaining these spin-offs, the significant risks involved, and uncertainties about whether the results of this research will be patentable, make it easy to understand why scientists have sought funding from the government. This funding is justified to the public in terms of its potential payoff in health-care benefits: new pharmaceuticals and treatments for genetically based diseases. Yet Rosenberg maintains that the centralized, top-down approach embodied in the HGP is not likely to produce such gains, and that more traditional grant-award processes, based on peer review of research proposals, would better serve to target funding to the most promising research in molecular biology.

The justification of genetic research in terms of its expected benefits is the subject of Allen Buchanan's contribution to this collection, "Choosing Who Will Be Disabled: Genetic Intervention and the Morality of Inclusion." Buchanan observes that proponents of public financing for the Human Genome Project and other genetic research appeal to an underlying ethic that appears to be universalistic and progressive: genetic science is to be deployed to improve the lives of all human beings. Some opponents of this research, however, including some advocates for the rights of disabled persons, fear that new developments hark back to the discredited eugenics movement that began in the late nineteenth century. These critics charge that the effort to prevent genetic defects expresses a devaluation of the lives of the disabled and rests on a system of values that is exclusionary and discriminatory rather than universalistic and progressive. At the very least, these critics complain, the pursuit of human improvement threatens serious injustices against the less than perfect, for the sake of mere beneficence. Buchanan argues that even though the dangers of exclusionary and discriminatory uses of genetic technology are real, the issue is not accurately posed as a conflict between justice and mere beneficence. Under some circumstances, he maintains, the failure to utilize technologies for intervention can itself constitute an injustice, not just toward those who can be spared serious disabilities but also toward other members of society. Nevertheless, Buchanan sees significant risks in the use of genetic technology to enhance human abilities: if such enhancements are available only to some, then those who are left behind may well face new forms of discrimination in employment, medical insurance, and other areas of their lives.

The moral implications of genetic engineering are also the subject of H. Tristram Engelhardt, Jr.'s essay "Germ-Line Genetic Engineering and Moral Diversity: Moral Controversies in a Post-Christian World." Engelhardt contends that germ-line engineering—the ability to redesign the human genetic inheritance, so that genetically engineered changes can be passed on to subsequent generations—raises the question of whether it is possible to articulate, in secular terms, any substantive moral constraints which could guide this undertaking. Notions of human nature and human excellence, Engelhardt maintains, are religiously or culturally dependent, and all substantive accounts of morality presuppose agreement on certain key moral assumptions. Thus, it is not possible to resolve controversies over how germ-line genetic engineering should be used without presupposing a particular religious or moral commitment. In a post-Christian world in which we no longer turn to religion for guidance, and in the absence of agreement on basic moral premises, Engelhardt argues that the only moral constraints that can guide developments in genetic engineering are the requirements not to use persons malevolently or without their permission. As a consequence, secular morality leaves open the possibility that human beings might be engineered with a number of radically different natures—and with different expectations regarding aging, suffering, disability, and death. Moreover, Engelhardt argues, we can draw no substantive moral distinction between using genetic engineering to cure diseases and using it to enhance human abilities and functions; indeed, we can expect scientists to turn their attention toward ways of adjusting human nature so that human beings may be better adapted to the environments in which they live.

As Engelhardt notes, genetic research raises questions about the morality of manipulating human nature. These questions—as well as issues relating to the treatment of human subjects in genetic studies, and the direction genetic research should take—have become an area of inquiry within the Human Genome Project itself. In "Self-Critical Federal Science? The Ethics Experiment within the U.S. Human Genome Project," Eric T. Juengst explores the ongoing attempt to deal with these issues in the HGP's Ethical, Legal, and Social Implications (ELSI) program. Juengst, a former director of the ELSI program, gives a brief account of the program's history and discusses various criticisms that have been raised against it. Some supporters of the HGP have claimed that the ELSI program threatens to undermine a worthwhile endeavor by creating unwarranted alarm about the implications of genetic research; some opponents of the HGP have viewed the ELSI program as an attempt to buy off the project's critics. Juengst argues, however, that the ELSI program is designed to minimize these potential difficulties, since ELSI research projects are initiated by nongovernment researchers who apply for grants through a time-tested peer-review process. Other critics of the ELSI program have argued that it is of questionable value because it lacks any formal mechanism for influencing policy in the area of genetic research and biotechnology. Juengst shows, however, that the program has influenced policy through informal channels—as is demonstrated by the program's success in formalizing guidelines for protecting the privacy of individuals and families who participate in genetic studies. Indeed, Juengst argues that the ELSI program should not evolve into a more formal commission designed to influence policy, since such a move would play into the hands of its critics. A better approach, he suggests, would be to continue to foster a community of researchers, interested observers, and critics who can engage in public deliberation about the implications of the HGP and propose policy changes through informal means.

Juengst's essay touches on some of the problems that can arise when governments become involved in funding and regulating scientific research. Henry I. Miller's contribution to this volume, "When Politics Drives Science: Lysenko, Gore, and U.S. Biotechnology Policy," explores these problems, focusing on the policies of the current United States administration. Miller sees disturbing parallels between the Lysenko era of Soviet biology beginning in the 1930s—which stunted progress in genetics and agriculture in the Soviet Union for decades—and current biotechnology policy in the United States. Lysenko and his followers ignored the scientific consensus of their time by advocating and practicing discredited Lamarckian biology, and Miller argues that the Clinton administration's approach to regulating the purported risks of the new biotechnology is contrary to the worldwide scientific consensus that biotechnology oversight should be both consistent with scientific principles and aimed at reducing risk, rather than trying, unrealistically, to eliminate it entirely. The administration's flawed policies, he contends, have adversely affected research, the development of new pharmaceuticals and medical treatments, and the availability of important consumer products. The leading figure in the administration's science policies is Vice President Albert Gore, and in the course of the essay, Miller sketches and critiques Gore's views on science and the role of government, and discusses instances in which the administration has demonstrated intolerance toward dissent on scientific issues and hostility toward pluralism in policymaking. He concludes that the administration's policies are at odds with sound scientific practice and leave decisions about the course of research vulnerable to political and ideological influences.

The next two essays deal with the impact of a specific area of government policy—the protection of patents—on the development of scientific and technological innovations. In "Biotechnology and the Utilitarian Argument for Patents," Michele Svatos analyzes defenses of patent systems which appeal to the contributions such systems make to human well-being. She notes that a utilitarian argument for patents, or for their extension to a new industry such as biotechnology, must show three things: it must show that patents make a significant contribution to stimulating innovation, that patents are the best way among the alternatives to stimulate innovation, and, at a more basic level, that stimulating technological innovation is itself justified on utilitarian grounds. Proponents of patents often simply assume that these three conditions are met, but Svatos maintains that there are strong reasons to doubt each of these three points. Using illustrations from agribusiness and the pharmaceuticals industry, she shows that the fear of infringing patents often inhibits innovation or leads to wasteful spending on efforts to "work around" a patented invention and achieve the same results by other means. She argues that alternatives to patents, such as tax incentives or subsidies, might be just as effective as patents at stimulating research and development, and that the kind of developments encouraged by patents—such as genetically engineered crops designed to tolerate greater use of fertilizers and pesticides—may not be beneficial all-things-considered, since they may harm the environment or exacerbate problems of overproduction in agriculture. Ultimately, Svatos says, we must either reject (or radically revise) the patent system on utilitarian grounds, or look to natural rights or considerations of distributive justice as the system's real foundation.

Like Svatos, Robert P. Merges is concerned with the impact of patents on scientific research. In his essay "Property Rights Theory and the Commons: The Case of Scientific Research," Merges describes a "creeping propertization" of science, in which patent rights play an increasing role in determining the kind of research that gets done and the level of cooperation among scientists. He recognizes that traditional science has always been subject to an elaborate system of informal property rights, but suggests that the growing use of formal rights poses a real challenge to the conduct of "pure science," as scientists are forced to curtail their inquiries in certain areas for fear of infringing on patents held by others. Scientists are already beginning to adapt to this new environment, however, as developments in the biotechnology community indicate. Merges shows that members of this community recognize a two-tiered system of property rights: one tier of relatively open, informal rights, which allow members of the community to share methods, findings, and research tools, including biological materials; and another tier of more formal rights, especially patents, which are exercised in commercial dealings with nonmembers. Merges finds these developments encouraging, and proposes a number of policy changes designed to strengthen the system. These changes would include an exemption from liability for patent infringement in the case of pure research conducted with federal funding, and the exclusion of certain areas of research from patentability altogether, in cases in which the administration costs of patents are deemed disproportionate to the expected benefits.

While Svatos and Merges address the relationship between patents and innovation, Svetozar Pejovich explores the more general connection between private property and technological development. In "Property Rights and Technological Innovation," Pejovich notes that the application of knowledge in the form of new technology involves risk, and requires that resources be drawn away from other uses; thus, the pace of technological innovation will vary depending on the ability of innovators to employ resources and to make decisions based on their assessment of risks and potential benefits. Their ability to do this, Pejovich argues, depends on the system of property rights within which they operate. To support this contention, Pejovich analyzes three types of property rights in business firms: privately owned firms under capitalism, labor-managed firms in decentralized socialist states, and state-owned firms in centrally planned economies. He maintains that a system of private property is best able to ensure that innovators have the necessary freedom and incentives to develop new technologies and integrate them into the economy. In labor-managed firms, workers have strong incentives to distribute profits among themselves rather than investing them in risky research-and-development efforts that may pay off, if they do pay off, only in the long term—perhaps long after the current workers have left the firm. In state-owned firms, decisions are made by extensive layers of committees, whose members face strong incentives not to disrupt the system: any would-be innovator faces great personal costs in pushing his idea through the official channels, but must share the benefits of the innovation with his colleagues and superiors. Pejovich argues that only a capitalist system, with private ownership and freedom of exchange, can afford innovators the flexibility they need to undertake risky ventures and bring new products to market. He maintains, moreover, that only a competitive market can properly assess the value of innovations, in terms of their voluntary acceptance by consumers. The slow rates of economic progress and technological growth in underdeveloped countries, Pejovich concludes, have been due to the inability or unwillingness of these countries to adopt and enforce the institutions of capitalism.

The propriety of treating animals as resources for human use is the focus of R. G. Frey's contribution to this volume, "Medicine, Animal Experimentation, and the Moral Problem of Unfortunate Humans." Frey discusses recent strides in medical science and technology which hold out promise for the mitigation and removal of some of the most terrible human illnesses—including developments in cross-species transplantation and in genetic engineering of animals on behalf of gene therapy in humans. He notes, however, that these medical uses of animals for human benefit occur in an intellectual and ethical environment in which the trade-off between animal sacrifice and human gain is the subject of intense moral scrutiny. We need to be able to justify this use of animals, Frey contends, and his essay sets out the beginnings of such a justification—one that permits a good deal of animal experimentation while at the same time accepting that animals count morally, that their lives are of value, and that discrimination on the basis of species is improper. His central premise is that animals, like humans, are experiential beings, whose lives can increase or decrease in value depending on how they are treated. Thus, if we seek to justify experiments on animals, but find them unjustifiable when conducted on humans, we must discover some characteristic of humans which ensures that human lives, no matter how low their quality, will always be more valuable than animal lives, no matter how high their quality. Yet Frey argues that any characteristic we might propose—such as rationality, intention, or the capacity to make choices—will be of questionable moral relevance, and, in any case, will not be possessed by at least some unfortunate human beings. He concludes, then, that if the appeal to benefit justifies the experimental use of animals in medicine, it will also justify the use of some human beings.

The collection's next three essays relate to advances in computer technology and their implications. David Friedman's "A World of Strong Privacy: Promises and Perils of Encryption" explores a number of new and emerging technologies—public-key encryption of messages, anonymous remailers, and digital cash—which make possible a level of individual privacy previously unknown. Friedman suggests that these developments, coupled in the future with computer networks capable of supporting virtual-reality communications, will bring about a world in which a large part of human interaction is technologically secure from surveillance or interference. This level of privacy, he argues, will make possible a society of competing virtual communities with competing legal codes, in which the only sanction anyone can impose on anyone else is the refusal to communicate with him. It will make political censorship more difficult and freedom of association more secure. As Friedman notes, however, it will also make possible less-benign outcomes: pirate publishers will find it easy to violate the copyrights of books, music, or computer programs; and, more ominously, criminal enterprises will be able to conduct business on-line, dealing anonymously with their customers but committing real crimes against their victims. Strong privacy will make it difficult for law-enforcement agencies to deal with such problems, and two major government initiatives are already underway in the U.S. to control the emerging technologies: the International Traffic in Arms Regulations are being used to prevent the export of encryption programs to other countries, and a government standard for telecommunications encryption (the "Clipper Chip") has been proposed as a means of allowing authorized law-enforcement agents to gain access to encrypted communications. Nevertheless, Friedman doubts that these strategies will be effective in the long run, since export controls can be circumvented and since criminals have the option of pre-encrypting their messages before they transmit them over encrypted telecommunications lines. A future of strong privacy, he says, may be impossible to prevent.

While Friedman's essay focuses on the use of computers in communications, James H. Fetzer's essay deals with their use in safety-critical applications—applications in which the conclusions reached by computer programs can have a profound impact on human lives. In "Computer Reliability and Public Policy: Limits of Knowledge of Computer-Based

Systems," Fetzer examines the public-policy implications of "expert" computer systems, which combine a base of knowledge in a particular field with heuristic decision-making techniques in order to simulate human expertise. As an illustration, he describes the MYCIN system for the diagnosis of diseases of the blood, which takes inputs regarding a patient's condition, applies over five hundred decision rules based on current medical knowledge of blood disease, and renders a diagnosis and recommended treatment. While such systems can be extremely useful, their reliability is necessarily uncertain; as Fetzer observes, it is possible for errors to creep into such systems from several sources. The knowledge base on which the system is founded may be flawed or incomplete, because the human sources of the system's expertise were not fully informed about the relevant field; the "knowledge engineers" who gather information from human experts may introduce errors or distortions; the programmer who translates the information into a computer program may make mistakes that go undetected. Moreover, highly complex software systems can be extremely sensitive to small changes in conditions, making their performance difficult to predict. Since these systems are often used to make life-and-death decisions affecting human beings, Fetzer stresses the importance of submitting them to the most rigorous level of testing. Merely testing individual hardware and software components is not enough, he argues: only system prototyping—testing entire computer systems within the environments for which they are intended—can give us confidence in the safety of such systems.

As more and more sophisticated computer systems are used for tasks that involve decision making, some theorists have speculated that such systems might one day be held responsible for their decisions and actions. William Bechtel explores this possibility in his contribution to this volume, "Responsibility and Decision Making in the Era of Neural Networks." Bechtel focuses his discussion on complex computer systems known as neural networks, which have recently become popular as tools for modeling human mental functioning, including decision making. A key question about such networks is whether they should be thought of as having propositional attitudes—beliefs about the world which can bear on the decisions they make. The capacity for holding such beliefs is, of course, an important part of the framework we use to account for moral responsibility in human beings, and Bechtel argues that neural networks can indeed be said to hold such beliefs. In the course of the essay, Bechtel sketches a brief history of the development of neural networks in the field of artificial intelligence (AI) and outlines ongoing debates over how to characterize their functioning. He challenges the common objection that we should not assign responsibility to AI systems since they are designed by humans and simply carry out the instructions set forth in their programs. These systems, he notes, are so complex that it is often impossible for their designers to determine in advance how they will respond in a wide range of situations; moreover, many of these systems are designed to simulate learning, so that their reactions to given situations may change over time. In the end, he argues, many of the same reasons we have for attributing moral responsibility to human agents will lead us to attribute responsibility to future AI systems based on neural networks.

The final essay, Susan Haack's "Preposterism and Its Consequences," examines the impact that research practices in the sciences have had on the way philosophical research is carried out. Haack argues that as philosophers have emulated the scientists' system of grant-funded research projects, the quality of philosophical research has significantly declined. The grant-seeking mentality encourages philosophers to inflate the importance of their research and promotes inquiry into trendy areas that are likely to attract funding. This creates a research environment which, Haack contends, is inhospitable to genuine inquiry. Similarly, the proliferation of philosophy journals, and of philosophy books put out by university presses, has led to an increase in the quantity, but a decline in the quality, of published work. This leads to a waste of energy and resources, a flood of articles that no one has the time to read, and a flood of books that soon go out of print—with the result that it becomes increasingly difficult to determine which works are actually of value. As the pressure to publish increases, philosophers are able to devote less time to developing their theories and polishing their work; yet, as Haack argues, worthwhile philosophical inquiry is a long-term endeavor—it is susceptible to false starts and dead ends, and may come to fruition only after many years, if at all. The current system, she concludes, is detrimental to the pursuit of serious philosophical research.

These thirteen essays—written by prominent philosophers, economists, and legal theorists—explore the challenges posed to our moral theories and public institutions by ongoing advances in research and technological development. Taken together, they offer valuable insights into the nature of scientific innovation and its implications for our social policies and practices.

## ACKNOWLEDGMENTS

The editors wish to acknowledge several individuals at the Social Philosophy and Policy Center, Bowling Green State University, who provided invaluable assistance in the preparation of this volume. They include Mary Dilsaver, Terrie Weaver, and Pamela Phillips.

We wish to thank Executive Manager Kory Swanson, for his tireless administrative support; Publication Specialist Tamara Sharp, for her patient attention to detail; and Managing Editor Harry Dolan, for editorial assistance above and beyond the call of duty.

# CONTRIBUTORS

**Alexander Rosenberg** is Professor of Philosophy and Director of the Honors Program at the University of Georgia. In addition to coauthoring *Hume and the Problem of Causation* (1981), he has written four books in the philosophy of social science, particularly economics, and three books on the philosophy of biology, focusing primarily on the relationship between molecular genetics and functional biology. He has received fellowships from the Guggenheim Foundation, the National Science Foundation, and the American Council of Learned Societies, and in 1993 he was awarded the Lakatos Prize in the Philosophy of Science for *Economics—Mathematical Politics or Science of Diminishing Returns?* (1992). His most recent book is *Instrumental Biology, or The Disunity of Science* (1994). In 1994-95, he taught philosophy at Oxford University.

**Allen Buchanan** is Grainger Professor of Business Ethics and Professor of Philosophy and Medical Ethics at the University of Wisconsin, Madison. He has written numerous articles in ethics, epistemology, political philosophy, bioethics, and other areas of applied ethics, and is the author of *Marx and Justice: The Radical Critique of Liberalism* (1982), *Ethics, Efficiency, and the Market* (1985), *Deciding for Others: The Ethics of Surrogate Decision Making* (with Dan W. Brock, 1989), and *Secession: The Morality of Political Divorce from Fort Sumter to Lithuania and Quebec* (1991).

**H. Tristram Engelhardt, Jr.** is Professor in the Department of Medicine, Baylor College of Medicine, and in the Department of Philosophy, Rice University. A member of the Center for Medical Ethics and Health Policy, he serves as editor of the *Journal of Medicine and Philosophy* and coeditor of *Christian Bioethics: Non-Ecumenical Studies in Medical Morality*. He is also coeditor of the book series "Philosophy and Medicine: Philosophical Studies in Contemporary Culture," published by Kluwer Academic Publishers, and of the series "Clinical Medical Ethics," published by Georgetown University Press. His most recent volume is a second edition of his book *The Foundations of Bioethics* (1996).

**Eric T. Juengst** is Associate Professor of Biomedical Ethics at the Case Western Reserve University School of Medicine. He received his Ph.D. in philosophy from Georgetown University in 1985 and has taught at the medical schools of Penn State University and the University of California at San Francisco. From 1990 to 1994, he was Chief of the Ethical, Legal, and Social Implications Branch of the National Center for Human Genome Research at the U.S. National Institutes of Health.

**Henry I. Miller** is Robert Wesson Fellow of Scientific Philosophy and Public Policy at the Hoover Institution, Stanford University, and Consulting Professor at Stanford's Institute for International Studies. He graduated from the Massachusetts Institute of Technology with a B.S. degree in life sciences and attended the University of California, San Diego, receiving the M.S. and M.D. degrees. After completing his clinical training in internal medicine at the Beth Israel Hospital in Boston, Dr. Miller spent three years as a Research Associate at the National Institutes of Health. He joined the Food and Drug Administration in 1979 and served in a number of posts involved with the new biotechnology, including Special Assistant to the Commissioner and, from 1989 to 1993, founding director of the FDA's Office of Biotechnology. His research focuses on a variety of public policy issues related to science and technology, particularly biotechnology. He is the author of more than 150 publications.

**Michele Svatos** is Assistant Professor of Philosophy at Iowa State University. Her work is in virtue ethics, bioethics, intellectual property, and philosophy of economics. She is currently working on a book manuscript entitled *The Foundation and Structure of Virtue Ethics*.

**Robert P. Merges** is Professor of Law at the University of California, Berkeley, School of Law (Boalt Hall). He is the author of numerous articles on the law and economics of intellectual property, as well as the leading law school casebook on patent law. He has testified before Congress many times on intellectual property matters. Among other professional activities, he serves as a special consultant to the Howard Hughes Medical Research Foundation.

**Svetozar Pejovich** is Professor of Economics at Texas A&M University and Senior Research Fellow at the International Centre for Economic Research, Turin, Italy. He is the author of *Economic Analysis of Institutions and Systems* (1995), *The Economics of Property Rights: Towards a Theory of Comparative Economic Systems* (1990), and *Socialism: Institutional, Philosophical, and Economic Issues* (1987).

**R. G. Frey** is Professor of Philosophy at Bowling Green State University and Senior Research Fellow of both the Kennedy Institute of Ethics at Georgetown University and the Westminster Institute of Ethics and Public Policy at the University of Western Ontario. He received his D.Phil. from Oxford University in 1970, and has taught at the University of Liverpool, at St. John's College, Oxford University, and at the University of Toronto. He is the author of *Interests and Rights* (1980) and *Rights, Killing, and Suffering: Moral Vegetarianism and Applied Ethics* (1983). In addition, he is the editor of *Utility and Rights* (1985), and the coeditor (with Christopher W. Morris) of *Liability and Responsibility: Essays in Law* *and Morals* (1991), *Violence, Terrorism, and Justice* (1991), and *Value, Welfare, and Morality* (1993).

**David Friedman** is Professor of Law at Santa Clara University, specializing in economic analysis of law and computer law. He received a bachelor's degree in chemistry and physics from Harvard University in 1965 and a doctorate in physics from the University of Chicago in 1971. He is the author of two books and many articles, mostly on economics, law, and political theory. He has taught economics at Virginia Polytechnic Institute, the University of California at Los Angeles, the University of California at Irvine, Tulane University, the University of Chicago, and Cornell University.

**James H. Fetzer** is Professor of Philosophy at the University of Minnesota, Duluth. The author of *Scientific Knowledge* (1981), *Artificial Intelligence: Its Scope and Limits* (1990), *Philosophy and Cognitive Science* (1991), and *Philosophy of Science* (1993), he is the coauthor, editor, or coeditor of twelve other books. In addition, he is the editor of the journal *Minds and Machines*, a coeditor of the journal *Synthese*, and the editor of the series "Studies in Cognitive Systems." He has extensive publications in the philosophy of science, cognitive science, artificial intelligence, and computer science, including more than eighty articles and reviews.

**William Bechtel** is Professor in the Philosophy-Neuroscience-Psychology Program at Washington University. He works in both the history and philosophy of biology and the conceptual foundations of cognitive science and neuroscience. Currently, he is engaged in a study of the development of cell biology as a scientific discipline in the period from 1945 to 1965. His books include *Connectionism and the Mind* (with Adele Abrahamsen, 1990) and *Discovering Complexity: Decomposition and Localization as Scientific Research Strategies* (with Robert C. Richardson, 1993). He is also the editor of the journal *Philosophical Psychology* and the coeditor, with George Graham, of *The Blackwell Companion to Cognitive Science*.

**Susan Haack** is Professor of Philosophy at the University of Miami. She was educated at Oxford University and Cambridge University, and has taught at the University of Warwick, U.K. Her books include *Deviant Logic* (1974), *Philosophy of Logics* (1978), and, most recently, *Evidence and Inquiry: Towards Reconstruction in Epistemology* (1993). She has also written numerous articles on philosophy of logic and language, epistemology and metaphysics, pragmatism, and feminism. *Deviant Logic, Fuzzy Logic*, a second, expanded edition of her first book, is scheduled to be published by the University of Chicago Press in 1996. She was president of the C. S. Peirce Society in 1994, and received the University of Miami's award for excellence in teaching during the same year.

# THE HUMAN GENOME PROJECT: RESEARCH TACTICS AND ECONOMIC STRATEGIES*

By Alexander Rosenberg

In the Museum of Science and Technology in San Jose, California, there is a display dedicated to advances in biotechnology. Most prominent in the display is a double helix of telephone books stacked in two staggered spirals from the floor to the ceiling twenty-five feet above. The books are said to represent the current state of our knowledge of the eukaryotic genome: the primary sequences of DNA polynucleotides for the gene products which have been discovered so far in the twenty years since cloning and sequencing the genome became possible.

## I. The Allegory of the Phone Books

In order to grasp what is problematical about the Human Genome Project (HGP), I want you to hold on to this image of a stack of phone books, or rather two stacks, helical in shape. Imagine that each of the phone books is about the size of the Manhattan white pages, and that the two stacks of phone books reach up a mile or so into the sky. Assume that the books are well glued together, and that there are no gusts of wind strong enough to blow the towers down. The next thing you are to imagine is that there are no names in these phone books, or on their covers—only numbers. We do know that each phone number is seven digits long, and we know that the numbers have been assigned to names listed alphabetically, but without the names we can't tell to whom a number belongs. Moreover, the numbers are not printed in columns down the pages that will enable us to tell where one phone number ends and the next begins. Instead of being printed in columns down the page, the numbers begin at the top left and fill up the page like print, without any punctuation between them. They are grouped within area codes, of course, and we can tell when one area-code list stops and another begins, but we don't know the area codes, still less what geographical areas they cover.

Sounds like a set of phone books that would be pretty difficult to use, doesn't it? Well, let's make them harder to use. Of course, none of the individual phone books have names or any other identifying features on their covers. In fact, the books don't have covers, and, what's more, the

* I am grateful to Everly Fleischer for advice on an early draft of this essay, and to Elizabeth Willott for extended criticism of the penultimate one.

binding of each directory was removed before the stack was constructed, and a random number of successive pages of adjacent phone books were rebound together. This rebinding maintains the order of pages, but it means that each volume begins and ends somewhere within each directory, and there is no indication of where these beginnings and endings are.

Can we make our mile-and-a-half-high double stack of phone books even harder to use? Sure. Imagine that somewhere between 90 and 95 percent of all the phone numbers in all the phone books have been disconnected, or have never even been assigned to customers—and of course we don't know which ones they are. These unused numbers look just like sequences of assigned phone numbers; they even have area-code punctuation, though there is no geographical area assigned to these area codes. Remember, we can't tell which area codes represent a real area and which do not. We do know that between 5 and 10 percent of the numbers are in area codes which have been assigned, and that within these assigned area codes there are long lists of phone numbers of real phone-company customers. Although we don't know which are the area codes that are real, nor where they are in the directories, we do know some interesting things about these area-code phone number listings. First, sometimes area codes and their phone numbers are repeated one or more times rather close together in a single volume, and sometimes they are repeated in distant volumes in the stack. Second, sometimes there are sequences of phone numbers which are very similar in digits to the numbers in a real area code, but their area codes are unassigned and all the phone numbers are unused. Even within almost all of the real area codes, the lists of assigned phone numbers are interrupted by long sequences of digits which, when grouped into phone numbers, are unassigned; sometimes within a real area code there are several of these sequences, longer than the sequences of assigned phone numbers within the area code.

Perhaps you are tiring of all the bizarre details of this idea of telephone numbers impossible to read. So I will stop adding detail to our picture. But don't let go of the picture. Imagine that someone, a numerologist, say, now proposes to you that for three billion dollars of the U.S. government's money, he will put together a team that will transcribe all the digits in the mile-and-a-half-high double stack of phone books into a computer. It's not the phone numbers he offers to transcribe, just the digits—one after the other—unsegmented into the phone numbers. The numerologist promises to make the list of digits available to anyone who asks for it, free. Assume further that three billion dollars is the cost of copying out the numbers, with no hidden profit for the numerologist.

I suppose one's first reaction to such a proposal would be to thank the numerologist for his offer, but to decline it on the grounds that the list of digits is of no immediate use to anyone, even if we were going to have a very large party and wanted to invite everyone who had a phone number.

But since it is in our nature as philosophers to wonder, we ask our numerologist, "What's in it for you? Why would you do this transcription at cost, without any profit?"

Imagine that our numerologist is candid and comes clean as follows: He is not really a numerologist, but rather represents a relatively large number of privately held direct-sales companies, each of which has a potentially very useful product, which it can only sell over the telephone. The companies know that there are enough potential customers out there to go around, so that each of their shareholders can become rich through the sale of the very useful product they can manufacture, if only they had the phone numbers of the customers. So, our numerologist/direct-sales-marketing representative says that if the companies he represents had all the digits, they could sell the products, make every customer better off, and become rich themselves.

There are two responses one should make to the numerologist's admission. The first is: Even if you can segment the three billion digits into phone numbers, why should the government pay for the phone lists, if you and the consumers are the ones to profit? The second and more important response is: Surely putting all those digits from all those books into a large computer file, without being able to tell the meaningless ones from the meaningful ones, just for starters, is not the best way to get in touch with potential customers.

Consider the first question: Why should the government pay for the phone list? The answer given on behalf of the direct-sales-marketing companies is that their products are guaranteed to help people stay healthier and live longer. But in that case, if they think putting all these phone numbers in a computer memory is so valuable, why don't they arrange to fund the project themselves, and reap the rewards by selling the products? The answer we get is that their capital is tied up in even more valuable investments, and besides, there is a free-rider problem. If any of them get together to fund the transcription, the disks on which the transcription is recorded could easily fall into the hands of other members of the trade association without these other firms paying. So, we might reply, what's it to us? Why should the government get you out of this predicament? If it does, will you cut the government in on your profits from using the phone numbers? Oh no, comes the reply. That would be a disincentive to developing new products to sell to people on the phone list.

But wait a minute, let's consider the second question. What's the use of a transcription of all these digits? Aren't there far better ways to get the names of customers with telephones? In fact, is this any way of getting the names of customers at all? Well, comes the response, what if developing the technology to transcribe all these phone numbers will also enable us to identify the real area codes, to segment the digits into meaningful phone numbers, and to begin to tell which ones are actually in use?

That might justify some investment in transcribing the phone numbers. Unfortunately, our numerologist can give us no such assurance. At most he can promise that once we have the total list of real area codes, 5 to 10 percent of the list of digits will become valuable. Are there ways of identifying these area codes? we ask. Certainly, says our interlocutor. Well, what are you waiting for, go and find them. When you have done so, you may or may not have any use for the transcription of all the digits. Until then, however, you would be wasting your time, or someone else's, along with a lot of money, government or private, to transcribe all these digits, including the ones in the unassigned area codes and the numbers with no customers.

This allegory, I suggest, pretty well matches the biochemical facts about the human genome, the molecular structure of the nucleic acids that compose it, the prospective payoff to sequencing the three billion base pairs of the human genome, and the policy advocated by the proponents of the HGP. Here is a brief explanation of my simile between the human genome and the mile-and-a-half-high double stack of phone books: The human genome contains about three billion base pairs of purine and pyrimidine nucleic acids; these are the digits in our "phone numbers." It is hoped that the average cost of providing the whole sequence can be brought down to one dollar per base. Three of these bases constitute a phone number with three digits—a codon of three nucleic acid bases. Ninety to 95 percent of these sequences code for DNA that has no role in gene transcription—this is the so-called junk DNA.[1] They compose phone numbers that are not in use. Of the 5 to 10 percent of the nucleotide sequences that do code for proteins, we know little that distinguishes them from the noncoding "junk." These sequences of codons that do code for gene products are the phone numbers in real area codes. Unfortunately, we cannot tell them from area codes that contain only "phone numbers" not in use. In our story we didn't know how many area codes there were, where they were in the phone books, how often they were reprinted, or how many corrupt sequences of meaningless phone numbers they contained.

Similarly, we do not know whether there are 50,000 genes or 100,000. We don't know their nucleotide size, the number of their copies, their locations, the number of stretches of meaningless numbers—the introns within each of them. The DNA for gene products is dispersed throughout the noncoding part of the genome. Within regions that code for gene products, there are long stretches of polynucleotides that, like nonsense or junk DNA, code for nothing, and whose messenger RNA sequences are deleted before protein synthesis. Some gene sequences are repeated two

[1] Molecular biologists are sensitive to the fact that calling 95 percent of the human genome "junk DNA" undercuts the rationale for sequencing the whole genome. As a result, some are suggesting that the scientific community was over-hasty in coming to the unanimous conclusion that DNA sequences with no known possible function are "nonsense."

or more times throughout the genome, on the same or different chromosomes, as are some stretches of junk DNA. Sometimes the same strand of DNA can code for two different gene products depending on codon-punctuation. Although we know what the start and stop codons are, we don't know how to segment the sequence of bases to tell either where a gene for some product begins, or which of the possible triplets of successive bases is the reading frame for the product—we don't know which among the digits in a sequence is the first digit of a phone number, even though we know that each phone number is three digits (three nucleotides) long.

## II. Straw Allegory?

How can proponents of the HGP defend its scientific integrity? One thing they cannot do is respond to the allegory with a denial that the HGP really contemplates sequencing three billion base pairs of mainly nonsense DNA as one of its primary missions. Such a reaction would of course grant the aptness of the allegory and admit the pointlessness of the project of completing the sequence. If sequencing the entire genome were not integral to the original or current aim of the HGP, its proponents would of course be guilty of seriously misleading the governments which support the project. The fact is, however, that sequencing the whole human genome has been and still is the goal of the HGP.

Writing in the fall of 1993 in *Gene*, James Watson, the original director of the National Center for Human Genome Research, described the HGP as follows:

> Its mission was not only to make much higher resolution genetic maps but also to assemble all the human DNA as overlapping cloned fragments running the entire length of all the human chromosomes. In their turn, these DNA pieces were to be sequenced and their respective genes revealed. Upon completion of the Human Genome Project we would then know how many human genes exist and so whether the then estimated 100,000 number was either too low or too high.[2]

But making physical maps of the human genome at varying scales and determining the primary sequence of all the DNA will not answer these important questions about how many genes there are.

In October 1993, Francis Collins, who replaced James Watson as director of the National Center for Human Genome Research, and David Galas, associate director of the Department of Energy's Office of Health and Environmental Research, wrote:

[2] James B. Watson, "Looking Forward," *Gene*, vol. 135 (1993), pp. 309–15.

> Although there is still debate about the need to sequence the entire genome, it is now more widely recognized that the DNA sequence will reveal a wealth of biological information that could not be obtained in other ways. The sequence so far obtained from model organisms has demonstrated the existence of a large number of genes not previously suspected. . . . Comparative sequence analysis has also confirmed the high degree of homology between genes across species. It is clear that sequence information represents a rich source for future investigation. Thus the Human Genome Project must continue to pursue its original goal, namely, to obtain the complete human DNA sequence.[3]

This passage is quite revealing for what it omits. It is certainly true that knowing the entire sequence would provide a wealth of information—but what kind of information, biological or physical? Collins tells us it is biological; yet this is not clear.

What is the difference? Biological information is information about the functions of systems. Physical information is information about physical composition and structure. Knowledge of physical composition and structure is of little use in determining function. For example, knowing that what British speakers call a "rubber" is composed of that material is of little help in learning its use. The American term "eraser" identifies the same object by its function. It is such functional identifications that biologists seek first. Uncovering structure is a later goal of inquiry, a goal that requires prior functional or biological information. But characterizing the primary sequence of the human genome is a paradigmatically structural inquiry, not a functional one. By itself, sequence data can provide no information about functional units like genes, or even homologies—similarities of primary sequences—among them.

Despite Collins and Galas's claim, the sequences so far obtained for simpler organisms do not demonstrate the existence of hitherto unsuspected genes, because sequence data cannot demonstrate this. In genomes as complicated as the mammalian one, sequence data can only help *localize* genes—functional units—whose existence has already been established by genetic techniques—i.e., breeding experiments or pedigree studies in the lineage of interest or some suitable model organism. Establishing sequence homologies between known genes of model organisms and parts of the DNA of humans is of the highest biological importance. First, however, we must identify the gene of the model system, then localize and sequence it, and finally hybridize it with human genomic DNA. The result will be the identification of a human gene, which can then be sequenced! Note that prior sequencing of the whole

[3] Francis Collins and David Galas, "A New Five Year Plan for the U.S. Human Genome Project," *Science*, vol. 262 (1993), p. 46.

human genome need play no part in this process, and cannot help divide up the human genome into genes. And except for genes which are physically unique to our species, of which there is no reason to think there are any, knowing the whole sequence of the human genome is unnecessary and insufficient for the identification of any genes. It certainly cannot tell us how many genes there are! Nevertheless, Collins and Galas's statement unequivocally commits the HGP to providing the whole sequence long before we have the functional information that might make it worth having.

In an article based on an interview with Director Collins, *Science* reporter Leslie Roberts wrote:

> Despite the slow progress, there is little sentiment for abandoning the goal of all-out sequencing. . . . But some thought is being given to a short cut called one-pass sequencing. The original plan calls for sequencing the whole genome several times to ensure an error rate of 0.001%. "Suppose we try one-pass coverage with 1% error rate but it only costs one tenth as much?" asks Collins. The idea, then, would be to return to the really *interesting* regions and sequence them again.[4]

The questions raised by this claim are: What are the interesting regions, how are they identified, and what can we do once we have identified them? But the answers to *none* of these questions will emerge from a complete sequence of the human genome. And that is what is wrong with Watson's claim quoted above as well. The interesting regions are the ones whose gene products are implicated in the production of proteins in the ribosomes, or the regions of DNA which produce messenger RNA for enzymes and other proteins, or the regions which produce enzymes that control the gene's expression of other enzyme- and protein-producing parts of the DNA, or enzymes that control the controllers, etc. How are these genes to be identified? They are not to be identified from "the bottom up," because we do not know *ab initio* which DNA sequences do any of these things; rather, we must work from gene products back to DNA sequences.

It is true that once we know where a functional gene's sequence lies on the chromosome and can isolate it, the sequence can tell us a great deal about the gene product. This is true because the genetic code has been broken and we know which amino acid molecule—the building block for proteins—is coded by which sequence of three DNA bases—the so-called "codon." Instead of analyzing proteins directly, we can analyze the gene sequence, and it can tell us more about the protein it codes for, and tell us

[4] Leslie Roberts, "Taking Stock of the Genome Project," *Science*, vol. 262 (1993), p. 21. It is worth noting that unless the 1 percent error areas are identified, the entire genome will have to be resequenced to locate the areas to be double-checked.

faster, because we have technical means of breaking down the DNA to read off its sequence, and we do not have equally powerful techniques for breaking down the protein and reading off its sequence of amino acids. It is the advent of these means for sequencing DNA which has made nucleic acids the locus for biotechnological research to design new pharmaceuticals, and has whetted molecular geneticists' appetites for the HGP.

To establish the existence of a gene (or a mutation within a gene) functionally requires identifying its product—the phenotype which it codes for and which assorts in a family of organisms in accordance with well-known regularities of population genetics. Suppose the phenotype is an abnormality, as it often is in current research, which results from a biochemical defect in the gene product. In this case, we may be able to make very great therapeutic advances without knowing much about the full DNA sequence, where it is, how long it is, how often it is repeated, etc. All we need to do is isolate the messenger RNA (mRNA) for the particular gene product, usually expressed most heavily in normal organs and tissues whose defective function we seek to understand. Thus, the brain will be richer in gene products which effect neural processes than the liver; and the richest harvest of mRNAs from the liver will be for gene products involved in storage of glycogen, and filtering of hemoglobin. Having identified high concentrations of the mRNA distinctive to the tissue, without proceeding back to the gene, we can employ well-known methods[5] to make synthetic genes and make large numbers of copies of them. Once inserted in the right vectors, these synthetic genes can produce enough protein product to provide drugs which will treat hereditary disorders.

It has not escaped the attention of researchers that being able to produce these synthetic genes—complementary DNAs or cDNAs – from mRNAs is a far more attractive route to understanding gene expression and gene regulation than sequencing the whole genome. Indeed, this realization is at the basis of a potentially lucrative research program in pharmacology. After all, by mixing, say, radioactively labeled cDNAs with the genome, and observing where the radioactive cDNA molecules bind to the genome or "hybridize," molecular geneticists can zero in on the 5 to 10 percent of the DNA that codes for gene products—i.e., the genes—without wasting any time sequencing junk. Accordingly, few researchers are asking for government subsidies to produce cDNAs; instead, they are attempting to patent them.

Of course, it is true that once we have identified a gene through its function—sometimes the immediate gene product, sometimes an observable phenotypic trait—we can begin to try to localize the gene to a chro-

[5] In particular, two discoveries make this procedure possible. A viral enzyme, reverse transcriptase, has been isolated, which will build a complementary DNA chain onto a single-stranded DNA or RNA template. Polymerase chain reactions, chemical processes which can be fully automated, enable another enzyme to build up vast numbers of copies of a sequence of DNA bases quickly and cheaply.

mosome. What is needed is to identify a detectable abnormality in the chromosome which co-varies systematically with the product or phenotype. Once we have done this, we can zero in on the locus on the chromosome and sequence the DNA to find out exactly what the genetic cause is. For this reason it is important to produce physical maps of the genome at a fairly high degree of resolution. However, such a physical map is very far from the full sequence. It is composed of tens of thousands of sequence tagging sites—each a few thousand base pairs long—not repeated elsewhere in the genome, of which 90 to 95 percent will be unrelated to any functional domain of the DNA. Constructing such a map is an integral part of the HGP. Indeed, many scientists and commentators will say it is the most important part of the project. But even a physical map of landmarks is without interest in the absence of pedigree studies that can reveal when it is worth analyzing chromosomes for distinctive markers that will physically localize genes to DNA sequences. To be useful, physical maps and DNA sequences need to be preceded by genetic research that can narrow down the focus of sequencing from the whole genome to the functional units.

Those who identify physical mapping as the central goal of the HGP implicitly demote sequencing the whole human genome to a derivative status. Far from being derivative, it should be no part of the project's expected goals at all.

## III. The Manhattan Project, the AIDS Crusade, and the HGP

Perhaps getting the government to support sequencing the entire human genome is part of a strategy for providing the community of molecular biologists with opportunities that they would not otherwise have, and which they cannot even identify or imagine. To see why this possibility is worth exploring, consider some other large scientific programs. First, recall the Manhattan Project, an undertaking of breathtaking size whose magnitude has been obscured by inflation. The two billion 1942–1945 dollars spent on the project to develop atomic weapons would equal a hundred billion dollars today. However, have you ever asked yourself what the motivation of the theoretical physicists was? There was serious disagreement among them about the practicability of an atomic weapon. Some argued that its mere possibility was enough reason to justify a research program. Moreover, if the U.S., Canadian, and British governments could be convinced to support research aimed at building a war-ending weapon, the spin-off for experimental and theoretical research of the sort which interested all physicists could be phenomenal. Resources devoted to fundamental physics would, as a result, certainly be many orders of magnitude greater than they could expect in even a prosperous peacetime economy. It is worth exploring whether for some of the more influential of these scientists the real objective was increased understanding of fundamental physical processes. Many participants rated the chances of producing a successful bomb rather low at first, but recognized that the project would give them far more money to explore far more physics than they had ever anticipated. Who can blame them? It was rational to encourage the government to believe that a weapon was feasible, and there was no one to gainsay how they spent the money, not even Leslie Groves. When they succeeded, the outlook for further support of fundamental research, with a national defense rationale, became even brighter, and spun off into support of all kinds of things.

After the war, J. Robert Oppenheimer came close to admitting the motivation of the Manhattan Project physicists:

> When you come right down to it the reason we did this thing is because it was an organic necessity. You can't stop such a thing. If you are a scientist you believe that it is a good to find out how the world works; that it is a good to find out what the realities are. . . .

More recently the molecular-biology community has come to the same realization: by harnessing the desire to understand the human immune system to public anxiety about the threatened spread of AIDS, immunology has acquired vastly more resources than it might otherwise have expected to support its aim of understanding the immune system. The character of the immune system is one of the most vexing of biological mysteries; the immune system also seems basic to our understanding of both genetics and neurophysiology. But its complexity made the likelihood of breakthroughs in theoretical illumination improbable. The opportunity presented by the threat of AIDS to assert research priority changed the probabilities. It is now no longer clear that the AIDS epidemic will break out among heterosexuals who avoid intravenous drug use. There remains, however, an influential portion of the population who continue to advocate a distribution of research support to the study of HIV and AIDS disproportionate to its incidence in the U.S. population. By making common cause with this group, and providing scientific and medical grounds that substantiate the group's warnings about the risks to the general population, the immunology community has assured itself of the resources to support a large number of scientists' attempts to make progress in basic understanding of all aspects of the immune system.

Claims about the value of sequencing the entire human genome are mysterious enough to make one suspect that the molecular geneticists have learned well the lesson of the Manhattan Project and the AIDS interest groups. Passing acquaintance with molecular genetics shows how useless knowing the whole sequence is by itself. Even when we have acquired the technology needed to make knowledge of the sequence possible, knowing the sequence will not add much to our therapeutic powers. But the goal of sequencing the entire human genome is one that can be more easily understood, will provide vast resources for more significant research, and can be urged as a visible national and international goal.

By comparison to the Manhattan Project, the HGP is small beer. At a dollar per base pair, it will come in at three billion dollars. At four dollars per base pair it would still be cheaper than the Superconducting Supercollider would have been, and an order of magnitude cheaper than just building the space station will be, not to mention keeping it occupied. In the grand scheme of things, the HGP is not really "big science." However, its institutional impact will be like that of big science.

Big science differs from what will inevitably be called "small science" not because of the size of the total budget, but because of the organization of effort, the assignment of problems, and the methods for dealing with them. Typically, in "small science" the individual scientist is the initiator of his or her own research program, its component problems, and the methods for dealing with them. The interest or significance of the problem, the adequacy of the scientist's resources for dealing with it, and the likelihood of success is often measured by peer-review for granting agencies which provide the funds for research. Nevertheless, the initiative in undertaking research remains with the individual scientist or a small team. The direction of scientific authority is from the bottom up. Bottom-up science has several important features: First, it harnesses the individual scientist's interest in the problem, and as a result produces far more effort for the same investment than other ways of assigning problems. Second, it exploits the fact that scientific knowledge is both vast and decentralized; a scientific command economy cannot absorb and deploy the information scientists produce as efficiently as a decentralized one in which individuals have strong incentives to seek out relevant information. Third, bottom-up research reduces the bureaucratization of science: it minimizes featherbedding, cuts off projects which have outlived their scientific value, and reduces the transaction costs of research. But a program which assigns long stretches of DNA to scientists, or their technicians, for sequencing must by its nature be a top-down enterprise. Thus, far from exploiting the advantages of decentralized research, the HGP's coordination problem can only be solved by centralization. The quality of its product—reliable sequences—is likely to suffer, as the cost of its administration inevitably grows beyond any reasonable return on investment.

## IV. Private Choice and Public Goods

Despite the problems of top-down science, and despite the HGP's doubtful payoff in worthwhile scientific information when compared to other problems in molecular biology at which we could throw money, few in the molecular-genetics community dissent from support for the HGP's objective of sequencing the entire human genome. From the perspective of rational choice theory this should be no surprise. Given the aims and objectives of scientists and the biotech companies, given the patent laws, and given the nature of the human genome, the incentives molecular biologists have to secure a government-supported project to sequence the human genome are very strong.

The entire sequence of the human genome is a piece of information; and to produce this information, a good deal of further information needs to be provided. If the allegory of the phone books is apt, then given the present state of knowledge, having the entire human genome "on disk" is of little informational value. However, there is no doubt that the research program of the HGP will generate a large number of technological breakthroughs necessary for producing the sequence: research methods, computer programs, informatics, reagents, assays, pieces of machinery for automated sequencing, etc. The HGP requires the joint problem-solving skills of biochemists, physicists, engineers, mathematicians, and computer scientists. The real value of the breakthroughs required to sequence the whole genome is that as "spin-offs" they are crucial to answering currently pressing research questions that the scientists and commercial biotechnology firms have. These questions are not about the sequence of the human genome as a whole, but about functional units of it which have scientific and commercial interest. It may well turn out, of course, that for reasons no one can now identify, having the entire sequence of the human genome will be valuable information. But to act on the supposition that it will be is a very expensive gamble. Why then the strong pressure from the molecular-biology community to establish and maintain the HGP?

We can shed considerable light on why leading figures in molecular genetics have committed us to the HGP, and perhaps draw some policy-relevant normative conclusions by applying a little of the economics of information to the project.

The first thing to know about information generally is that it is unlike most other commodities. Other things being equal, economically valuable information always benefits larger-scale producers over smaller ones—since the costs of discovery are the same for each, but can be spread over a larger production run by larger producers. This means that larger concerns can outbid smaller ones for information, and that concerns with exclusive rights to some valuable information will grow larger than others. The result will be a loss of general welfare well understood in the economics of monopoly and monopolistic competition.

The second thing of importance about information is its nonappropriability. An individual who has acquired some information cannot lose it by selling or giving away to others a nonexclusive right to use it. Moreover, information acquired at great cost in research, or purchased for nonexclusive use, can be sold very cheaply, or even given away. Consider what happens to a piece of software newly introduced in an office. The market price of a token of information generally is much smaller than the cost of research to develop the first token. The information cannot be fully appropriated by a purchaser since the seller can sell to others. Nor can a seller recapture its full commercial value in the price charged for selling a token of the information, because this value includes returns to purchasers who resell. Thus, the production of new information is always below the optimum level, *ceteris paribus*. According to established economic analyses, then, a competitive economy always underinvests in research and development. This is a form of market failure.[6]

Because it is nonappropriable, and not provided at optimum levels, information has an economic role rather like that of a public good. An economically rational individual will invest resources in the discovery of new information up to the level of the marginal expected value of the information to the discoverer. But the expected value of the new information to all researchers is the sum of the marginal expected value to each of them, and will be larger than the expected value to the individual discoverer or inventor alone. Unless some part of the marginal value to other potential users can be captured by the discoverer or inventor, he will lack the purely economic incentive to invest in research up to anywhere near the point at which the costs of research equal the benefits to the whole economy of the research. This leads to underinvestment, because of the scope for "free-riding."

Solutions to problems of market failure in the provision of public or other nonappropriable goods usually involve governmental coercion. In the case of information, such coercion comes in the form of patent protection. The solution to the problem of undersupply is the establishment of governmentally enforced copyrights or patent rights in the discovery of the information. Patent and copyright protection enables the first discoverer to secure some of the marginal value that other users can produce by implementing the discoverer's information. Thus, it encourages individual investment at levels closer to the optimal level of investment for the whole economy. Patent protection is not a perfect solution to the underproduction problem; it cannot shift the market to a welfare-optimum equilibrium. No invention has a perfect substitute, and therefore an exclusive right to sell the invention allows its owners to charge a noncompetitive price for their information. This reduces consumption of information by raising its cost. Thus, patents and copyrights alleviate the underproduction problem while fostering an underutilization problem.[7]

Now, in the case of much biotechnological research, the resulting equilibrium does lead to investment in research. Witness the development of new products, the explosion of new firms, and their attraction of venture

[6] See Kenneth Arrow, *The Economics of Information* (Cambridge, MA: Belknap Press, 1984), pp. 142–43.

[7] For further discussion, see Jack Hirshleifer and John G. Riley, *The Analytics of Uncertainty and Information* (Cambridge: Cambridge University Press, 1992), ch. 7.

capital. In the case of the DNA sequence of Homo sapiens, however, patent protection is unlikely to have the same mitigating effects. Patents are unlikely to result in either the sequence or the spin-offs being produced at anything near optimum levels.

To begin with, there are reasons to think that neither the whole sequence nor large portions of it are open to patent protection. U.S. patent law restricts patents to new or useful processes, machines, manufactures, or compositions of matter, or useful improvements of them, including genetically engineered living organisms.[8] But it excludes as unpatentable those scientific discoveries that cannot be immediately used for any human purpose. Absence of immediate utility would presumably exclude both the primary sequence of base pairs and most physical maps of the human chromosome until discovery of the functional units with which their landmarks are correlated. Patents are also unavailable for so-called "obvious" extensions or applications of prior information. Thus, attempts to patent large numbers of cDNAs produced by means well-understood by all researchers have been challenged as failing the "nonobviousness" test. Since these cDNAs are far more immediately useful than either the whole sequence, large parts of it, or a physical map of the whole chromosome, the likelihood of patent protection for any of these latter seems low.

However, usefulness and nonobviousness are tests which some of the spin-offs may satisfy. Technology useful for mapping and sequencing alone may not be any more patentable than the sequences are, because of either nonusefulness or obviousness;[9] and even if they were patentable, these innovations would probably be restricted in their foreseeable use to the HGP labs alone, and therefore would probably not be lucrative enough to net returns to their discoverers. However, some of the spin-off technologies will be of great value in producing useful things like gene products with significant pharmaceutical value. Thus, no single researcher or group has an economically measurable incentive to provide the whole sequence, because there is no patent protection available for it; nor do researchers have material incentives to produce technologies that do nothing but sequence. However, beyond the most obvious improvements in informatics and sequencing technologies, researchers cannot tell when spin-offs will turn out to be of great value, and will be patentable.

Eventually, the sequence will have value, once we have a great deal more functional information; but no one can predict how much value it will have, scientific or economic. Similarly, the spin-offs are sure to be harnessed to technological breakthroughs; but the probable time required

[8] Rebecca S. Eisenberg, "Patent Rights in the Human Genome Project," in George J. Annas and Sherman Elias, *Gene Mapping* (New York: Oxford University Press, 1992), p. 227. See also V. Sgaramella, "Lawyers' Delights and Geneticists' Nightmares: At Forty, the Double Helix Shows Some Wrinkles," *Gene*, vol. 135 (1993), pp. 299–302.

[9] Eisenberg, "Patent Rights in the Human Genome Project," p. 227.

for breakthroughs to be harnessed profitably is long, and the probabilities that any particular lab will secure returns from these breakthroughs is very small. Consider the transistor or the laser: the former was at first expected only to help produce better hearing aids; the latter was invented at Bell Labs but was almost not patented, since it had no evident application in telephone technology, and would not until the advent of fiber optics twenty-five years later. No one anticipated its role in the household compact-disc player. No lab has an economic incentive to invest in the production of the sequence or the spin-offs alone, nor a nonnegligible rational expectation of inventing patentable and lucrative spin-offs.

How should an (economically) rational molecular-genetics laboratory respond to this degree of uncertainty about information which may or may not be patentable, the well-known consequences in underinvestment in research and development, and the potential public-goods effects of the sequencing project for the molecular-genetics community? Let us raise the question for labs, and not for individual researchers, both because the unit of research nowadays is the lab, and because in the present context, the role of labs is rather like that of individual business firms—in fact, some of the participants in the HGP are private companies. How a rational molecular-genetics lab might respond to this state of affairs depends on whether the lab is already a relatively large one or not.

The fact that sequence and spin-off information is a public good for molecular-genetics labs is no incentive to the individual researcher to provide it; it is an incentive to free-ride on the willingness of others to provide the good. Could researchers in molecular genetics enter into an enforceable agreement among themselves to produce the sequence and the spin-offs? They could do so, provided they were willing to work together to secure a coercive agent to enforce the agreement, and to provide the resources to develop the technology to determine the sequences.

This last requirement is the most difficult one, of course. Not only do individual labs not have control over sufficient disposable research funds to pool together, but if they did, each laboratory would have an incentive to understate its resources. However, suppose they mutually agreed to propose that the government provide these resources, subject to each principal investigator's surrendering the patent right to information that might be generated. In return for this subvention, the larger labs surrender their right to patent sequences and some spin-offs.

If the analysis of patent rights sketched above is correct, the expected value of this right is very low: the sequence information that is predictably forthcoming cannot be patented and the spin-off information which might be patentable is unlikely for any given lab. The expected value of patent rights is thus equally low for small labs and large ones. Accordingly, large labs will surrender patent rights "cheaply," and labs too small to participate will not complain, even though they have not been made parties to the contract, and secure no governmental support from it. Note that federal support of the HGP does not prohibit the patenting by researchers of useful, nonobvious discoveries made while supported by HGP funds.

So, by offering the sequence of the human genome as a nonpatentable public good to all labs in exchange for the funds to carry out HGP research, the large labs give up little in return for a great deal. And the larger the lab, the greater the economies of scale it will be able to apply for any unit of foreseeable spin-off information. Corporations pursuing research in biotechnology will happily support this strategy, since their immediate commercial interests are limited to foreseeable spin-off technology, and the expected value of this technology for each of them is sufficiently similar so that none will have an incentive to oppose a no-patentability policy.

The HGP is a good deal for the molecular-genetics community. Or rather, it is a good deal for those participants which can secure recognition as HGP research centers, or association with a center. This will include the larger labs in universities, and of course the National Laboratories operated for the Department of Energy by leading universities. Moreover, to the extent that the allocation of funds for the HGP does not reduce support for other molecular-biological research, smaller laboratories which have no stake in the HGP will have no grounds to complain, and some interest in acquiescing: they may profit from the spin-offs—reagents, assays, informatics, etc. And the small labs have incentives not to criticize the programs of established figures in the field who have advocated the HGP in public debate.

But is the trade-off—three billion dollars in exchange for the sequence and the spin-offs that may not be patentable anyway—worth it to the governments and citizens whose taxes support the research? Is the exchange between the large labs and the government equitable? Beyond equity, does it provide incentives to pursue the most pressing questions, the most promising lines of inquiry, the highest quality research, in molecular biology? Affirmative answers to these questions are doubtful. The multiplication of small, medium, and large biotechnology firms—none of them blindly sequencing the human genome, all of them seeking the sequences that code for gene products—suggests that the HGP is not the most promising line of inquiry for biomedical discoveries; interest in other sequences, like those of yeast, E. coli, C. elegans, the mouse, seems very great, but little research is devoted to sequencing for its own sake the entire genomes of these creatures.

If the government's intention in providing support for the HGP is its expected payoff for health care, then the exchange cannot be a fair one. For were the expected payoff high enough, the costs would have been internalized by the molecular-genetics community, especially the biotech firms. If the government's intention in providing support for the HGP is simply to support the best research being done, then surely the bottom-up system which has worked well in the traditional grant-award process, and in the processes used by the National Science Foundation and the National Institutes of Health, would more fully ensure high-quality work on the most pressing problems. Of course, if sequencing the human genome were a scientifically valuable immediate objective, given current knowledge, then the dimensions of the task, the efficiencies of the division of labor, the opportunity to spread capital costs widely, and the need to avoid duplication, would make top-down funding and direction sensible. But the antecedent of this conditional does not obtain. The whole sequence has no immediate value, and research into its functional domains can best be carried out under the auspices of bottom-up research.

The HGP thus raises some profound questions for the political economy of large-scale scientific research and governmental support. Exponents of government support for scientific research justify the support by appeal to its eventual instrumental value to the whole society and its intrinsic value in expanding understanding of the way the world works. Even those who might doubt that such objectives are within the proper sphere of government can accept another argument for the public support of science. The regulatory burden—animal care and human subjects oversight committees, toxic-waste prohibitions, fair employment practices, public disclosure requirements, as well as drug-free workplace-, conflict-of-interest-, anti-lobbying-, and other certifications—has so vastly increased the nonexperimental costs of scientific research (in the U.S. at least) that government is obliged to fund these intrusive mandates, in science and elsewhere.

But everything the theory of public choice tells us about the behavior of individuals and institutions suggests that the government must structure and administer the support of scientific research to maximize decentralization in decisions about the use of its funding. Only decentralizing the decision making about research subjects and strategies to the lowest level possible will harness most effectively the distributed knowledge of the scientific disciplines. Like other human institutions, modern science provides individuals with strong incentives to centralize decision making for their own direct interests or in the interests of institutions that indirectly benefit them. The HGP seems a transparent example of this tendency. The traditional system of providing support on the basis of peer reviews of individual proposals is by no means free from the defects of private choices in the public sphere, but it is manifestly freer from these defects than the HGP's state central planning mold.

*Philosophy, University of Georgia*

# CHOOSING WHO WILL BE DISABLED: GENETIC INTERVENTION AND THE MORALITY OF INCLUSION

By Allen Buchanan

## I. Hopes and Fears of the New Genetics

The Nobel prize–winning molecular biologist Walter Gilbert described the mapping and sequencing of the human genome as "the grail of molecular biology." The implication, endorsed by enthusiasts for the new genetics, is that possessing a comprehensive knowledge of human genetics, like possessing the Holy Grail, will give us miraculous powers to heal the sick, and to reduce human suffering and disabilities. Indeed, the rhetoric invoked to garner public support for the Human Genome Project appears to appeal to the best of the Western tradition's enthusiasm for progress: the idea of improving human lives through the practical application of scientific knowledge.

What is more, the rhetoric of the proponents of the new genetics is explicitly—almost self-consciously—*universalistic*: genetic science is to serve human beings generally, rather than any particular people or nationality or "race." In fact, the very understanding which the new science seeks and the manner in which it is sought seem to highlight the importance of what all human beings have in common rather than what differentiates us. And the human genome that is the object of an international network of sequencing and mapping projects is itself a constructed composite, not the genome of any particular person or even a composite representative of any particular group.[1]

Those who advocate social and private investment in the new genetics and support untrammeled scientific freedom to explore the human genome are aware that the "old eugenics"—the social policies of forced sterilization in the United States in the 1920s, 1930s, and beyond, and of the killing of "defective types" in Nazi Germany—casts a long shadow over their endeavors. In fact, the old eugenics was many different things. Some eugenicists of the late nineteenth and early to mid-twentieth cen-

[1] In other words, since all human beings have different genomes (except for identical twins), there is no such thing as *the* human genome. What the Human Genome Project aims at is sequencing many bits of DNA from many human beings to derive an understanding of what is common to all human beings, absent any errors in replication or mutations. The Human Genome Project was officially begun in 1989, but for several years previous to this there had been discussion, by Nobel prize-winners Walter Gilbert and James Watson, among others, of the idea of sequencing the entire human genome. For an excellent account of the scientific and political origins of the Human Genome Project, see Robert Cook-Deegan, *The Gene Wars: Science, Politics, and the Human Genome* (New York: W. W. Norton and Co., 1994).

 

turies endorsed coercive programs to "improve the human stock"; others insisted that improvement must come by strictly voluntary means. Some were racists, some were not. Some based their policy proposals on what we now see as pseudoscience; others were more scientifically informed.[2] At bottom, perhaps the only thing that they all had in common was a commitment to applying scientific knowledge of heredity to improve human lives. Some of the old eugenicists, however, held elitist and exclusionary (and in some cases ultimately genocidal) conceptions of what counts as the good type of human beings toward which improvement should aim.

Proponents of the new genetics, at pains to avoid the opprobrium that attaches to the old eugenics, emphasize that their aim is, first and foremost, to relieve human beings, *all* human beings, of the burdens of genetic disease. To the extent that the rhetoric—and the underlying ideology—of the new genetics focuses on an ethic that is both progressive and universalistic, it seems to avoid any but the most tenuous, nominal association with the old eugenics that is now nearly universally condemned. What could be controversial about the goal of reducing suffering, of removing disabling limitations on opportunities, for humanity in general, through the application of scientific knowledge? Surely the difference between the new genetics and the old eugenics is fundamental and clear: according to the proponents of the new genetics, the pursuit of progress through the application of scientific knowledge is based on a universalistic, nonexclusionary conception of the value of human lives, rather than on a pernicious view that what is valuable is the assumed distinctive characteristics of some particular race or nation or social class.

The rhetoric of universalistic progress has proven unconvincing to some, however. Where enthusiasts for the new genetics see universalism and progress, critics claiming to speak on behalf of the disabled see exclusion and moral retrogression. More specifically, the charge is that the very conception of progress that lies at the core of the ideology of the new genetics discriminates against and devalues disabled individuals, inflicting upon them what may be the gravest injustice possible: the rejection of their very right to exist. This view, which I shall label the "radical disabilities rights position," may not be held by the majority of disabled persons or of those who act as advocates for them. However, those who hold it are extremely vocal and impassioned.[3]

[2] For an excellent and influential history of eugenics in the United States, see Daniel J. Kevles, *In the Name of Eugenics: Genetics and the Uses of Human Heredity* (New York: Alfred A. Knopf, 1985).

[3] For what may be the most detailed and systematic statement of the radical disabilities rights position, see *Just Technology?*, an issue paper of the International League of Societies for Persons with Mental Handicap (North York, Ontario: L'Institute Roeher, 1994). It is important to note that there is no single disabilities rights position. Those active in the disabilities rights movement (or movements) have expressed a wide range of responses to

The source of this injustice is said to be a fundamentally flawed conception of the value of human lives.[4] Thus, the disabilities rights advocates' view stands the new genetics' claim to universalistic progress on its head. Not only is the alleged universalism indicted as discrimination and exclusion, but also the very notion of progress is seen to rest on a distorted view of the basic value that is supposed to guide the progress. The ability to control natural endowments which the new genetics promises will not lead to improvements for humanity in general, it is said, because it will harm the fundamental interests of some human beings, namely, those with disabilities.

According to this view, the conception of the value that is to guide progress under the aegis of the new genetics expresses and encourages the most profound moral ignorance—a radical misunderstanding of the basis of morality itself, namely the value of human lives. The value that drives the pursuit of "progress" through application of the new genetic science is not the value of human lives, but rather the value of human perfection as understood by those who deny the value of the lives of people with disabilities. If the inherent flaw of the old eugenics was its discriminatory and exclusive character, then the new genetics is equally flawed.

The disabilities rights advocates' critique of the new genetics is a rejection of the basic idea of striving *to make human lives better by selection based on genetic knowledge*.[5] "Selection" here includes not only choosing who will be born (through genetic testing and selective abortion to avoid the birth of individuals with defects such as Down's syndrome), but also choosing the characteristics of those who will be born by genetic interventions on gametes (sperm or egg cells) or embryos in order to eliminate or counteract genetic influences that would cause disease or disability. Furthermore, the charge is not simply that the effort at "improvement through selection" (in either of these ways) is unwise or in some way morally questionable. To repeat: the claim is that it is *unjust*—that it violates the most basic rights of disabled persons and is nothing less than a degradation of the core of morality, the proper appreciation of the value of human life.

Given the universalistic and progressive self-image of those who engage in or support the new genetics, these objections evoke incredulity if not indignation on the part of enthusiasts for the new genetics. It is tempting to dismiss the radical disabilities rights advocates' objections as hysterical, paranoid, extremist. This, however, would be a grave mistake, as we shall see; for there is a kernel of truth in these objections. Our emerging powers of genetic intervention do raise important and in some

---

the prospects of genetic intervention with human beings. No assumption is made here that what I have labeled the radical disabilities rights view is the dominant one.

[4] *Ibid.*, p. 8.

[5] *Ibid.*, p. 1.

respects novel issues of justice and exclusion—issues that the rhetoric of universalistic progress obscures. On closer examination, however, it will turn out that neither the disabilities rights advocates nor the enthusiasts for the new genetics have grasped the fundamental implications of genetic intervention for our understanding of justice, of the moral significance of disabilities, and of what may be called the morality of inclusion and exclusion.[6]

## II. Attack on the New Genetics: Objections on Behalf of the Disabled

There are a number of distinct objections advanced by disabilities rights advocates. No attempt is made here to evaluate or even to list all of them. (And no assumption is made that if one advances one of these arguments one endorses all of them). Instead, I shall concentrate on those objections that strike at the heart of the ideology of the new genetics—those that challenge the claim to universal, nonexclusionary progress.

Before proceeding to these most fundamental objections to the new genetics, however, I should note a distinct but related objection to "improvement through selection" that is often voiced by disabilities rights advocates: the charge that as the application of genetic science reduces the number of persons suffering from (genetically based) disabilities, public support for those who have these disabilities will dwindle.[7] Although I discuss this particular objection (which for convenience I label the "loss of support" argument) mainly to distinguish it from those with which I shall be concerned, it is frequently voiced and no discussion of the critical

[6] See Allen Buchanan, "The Morality of Inclusion," *Social Philosophy and Policy*, vol. 10, no. 2 (Summer 1993), pp. 233–57.

[7] A large number of objections to various actual or proposed uses of genetic technology have been voiced by those claiming to speak for the disabled and others as well. No attempt is made here to provide an exhaustive catalog of all such objections. However, it can be said that the unifying theme with respect to objections raised by disabilities rights advocates is one of *discrimination*: that discrimination (against people with disabilities) rests upon and expresses attitudes that *devalue* individuals with disabilities. More broadly, two general types of concerns about "eugenic abuses" of genetic intervention technology may be distinguished. On the one hand, there are fears of old-style *statist* eugenics policies, whereby individuals' reproductive freedom and even their lives would be at risk due to policies for "human improvement" that are given the force of law and directed by the state. On the other hand, there are apprehensions about *market-driven, "backdoor" eugenics*. With respect to the latter, the fear is that even if the state does not enforce eugenic policies, the cumulative effects of many individual choices under conditions in which genetic services are offered as a commodity in the market will lead to morally defective outcomes. Two examples of the dangers of market-driven, backdoor eugenics are frequently mentioned: (1) increasing imbalances in the ratio of males to females in countries such as India and China where detection of the sex of the fetus is undertaken for the purpose of aborting females, and (2) coercive social pressures to abort or avoid the conception of individuals with genetic defects either for economic reasons (if such individuals become uninsurable) or because of societal ideals of human perfection and the stigmatization of those who fall short of these ideals.

stance of disabilities rights advocates toward genetic intervention should ignore it. Three points are worth making.

First, the objection rests on a sweeping empirical generalization: that as the number of persons with a certain disability decreases, support for those who have the disability will also decrease. Without attempting to adjudicate the empirical issue, I would only point out that it is not enough to state the generalization. Data to support it must be supplied. Moreover, there is at least one instance of which I have knowledge in which reduction in the incidence of a genetic disease (through voluntary utilization of knowledge from carrier testing) allowed *more* resources to be used to support the smaller number of those who had the disease.[8]

Second, whether or not support will dwindle for individuals with a particular condition will depend upon a number of factors, not the least significant of which is whether the public is alerted in advance to the danger of reduced support. In fact, the prediction that as science reduces genetic diseases support will decrease is much less plausible today than it would have been twenty years ago, precisely because advocates for people with disabilities have achieved hard-won and impressive victories in alerting the public and policymakers to the need for support.

Third, even if there should turn out to be some loss of support for those suffering with certain genetically based disabilities as their incidence declines, it would not follow that seeking to reduce their incidence is wrong or even inadvisable, all things considered. The problem with the "loss of support" argument is that it only considers the interests of those who will have disabilities after a reduction in the incidence of the disabilities occurs. It entirely overlooks the interests that others have in *not having* disabilities.

It is of course true that in some cases preventing the disability will be achieved only by aborting a fetus in whom the genetic defect is detected, or by avoiding the conception of such a fetus. Here it would be incorrect to say that forgoing the prevention of the defect is contrary to the interest of anyone in not having a disability, simply because there is no individual whose condition is improved by removing or ameliorating the defect.

In other cases, however, it may be possible to correct defects in the embryo (or even in the gamete, that is, the sperm or the egg). In these instances it will be correct to speak of preventing an individual from having a disability and of the individual having an interest in avoiding the disability. Similarly, the application of genetic knowledge can prevent or remedy defects in less dramatic ways, not by manipulating the embryo's (or the gamete's) genes, but by producing chemicals that mimic the

[8] Philip Kitcher cites an actual case of this occurring with respect to support for persons with thalassemia anemia in Greece; see his *The Lives to Come: The Genetic Revolution and Human Possibility* (New York: Simon and Schuster, 1996).

products of normal genes or that counteract the deleterious effects of abnormal genes.[9] In these cases, too, we may correctly say that the application of genetic science makes identifiable individuals' lives better by preventing genetically based diseases and that such individuals have a legitimate interest in avoiding the damage to them which would occur if we did not intervene.

Once we recognize that a reduction in the incidence of genetically based diseases may be achieved without preventing the birth of individuals with genetic defects, and without even changing the individuals' genes, it becomes clear that the "loss of support" objection must be rejected, not only because it fails to give any weight to the interests individuals have in avoiding disabling defects, but also because, if valid, the objection would forbid us to take any measures, involving the use of genetic knowledge or otherwise, to reduce disabilities of any kind.

For example, if it is wrong to reduce the incidence of a genetic disease because a lower incidence of the disease may lead to a loss of support for those who suffer it, then it would also be wrong to treat babies' eyes at birth to prevent blindness due to contact with gonococcus bacteria. But surely it is not only permissible but morally obligatory to take steps to prevent babies from being blinded, if this can be done safely and effectively. So even if proponents of the "loss of support" argument could marshal strong empirical support for the generalization that when the incidence of genetically based disabilities decreases, support for those with disabilities will decrease as well, this would not suffice to show that limitations on efforts to prevent or remedy such disabilities are called for.

As we shall see later, this critique of the disabilities rights advocates' "loss of support" objection reveals three very general weaknesses of the arguments advanced on behalf of persons with disabilities which are considered in this essay. First, these arguments are not limited to genetic engineering with human beings, or even to *genetic* intervention more broadly conceived (including the use of genetic knowledge to mimic or modify the chemical products of genes, i.e., genetic pharmacology). If sound, they would rule out a wide range of traditional, "low-tech" interventions to avoid or remedy disabilities, as the example of treating newborns' eyes shows. Second, as the same example also indicates, the implications of the disabilities rights advocates' objections are not limited to attempts to prevent or remedy *genetically based* disabilities—they apply to all disabilities regardless of their source. Third, like the "loss of support" objection, the other disabilities rights advocates' arguments discussed below are flawed because they consider only *some* of the legitimate

[9] Examples of defects which might be treated in this way include one form of Gaucher's disease, Wilson's disease, and various forms of cystic fibrosis. See Kitcher, *The Lives to Come*.

interests at stake. As the foregoing critique of the "loss of support" argument shows, they do not even consider the interests of all persons with disabilities, much less those of all persons, those who are disabled and those who are not.

If some of the interests that are ignored by the disabilities rights advocates' arguments provide the basis for claims of justice, as I shall argue they do, then, ironically, those who advance those arguments make the same mistake they attribute to the enthusiasts for the new genetics: advocating practices that are unjust because they are discriminatory and exclusionary. More specifically, if, as I shall argue below, justice sometimes requires intervening to prevent or remedy disabilities, then it also requires that we give some weight to the interest people have in avoiding disabilities, not just the interests of people who will continue to have disabilities, as the "loss of support" argument would have us do.

## III. Justice and Genetic Intervention

Elsewhere I have argued in detail that there are or soon are likely to be cases in which justice is not only compatible with, but *requires* interventions to correct or prevent genetic defects, including interventions that involve direct modification of genes or modification of their expression through the application of genetic science.[10] The basis of this conclusion is the assumption that an adequate account of justice will include a place for a commitment to equal opportunity and that in some cases equal opportunity requires more than the removal of legal barriers to opportunity.

Equal opportunity, as a principle of justice, requires not only the dismantling of legal barriers to opportunity (e.g., racially discriminatory laws), but also removing or ameliorating the more extreme disadvantages in initial *social* assets (in particular the economic and educational deficits of the family one is born into), to the extent that this can be achieved without violating other rights that individuals have. The fundamental idea here is that of fairness—that it is not fair for individuals' most basic life-prospects to be significantly curtailed due to their bad luck in the "social lottery." More specifically, an individual should not be barred from opportunities for leading a good life, simply because he happens to have been born into a poor, uneducated family—something which he neither chose nor deserved.[11]

The same considerations of fairness that speak in favor of removing or ameliorating the more extreme disadvantages in persons' initial *social*

[10] Allen Buchanan, "Equal Opportunity and Genetic Intervention," *Social Philosophy and Policy*, vol. 12, no. 2 (Summer 1995), pp. 105–35.

[11] For a more detailed defense of this conception of equal opportunity, for references to its occurrence in recent literature on distributive justice, and for a discussion of how it differs from alternative conceptions of equal opportunity, see *ibid.*, pp. 114–25.

assets apply with equal force in the case of serious genetic defects. For genetic defects are undeserved, unchosen, and unavoidable by those who have them. Thus, if one believes that there should be *some* limitations on at least the more extreme inequalities that arise through socioeconomic systems in which one's initial (undeserved, unchosen, and unavoidable) social assets play a significant role in determining one's life-prospects, then there is at least a strong presumption that the same is true of serious disadvantages in natural assets.

To say that deficits in natural or initial social assets that result in serious limitations on opportunity are a concern of justice is *not* to say, of course, that justice requires that persons' opportunities be literally equal; and to that extent the label "principle of equal opportunity" is misleading. Instead, the conception of equal opportunity employed here relies upon the idea that there is an obligation to devote some social resources to preventing or correcting undeserved differences in initial social or natural assets that result in some persons' suffering significant limitations on their opportunities—limitations so serious as to interfere with their having reasonable prospects for a decent life. Thus, this conception of equal opportunity views as a concern of justice only those limitations that amount to something akin to *deprivations*. Although no attempt will be made here to mount a systematic defense of this conception, it can be said that it has at least two signal advantages over a strictly egalitarian interpretation of equal opportunity. First, it recognizes that there are significant limitations on what we owe other individuals, at least for conditions that we did not cause. In this sense the weaker (not strictly egalitarian) conception of equal opportunity acknowledges what I take to be a fundamental fact about morality, namely: that each of us has but one life to live, that it is perfectly proper for us to exhibit a preference, within limits, for our own projects and for the interests of those we hold dear, and consequently that we are not responsible, as a matter of justice, for correcting or preventing every disadvantage another person may suffer, even if it is not so serious as to prevent him from having a decent life. Second, when proponents of the strictly egalitarian conception say anything at all to try to justify its stringent demands, they tend to assume that it is required by the principle that we ought to show equal concern and respect for persons. However, this simply begs the question, since it is not at all obvious that equal concern and respect require something this demanding rather than commitment to a weaker conception of equal opportunity such as the one advocated here.[12]

Another important qualification on equal opportunity as I am understanding it here ought to be stressed. The principle of equal opportunity

[12] This idea that equal concern and respect for persons requires strictly equal opportunities, at least so far as it is feasible to achieve such a condition, is suggested by John Rawls's discussion of "fair equality of opportunity" in *A Theory of Justice* (Cambridge: Harvard University Press, 1971), p. 100.

must be applied in such a way as to recognize the legitimacy of inequalities that result from people's free choices over time, at least so far as they only primarily affect those who have made the choices. Even if all persons began with equal initial social and natural assets, inequalities in opportunity would surely arise over time, as the cumulative result of their choices, which in turn would reflect not only their preferences, but also their commitment to and self-discipline in acting so as to satisfy those preferences. For example, some individuals will choose to invest more of their income and time in advanced education and training than others, with the result that their opportunities will be correspondingly greater. Such emerging differences in opportunities are not in general a concern of justice. This qualification signals another sense in which equal opportunity, properly understood, does not require strictly equal opportunities. A better term might in fact be "fair opportunity."[13]

My claim, then, is that justice can require genetic intervention in certain circumstances. This claim has an important implication for an assumption that appears to be at work beneath the surface of the disabilities rights advocates' charge that the project of reducing the incidence of genetic defects through the application of the new genetic science treats disabled people unjustly by putting them at risk of being deprived of the support to which they are entitled. That assumption is that only beneficence, not justice, speaks in favor of genetic intervention, while justice (to individuals with disabilities) speaks against it. A further assumption is that if this first assumption is granted, then the scales of the moral balance must tip toward the stance of opposing genetic intervention (a stance which the disabilities rights advocates favor), because when justice and beneficence conflict, justice trumps.[14]

In other words, at least some disabilities rights advocates appear to invoke the following argument, albeit rather implicitly:

(1) Pursuing the expected benefits of genetic intervention is not required by justice, but only by beneficence. (The "mere" benefits assumption)
(2) Pursuing these ("mere") benefits creates a serious risk of fundamental injustices to people with disabilities.

[13] Alternately, since some genetic defects (e.g., Huntington's chorea, Lesh-Nyan syndrome, Tay-Sachs disease and sickle-cell anemia) not only grossly limit opportunities but cause severe suffering and premature death, *the obligation to prevent harm* can also provide a moral mandate for genetic intervention. Even if the obligation to prevent harm is not understood to be an obligation of justice, if the harm is sufficiently serious, it may have great moral weight and in some cases might even justify interventions, as in the case of the prevention of prenatal harms, that are performed without the consent of the woman carrying the fetus. At the very least, it could be argued that in cases where an extremely serious harm could be avoided without violating anyone's rights, the obligation to prevent harm justifies the use of public resources for intervening.

[14] *Just Technology?* pp. 24–25.

(3) When considerations of justice and those of beneficence conflict, justice overrides, at least where the fundamental rights of persons are concerned.
(4) (Therefore) we should not undertake genetic interventions.

This argument is flawed for two reasons. First, some benefits are not "mere benefits." Achieving a great good or averting a great harm for a great many people can be obligatory, not merely laudable. Indeed, there can be cases in which such an obligation may "trump" an obligation of justice. But second, and more importantly, as I have just argued, justice, and more specifically equal opportunity as one component of justice, sometimes requires genetic intervention. Therefore, it is a mistake to say that we are faced with a conflict between justice and beneficence. Instead of an unequal contest between the most fundamental demands of justice—those pertaining to the basic rights of persons—and less weighty obligations of beneficence or merely desirable goals of doing good or preventing harm, we have a conflict between fundamental demands of justice: on the one hand, the obligation to prevent or correct or ameliorate serious limitations on opportunity caused by genetic defects; on the other, the obligation to avoid injustices to individuals with disabilities, including the reduction of support to which they are entitled. What we do *not* have is a conflict between the pursuit of merely desirable ends and the commitment to justice, or even a clash between obligations of beneficence and more fundamental obligations of justice.

Once it is recognized that genetic intervention may enable us to remove or prevent serious disabilities and thus enhance individuals' opportunities, it would be deeply ironic—and inconsistent—to argue that respect for the rights of the disabled bars us from employing genetic intervention for this purpose. After all, the most powerful argument to support changing the physical environment to lower barriers to access for people with disabilities is that equal opportunity, as a matter of *justice*, not merely of charity or beneficence, requires this. In other words, what has been distinctive and peculiarly powerful about the disabilities rights movement that issued in the Americans with Disabilities Act in the U.S. and similar legislation elsewhere is that it has insisted that equal opportunity is a matter of justice. That is why it is called the disabilities *rights* movement. But if so, then it is arbitrary and inconsistent to argue that justice requires removing barriers to opportunity that are part of the social environment, but can never speak in favor of removing barriers that result from the individual's genetic constitution. Put most simply: The same conception of equal opportunity that supports the disabilities rights movement in general, also makes it implausible to say that genetic intervention is a matter of beneficence, not justice.

There is another way in which justice bears on genetic intervention. The commitment to equal opportunity might also, under certain circumstances, require measures to ensure that the use of genetic science to enhance certain desirable characteristics does not *create* a new class of disabled persons. If those who enjoy vastly more favorable initial *social* assets could use their wealth to secure markedly better genetic assets for their children or themselves, those who lacked access to "genetic enhancement" might suffer limitations on their opportunities so severe that they would count as disabilities. Justice would presumably require either making such enhancements available to all (not just those who could afford them) or not allowing anyone to have access to them.

## IV. The Expressivist Objection: "Genetic Intervention Devalues Disabled Individuals," Depriving Them of Their Fundamental Status as Persons of Equal Value

The expressivist objection, or rather family of objections, focuses on what may be called the expressive character of decisions to use genetic interventions to prevent or remove disabilities, and hence on the expressive character of the enterprise of developing and deploying scientific knowledge for such interventions. The claim is that the commitment to developing modes of intervention to correct, ameliorate, or prevent genetic defects expresses (and presupposes) negative, extremely damaging judgments about the value of disabled persons. These judgments are said to betray a profound miscomprehension of the core concept of morality: the value of human life.

The implication of this objection is that the error is not merely a mistake in moral theory. To express these negative judgments about disabled people is itself an injury to them, a violation of their most fundamental right, the right to be regarded as persons of equal worth. In addition, the social acceptance of the enterprise that expresses these negative judgments, the project of using genetic knowledge for improvement through selection, puts disabled persons at risk in more concrete ways. Those who are not regarded as members of the community of equal persons, those whose fundamental value is denied, are likely to be neglected and abused, if not exterminated.

The negative judgments that are alleged by the radical disabilities rights advocates to be expressed in the new genetics are these:

(1) The lives of individuals with disabilities are not worth living.
(2) Only perfect individuals should be brought into the world (and imperfect individuals have no right to exist).

Disabilities rights advocates would reject the first judgment, emphasizing that persons without disabilities tacitly make this judgment either because they are ignorant of the joys and fulfillments that even severely disabled individuals experience, or because they assume the truth of the second judgment.

It can hardly be denied that people who have not experienced serious disabilities themselves, or been close to people who are seriously disabled, sometimes—perhaps often—fail to appreciate what it is like to be disabled. They may focus on the suffering and limitations of the disability, underestimating both the positive experiences the disabled can have and the capacity of human beings to adapt their expectations and their pursuits to changes in their abilities.[15]

However, even if it is true that many people without disabilities underestimate the quality of life that people with disabilities can and often do enjoy, it does not follow that those who are not disabled believe that disabilities generally, even serious disabilities, make life not worth living. It is certainly true that some people believe that there are some disabilities so severe that they make life not worth living. But this belief, whether it is justified or not, does not in any way imply that *all* disabilities, or even all serious disabilities, make the lives of those who have them not worth living.

What, then, would lead disabilities rights advocates to conclude that the enthusiasm for using genetic science to reduce the incidence of disabilities expresses the judgment that disabled lives are not worth living? The answer, apparently, is that the disabilities rights advocates believe that central to the new genetics is the decision to prevent disabilities *by avoiding the birth of disabled individuals*—and that this decision must rest upon the judgment that life with those disabilities would not be worth living or that less than perfect individuals ought not to exist or have no right to exist.[16]

It should be noted that as a general form of argument the expressivist objection appears to be invalid. An example that has nothing to do with genetic intervention or genetic defects will clarify this point. Suppose that a woman is faced with the choice between (1) conceiving a child now, knowing that the child will be born into circumstances in which it will suffer serious illnesses that will have lifelong effects and that it will perhaps die at a very young age, or (2) waiting a few months to conceive, with the result that the child will be born in favorable circumstances. (Imagine, for example, that the woman is a refugee, living in wretched conditions in a camp, but knowing that she will be transported to safety in one year.) Surely the woman's decision to postpone conceiving a child until it could be born in safe and healthy conditions need not be an expression either of the belief that if the child were born in the unfavor-

[15] See Allen Buchanan and Dan W. Brock, *Deciding for Others: The Ethics of Surrogate Decision Making* (New York: Cambridge University Press, 1989).

[16] *Just Technology?* pp. 6–7.

able conditions its life would not be worth living or of the belief that it would have no right to life if it were born in these unfortunate conditions.

Presumably, to say that a decision expresses (or presupposes) a judgment is to say either (a) that (as a matter of psychological fact) one could be *motivated* to make a decision of this sort only if one subscribed to the judgment (and that hence one couldn't make the decision if one did not believe to be true what the judgment affirms), or (b) that one cannot *rationally* make the decision without believing what the judgment affirms.

The first thing to notice is that even if the expressivist objection were granted, it would only apply to *some* uses of genetic science to prevent disabilities—namely, those which involve avoiding the conception of fetuses that will have disabilities or which involve aborting fetuses that are found to have disabilities. It would leave unscathed other ways in which genetic science might be used to reduce the incidence of disabilities—for example, gene surgery on embryos or gametes or the employment of genetic pharmacology to correct or mitigate the effects of genetic defects. In order to make this point clearer, it is useful to distinguish the following four types of intervention for preventing or correcting genetic defects:

(i) Removing or counteracting or mitigating a genetic defect that will be disabling by "switching off" the defective gene or by altering its effects by inserting normal genes, through gene surgery on embryos or gametes or on individuals after they are born (e.g., by inserting normal genes into stem cells in bone marrow).

(ii) Avoiding conceiving a fetus with a genetic defect after genetic testing reveals that there is a significant risk of the defect, by using contraceptives (as when both prospective parents are found to be carriers for a recessive defect such as cystic fibrosis, or when one prospective parent is determined to have a serious autosomal dominant defect such as Huntington's chorea).[17]

(iii) Avoiding conceiving a fetus with a genetic defect (after genetic testing) by utilizing artificial insemination or embryo transplant.

(iv) Preventing the birth of an individual with a genetically based defect (such as Lesh-Nyan syndrome, Down's syndrome, Fragile X syndrome, or spina bifida) by aborting the fetus if a prenatal test for the defect is positive.

It should be evident that opting for the first form of intervention in no way presupposes a judgment that only perfect individuals should exist or that disabled lives are not worth living, anymore than performing con-

[17] In the case of a recessive genetic disorder, the disorder only occurs if the individual has two copies of the gene in question, one from each parent. In the case of an autosomal dominant genetic disorder, only one copy is required.

ventional surgery to restore a blind person's sight does. In either case the motive is the desire to remove serious limitations on the individual's opportunities. One can be motivated by this desire and rationally decide to act on it without believing either that the individual's life with the limitation is not worth living or that only perfect individuals should exist.

Similarly, the second and third options for avoiding genetic defects need not express or presuppose either of the judgments that the expressivist objection attributes to enthusiasts for the application of genetic science to the reduction of disabilities. To be willing to undertake either of these options, all that is necessary is the desire not to bring into the world an individual whose opportunities will be severely limited and who may also experience considerable suffering.

There are a number of considerations that might account for this desire, any of which would make the decision fully coherent and rational.

First, one may simply wish to be spared avoidable and serious strains on one's marriage or on one's family. Or one may wish to avoid putting additional pressure on limited social resources to support disabled individuals. Given that one can act on these desires without violating anyone's rights, there is nothing morally suspect, and there may be much that is morally admirable, about such desires.

Acting on these desires does not violate anyone's rights, because there is no existing individual who has rights that might be violated. In options (ii) and (iii), it is the coming into existence of an individual that is avoided; no individual's existence is terminated. So even if one believes that fetuses are persons with all the rights that persons have, including the right not to be killed, avoiding disabilities by avoiding conception does not violate anyone's rights and need not express any negative judgment to the effect that disabled lives are not worth living or that imperfect individuals ought not to exist or have no right to exist. Furthermore, to judge that it is morally permissible to avoid bringing a disabled person into the world, one need not judge that disabled persons *ought not to be born*, anymore than judging that it is not wrong to refrain from getting a Ph.D. commits one to judging that one ought not to get a Ph.D.

Only option (iv) for avoiding disabilities holds any prospect of being vulnerable to the expressivist objection, because only here is there a decision to terminate a life that will involve a disability. Notice, however, that even in this case the decision to intervene—to abort a fetus with a serious genetic defect—need not express either of the two alleged negative judgments about individuals with disabilities. If one decides to terminate a pregnancy after learning that the fetus one is carrying has Down's syndrome, one may simply be motivated by the very same desire that motivates the decision to undertake any of the other three options for avoiding disabilities: the desire not to bring into the world an individual with seriously limited opportunities.

Here, too, this desire may be based upon any of several quite morally unexceptionable considerations. One may wish to avoid serious strains on one's marriage, on one's ability to fulfill responsibilities to one's other children, or on scarce social resources, and yet consistently believe that the lives of many, indeed of all Down's syndrome individuals are worth living and that every child and adult with Down's syndrome has the same right to life as any other person. Nor need one believe that only perfect individuals ought to exist. Nor need one erroneously lump Down's syndrome together with much more serious conditions such as Lesh-Nyan syndrome.

All that is required to render the desire to abort a fetus with a genetic defect consistent with the belief in the equal worth and rights of all persons, disabled or not, is the belief that *fetuses* (or at least fetuses up to and including the stage of development at which the abortion is to be performed) are not persons and hence do not have the rights of persons.

To repeat the essential point: To believe that one *may* avoid a serious disability by selective abortion, one need not believe that individuals with that disability *ought not* to be born. All that is necessary is that one believe that they have *no right to be born*. Furthermore, one can—and many people apparently do—consistently believe both that fetuses, whether disabled or not, have no right to be born (because they are not persons), while believing that all persons, including disabled ones, have a right to exist, and hence not to be killed (because they are persons).

Finally, there is nothing inconsistent about believing that—given one's particular circumstances (recall the case of the refugee)—one ought not to bring a disabled child into the world *and* that it is not the case that children with disabilities (generally) ought not to be born. (Similarly, one can believe that one ought not to marry without believing that marriage should be prohibited.)

Perhaps those who advance the expressivist objection will still not be satisfied with this rebuttal. The appeal of the expressivist objection is its simplicity. Thus, a person with a disability, impatient with the subtleties and hair-splitting of the preceding arguments, might reply: "No analysis of the possible motives or of the coherence of the possible reasons for preventing disabilities can erase one simple fact: when you endorse the application of genetic science to reduce disabilities, *you are saying that people like me ought not to exist*. And when you say that people like me ought not to exist you devalue me in the most fundamental and threatening way. Your conception of the value of human life denies that my life, imperfect as it is, has value."

In advocating the use of genetic science to reduce disabilities one *is* saying that avoidable disabilities ought to be avoided, and in that sense one *is* saying that our world, in the future, should not include the existence of so many people with disabilities. But it is not the people who have disabilities which we devalue; it is the disabilities; and one need not and should not wish to reduce the number of people with disabilities by taking the life of any person who is disabled.

We devalue disabilities because we value the opportunities and welfare of the people who have them—and it is because we value people, all people, that we care about limitations on their welfare and opportunities. We also know that disabilities, as such, diminish opportunities and welfare, even when they are not so severe that the lives of those who have them are not worth living. Thus, there is nothing incoherent or disingenuous in our saying that we devalue the disabilities and wish to reduce their incidence *and* that we value all *existing* persons with disabilities—and value them equally to those who are not disabled.

One last example may help to dispel the charge that when we seek to reduce the frequency of disabilities we thereby devalue persons who have disabilities. Suppose that a parent, as parents often do, encourages her child to work hard in school by pointing out that if he does not, his career options will be limited to "menial" jobs in which there is little potential for development of new skills and little prospect of advancement. Must we say that such a parent devalues persons who do "menial" jobs? No such attitude is implied in the advice the parent gives or in her motives for doing so.

Of course, it may still be true that some parents who have always engaged in "white-collar" work will underestimate the opportunities for development of skills and the satisfaction that even some of the least skilled "blue-collar" jobs sometimes offer. Nevertheless, the advice the parent gives may be sound: she may be correct both in her judgment that this individual would be happier and more fulfilled with a different kind of job and in her prediction that doing well in school is a prerequisite for getting such a job. She may only be expressing concern for the well-being of her child in the light of a realistic estimate of the educational and economic facts of life, without in any way denigrating persons who perform "menial" labor.

None of this is to deny that some "white-collar" workers look down on "blue-collar" workers, or that some "abled" persons devalue the "disabled." The expressivist objection must show more than this, however. It must show that the very decision to attempt to avoid or correct defects that cause disabilities devalues people with disabilities. It clearly does not.

One last thought experiment will clarify our observation that devaluing disabilities need not imply devaluing persons with disabilities. Suppose God tells a couple: "I'll make a child for you. You can have a child that has limited opportunities due to a physical or cognitive defect or one who does not. Which do you choose?" Surely, if the couple says they wish to have a child without defects, this need not mean that they devalue persons with disabilities, or that they would not love and cherish their child if it were disabled. Choosing to have God make a child who does not have defects does not in itself in any way betray negative judgments or attitudes about the value of individuals with defects.[18]

The disabilities rights advocate might concede this point but offer one last argument: "Even if the decision to use or develop genetic intervention does not necessarily express such negative attitudes, such attitudes are all too common in our society. In fact, they are so widespread and pronounced that many individuals with disabilities experience greater limitations on their opportunities as a result of stigma than from their physical or cognitive defects. Undoubtedly, these negative attitudes are part of the motivation for the willingness to develop and use genetic-intervention technologies. We should not encourage these attitudes by giving them a powerful vehicle for their expression."

This argument might be telling if there were nothing of great consequence to lose by following its advice. However, there is: the chance to avoid or correct serious limitations on individuals' opportunities. Accordingly, the wiser course of action is to continue the laudable fight to change negative attitudes toward people with disabilities rather than to refrain from using genetic-intervention technologies to accomplish the same goal that has inspired the disabilities rights movement's greatest triumphs in overcoming physical barriers in the social environment. For it is crucial to remember that the strongest argument in favor of removing physical barriers to access is that this is necessary to achieve equal opportunity and that equal opportunity is a matter of justice, something to which all individuals have a right.

I can now summarize the main points of this complex discussion of objections to genetic intervention sometimes voiced by or on behalf of people with disabilities. To be sound the expressivist objection must either (1) deny that we can devalue and seek to avoid disabilities without devaluing disabled persons, or (2) assume—and defend—the view that fetuses are persons, with all the rights that persons have, and that hence avoiding disabilities by aborting fetuses with disabilities is exactly like reducing the number of disabilities by exterminating disabled children and adults.

The first alternative is wholly unconvincing. There are many instances in which we devalue (and seek to eliminate or ameliorate) certain characteristics of individuals without devaluing the individuals themselves. For example, we seek to prevent hypertension without devaluing people with hypertension.

The second alternative comes at a steep price: not only must the disabilities rights advocate adopt and defend an account of personhood which shows that fetuses have the properties necessary for personhood, but he must also acknowledge that the fundamental error of those who advocate selective abortion to avoid disabilities is *not* that they devalue

[18] This thought experiment was suggested to me by Dan W. Brock.

disabled individuals, but that they fail to recognize that fetuses, whether disabled or not, are persons. Since virtually no one (at least in this country) who defends the new genetics does so on the grounds that *persons* with disabilities may be killed or ought to be killed or have no right to life, this admission in effect robs the expressivist objection of its distinctive interest. It is simply the view that abortion is murder, and has nothing to do with genetic intervention as such. Moreover, if what is wrong with such interventions is that they are instances of murdering persons, then the fact that it is disabled persons who are singled out as victims, though it would be a distinct wrong, would be of secondary importance. Unless one is persuaded, as I and many others are not, that fetuses are persons, one will not in the end find the expressivist objection—or rather the anti-abortion position that it reduces to—compelling.

Furthermore, even if one were to assume that fetuses are persons, and hence that killing them to reduce the incidence of disabilities is morally indistinguishable from gassing disabled children and adults, this would have no implications whatsoever for the other three options for genetic intervention to avoid disabilities. None of these three options involves killing a fetus, and hence none can be described as killing a person, even if we assume that fetuses are persons. Therefore, endorsing these modes of reducing disabilities does not express or presuppose a judgment that disabled children or adults have no right to life.

So advocating the fourth mode of intervention (selective abortion) is tantamount to saying that people who are disabled have no right to exist, only on the assumption that fetuses are persons. Opting for the first, second, and third types of intervention has no implications at all for the worthiness or unworthiness of disabled people as such to live, regardless of which view of the status of fetuses is adopted. What appeared to be a distinctive objection to the new genetics turns out to be a familiar and far from novel objection to the age-old practice of abortion.

Finally, the decision to try to avoid or correct disabilities, by genetic intervention or other methods, need not express any negative evaluation of people with disabilities. Instead, it may be an expression of a commitment to the value of all persons and to the importance of removing barriers to their opportunities. Thus, while advocates for people with disabilities have rightly emphasized that the stigmatization of disabilities adds additional harms to the disabilities themselves, a consistent commitment to equal opportunity requires that we try to reduce both the stigma and the physical causes of disabilities.

The morally optimal combination of attitudes would be this: a commitment to correcting or preventing disabling defects out of respect for equal opportunity for all, along with a caring acceptance of persons who have disabilities. As I have argued, there is nothing inconsistent or incoherent about this combination of attitudes; indeed, there are many parents who exhibit it. The proper course of action, then, is both to encourage respect for those who have disabilities by attacking the tendency to stigmatize and to fail to appreciate the quality of the lives of people with disabilities, and at the same time to act consistently on the commitment to equal opportunity by taking advantage of new possibilities to intervene.

## V. The Social Construction of Disability

We saw earlier that it is a mistake to assume, as disabilities rights advocates seem to do, that the choice as to whether or not to forge ahead in efforts to use genetic science to reduce disabilities is the choice between (1) pursuing merely desirable goals (improving some individuals' lives) at the risk of serious injustices (to disabled persons), and (2) forgoing the pursuit of these goals to avoid the risk of these injustices. The point there was that justice can speak in favor of genetic interventions when they are needed to assure equal opportunity by preventing undeserved and unchosen serious limitations on opportunity.

There is, however, a second, more subtle way in which justice bears on the uses of genetic interventions and other attempts to prevent or remedy genetic defects that cause disabilities. A more comprehensive view of justice, which I will develop below, will include the idea that those who are not disabled can have a legitimate interest in reducing the incidence of disabilities in *others* (through the use of genetic intervention), quite independently of the interests that individuals have in not *being* disabled themselves. To grasp the implications of this view, it will first be necessary to clarify the concept of a disability. Doing so will also strengthen and clarify the conclusion that using knowledge of how genes work may be required as a matter of equal opportunity.

To be disabled is (1) to be unable to perform some significant range of tasks or functions (2) that individuals in a reference group of which one is considered to be a member (for example, adults) are ordinarily able to do, at least under favorable conditions, (3) where the inability is not due to simple and easily corrigible ignorance, or due simply to a lack of the tools or means ordinarily available for performing such tasks or functions. Each of the three elements of the analysis of the concept of a disability will be explained in turn.[19]

*(1) The task-relative nature of disability.* One may be able to perform a certain range of tasks or functions but unable to perform many others. Accordingly, in ordinary parlance we distinguish, somewhat misleadingly, between being partially disabled and being totally disabled—even though many if not most of those who are labeled totally disabled are in fact able to perform some tasks or functions. (It has been one of the great

[19] Although this definition of "disability" is my own, it is not wholly novel. I believe it is merely an explicit elaboration of a distinction that is commonly made between a defect and a disability.

successes of the disabilities rights movement to make more people aware that one can be disabled in some respects but not in others. Hence the term "persons with disabilities" is said to be preferable to "disabled persons," to the extent that the latter may suggest a global, or all-encompassing condition of being disabled.)

*(2) The reference-group–relative nature of disability.* Where no members of a certain group are able to perform certain tasks, and where the group is identified by reference to features other than this inability, we usually do not speak of any one of them being disabled (relative to those tasks). For example, because no infants are able to drive automobiles, we do *not* say that any infant is disabled in this regard.

*(3) Disabilities are inabilities that are not remediable by simply providing information or by simply supplying the tools or means ordinarily available for the tasks in question.* If I am unable to perform a range of tasks only because I have not been given the instructions for doing so (and most people, or most people who, like me, are adults and competent, would not be able to perform that range of tasks without being supplied instructions), or only because I lack the tools or means typically available for and used to perform the tasks, then I am not disabled (so far as these tasks go). (For example, if I am unable to tie special knots but could readily tie them if told how to do so, then I do not have a knot-tying disability. If I am unable to hammer a nail only because I lack a hammer, I am not disabled.) On the other hand, if I am blind and as a consequence of my blindness am unable to perform a range of tasks which others who are otherwise like me can perform, and which I could perform were it not for my blindness, then I have a (visual) disability.

*Distinguishing between disabilities and defects.* Disabilities, thus understood, are not the same as physical or psychological *defects*, though defects, unless compensated for, corrected, or prevented, can result in disabilities. Whether a defect results in a disability depends upon the social context. An illustration will clarify this crucial point.

Suppose that one were a member of a society in which everyone had a defect of the optic nerve that made unaided vision impossible (say, a lesion that blocked transmission of electrochemical messages necessary for stimulating the visual cortex). Suppose also that, like everyone else, one were supplied with an artificial vision apparatus that enabled one to discriminate objects as well as anyone else in one's society. In this context, relative to this reference group (members of one's society) and relative to the tasks its members are ordinarily able to perform and called upon to perform on the basis of visual discrimination, one would not have a visual disability, at least if the widespread use of such visual apparatuses had for some time become standard practice.

A psychological or physical defect, at least what may be called a functional (as opposed to a cosmetic or aesthetic) defect, is the lack of a capacity required for the performance of a normal function for members of the species in question. Thus, in the example above, there is a defect in the optic nerve if a condition in that nerve (the presence of a lesion) causes the lack of the capacity to transmit messages to the visual cortex, as a normal (human) optic nerve would.

Some defects, however, have no debilitating effects, simply because they involve a lack of capacities which are not necessary for the performance of the tasks the individual is required to perform or seeks to perform in his social environment. For example, I may have a hearing defect that makes me unable to discriminate among certain notes in a particular frequency range, but this is not a disability if the ability to distinguish those notes is not needed for any task which people in my society are ordinarily expected to perform.

Therefore, although every functional defect constitutes an *inability*, not all defects result in *disabilities*, because it is only those inabilities that interfere with the performance of socially significant tasks (in one's social environment, relative to one's reference group) that count as disabilities. And as the example of the artificial visual apparatus shows, whether a defect prevents one from performing a task will depend upon what alternative ways of getting the task done are available and how commonly employed these alternatives come to be. (In a society in which eyeglasses are readily available and used by many people, myopia is not considered a disability.) For this reason it is generally better to speak of birth defects rather than birth disabilities.

## VI. Appreciating the Full Range of Options for Preventing or Removing Disabilities

Disabilities rights advocates rightly stress that individuals can benefit from learning to cope with disabilities. Nevertheless, disabilities, as such, are undesirable. They are undesirable—for those who have them—because they interfere with opportunities for performing significant tasks and for full participation in valued social interactions. It is therefore a mistake to say that disabilities are not undesirable or that they are not necessarily a disadvantage to those who have them.

It is also true, as disabilities rights advocates emphasize, that individuals who have disabilities do not always suffer from them (that is, experience physical or psychological pain or distress). Nevertheless, disabilities, as limitations on significant opportunities, are by definition undesirable, even when they do not cause suffering. They are disadvantages.

Some disabilities are preventable or removable disadvantages. Understanding the complex relational character of disabilities enables us to appreciate the full range of possibilities for removing or preventing disabilities and then to begin to articulate the different types of moral reasons that can speak in favor of realizing some possibilities rather than others.

The key idea is that a disability is a *mismatch between the individual's abilities and the demands of a range of tasks*. Given that this is so, there are in principle two main options for removing or preventing disabilities: *changing the individual* or *changing the social environment that defines the tasks*, what I shall call the infrastructure for interaction. (The infrastructure for interaction includes two chief elements: the physical infrastructure, for example, buildings, machinery, etc., and the institutional infrastructure, roughly the rules and norms of interaction.)

The individual may be changed in either of two ways: by improving his or her abilities through education or training or other nongenetic means (including ordinary medications); or by improving his or her abilities through modifying the genetic bases of these abilities or by modifying or counteracting the deleterious effects of his or her genetic defects through genetic pharmacology (pharmaceutical interventions utilizing knowledge of the functioning of the relevant genes). Utilizing all of the foregoing distinctions, we have the following list of types of options for removing or preventing disabilities.

1. *Removing disabilities by changing relevant features of the physical infrastructure of social interaction.* This option has been endorsed, with increasing success, by disabilities rights advocates. Examples include captioned television broadcasts and curb-breaks and ramps for wheelchair access. If these changes in the physical infrastructure were universal in a given society, then, relative to those tasks which they were previously unable to perform in the absence of these measures, persons would no longer be disabled. They would, of course, continue to have whatever physical defects previously caused their disabilities.

2. *Removing or preventing disabilities by changing the individual through education, training, or other nongenetic means.* Hearing-enhancing technology and, more radically, technology that serves as a complete substitute for natural hearing, are examples of this option. The special diet given to babies born with PKU (phenylketonuria) to prevent the buildup of a chemical that would produce mental retardation, or the regimen of phlebotomies to deplete or prevent excessive iron-storage for persons with nonacquired hemochromatosis, are additional instances of this second option. Finally, any special educational or training intervention (such as speech therapy or the inculcation of special strategies for mitigating the effects of a learning disability) also falls under this heading.

3. *Changing the individual by changing his or her genome or by pharmaceutical intervention based on genetic knowledge.* Included here would be gene surgery which inserts normal genes into an embryo or gamete containing a defective gene, or techniques of "switching off" defective genes in the embryo or gamete, as would pharmaceutical therapies utilizing the genetically engineered products of normal genes. All of these interventions involve preventing or removing *disabilities* by removing *defects* in the individual's genome or by using knowledge of the functioning of genes to modify or counteract the effects of the defective genes.

4. *Removing disabilities by changing the nonphysical—i.e., institutional—infrastructure of social interaction.* This option is less familiar than the preceding three, but is in principle extremely important nevertheless. A small-scale, greatly simplified example will illustrate.

Suppose that one wishes to play a card game in which everyone in a mixed group of individuals ranging from age five to age fifty can successfully participate. The "institutional infrastructure for social interaction" here is (mainly) the rules of the game. Choosing an institutional infrastructure means choosing which game, defined and governed by which set of rules, will be played.

If the game chosen is contract bridge, it is more than likely that some individuals in the group will not be able to participate successfully. Even if they are given instructions on how to play this complex card game, the youngest members of the group may not be able to play with even minimal proficiency. However, there is another option: a simpler game (a less demanding institutional infrastructure for social interaction) can be chosen in which everyone will be able to participate successfully. The point is that whether a given individual or class of individuals will be able to perform the tasks required by the institutional rules of interaction will depend, not just upon what skills and talents the individuals have, but also upon the character of the demands of the forms of interaction specified by the rules. An individual will be able to participate successfully in the interaction if there is a fit between his or her abilities and the demands of the form of interaction, and will be disabled if not.

If, instead of a limited sphere of interaction (a card game), we focus on what may be called the dominant institutional infrastructure for productive interaction or, more simply, what I shall call "the dominant cooperative scheme" in a society, then it becomes clear that *choosing the dominant cooperative scheme means choosing who will and who will not be disabled.*[20]

A dominant cooperative scheme such as that found in the contemporary U.S. and other developed countries requires individuals to have a complex array of literacy and numeracy skills if they are to participate effectively in it. These skills may not be needed to thrive in other, "less developed" societies in which the division of labor is not so elaborate and in which contractual interactions are neither so ubiquitous nor so complex. Accordingly, some individuals may be disabled ("cognitively impaired" or "mentally handicapped" or "mentally retarded" or "learning disabled") in our sort of society, but not so in another.

Typically, rough and ready classifications of abilities, along with equally crude legal conceptions of "competence," serve to qualify some persons for entering into contracts, marrying, disposing of property, etc., and to disqualify others from doing so. It is tempting to assume that these "gate-

[20] See Daniel Wikler, "Paternalism and the Mildly Retarded," in *Paternalism*, ed. Rolf E. Sartorius (Minneapolis: University of Minnesota Press, 1983), pp. 83–94; and Allen Buchanan, "Justice as Reciprocity versus Subject-Centered Justice," *Philosophy and Public Affairs*, vol. 19, no. 3 (Summer 1990), pp. 227–52.

keeping" standards and categories, these devices for excluding certain individuals from participation in complex interactions, are (or at least in principle should be) based on purely *paternalistic* considerations—that is, that minors or the severely retarded are excluded from entering into contracts, for example, simply in order to protect *them*.

On reflection it becomes apparent, however, that those who are able to participate in such complex interactions can have an interest in excluding from participation those who are not. As the example of very young children playing contract bridge with adults shows, participation by "disabled" individuals can cause discoordination and can reduce the benefits which the "abled" might otherwise reap from the form of interaction in question.

It is important to note, of course, that dominant cooperative schemes (for entire societies) have never been *chosen*, strictly speaking. Instead, they have emerged, not according to any overall conception or plan, or as the result of collective deliberation concerning alternatives, but rather from the cumulative (and largely unanticipated) effects of many interactions among many generations of individuals. However, at certain critical junctures in a society's history, it may be possible to exercise some degree of choice, over some important elements in the dominant cooperative scheme. On the threshold of the genetic revolution, we now find ourselves at such a juncture.

The opportunity to choose key elements of a dominant cooperative scheme (in the absence of authoritarian political power) can arise when two conditions are satisfied: (1) there is an anticipation of the emergence of a new technology that will have a significant impact on the nature of the dominant cooperative scheme; and (2) there are political institutions that enable some or all citizens to have an effective voice in consciously determining whether or how the technology about to emerge will be deployed. The extent to which the character of the dominant cooperative scheme becomes an *object of social choice*, as the physical infrastructure for interaction has already become (since the movement for physical access for the disabled), depends upon two factors: our will to make it so and the adequacy of our political institutions to give effect to that will.

## VII. Why Choosing a Dominant Cooperative Scheme Is a Matter of Justice

The choice of a dominant cooperative scheme is a matter of justice because this choice will determine who is disabled and who is not—and whether a person is disabled has profound significance for his or her status in society, opportunities, and overall life-prospects. Because of the economic and social advantages of being able to participate effectively in the dominant cooperative scheme, individuals have a fundamental interest in not being disabled, in having access to a dominant cooperative scheme whose demands are matched by their abilities.

It is crucial to understand, however, that this is only one side of the story. Each individual also has an important interest in having access to a dominant cooperative scheme that is the most productive and rewarding form of interaction in which he or she can participate effectively. Just as those who are disabled, and hence not able to participate effectively in a cooperative scheme, are at a disadvantage, so those who could participate in a more productive and rewarding scheme, but are barred from doing so, also lose something of value.

The fact that there are two legitimate interests at stake in questions concerning just schemes of social cooperation is tacitly recognized in the most significant legislation addressing the needs of people with disabilities to date, the Americans with Disabilities Act (ADA), passed in 1990. This law recognizes the legitimate interest in inclusion by requiring employers (private and public) to undertake *accommodations* to the special needs of those with disabilities. What this means is that some compromises with efficiency are required in the name of equal opportunity for those with disabilities. The ADA also adds the qualifier that all that is mandated is "*reasonable*" accommodation, thus signaling that the interests of employers (and workers who do not have disabilities) are also legitimate and should be accorded some weight.[21]

The choice of dominant cooperative schemes raises profound and difficult questions of justice precisely because different groups of individuals, due to differences in their abilities, can have conflicting interests in the choice of a dominant cooperative scheme. The example discussed earlier will make this clear.

The youngest persons in our imagined card game have an interest in the game that is chosen being one in which they can participate effectively—a simpler game. The older persons have an interest in the game that is chosen being a more complex and demanding game which gives them greater pleasure, is more challenging to them, etc.

This is not to say that the opposition of interests between the two groups need be total. It may be that some of the older people (for example, the grandparents of the youngest children) may also have an interest in being in a game that includes everyone. However, when the choice of a dominant cooperative scheme is at stake, and extremely large numbers of unrelated people are involved, we cannot count on such an interest in inclusion being universal or dispositive.

There is another feature of the choice of a card game that is absent in the choice of a dominant cooperative scheme for society. In the former case it may be feasible to resolve the conflict of interest by forming two different games, suited to the respective capacities of the two groups. However, for most people in most societies—especially as the global economy increasingly homogenizes the dominant cooperative frameworks of all

[21] Public Law 101-336, Title 1, Section 101 (9) in *United States Statutes at Large*, vol. 104, Part I.

societies or, rather, forges one world society defined by a single dominant framework—this is not a realistic option. Most will have no choice but to try to participate in the dominant cooperative framework. Inability to do so effectively will have grave consequences, for one's economic well-being, one's social status, one's self-esteem.

Two more examples will illustrate what is at stake here. Suppose that advances in immunology based on increased knowledge of genes makes it possible to enhance resistance to common illnesses, including the common cold, flu, etc. (The mode of intervention might be gene therapy or, more likely, genetic pharmacology utilizing drugs that stimulate the immune system.) Those who can afford health insurance that covers these interventions will be sick less often, and their illnesses will be less severe. Suppose also, as is now the case, that most people have access to health insurance and hence to this beneficial intervention, but that there is a significant proportion of the population, say 15 percent, who do not (as is also the case at present in the United States).

Standard employment contracts might come to be geared to the health needs of the majority—those who have benefited from immunological enhancement: the number of sick-leave days that employers offer to workers would reflect the risk of illness which the (enhanced) majority have. Under such conditions, those who lack access to the intervention in question would face severe limitations on employability, because they would not be able to meet prevalent expectations for work performance. Unequal access to enhancement technology would function to exclude them from the dominant cooperative scheme.

A somewhat more speculative example might be devised based on the fact that the dominant cooperative scheme is increasingly grounded in information technology. Suppose that our growing knowledge of genes that code for proteins that affect the brain eventually makes it possible to enhance certain significant aspects of cognitive and perceptual performance: those who are fortunate enough to be able to afford access to enhancements have faster rates of neural processing, the capacity to recognize and recall longer strings of symbols, and the ability to perform longer sequences of complex operations involving information management at higher speeds. If a majority or even a substantial minority of the population enjoyed such enhancements, their greater capacities might influence the direction of technology development (just as the increase in average height of recent generations has influenced architectural specifications, the dimensions of furniture, and the distance between the driver's seat and the brake pedal in automobiles). Computer hardware and software design might exploit these enhanced perceptual and cognitive abilities, with the result that those who lacked them could not operate the new systems effectively, if at all. Again, enhancement for some would result in exclusion for others.

This is not entirely a "science fiction" example. Persons with disabilities are already in many cases barred from computer technologies, simply because the operating mechanisms (keyboards, screens, the "mouse," etc.) are designed for those who are not disabled. If new information technology continues to evolve without any attempt to widen access to it, then the limits on opportunity that people with disabilities already face may be exacerbated as employability and educational advancement come to depend more and more upon the ability to use information technology.

There is at the time of this writing at least one large-scale grant project that addresses an important aspect of the general problem: access to the "information superhighway." The aim of this project is to help to ensure that equipment will be designed to minimize barriers to access to the internet and its successor technologies. The rationale for this endeavor rests on the same insight which our hypothetical example of cognitive and perceptual enhancement conveys: If technology is designed only with reference to "normal" abilities, then it may restrict rather than widen opportunities for some. And this is true regardless of whether those who do not have "normal abilities" suffer from genetic or other defects due to trauma or nongenetic disease, or whether they are simply the poor who cannot afford the enhancements that set a new level of normality with reference to which technology is designed.

Both *the interest in inclusion*, the interest in having access to a dominant cooperative scheme in which one can participate effectively, and the interest in having access to the most productive scheme in which one can participate successfully, what I shall call *the maximizing interest*, are legitimate interests. And because both are legitimate—that is, in no way intrinsically immoral—and since both are very important interests for those who have them, the problem of justice cannot be resolved by simply dismissing either interest and fully satisfying the other.

Another way to frame the problem of justice in the choice of dominant cooperative frameworks is this: Satisfying the interest in inclusion imposes costs on those who could benefit from a more demanding scheme; satisfying the maximizing interest imposes costs on those who would be excluded from effective participation in it. Remarkably enough, theorists of justice have not only failed to provide a principled account of how these conflicting interests ought to be balanced; they have almost without exception failed even to identify the problem as a problem of justice. Instead, they have framed the most basic problem of justice as that of how to determine the fair distribution of the burdens and benefits of cooperation, on the assumption that the basic character of the cooperative scheme is given. The more fundamental problem of justice, however, is that of choosing the cooperative scheme itself. Both the choice of the rules for a fair distribution of burdens and benefits *within* a cooperative scheme and the choice *of* a cooperative scheme are problems of justice, because both have profound and enduring effects on persons' most basic opportunities, welfare, and status.

Precisely because this is a problem of justice, in particular a problem of balancing legitimate and fundamental interests, it is a mistake to assume, as disabilities rights advocates tend to do, that the "abled" have an *unlimited* obligation to modify the physical and institutional framework for interaction so as to accommodate, as fully as possible, the interest in inclusion of the "disabled." For this reason, we must reject the disabilities rights advocates' slogan that we should "change society, not individuals." Rather, the problem of justice is to achieve a proper balancing of the conflicting interests (as the ADA's requirement of "reasonable accommodation" implies).

Such a balance may—and I believe should—generally give *greater* weight to the interest in inclusion. This is not to say, however, that no weight whatsoever should be given to the maximizing interest. And from this it follows that in some instances a proper balancing of the conflicting interests, or, more positively, a just effort to achieve a better fit between individuals' abilities and the demands of the dominant cooperative scheme, may require changing individuals, through genetic means or otherwise. In other words, it may be necessary to change both society and individuals. (None of this is to say, of course, that every way of changing individuals is permissible. For example, in cases where the individual is able to consent to genetic intervention, effecting changes is permissible only if consent is given.)

## VIII. Conclusions

Disabilities rights advocates rightly stress the risks of injustice that are the dark side of the rapid growth of genetic technology. Understandably, as advocates for the disabled they concentrate on the injustices to the disabled. Some of the objections they raise are profound and disturbing. They perform a great service by challenging unspoken assumptions and hidden motivations that might otherwise go unexamined in the rush of enthusiasm for improving the human condition through the application of scientific knowledge.

However, though the risks of injustice to disabled people are real, the arguments and slogans of the disabilities rights advocates in some cases cast only a partial light on the relationship between justice and genetic intervention. That relationship, I have argued, is complex. Although some uses of genetic technology undoubtedly would violate the rights of the disabled, it is a mistake to say that the core ideology of the new genetics, the project of improving human lives through the application of genetic science, *as such* devalues disabled people or violates their rights, much less that it rests on a twisted conception of what the value of human life is.

Disabilities rights advocates apparently assume that the ideology of the new genetics gives a central role to improvement through selection—the application of genetic science to determine which genes persons will have, where this sometimes is to be achieved by determining which sorts of persons will be born. It is important to point out, however, that the defining project of the new genetics is more accurately described in a less restrictive fashion as the use of knowledge about the functioning of genes to improve human lives. This includes improvement by selection, but also encompasses other modes of intervention such as genetic pharmacology.

Even if we were to limit the project of the new genetics to improvement by selection, it would still not be correct to characterize the project as being based on a commitment to *perfectionism*, if this means a devaluation of persons who are imperfect, rather than merely an attempt to improve people's lives. Since disabilities are limitations on persons' opportunities, a sincere concern for the opportunities of all persons, rather than any notion that only perfect individuals ought to exist, grounds obligations of justice to remove or prevent disabilities.

Because justice, not the false promise of perfection, requires efforts to use genetic science to reduce disabilities, it is also a mistake to contend that the choice we are faced with is either to run the risk of fundamental injustices to the disabled for the sake of merely desirable goals of improvement or to avoid the risk of injustices to them by forsaking goals that are merely desirable but not required by justice. In some cases justice, in the name of equal opportunity, demands intervention.

Although the disabilities rights advocates are correct to adopt a critical stance toward the professed universalism of the new genetics' ideology of improving human lives through the application of genetic science, the ethics of inclusion and exclusion is a much more complex domain than their criticisms suggest. Justice not only requires intervention for the sake of equal opportunity, but also may require changing individuals, *as well as* society, in order to cope with the most basic problem of social justice: the choice of a dominant cooperative scheme.

Finally, the present investigation has led to the conclusion that in choosing to deploy or not deploy our newly emerging powers for genetic intervention, we are choosing who will be disabled, in several senses. If, as some fear, "genetic improvement" is available to some, but not all (as it will be if access is according to ability to pay), then in effect we may be choosing a new dominant cooperative scheme which excludes those who are not "enhanced" from full participation—and thereby creating a new class of disabled individuals who do not suffer from any condition which we would now recognize as a genetic defect. If, in order to avoid this possibility, we choose not to develop the capacity to intervene, we also choose who will be disabled—by depriving ourselves of the means to intervene to correct or avoid genetic defects which will, given the nature of our cooperative scheme, result in disabilities.

*Business Ethics, Philosophy, and Medical Ethics,*
*University of Wisconsin, Madison*

# GERM-LINE GENETIC ENGINEERING AND MORAL DIVERSITY: MORAL CONTROVERSIES IN A POST-CHRISTIAN WORLD

By H. Tristram Engelhardt, Jr.

## I. Introduction: Human Nature in the Plural

The prospect of germ-line genetic engineering, the ability to engineer genetic changes that can be passed on to subsequent generations, raises a wide range of moral and public policy questions.[1] One of the most provocative questions is, simply put: Are there moral reasons that can be articulated in general secular terms for accepting human nature as we find it? Or, at least in terms of general secular moral restraints, may we reshape human nature better to meet our own interests, as we define them? This question in turn raises the further question of whether human nature as it now exists has a moral standing akin to sacredness that can be understood in nonreligious terms. This essay will take as a given that it is not possible to show in general secular moral terms that human nature has a sanctity or special moral standing that should guide secular health-care policy.[2] In addition, as this essay shows, it is not possible through appeals to considerations of authorizing consent or beneficence toward others to remedy this failure to establish a sanctity or special moral standing for human nature. Absent a religious or culturally normative understanding of human nature and given the availability of germ-line genetic engineering, there is a plurality of possibilities for refashioning our nature. The unavailability of substantive secular moral constraints on germ-line genetic engineering discloses a secularly licit plurality of possibilities for human nature. The likelihood that we will be able to refashion our human nature reveals how few general secular moral constraints there are to guide us. Paradoxically, the more we are able to reengineer our human nature, the less guidance is available. The plurality of possible conceptions of human well-being that can be pursued through germ-line genetic engineering challenges our self-understanding as humans. Given human freedom, and in the absence of taken-for-granted religious or

[1] A considerable literature has developed regarding the moral and public policy implications of the genome project, as well as of the prospects of genetic engineering. See *ELSI Bibliography: Ethical, Legal, and Social Implications of the Human Genome Project* (Washington, DC: U.S. Department of Energy, May 1993); and *ELSI Bibliography*, 1994 Supplement (Washington, DC: U.S. Department of Energy, September 1994).

[2] H. Tristram Engelhardt, Jr., "Human Nature Technologically Revisited," *Social Philosophy and Policy*, vol. 8, no. 1 (Autumn 1990), pp. 180–91.

 

cultural moral constraints, the likelihood of germ-line genetic engineering opens the possibility of human nature in the plural.

In this essay, the term "human nature" identifies more than merely the incarnation of a mind in a body. "Human nature" is used to identify those particularities of mind and body that mark humans as an identifiable species of rational animals. In this sense of "human nature" and given significant germ-line genetic engineering, numerous human species may once more be identifiable within the genus Homo, as was the case in the past (e.g., Homo neanderthalensis). They could be identified as distinct not merely through an appeal to an absence of cross-fertile mating, but through reference to substantial differences that would be the result of refashioning human nature in the pursuit of alternative ideals of human well-being. I acknowledge at the outset that the ways in which humans realize their nature are always determined in part by environment and culture, and presume as well that the genetic material available for determination by environment and culture is primarily afforded in terms that can be acted upon by germ-line genetic engineering. Significant genetic restructuring would then lead to speciation in the sense of (1) creating significantly different human forms and (2) producing infertile mating across types of humans. To talk about changing human nature is to talk about changing our current genetically based constellation of strengths and weaknesses. Of all scientific innovations, germ-line genetic engineering promises to be the most radical and intimate.

In exploring concerns raised by the prospect of germ-line genetic interventions, I do not assume that within the next few decades sufficient strides will have been made in germ-line genetic engineering so as to allow a significant reshaping of the human genome. My assumption is rather that such abilities will be realized over the next centuries. It is only within the last two hundred years that anatomy, pathology, physiology, biochemistry, microbiology, etc., have become basic sciences in the sense of being foundational to the clinical practice of medicine. My assumption is that over the next centuries the genetic sciences and technologies will emerge as cardinal basic sciences in providing a key to the traditional basic sciences. The genetic sciences and technologies will likely be used in effecting major genetic restructurings of both human anatomy and physiology.

We have the luxury of being able to reflect on the moral quandaries we will face, if such advances occur. This essay offers an exploration of one among the issues that will need to be addressed: Are there substantive or only procedural constraints on the refashioning of human nature? As we turn to making ourselves our own objects in the sense of determining how to reshape ourselves through our own technologies, can we articulate any firm moral constraints or guidelines? As we confront the most revolutionary opportunity with regard to our own nature, are we at the same time radically despoiled of firm guideposts? Or, does the very possibility of being able to reshape our nature despoil us of the possibility of securing substantive constraints and helpful moral direction? Can we discover content-full secular moral norms, or are we left with agreement and moral diversity—a likely plurality of outcomes?

## II. Humanity, Humanitas, and the Normatively Human

From Greco-Roman times, in legal codes such as the Institutes of Gaius and the Justinian Code, a notion of the normatively human has directed reflections concerning morality and public policy. When Napoleon remarked regarding Goethe, "Voilà un homme!"[3] he was not identifying species membership, but rather affirming a particular notion of human excellence. Napoleon was using "homme" against a history of celebrating the normatively human. In the Greco-Roman world, many took pains to understand the term *philanthropia* as not merely love of one's fellow man, but rather as an endorsement of those traits that are most excellently human.[4] These concerns became tied to the term *humanitas* and its cognates: Cicero helped popularize these and joined them to the phrase *studia humanitatis*.[5] In the term's various usages in *humanissime* (being very kind), *humanitas* (kindness), *humanitas* (urbanity), *sensus humanitatis* (a feeling of humanity), Cicero is drawing on a view of what distinguishes humans from other animals.

At stake is not merely a description of biological characteristics, but an affirmation of the ways in which humans deport themselves with excellence and grace. Aulus Gellius, in the mid-second century A.D., ties together these various interests in refinement, education, erudition, and the normatively human:

> Those who have spoken Latin and have used the language correctly do not give to the word *humanitas* the meaning which it is commonly thought to have, namely, what the Greeks call "philanthropia," signifying a kind of friendly spirit and good-feeling towards all men without distinction; but they gave to *humanitas* about the force of the Greek *paedeia*; that is, what we call *eruditionem institutionemque in bonas artes*, or "education and training in the liberal arts." Those who earnestly desire and seek after these are most highly humanized. For the pursuit of that kind of knowledge, and the training given by it,

[3] Emil Ludwig, *Napoleon*, trans. Eden and Cedar Paul (New York: Modern Library), p. 322.

[4] See, for example, Werner Jaeger, *Humanism and Theology* (Milwaukee: Marquette University Press, 1943), esp. p. 87; see also Jaeger, *Paideia: The Ideals of Greek Culture*, 3 vols. (Oxford: Oxford University Press, 1943–45).

[5] Franz Beckmann, *Humanitas* (Münster: Aschendorff, 1952).

> have been granted to man alone of all the animals, and for that reason it is termed humanitas, or "humanity."[6]

Though Gellius is manifestly concerned with the cultural and intellectual environment that will educate sensibilities and produce refinement, the Latin *humanitas* suggests that one is drawing the excellences of human refinement out of human nature, so that they can be given full expression. A background human nature, which can be expressed in certain excellences, is presupposed by the ancients and continues in the humanities to the present. The humanists of the Renaissance understood themselves as cultivating the truly human,[7] as did theorists of the second humanism at the beginning of the nineteenth century, such as Wilhelm von Humboldt (1767–1835) and Friedrich Niethammer (1766–1848).[8] The same can be said regarding theorists of the new humanism, such as Irving Babbitt (1865–1933) and Paul E. Moore (1864–1937), or those of the third humanism, such as Horst Rüdiger (1908– ) and Werner Jaeger (1888–1961), writing at the end of the nineteenth and the first half of the twentieth centuries. The attempt was again to preserve an accent on those marks of excellence that distinguish humans.[9] A complex set of moral and aesthetic concerns have been expressed around a cluster of concepts associated with that which is normatively human.[10]

These reflections concerning the normatively human involve a cluster of aesthetic and moral ideals, each of which presupposes particular sensibilities, aesthetic responses, intelligences, and responses to the world. In antiquity, a unity could be given to the normatively human by accepting a particular cultural perspective as canonical. Thus, for the Roman world, *humanitas* was unproblematically associated with *romanitas*. *Homo humanus* was *Homo romanus*, as opposed to *Homo barbarus*. Those humans who acted *romaniter* were equivalent to those who acted *humaniter*.[11] These associated understandings were embedded in an intact set of moral practices and traditions. Stoic and Roman reflections on natural law provided a theoretical grounding in human nature of the values associated with the normatively human. There was a human nature, and it had value impli-

[6] *The Attic Nights of Aulus Gellius*, trans. John C. Rolfe (Cambridge, MA: Harvard University Press, 1978), XIII.xvii.1, vol. 2, p. 457.

[7] Paul O. Kristeller, *Renaissance Thought* (New York: Harper and Row, 1961).

[8] See, e.g., Friedrich Niethammer, *Der Streit des Philanthropinismus und Humanismus* (Jena: Frommann, 1801).

[9] See Norman Foerster, ed., *Humanism and America* (New York: Farrar and Rinehart, 1930); Richard Newald, *Probleme und Gestalten des deutschen Humanismus* (Berlin: Walter de Gruyter, 1963); and Horst Rüdiger, *Wesen und Wandlung des Humanismus* (Hamburg: Hoffmann and Campe, 1937).

[10] H. Tristram Engelhardt, Jr., *Bioethics and Secular Humanism: The Search for a Common Morality* (Philadelphia: Trinity Press International, 1991).

[11] Martin Heidegger, "Brief über den 'Humanismus'," in Heidegger, *Wegmarken* (Frankfurt/Main: Vittorio Klostermann, 1976), esp. pp. 319f.

cations.[12] Final grounding and focus was provided by the Judeo-Christian appreciation of a single God creating a single nature. This appreciation was further strengthened in the Christian recognition of the Incarnation as the unique bond between human nature and the nature of God.[13] All of this fortified the expectation that the normatively human could be identified and could guide policy.

## III. The Loss of Human Nature as a Given for Moral and Political Theory

Against the prospect of germ-line genetic engineering and in a post-Christian world, this expectation is brought into question. The normatively human, insofar as it depends on particularities of inclination, sensibility, and intelligence, is in principle open to being recast through the intrusions of germ-line genetic engineering, as one becomes able to engineer and direct human evolution. Indeed, the mapping of the human genome, the demonstrated feasibility of somatic cell genetic engineering (genetically based changes that cannot be passed on to one's offspring), and the clear possibility of significant germ-line genetic engineering change the relationship of humans to human nature. Human nature, which is still a relatively unalterable given, would become a cardinal point in the human refashioning of the human condition. Whether understood as the gift of God or merely as the deliverance of spontaneous mutations, random selection, genetic drift, cosmic happenstance, and biochemical constraints, human nature has until now been regarded as placing constraints on human freedom. Indeed, it has served as a point of orientation for morality, political theory, and the biomedical sciences. The character of human nature has provided a point of departure for articulating natural law, understanding human sympathies (and their limits), establishing governmental responses to the improvidence of humans, and framing human expectations regarding the roles of government. Human nature as given to us by God or produced for us by evolution has been a secure starting-point not only for arguing what could and should be done, but also for arguing what could not or should not be done. Human nature has been given a more central place than the general character of the universe, for here nature shapes the starting-point of all human undertakings.

Human nature provides bases for expectations regarding aging, suffering, disability, and death. It grounds taken-for-granted, normal, or ordi-

[12] Greek, Stoic, and Roman thinkers such as Chrysippus (279–206 B.C.) and Cicero (106–43 B.C.) developed the Greek distinction between positive law (*dikaion nomikon*) and natural law (*dikaion physikon*). This distinction came to be incorporated into Roman laws such as the Institutes of Gaius (A.D. 161). See, for example, Francis de Zulueta, *The Institutes of Gaius*, 2 vols. (Oxford: Clarendon Press, 1976).

[13] I explore the difficulties of transferring a religious notion of the sanctity of nature into a serviceable secular moral concept in "Human Nature Technologically Revisited" (*supra* note 2). See also Kurt Bayertz, *Sanctity of Life and Human Dignity* (Dordrecht: Kluwer, 1996).

nary expectations regarding human abilities and limitations. It predisposes human beings to accept certain sufferings as natural (e.g., the pain of teething and childbirth) and to view death at certain ages (e.g., in the late nineties) as being acceptable. The likely range of human abilities and limitations is determined by the interaction of humans with the environment and other organisms. Whether a particular environment or set of organisms is threatening, neutral, or congenial depends as much on the character of humans as on the character of the environment or the organisms. The sensitivity of humans to various materials in the environment makes such materials into pollutants. The circumstance that humans can contract tuberculosis, hepatitis, and AIDS makes the organisms associated with these phenomena infectious agents. As one is able to refashion human nature, one will also be able to change the ways in which the environment and other organisms are regarded. One will also change what limitations and abilities are regarded as normal or natural.

This is as much the case with respect to the complex cultural environments in which post-industrial humans live, as with regard to environments understood in more physical terms. Human institutions, laws, and expectations are in great measure framed in terms of expectations regarding human capacities to learn, to know, and to respond effectively. Policies regarding education, police, and welfare are all governed by expectations regarding the usual responses of humans. Such appeals, however, presume that human nature is a given, a source of perennial guidance and constraints. Adaptation is primarily directed toward changing the environment, not toward changing the character of humans. Everything is different if human nature, which supplied enduring content to concrete moral concerns, can itself be changed. Though there will surely be physical, chemical, and biological limits to any self-refashioning of human nature, the particular content of our human nature is now open for significant recasting by genetic engineering. Our human nature, our most intimate place in the cosmos—that in terms of which we have framed much of morality and public policy—is about to become the focus of our manipulating and transforming energies.

## IV. From Sanctity to Happenstance: The Loss of Ultimate Orientation

There are likely to be substantial cultural constraints on facing the problem of determining whether secular morality can offer firm guidelines or constraints as we move genetically to reengineer our human nature. The difficulties may lie in the remaining, unnoticed influences on secular thought of the cultural force of once widely acknowledged theological commitments.[14] Within the Judeo-Christian religions, there are substantial grounds for hesitations regarding intervening in the human

[14] The reader should be given notice: the author is an Orthodox Christian who holds that, although reason does not provide canonical moral content, revelation does.

genome. After all, once one acknowledges that human nature is created by God, even if created through evolution, the basic design of human nature can be recognized as having a fundamental status through divine endorsement. Indeed, the basic design of human nature can be recognized as having a kind of sanctity or moral standing because, as emphasized in the first chapter of Genesis: the goodness of human nature is guaranteed by God. Moreover, the Christian recognition of the significance of the Incarnation, of God becoming man, includes a divine affirmation and acceptance of human nature now redeemed from the Fall. The normatively human can then be recognized in Jesus Christ, through Whom human nature is affirmed by being united to God. The Judeo-Christian heritage discloses a central metaphysical anchor in the reflections on human nature. It indicates where to look for constraints when one turns to refashioning that nature.

Within a secular culture that no longer recognizes humans as creatures of God, much less as having a nature taken on by God through the Incarnation, this cosmic centrality of human nature is lost. This circumstance is more profound than the cosmic disorientation engendered by Copernicus, Giordano Bruno, and Galileo Galilei, who placed the world in a cosmos in which humans were no longer the center. The post-Darwinian, post-Christian worldview removes human nature from the moral center of things. Human nature becomes the outcome of biological and chemical forces, happenstance and chance, so that its particular characteristics no longer have a claim as moral constraints on human technological powers. There may still among the secular be an agonizing sense that human nature must in some sense be sacred. However, that sense of sanctity cannot coherently be articulated without a source of holiness. A transcendent purpose or grounding for an overriding value is not available, because the secular is immanent. There remains instead a cluster of vague intuitions regarding the impropriety of radically reconstructing human nature. In a post-Christian secular society, those vague intuitions can no longer be placed within the traditions and moral practices that originally gave them their force and substance.

## V. Secular Moral Constraints: Some Guidance, No Specific Content

The cardinal difficulty is that one cannot resolve moral controversies in morally substantive terms (i.e., other than by indicating formal contradictions) without presuming a particular moral vision. In order to know which choices maximize benefits over harms, one must already be able to compare different kinds of harms and benefits (i.e., liberty harms and benefits, equality harms and benefits, etc.). In order to maximize preference satisfaction, one must know how to compare rational versus impassioned preferences, as well as know the correct discount rate for time. In order for an appeal to a hypothetical-choice theory to deliver an answer, one must have already outfitted the chooser with one among the many possible moral senses or thin theories of the good. That is, if one wishes to resolve a moral controversy in substantive terms, one must already agree on basic moral premises or on an account of moral evidence (which will presuppose a particular guiding moral sense, thin theory of the good, etc.). Substantive, not merely formal, resolutions of moral controversies require substantive guidance so as to be able to choose among alternatives. The attempt rationally to discover moral content either begs the question or involves an infinite regress.

In such circumstances, by sound argument one cannot decide moral controversies about the substantive nature of justice, beneficence, or constraints on refashioning human nature without first considering important substantive issues of moral controversy. However, without agreeing to background moral premises, one can still resolve moral controversies by decision, by agreement of all involved. Such a way of resolving moral controversies will not presuppose a particular moral content or rely on a preponderant consensus. It will instead approach the resolution of controversies on the basis of the authorization of those involved. As a result, contracts and market transactions become the paradigm example of moral controversy resolution and moral authorization. The appeal to agreement becomes the one way of resolving controversies in a morally authoritative way that does not presuppose either a religious revelation or the acceptance of a particular content-full moral view. One finds by default a possibility for the resolution of moral controversies where the authority for the resolution is that of agreement and where the resolution's grammar requires for its possibility using others only with their consent. Appeal to consent is not as such valued, but is integral to a cardinal practice of moral controversy resolution. Those who enter into this practice can understand the general secular morally authoritative resolution of moral controversies without agreement regarding particular content-full moral premises. Those who do not enter will lack any such basis for common morally authoritative action and will in this sense be secular moral outlaws. The appeal to agreement is the disclosure of a secular moral possibility, a kind of transcendental possibility.[15]

As a surrogate for appeals to moral constraints grounded in our character as humans, the appeal to consent or permission offers no content-full guidance. Consent, absent the incorporation of particular notions of the good or the right, involves mere permission: bare concurrence or agreement. To require more from consent than mere agreement in the absence of coercion on the part of those one agrees with, is to build into permission particular notions of benefits, harms, and proper conduct, as is the case with the various legal requirements for free and informed

[15] This argument is developed more fully in H. Tristram Engelhardt, Jr., *The Foundations of Bioethics*, 2d ed. (New York: Oxford University Press, 1996), chs. 1–4.

consent. Consent by itself requires only permission. Permission requires at most a procedural resolution of controversies (e.g., through consent or contract). It does not by itself bring with it any specific moral content, for the primary authority of consent is not the good of liberty but bare conveyance of authority. Indeed, one can freely decide to limit one's own freedom; for example, one can give permission to have one's range of liberty limited, as one does by joining the French Foreign Legion.

Consent as mere permission requires at most that all actual persons involved give actual agreement. With respect to future persons, such as children to be produced through genetic engineering, an appeal to consent or permission also offers little guidance. This should not be unexpected. After all, children never consent to being born. Moreover, unless children are brought into an existence not worth living by their own lights, it is impossible on the basis of requirements of permission to justify an objection to their creation, to their being brought into existence in an acceptable, albeit nonoptimal, circumstance. If children's characters are determined in part by their disposition to value certain states, then, given that germ-line genetic engineering will shape their very proclivities and dispositions, they will judge whether they are harmed or benefited in terms of those new proclivities and dispositions. They can be said to have been created in violation of obligations of consent or permission only if one has grounds to hold that those created would refuse to agree to their creation by sincerely wishing never to have been. Since the future is always opaque, the most that can be required of those producing children under the appeal to permission is that they not produce children in circumstances in which they could anticipate that the children would rather not exist.

It is not simply that one cannot appeal to permission to gain substantive guidance; one equally cannot invoke substantive notions of beneficence in setting moral impediments to reshaping human nature in fundamentally new ways. What will count as doing good depends on the views, character, and nature of the person receiving the good. In addition, substantive understandings of altruism or beneficence presuppose taken-for-granted background understandings of the nature, interests, character, and inclinations of humans—including the value assigned to various kinds of liberty. Such understandings give content to notions of the good. But if that very nature, set of interests, and cluster of inclinations are themselves available to be reshaped, so, too, is the content-full character of what will count as beneficent interventions. As one alters what can be the basis of successfully beneficent actions toward others, one changes what must count as concrete rules for beneficent actions. With germ-line genetic engineering which could produce humans with new sympathies and inclinations, those so produced would then presumably be as satisfied with their existence as we are, only by new standards. In any event, to quiet some moral scruples and to focus this inquiry more narrowly, one need only imagine that genetic engineering will be able to produce children as reliably and safely as is now possible through ordinary feral, in vivo means, so as to meet currently accepted standards of responsible reproduction.

This is not to say that one cannot morally rule out interventions that are malevolent or likely to produce outcomes which the recipients can be anticipated to abhor. Malevolence violates morality without invoking any particular moral content, by being directed against morality. To produce children malevolently—that is, to produce children in circumstances that the producers hold to be improper, even if those produced would find them acceptable—is to act contrary to morality as directed to the good. In addition, judgments can be made regarding matters of beneficence, given some substantive agreement regarding the nature of the good. For example, one can envisage that there will be some avoidable outcomes of germ-line genetic engineering, which are easily worse than other outcomes, so that some alternatives can be judged to be preferable. Such comparisons of alternatives can provide guidance insofar as they exhibit a commonality sufficient to allow judgments of better and worse outcomes, preferable and less preferable alternatives.[16]

Novel moral challenges arise from the possibility of substantially different ways of refashioning human nature, which would allow the pursuit of different constellations of goods, so that one would need to compare quite different and mutually exclusive benefits. Given no morally neutral way of choosing among most substantively different visions of the good (i.e., other than the constraints set by permission and nonmalevolence), it is not possible to determine which radical reengineerings of human nature are morally impermissible. Imagine, for example, that one could genetically engineer either gills to allow "breathing" under water or lungs to live in a very low oxygen environment. Imagine also that one could engineer the ideal sedentary philosopher able to sit for hours reading philosophical tomes and swilling large portions of good port without any adverse health outcomes. Genetic engineering will very likely offer not just better or worse outcomes, but outcomes that realize fundamentally different biological and physiological excellences. It is this possibility of divergent excellences that offers the most novel challenge. Genetic engineering allows the pursuit of different understandings of health and well-being in the absence of substantive guidance regarding what is morally licit.

From the foregoing it does not appear possible to secure secular moral guideposts and constraints on germ-line genetic engineering beyond rather formal ones such as: (1) do not use actual persons without their consent, (2) do not act against future persons in ways one presumes they would not find acceptable, (3) do not act with malevolent intent against future

[16] See Derek Parfit, *Reasons and Persons* (Oxford: Clarendon Press, 1984), esp. pp. 371–417.

persons, and (4) when commensurable goods are at stake, all else being equal, attempt to maximize the good. Some risky undertakings may violate these conditions so as clearly to be proscribable. One is left with a vast range of possibilities open to be chosen in the absence of general secular moral constraints. Faced with the prospect of being able to refashion human nature, it is not possible to find a content-full, normative, secular understanding of human nature to guide the unparalleled project of refashioning the character of human nature and of shaping evolution by genetic engineering.

Insofar as one seeks to give substantive moral guidance, one asks a question that cannot be answered in the terms in which it is posed. There are no general secular moral restraints on interventions into the human genome that can establish on principle the moral impropriety of refashioning human nature. To arrive at such restraints would require showing (1) that intervening in the human genome is in some sense in principle immoral, or (2) that the use of genetic engineering would always cause more harm than benefit. To show that germ-line genetic interventions are in principle impermissible would require establishing that the current status of the human genome has a sanctity that cannot be established in general secular terms. Secular moral concerns that do not involve moral obligations regarding permission and nonmalevolence collapse into concerns about how most prudently to maximize benefits over harms. Even to show that genetic engineering in general will cause more harm than benefit would require comparing imponderable risks of (1) possible noxious outcomes due to genetic intervention versus (2) possible noxious outcomes due to the unavailability of genetic engineering (which could, e.g., protect humans against new and highly virulent lethal viruses). Such concerns regarding imponderable outcomes at best cancel each other out. Particular rankings of benefits and harms must take into account how benefits and harms will likely be perceived by those who come into existence as the result of genetic engineering. All of this depends on particular persons in particular communities with particular human natures.

## VI. Genetic Engineering: Facing the Possibilities

The challenge is to place the enterprise of germ-line genetic engineering within a coherent moral understanding, a set of moral practices, and a moral tradition, such that particular undertakings can be seen to be appropriate and others forbidden. To recast arguments from Alasdair MacIntyre regarding the broken character of Western moral practices (i.e., the view that to resolve moral controversies coherently, one must share intact moral understandings and practices, and such common moral understandings are no longer available in the West), the difficulty is that a framework within which to understand which interventions in human nature are appropriate or inappropriate is no longer at hand, beyond requirements that one act with consent, not be malevolent, and attempt to achieve the good. Since there is no agreement about the nature of the good or the good of human nature, substantive guidance has been lost. Content-full guidance requires intact moral practices and traditions, as MacIntyre has argued.[17] In the absence of such traditions, such as those supplied by an intact religious or cultural perspective, disinclinations to engage in significant germ-line genetic engineering directed toward enhancing particular human abilities or creating new ones will at best appear to be taboos.

Faced with the challenge of justifying general secular moral constraints regarding the refashioning and recreation of human nature, one encounters numerous understandings of what is morally significant concerning human nature and of which evolutionary goals should be invoked in guiding evolution. Confronted with numerous competing understandings of the normatively natural and of the goals appropriate to humans, one can recast a phrase from MacIntyre and ask *which* human nature, *whose* evolutionary goals should guide germ-line genetic engineering. As we face the possibility of reconstructing ourselves to meet our own goals, who is the *we* to define the goals? Which goals should be normative? Once the normativity of a theological context is lost, the normative and univocal character of the design of human nature is lost as well. Different moral communities with different framing moral premises and different rules of moral evidence and inference will likely endorse different goals.

## VII. Disease, Health, and Human Enhancement

Because of the deservedly bad reputation that has befallen eugenics in this century because of the moral atrocities of the National Socialists, as well as out of other considerations, there has been an attempt to draw a line between medical interventions to cure diseases and those to enhance function. If one could find firm moral grounds for only treating diseases but never enhancing human functions, then many of the difficult questions regarding how much enhancement is proper could be clearly answered. Interventions aimed at curing disease would not involve the question of the extent to which human nature may or may not appropriately be recast through human germ-line genetic interventions. It is for this reason that somatic cell and germ-line genetic engineering would be relatively unproblematic, if they were directed only toward restoring individuals to age- and sex-appropriate, species-typical levels of species-typical functions.

[17] See Alasdair MacIntyre, *Whose Justice? Which Rationality?* (Notre Dame, IN: University of Notre Dame Press, 1988); and MacIntyre, *After Virtue* (Notre Dame, IN: University of Notre Dame Press, 1981).

The difficulty is in understanding why medicine should be restricted to treating only failures to achieve age- and sex-appropriate species-typical levels of species-typical functions, since medicine regularly treats states of affairs that do not satisfy these restraining conditions.[18] Presbyopia, decay of teeth and bones, glucose intolerance after age seventy, benign prostatic hyperplasia in elderly males, and osteoporosis tied to menopause are among the long list of species-typical characteristics and levels of functions to which medicine regularly turns its therapeutic powers. Indeed, the actual practice of medicine does not appear directly concerned with what is species-typical, but rather with what involves unacceptable losses in function, grace, or anatomical form, unacceptable levels of pain or suffering, or what is appreciated as a premature death. Medicine has traditionally been concerned with ameliorating pain and suffering as well as helping individuals achieve the goals they are hindered in realizing, due to the limitations of anatomy, physiology, and psychology.[19]

This complaint-oriented character of medicine is in practice constrained by appeals to usual or ordinary levels of human function, pain, grace, and life expectancy. Such appeals serve to delegitimate complaints, restrain social expectations, or limit the use of scarce resources in terms of a set of usually implicit background understandings of what it is reasonable to seek through medical interventions. Invocations of what is "typical" are used to justify or delegitimate demands for health care. If a ninety-year-old man complains that he has trouble with some shortness of breath after running up three flights of stairs, it is not at all unreasonable to reflect that most men are dead at the age of ninety, and for him to expect the vigor of youth is unreasonable. To want the same well-being as a twenty-year-old is to expect a state of affairs that is not only not species-typical for sex and age, but also not feasible. Once it becomes feasible, the project of allowing individuals to realize species-atypical levels of function for age becomes reasonable. The medical expectations of individuals are placed within the usual and the typical. Notions of disease and illness are freighted with a complex set of subtle evaluations regarding what it is reasonable to expect in aid and treatment from others and what one should accept as one's lot in life.

Notwithstanding contrary trends in the history of medicine, with its culturally conditioned notions of disease and accounts of treatment, considerable energies have been invested in attempting to provide an account of disease and health not dependent on particular, culturally determined understandings. These efforts have in part been expended in the service of establishing an account of medicine that can transcend

[18] See Christopher Boorse, "Health as a Theoretical Concept," *Philosophy of Science*, vol. 44 (1977), pp. 542–73.

[19] See Engelhardt, *The Foundations of Bioethics*, 2d ed., ch. 5.

cultural vagaries. Such efforts have often been combined with a concern to distinguish responses to mere human whim from interventions to treat true somatic diseases.[20] With the advent of concerns with health-care cost containment and the allocation of scarce medical resources, these arguments have been directed to distinguishing between mere desires brought to medicine for fulfillment and true medical needs demanding attention.

The goal has been to find a culture-independent border between those interventions that are truly medical (in that they respond to true diseases) and those that are not truly medical (in that they respond to conditions that are not true diseases, but mere dissatisfactions with elements of the human condition). Were such a border available, one could then direct the energies of physicians and the resources of society toward addressing real medical needs and not face the prospect of a health-care system without firm boundaries regarding what it is committed to treating. A leading strategy has been to identify as diseases those states of affairs that involve deviations from species-typical levels of species-typical functions. The assumption has been that, if one could identify those medical needs which are based on the failure to realize a species-typical level of species-typical function, one would not be hostage to particular cultural understandings of the goals of medicine that might be overexpansive. One could draw a distinction between when medicine is invited to respond to mere human desires and when it is invoked to respond to true human needs.[21] One would also have guidance in the proper use of germ-line genetic engineering. One would find limits to germ-line genetic engineering that have their basis in the true character of diseases and, derivatively, in the proper goals of medicine.

The difficulty lies in the heterogeneous character of the states traditionally addressed therapeutically by medicine. Medicine responds to the absence of (1) age- and sex-appropriate levels of usual human functions, (2) acceptable grace in deportment (e.g., freedom from uncontrollable rhythmic motion), (3) acceptable anatomical form, (4) acceptable freedom from pain, suffering, and vexation, and (5) acceptable freedom from premature death. Any account of appropriateness, acceptability, or prematurity depends on what is usually expected from humans of a particular age and sex. Once one can alter that which is usual, the hope of discovering clear lines evanesces. In addition, once one recognizes the pleomorphic character of human form and function, it becomes difficult to identify particular deportment, form, levels of function, and freedom from suf-

[20] See Edmund D. Pellegrino and David C. Thomasma, *A Philosophical Basis of Medical Practice* (New York: Oxford University Press, 1981); Pellegrino and Thomasma, *For the Patient's Good* (New York: Oxford University Press, 1988); and Leon Kass, "Regarding the End of Medicine and the Pursuit of Health," *The Public Interest*, vol. 40 (Summer 1975), pp. 11–42.

[21] Norman Daniels, *Just Health Care* (New York: Cambridge University Press, 1985).

fering as those which are species-typical in the sense of species normative. Moreover, and crucially, insofar as there are diverse ecological niches within which humans now or in the future might wish to thrive, and insofar as there are different and indeed competing notions of human excellence and thriving, there will be numerous competing notions of how humans ought appropriately to understand health or successful adaptation.

An examination of concepts such as disease, health, and successful adaptation discloses a connection between those concepts and various moral and nonmoral values and goals. To be diseased is not to be able, because of biological or psychological hindrances, to do the things one takes to be appropriate, to live an appropriate lifespan, or to have acceptable grace in deportment. Or it is to be subject to pain or suffering considered to be inappropriate. In great measure, in the history of medicine problems have been considered medical insofar as medicine has been able to address them. To treat a problem as medical is to place it within biological and psychological causal accounts, and to expect that medicine can provide prognoses, if not therapeutic benefits. Medicine also brings special role-expectations (i.e., the sick role generally absolves one from being guilty for being ill, though one may be guilty for having become ill, for having knowingly done things that would harm one's health; it excuses one from certain social duties and may vest one with special welfare rights; the sick role also identifies medical experts and obliges one to seek medical intervention).[22] The social practice of medicine is one directed toward prevention, treatment, cure, and care, not toward punishment, and thus stands apart from other social practices such as the law. Given established human expectations and scarce medical resources, energies are more frequently directed to those hindrances, pains, and limitations that are accepted as inappropriate for men or women of particular ages. But what appears crucial is the feasibility, the costs involved in ameliorating a limitation or burden.

This analysis undermines the possibility of discovering in the results of evolution a morally significant line between diseases and various competing, positive notions of health. Medicine as a social practice is directed toward clusters of complaints that are acknowledged as warrants for medical intervention. These, however, are dependent on particular value expectations. Medically cognizable diseases, illnesses, disabilities, impairments, disorders, and problems are states of affairs that fail to meet particular accepted ideals of function, form, deportment, grace, freedom from pain, and risk of death, and whose treatment is understood within estab-

[22] Talcott Parsons, "Definitions of Health and Illness in the Light of American Values and Social Structure," in *Patients, Physicians, and Illness*, ed. E. G. Jaco (Glencoe, IL: Free Press, 1958), pp. 165–87.

lished therapy roles.[23] Once these ideals and expectations change, the goals of medicine change.

## VIII. CONCLUSION

Germ-line genetic engineering has the prospect of being the case of scientific innovation par excellence. It may well be able to change the very ways in which humans can understand the task of adapting to their environment and establishing successful social structures. It may well be able to change our concerns regarding what is an environmental threat. It has the prospect of changing the range of social problems to which governments may be moved to attend. But this is only one dimension of germ-line genetic engineering's moral significance. As significant is the possible plurality of human well-beings and ways of fashioning human nature, which it by default discloses. This plurality reveals our inability in general secular moral terms to discover which way of fashioning human nature should determine our future. It therefore presents the possibility that numerous possible future alternatives may be chosen, fracturing mankind into numerous different species of humans. By raising the possibility of substantially changing the character of human responses to the environment and other humans, germ-line genetic engineering discloses how little guidance general secular moral reflection can provide. Any attempt rationally to discover which particular moral content should be guiding or normative either begs the question or involves an infinite regress. As with most significant secular moral and public policy challenges, one finds individuals faced with the choice of creating policy in the absence of general secular, rationally discoverable content-full norms.

*Medicine and Philosophy, Baylor College of Medicine and Rice University*

[23] H. Tristram Engelhardt, Jr., "Clinical Problems and the Concept of Disease," in *Health, Disease, and Causal Explanations in Medicine*, ed. L. Nordenfelt and B. I. B. Lindahl (Dordrecht: D. Reidel, 1984), pp. 27–41.

# SELF-CRITICAL FEDERAL SCIENCE? THE ETHICS EXPERIMENT WITHIN THE U.S. HUMAN GENOME PROJECT

By Eric T. Juengst

## I. Introduction

On October 1, 1988, thirty-five years after co-discovering the structure of the DNA molecule, Dr. James Watson launched an unprecedented experiment in American science policy.[1] In response to a reporter's question at a press conference, he unilaterally set aside 3 to 5 percent of the budget of the newly launched Human Genome Project to support studies of the ethical, legal, and social implications of new advances in human genetics. The Human Genome Project (HGP), by providing geneticists with the molecular maps of the human chromosomes that they use to identify specific human genes, will speed the proliferation of a class of DNA-based diagnostic and risk-assessment tests that already create professional ethical and health-policy challenges for clinicians. "The problems are with us now, independent of the genome program, but they will be associated with it," Watson said. "We should devote real money to discussing these issues."[2] By 1994, the "ELSI program" (short for "Ethical, Legal, and Social Implications") had spent almost $20 million in pursuit of its mission, and gained both praise and criticism for its accomplishments.

In this essay, I offer an evaluation of the ELSI experiment as one example of how society and the scientific community might go about addressing the policy issues raised by scientific innovation. My assessment is drawn from my experience as one of this experiment's principle lab techs and bottle-washers during my tenure as Chief of the ELSI Branch at the National Institutes of Health (NIH)'s National Center for Human Genome Research (NCHGR) between 1990 and 1994. Like any lab manager, I have both allegiances to the enterprise and reservations about the methods chosen—particularly when they leave unsightly stains on the glassware. For science policy experiments, one of the most troublesome precipitates is the buildup of false expectations. In fact, as I hope will become clear below, my main goal with this essay is to scrub off just such an encrustation.

[1] Harold Schmeck, "DNA Pioneer to Tackle Biggest Gene Project Ever," *New York Times*, October 4, 1988, pp. C1, C6.

[2] Leslie Roberts, "Genome Project Gets Underway at Last," *Science*, vol. 243 (January 13, 1989), pp. 167–68.

This is not a philosopher's philosophical essay. It is intended to be a piece of "science policy analysis," and, as such, remains faithful to the conventions of no particular intellectual discipline. Developing public policy about scientific innovation is a promiscuous business. It makes strange bedfellows and inevitably infects the purer modes of discourse it picks up with dubious social agendas. In the spirit of this eclecticism, I have given this essay a hybrid genre-type: it takes the form of proposal, flanked by two brief histories, an opening argument, and a parting shot. Since that seems to describe the intellectual basis of most of our public policies about science, it should work just fine.

In brief, the theses I would like to pursue through the next five sections are the following:

1. The two intrinsic critiques of the ELSI program—that it necessarily amounts to either alarmist hype (because there are no special issues here) or public relations (because it cannot bite the hand that feeds it)—will both continue to be wrong as long as the program's original concept as a source of independent explorations of the social context of genome research is preserved.

2. The extrinsic critique of the ELSI program—that it is not an effective agent of change—is also being belied by the program's emerging track record of practical accomplishments. Cultivating a community of committed and expert genomics-watchers turns out to provide an admirably flexible capacity to develop and influence policy: an "un-commission" for professional and public policy on genetic issues.

3. On the other hand, the direction in which the ELSI program has been taken during the Human Genome Project's efforts to increase the pace of the program's accomplishments is not promising. By striving to recast the ELSI program as a more traditional commission, the HGP plays into the hands of its critics, and neglects the strengths and protections that the program's original conception supplies. Fortunately, it is not too late to regroup, and in Section IV of the essay, I propose steps the program can take to preserve its commitment to building a community while it becomes more "proactive."

4. The best evidence for the power of the "un-commission" is the ELSI program's most successful cascade of practical accomplishments to date: efforts to address questions about the conduct of genome research itself that were not even on the program's original agenda.

5. In the current national political climate, characterized by a receptivity to special pleading by specific constituencies and an (incompatible) commitment to cost-cutting, it is worth considering whether, in lieu of clamoring for a new (traditional) national bioethics commission, it wouldn't be better to pursue the "un-commission" approach for a wider array of bioethical and science policy issues.

## II. The Very Idea of ELSI

It is a common misapprehension that the "ELSI set-aside" within the Human Genome Project's budget was an idea that Congress imposed upon the National Institutes of Health (NIH) when it approved that federal agency's plans to add a National Center for Human Genome Research to its roster of research institutes in 1989. Actually, the congressional appropriations subcommittee that funds NIH was as surprised and skeptical as the rest of the biomedical research community about Dr. Watson's initial announcement.

The fact that there were ethical and social issues to be attended to in genome research was not news. Both of the major feasibility studies for the Human Genome Project, by the quasi-governmental National Research Council of the U.S. National Academy of Sciences[3] and by the U.S. Congress's own Office of Technology Assessment,[4] contained sections forecasting the major ethical and social implications of mounting such an initiative. Chief among these were concerns about the potential commercialization of genetic science, the discriminatory use of genetic test results to stigmatize individuals or exclude them from social opportunities, and fears that genetic testing would be open to infection by social agendas and professional values that might curtail the autonomy of those who might avail themselves of the technology. In 1988, witnesses had urged Congress to take these implications seriously, in the presence of the agency personnel and scientists who would shortly thereafter gather to design the HGP.[5] No one had suggested, however, that the project itself should fund the work involved in articulating and addressing the social sequelae of genome research: for that, we have Watson to thank, and—perhaps the real hero of the story—the anonymous reporter who triggered his announcement.

To the agency's credit, the NIH stood by Watson's decision, and incorporated this new mission into its joint efforts with the Department of Energy (DOE) to create a formal plan for the first five years of the U.S. Human Genome Project.[6] The work of the ELSI branch was structured by two goals in that initial plan: to "[d]evelop programs addressed at un-

[3] National Research Council, *Mapping and Sequencing the Human Genome* (Washington, DC: National Academy Press, 1988).

[4] Office of Technology Assessment, U.S. Congress, *Mapping Our Genes: Genome Projects—How Big? How Fast?* OTA-BA-373 (Washington, DC: U.S. Government Printing Office, 1988).

[5] Tom Murray, "Testimony," *OTA Report on the Human Genome Project Hearing*, One Hundredth Congress, Second Session, Serial No. 100-123 (Washington, DC: U.S. Government Printing Office, 1988), pp. 52–74.

[6] The Department of Energy's interest in the Human Genome Project stems from its own research efforts to develop tools for measuring the biological effects of low levels of radiation in the environment. For a detailed political history of the DOE's involvement in the genesis of the Human Genome Project, see Robert Cook-Deegan, *The Gene Wars: Science, Politics, and the Human Genome* (New York: W. W. Norton, 1994).

derstanding the ethical, legal and social implications of the human genome project," and to "[i]dentify and define the major issues and develop initial policy options to address them."[7] The methods for achieving those initial goals were also prescribed in the plan: to adapt existing NIH review and funding mechanisms to create extramural grant support for research, education, and public participation projects on these issues, to collaborate with other institutes and agencies on initiatives of mutual interest, to encourage international collaboration in this area, and to work closely with those in the field to refine the research agenda, solicit public discussion, and communicate the results of the work to policymakers and society. The ELSI program was budgeted to scale up from 3 percent to 5 percent of the grant-making monies allocated to the NIH's new National Center for Human Genome Research over the first three years. Moreover, the Department of Energy, as joint sponsor of the plan, also found itself subscribing to the ELSI goals and, in 1989, was embarrassed into contributing 3 percent of its genome research funding to the effort as well.[8] By October 1, 1990, when the U.S. Human Genome Project officially started its fifteen-year clock, social-impact assessment was part of the package of any self-respecting genome research initiative: as new genome research programs were established in other countries and within universities and research labs, ELSI-type efforts of varying styles and sizes were incorporated into them as a matter of course.[9]

Of course, there were still those inside the NIH who were willing to challenge Watson on the wisdom of his move. "I still don't understand," one senior official said after hearing Watson describe his plans at a 1990 briefing for the assembled directors of the NIH institutes, "why you want to spend all this *money* subsidizing the *vacuous pronunciamentos* of self-styled *'ethicists'*!?" When Watson responded that, for better or worse, "the cat was out of the bag" with respect to the public's concern over the ethical issues, the official retorted: "But why *inflate* the cat? Why put the cat *on TV*?"[10]

Why indeed? Why should the Human Genome Project fund its own social-impact studies, when there are all of us professional science-watchers around who would probably do the work anyway?

Suspicions about the very idea of an ELSI program came from both advocates and opponents of the HGP as a scientific venture. Pro-

[7] U.S. Department of Health and Human Services, U.S. Department of Energy, *Understanding Our Genetic Inheritance: The U.S. Human Genome Project—The First Five Years,* NIH Publication No. 90-1590 (Bethesda, MD: National Institutes of Health, 1989).

[8] Edward J. Larson, "Half a Tithe for Ethics," *National Forum: Phi Kappa Phi Journal*, Spring 1993, pp. 15–17.

[9] Eric Juengst, "Human Genome Research and the Public Interest: Progress Notes on an American Science Policy Experiment," *American Journal of Human Genetics*, vol. 54 (1994), pp. 121–28.

[10] Personal communication, NIH Institute Directors' Briefing on the NCHGR, June 15, 1990.

genomicists, like the NIH official quoted above, saw it as at best a waste of (increasingly scarce) NIH research dollars, and at worst an overblown hand-waving that could backfire badly on the scientific community if it actually succeeded in getting the public's attention. Anti-genomicists suspected that the program was, at best, a clever attempt to create a screen of ethical smoke behind which the HGP's juggernaut could build up speed, and, at worst, an attempt to buy off the very critics who might otherwise make trouble for the scientists.[11] The Council for Responsible Genetics, a public interest group with its roots in the recombinant DNA debate of the 1970s,[12] announced that, although it shared an interest in the issues to be addressed by the ELSI program, it would not be approaching the NIH for financial support, in order to preserve the independence of its views.[13] Congress, incarnate in the form of appropriations subcommittee member David Obey (D, Wisconsin), heard from both sides, and pressed Watson hard at the next round of appropriations hearings in 1990 to explain his rationale and goals for this new program.[14]

Watson's actual responses to these questions at that time were earnest, but anecdotal and programmatic.[15] However, he would later say that what he meant was this:

> It is a twentieth-century truism that science is not done in a vacuum and should not be pursued as if it could be. Good science affects its social context, and the practical effects of good basic science are often the most wide-ranging of all. Science, in turn, is constantly affected by the professional norms, social policies and public perceptions that frame it. Doing science in the real world means anticipating those interactions and planning accordingly. By pursuing the study of the ethical, legal and social implications of its scientific initiatives, the NCHGR assumes its responsibility to help make that planning timely, well informed, and productive. . . . The genome project is very basic science indeed: by the same token, however, the potential for the social impact of the HGP is proportionately broad. . . . Doing the Genome Project in the real world means thinking about these outcomes from the start, so that science and society can pull together to

[11] Ruth Hubbard and Elijah Wald, *Exploding the Gene Myth* (Boston: Beacon Press, 1993), p. 159.

[12] After the development of the first effective technique for recombining isolated pieces of DNA, discussion within molecular biology of the possible "biohazards" involved in performing this "genetic engineering" between species yielded a self-imposed moratorium on this research. In the wake of this moratorium, a wider public reaction occurred, leading eventually to the establishment of a public federal review process for all "recombinant DNA" research. For the history of this episode, see Sheldon Krimsky, *Genetic Alchemy: The Social History of the Recombinant DNA Controversy* (Cambridge, MA: MIT Press, 1982).

[13] Jonathan Beckwith, personal communication, February 11, 1990.

[14] Cook-Deegan, *The Gene Wars (supra* note 6).

[15] James Watson, "The Human Genome Project: Past, Present, and Future," *Science*, vol. 248 (1990), pp. 44–49.

optimize the benefits of this new knowledge for human welfare and opportunity.[16]

At its best, this position reflects a laudable willingness to look beyond the laboratory in conducting scientific work, in order to help society craft its science policy in an "evidentiary" rather than an "extemporaneous" fashion.[17] It is important to remember that the generation of molecular biologists behind the Human Genome Project were either personally involved in, or cut their scientific teeth during, the recombinant DNA debate (see footnote 12), and still look back on that episode as a success story of scientific self-policing. For (some of) them, participating reflectively in the public discussion of their work and incorporating the results into their research is accepted as a natural and necessary part of doing science, and the ELSI effort is what provides the resources, collaborations, and "data" necessary for doing that part.

At its crassest, this position is simply enlightened scientific self-interest. To the extent that the social environment of genetic research can influence their work, it makes sense for scientists to pay attention to developing a social context in which genetic research can flourish. If the Human Genome Project can help society develop policies that protect people from being harmed by genetic information, it helps create an environment conducive to its research program. From this perspective, it makes as much sense for a scientific resource-building project like the Human Genome Project to address the environmental factors that might inhibit the use of its tools as it does for it to address any other bottlenecks in its program.

Notice that under either interpretation, this "Watsonian" rationale for supporting social-impact studies assumes that the enterprise of genome research itself and the knowledge to be generated by it are unalloyed prima facie goods. There are dangers to be avoided in the responsible conduct of genome research, and abuses of genetic knowledge to be prevented; but the scientific goals of genome research and the biomedical strategy it supports—seeking for clues to the cure of disease at the molecular level—are accepted as intrinsically unproblematic. The question that the ELSI program addresses is the virtuous genome scientist's professional ethical question: "What should I know in order to conduct my (otherwise valuable) work in a socially responsible way?"

Clearly, this orientation does put some limitations on the ELSI program from the start. For example, it effectively forecloses any ELSI-sponsored

[16] James Watson and Eric Juengst, "Doing Science in the Real World: The Role of Ethics, Law, and the Social Sciences in the Human Genome Project," in George Annas and Sherman Elias, eds., *Gene Mapping: Using Law and Ethics as Guides* (New York: Oxford University Press, 1992), pp. xv–xviii.

[17] Benjamin Wilfond and Kathleen Nolan, "National Policy Development for the Clinical Application of Genetic Diagnostic Technologies," *Journal of the American Medical Association*, vol. 270 (1993), pp. 2948–54.

discussion of the relative value of the Human Genome Project compared to other uses of public funds. But perhaps this is as it should be. As George Annas and Sherman Elias, early grantees of the ELSI program, point out about their own list of "social policy research priorities for the Human Genome Project":

> Perhaps the most important social policy issue of all—should the Human Genome Project proceed at this time?—received no priority rating. This is unremarkable. The Project itself is not the appropriate funder for any research designed to give an "independent" or "objective" assessment of its own priority in scientific research. . . . In this regard, we found workshop participant Eric Lander's response to the question "Will the Human Genome Project distort research for molecular biology?" both instructive and accurate. His response: "It is much more likely to distort research in bioethics."[18]

Moreover, Eric Lander's wry point is another example of a problem that the ELSI program cannot take much direct interest in. It is true that an ELSI program could distort the research agenda of bioethics, by attracting scholarly attention to issues that, in the grand scheme of current issues in biomedicine and health policy, might not merit top priority. Again, however, if that is a public policy problem, it is not a problem for genomicists, who want to recruit as much of the best talent that they can to collaborate on their research. Hence, the question of the relative merits of a genetics-centered ELSI program compared with other public and professional bioethical needs is also not very high on ELSI's agenda.

So what should critics make of this Watsonian conception of ELSI, given the limitations it imposes on the program's domain? Genome scientists, nervous about the public policy consequences of "putting the cat on TV," can grant Watson's point about doing science in the real world, but still worry that his approach will distort the bioethicists' agenda too much: that is, that a mountainous amount of attention will be called to their problems which, in reality, are relative moral molehills. Is genome research really that problematic—so problematic as to be the only form of biomedical research to warrant the level of scientific caution represented by this unprecedented and ongoing funding for social-impact assessment?

Similarly, social critics who are worried about (their colleagues) being bought off by ELSI funds can applaud Watson's gesture, but still complain that the program's context ultimately prevents its grantees from being directly critical of the Human Genome Project itself. To take Annas and Elias's point further, how "objective" can ELSI grantees be about any issue that bears on genome research, when their funding is provided by

[18] George Annas and Sherman Elias, "Social Policy Research Priorities for the Human Genome Project," in Annas and Elias, eds., *Gene Mapping*, p. 275.

the genome research community on the assumption that genome research is a good to be protected?

### A. *Putting the cat on TV*

Is the celebrity status that ELSI gives to issues in genetics threatening to simply make matters worse by alarming the public, overselling the risks of genome research, or even exacerbating them (e.g., by giving insurance companies ideas)? What is special about these issues? It has become commonplace to point out that the Human Genome Project will give us molecular information that we can use to develop new risk-assessment tools for genetically influenced diseases well in advance of corresponding therapeutic or prophylactic breakthroughs, and most authors point to that "therapeutic gap" as the source of genomics' special moral burden.[19] Granted, the possibilities of acquiring and using this genetic information about individuals entail all the choices for public and professional deliberation that ELSI-ites enumerate ad nauseam:

> Choices for individuals and families about whether to participate in testing, with whom to share the results, and how to act on them; Choices for health professionals about when to offer testing, how to ensure its quality, how to interpret the results, and to whom to disclose information; Choices for employers, insurers, the courts and other social institutions about the relative value of genetic information for the decisions they must make about individuals; Choices for governments about how to regulate the production and use of genetic tests and the information they provide, and how to provide access to testing and counseling services; and Choices for society about how to improve public understanding of science and its social implications and increase the participation of the public in science policy making.[20]

But clinicians have coped with similarly lopsided diagnostic challenges in other settings,[21] from HIV testing to cholesterol screening, without making a special issue of them: why should genetic diagnostics uncomplemented by treatments merit special attention?[22] Indeed, the NIH/DOE Task Force on Genetic Information and Insurance, put together under the auspices of the ELSI program, argued that, as DNA-based risk assess-

[19] F. S. Collins, "Medical and Ethical Consequences of the Human Genome Project," *Journal of Clinical Ethics*, vol. 2 (1991), pp. 260–67; J. R. Botkin, "Ethical Issues in Human Genetic Technology," *Pediatrician*, vol. 17 (1990), pp. 100–107.

[20] Watson and Juengst, "Doing Science in the Real World," p. xvi.

[21] George Guyatt et al., "The Role of Before-After Studies of Therapeutic Impact in the Evaluation of Diagnostic Technologies," *Journal of Chronic Disabilities*, vol. 39 (1986), pp. 295–304.

[22] John Maddox, "New Genetics Means No New Ethics," *Nature*, vol. 364 (1993), p. 97.

ments become relevant for a wider spectrum of multifactor health problems, the distinction between "genetic" and "nongenetic" diagnostics is increasingly indefensible for professional and public policy purposes, and should be abandoned.[23] The members of this task force point out that, as the nosological line between diseases defined genetically and those defined environmentally becomes blurred by the discovery of the reciprocal influence of both kinds of causal factors, and as the technological domain of DNA-based diagnostics (e.g., "genetic tests") expands to include nongenetic diseases (like HIV disease and malaria), it will become increasingly arbitrary to single out some subset of genetic diseases or genetic tests for special regulatory attention. To this extent, they concur with the skeptics about the wisdom of "putting the [Genome Project's] cat on TV."

There are three answers to such a challenge: an incomplete one, a short one, and long one. The incomplete response is to argue that, while the issues provoked by genome research are not new in kind, it is nevertheless true that as the number and range of new gene-based tests expands, these issues will become concrete problems for more and more health-care professionals, patients, and policymakers. As the frequency of these problems increases, it is argued, moral economies of scale will kick in to change the way the problems are framed and resolved. "The sheer volume of new information and new technologies promised—or threatened—by the Genome Project gives the old questions new urgency and hints that relatively novel ones will emerge."[24] "It is primarily the complexity of that broadened context that gives these issues their urgency as social policy making problems."[25] Well, this may be true; but so far no one has explained this response well enough to decide how one would go about deciding whether it is true or not. In what ways should we expect to see existing moral problems change as their frequency increases?

The short answer is less mysterious, but has dramatic consequences. This is to concede that, in fact, there is little to distinguish human genetics from other parts of biomedicine in terms of the urgency or importance of the social challenges it raises, and then to draw the opposite conclusion from the skeptic's. Perhaps *all* the institutes of the NIH should put aside resources to support social-impact studies of the basic science research they sponsor! This response was recently embraced by a Health Sciences Policy panel of the National Academy of Sciences/Institute of Medicine

[23] NIH-DOE Working Group on Ethical, Legal, and Social Implications of Human Genome Research, *Genetic Information and Health Insurance: Report of the Task Force on Genetic Information and Insurance* (Bethesda, MD: National Center for Human Genome Research, 1993), p. 19.

[24] Thomas Murray, "Speaking Unsmooth Things about the Human Genome Project," in Annas and Elias, eds., *Gene Mapping*, p. 247.

[25] Eric Juengst and James Watson, "Human Genome Research and the Responsible Use of New Genetic Knowledge," *International Journal of Bioethics*, vol. 2 (1991), pp. 99–102.

deliberating on how best to make public policy on bioethical issues, and led to the same conclusion:

> The committee recommends that the National Institutes of Health provide funding mechanisms to support (1) the exploration by individual investigators of social and ethical aspects of biomedical technologies as they are developed and (2) the creation of a social and ethical knowledge base for all of biomedical science (e.g., extend the ELSI program to other institutes and programs within the NIH).[26]

The long answer to the question "Why pick on genomics?" draws on the short but dramatic social history of human genetics. It begins by pointing out that, whether it is entirely rational or not, public policy discussions about new advances in genetics in our society do seem to be animated by moral and social tensions that do not characterize policy-making in other areas: there is a special public interest and concern that needs to be addressed, if only for prudential reasons.[27] The argument then goes on to spell out the special features of predictive genetic testing, genetic explanations of illness, the professional ethos of medical genetics, and the historical and cultural context of contemporary genetic research that generate and make sense of those tensions as indicators of substantive policy problems.[28] It suggests that, in fact, for both extrinsic and intrinsic reasons, there is something "special" about the generation of new genetic tools that warrants special societal scrutiny.

In essence, those who would develop and use new genetic risk information find themselves caught in the scissors-action of two broad forces: our society's inclination to invest genetic information with occult power to define our identities and predict the future, and the lessons of our long history with other attempts to use genetics for the public good. The former inclination is understandable enough, given the deterministic paradigms that the public uses to understand genetic health problems: diseases like Huntington's disease or Tay-Sachs disease that do unfold in a lockstep manner and eventually consume the carrier's identity. But it also leads to the overinterpretation of more uncertain risk assessments,[29] the stigmatization of mutation carriers,[30] and social discrimination by those

[26] Ruth Bulger, Elizabeth Bobby, and Harvey Fineberg, eds., *Society's Choices: Social and Ethical Decision-making in Biomedicine* (Washington, DC: National Academy Press, 1995), p. 179.

[27] Eleanor Singer, "Public Attitudes towards Genetic Testing," *Population Research Policy Review*, vol. 10 (1991), pp. 235–55.

[28] Eric Juengst, "Patterns of Reasoning in Medical Genetics: An Introduction," *Theoretical Medicine*, vol. 10 (1989), pp. 101–7.

[29] Neil A. Holtzman, *Proceed with Caution: Predicting Genetic Risks in the Recombinant DNA Era* (Baltimore: Johns Hopkins University Press, 1989).

[30] Evelyn Fox-Keller, "Genetics, Reductionism, and Normative Uses of Biological Information," *Southern California Law Review*, vol. 65 (1991), pp. 285–91; Daniel Brock, "The

who think they have been told the future.[31] The history of social discrimination is replete with examples of well-meaning programs gone awry, including the involuntary-sterilization programs of the eugenics movement,[32] the XYY and sickle-cell screening programs of the 1970s,[33] and the dilemmas of genetic counseling under the emphatically individualistic "client-centered" ethos to which genetics professionals currently subscribe.[34] For those willing to learn from experience, all these episodes bear evidence of the volatility of genetic interventions, and the need for approaching new developments with caution and forethought.

This long answer is the one on which the Human Genome Project primarily relies in explaining its investment in social-impact assessment. Since the long answer is elaborated in many other places,[35] I will not fill in its details here. But notice one thing in passing: according to the long answer, the real burden borne by new genetic tests is not their novelty at all. Rather, it is the context into which they are delivered and through which they are understood that is the source of the challenges they pose. This explains the significance of the "therapeutic gap" for the ELSI program. Genetic tests do not pose radically novel issues during this gap; rather, it is just that this is when the new genetic tests are most traditionally "genetic." That is, it is during this technological gap that these tests behave most like our paradigms of genetic risk assessments (providing uncertain risk estimates of familial health problems we can do little about), and, as a consequence, pass on to their users the psychosocial burden and the professional ethical challenges traditionally associated with genetic explanations of illness. Against this backdrop of public and professional expectations, the prospect of a groundswell of new genetic tests is daunting. In the face of the pressures created by commercially driven efforts to disseminate convenient and technically accurate genetic risk assessments to a public that is likely to overinterpret the significance of the test results for themselves, their families, and their neighbors, geneticists must decide how much of their distinctive client-centered ethos they can afford to preserve, and policymakers must resolve regulatory dilemmas with long histories of controversy.

---

Human Genome Project and Human Identity," *Houston Law Review*, vol. 29 (1992), pp. 19–21; R. H. Kenen and R. M. Schmidt, "Stigmatization of Carrier Status: Social Implications of Heterozygote Genetic Screening Programs," *American Journal of Public Health*, vol. 49 (1978), pp. 116–20.

[31] Dorothy Nelkin and Laurence Tancredi, *Dangerous Diagnostics: The Social Power of Biological Information* (New York: Basic Books, 1989).

[32] Philip Reilly, *The Surgical Solution: A History of Involuntary Sterilization in the United States* (Baltimore, MD: Johns Hopkins University Press, 1991).

[33] Troy Duster, *Backdoor to Eugenics* (New York: Routledge, 1990).

[34] Alexander M. Capron et al., eds., *Genetic Counseling: Facts, Values, and Norms* (New York: Alan R. Liss, 1979).

[35] Cf. Robert Weir, "Why Fund ELSI Projects?" in Robert Weir, Susan Lawrence, and Evan Fales, eds., *Genes and Human Self-Knowledge* (Iowa City: University of Iowa Press, 1994), pp. 189–95.

In other words, to the extent that the Human Genome Project has an unusually strong need for social-impact studies (compared to other biomedical initiatives), that need stems more from the unusual cultural environment in which genome research is being pursued than from the novelty, complexity, or "sheer volume" of its specific products. This, of course, is what one would expect, given the ELSI program's basic assumptions about the prima facie value of the Project's work and the ELSI program's own role as the Project's "environmental interface."

Moreover, one consequence of embracing the long answer I have just set out is that it puts a premium on studies that will help illuminate the dynamics of that historical, social, and cultural context, rather than on narrow efforts to keep up with the individual spin-offs of genome research. Indeed, this emphasis was present in the solicitation that announced the program in 1990: its broad-based menu of nine research needs still ranges from "individual psychological responses to knowledge of genetic variation" to "uses and misuses of genetics in the past" to "conceptual and philosophical implications of the Human Genome Project."[36] In turn, this contextual orientation has been reflected in the research portfolio that the program has begun to build over its first years of grant-making.

### *B. Ethics with strings attached?*

There are also several ways to respond to the fear that the availability of research funding from the Human Genome Project will mute the voices of those who would otherwise be critical of genome research, either by professionally indebting them to the Project or by redirecting their attention "downstream" from the Project to its applications.

First, it is possible that at a subliminal level people's scholarly conclusions are influenced by their relationships with their funding sources: gratitude, intimidation, and funding-security anxieties could all come into play. But then, scholars who try for a grant and do not succeed, or those who conscientiously abstain from federal funding, are just as likely to be vulnerable to equally powerful subliminal influences: disappointment and frustration, or suspicion and pride. Either way, the influences are likely to be too subtle to do much about: they blend too quickly with all the other psychological background that any investigator brings to a study. As a result, it is hard to know what to do with this concern, except to be alert to systematic differences of opinion between the funded and unfunded that might expose some form of institutional pressure on the part of the NIH. Beyond that, it remains up to the professional integrity

[36] National Center for Human Genome Research, "Program Announcement: Ethical, Legal, and Social Implications of Human Genome Research," *NIH Guide to Contracts and Grants*, vol. 19, no. 4 (1990), pp. 23–26.

of the individual investigators to go where leads lead and to call conclusions as they see them.

Moreover, the ELSI program does have some built-in safety features to buffer its researchers from this kind of influence. The principle virtue of the program's design as an extramural, investigator-initiated, peer-reviewed grant-making program is that it places the researchers as far as one can from government influence and still provide them with public monies. In this respect, the ELSI program takes special advantage of the system that American scientists have devised to protect their own scientific freedom in the face of their need for public assistance. Federally funded scientific studies have long been classified as "federal demonstration projects," which is the most unfettered form of federal support. The academic latitude that this gives to investigators is a constant source of tension for the rest of the Human Genome Project (because of the freedom it gives them to wander from the Project's stated goals); it is the ELSI program's primary means of ensuring that its grantees' explorations of the context and implications of genome research are as unconstrained as possible. The fact that the one embarrassing political infringement on the sanctity of this system—the cancellation and subsequent reinstatement of a peer-approved ELSI conference grant—provoked a national controversy is an indication of how important and reliable a protection it usually provides.[37]

Finally, the contextual orientation of the ELSI program—that is, its focus on the cultural backdrop of genome research and its applications—also serves to foster critical inquiry about the HGP itself. Even though the program begins with a positive assumption about the value of genetic inquiry and asks the scientists' ethical question (How should we proceed?), it does not stop there. Inevitably, in examining the history, the conceptual assumptions, and the social context of *applied* genomics (e.g., DNA-based risk testing), the scholars pursuing these contextual studies will be led to explore the culture, dynamics, and values of the genomic juggernaut itself. The proof here is already in multiple puddings. For example, sociologist of science Stephen Hilgartner began by studying the impact of the Human Genome Project on "small science" in molecular biology in order to assess the claims that the Project would damage the tradition of decentralized, independent research within the field. He now writes about the dynamics of priority setting within the HGP, including the dynamics of the ELSI program.[38] In the course of analyzing the assumptions about genetics conveyed to the public through the popular media, Dorothy Nelkin dissects the metaphors that genome scientists use

[37] See John Marshall, "Violence Research: NIH Told to Reconsider Crime Meeting," *Science*, vol. 262 (1993), pp. 23–24.

[38] See, e.g., Stephen Hilgartner, "The Human Genome Project," in James Peterson et al., eds., *Handbook on Science, Technology, and Society* (Newbury Park, CA: Sage, 1992), pp. 1–32.

to promote their work.[39] Historian Lily Kay turns an exploration of the influence of postwar information theory in molecular genetics into a critique of the tacit conceptual underpinnings of genome research.[40] Sahotra Sarkar uses the genome project itself as the central case for a philosophical study of the strengths and limitations of "genetic reductionism" in biomedicine.[41] And so on. Together, the contextual orientation and the academic freedom built into the ELSI program actually encourage efforts to press against the HGP's prima facie assumptions. As one geneticist remarked at the end of an ELSI review meeting: "This is the only federal science program I've ever seen that feeds the dogs that bite it."

Moreover, it is even conceivable that ELSI's bite could hurt the Human Genome Project. The juggernaut is remarkably delicate in some respects: it runs on an annual budget that is in the hands of elected public representatives. If enough ELSI-ites, having scrutinized, clarified, and evaluated the forces influencing the social impact of new advances in genetics, were to argue in a politically persuasive way that, all things considered, now is *not* the time for our society to pursue such a project, they could effectively derail the HGP. It is instructive here to recall the fate of the last major federal initiative in human genetics, the National Genetic Diseases Act, which established an elaborate network of regional genetic-services organizations in the 1970s, only to have the tap steadily turned off by the bad press garnered by its mass carrier screening programs.[42]

This should have brought us to the end of this essay. Unfortunately, you cannot please all the people all the time from a Glass House like the NIH. For some, the contextual, critical studies I have been describing are the realization of their worst fears about the ELSI program. Such studies are more often than not "qualitative" and "normative," involving methods from the humanities, jurisprudence, and the social sciences that seem inordinately hard to operationalize in a grant application (and sound ridiculous in most attempts). They rarely end with policy recommendations. They usually appear as books (and NIH scientists consider proposals for such books as quaint as you would your graduate student's request to produce her dissertation as an illuminated manuscript). They almost always represent nothing more authoritative than the personal views of the authors (and their arguments and evidence). And they do nothing immediate either to reform the enterprise of genome research or to help the world prepare to live in its wake. It was not long before the action-

[39] Dorothy Nelkin, "Promotional Metaphors and Their Popular Appeal," *Public Understanding of Science*, vol. 3 (1994), pp. 25–31.

[40] Lily Kay, "Who Wrote the Book of Life? Information and the Transformation of Molecular Biology," in Michael Hagner and Hans Rheinberger, eds., *Experimentalsysteme in den Biologische-Medizinschen Wissenshaften: Objekt, Differenzen, Konjunkturen* (Berlin: Academie Verlag, 1994).

[41] Alfred Tauber and Sahotra Sarkar, "The Human Genome Initiative: Has Blind Reductionism Gone Too Far?" *Perspectives in Biology and Medicine*, vol. 35 (1992), pp. 220–35.

[42] Cf. Duster, *Backdoor to Eugenics*, pp. 58–63.

oriented folk in ELSI's audience—the engineers,[43] clinicians, and activists—began to complain that the program just looked like a welfare program for underemployed philosophers. "We've had enough of this Hastings Center stuff," these critics cried.[44]

## III. The ELSI Program and the Mechanistic Policy Worldview

It is this last critique—that ELSI cannot make policy—and the Human Genome Project's attempts to address it that have dominated the last two years of the ELSI experiment. In addressing this issue, the HGP has begun to build up a thick crust of problematic expectations about the ELSI program's role which, in my view, threatens to bury the very ability to put genome research in context that ELSI was created to provide.

The catalyst for this precipitate was in the ELSI mix from the beginning. The HGP did promise to "identify the most urgent issues and develop policy options to address them" in its first five-year plan; and when Representative David Obey pressed Dr. Watson for a plan for achieving practical results from his ELSI program, Watson was quick to reinterpret the program's promise as a policymaking agenda rather than a research goal.

In February and September 1990, two convocations of ad hoc external consultants were convened, both including the six consultants who had written the first five-year plan for the ELSI grant-making program in 1989 and both chaired by the chair of that initial working group, Dr. Nancy Wexler. This time, they met to help the NIH (and, by then, the DOE) to assign priorities among the program's issues for policy-development purposes, in response to Obey's queries. The two groups identified four categories of issues as "high priority areas" for policymaking purposes within the first five years of the HGP: (1) issues concerning the clinical integration of new genetic tests; (2) issues concerning the privacy of personal genetic information (such as genetic test results); (3) issues of unfair discrimination on the basis of personal genetic information (as in insurance underwriting and employment); and (4) issues in professional and public education. White papers were commissioned from outside experts on each of these topics, to help further refine the research agenda that the ELSI program might promote in each area.

By the end of the September meeting, however, the six consultants providing continuity from the prehistory of the ELSI program had also gained a distinct corporate identity as the "NIH-DOE ELSI Working

[43] Engineers make up a large cohort of "genome scientists," if not by professional affiliation then by personal inclination. The Human Genome Project, after all, describes itself as a "toolmaking" effort, and approaches its task accordingly.

[44] Leslie Roberts, "Taking Stock of the Genome Project," *Science*, vol. 262 (1993), p. 22.

Group," and a mission of their own. At Watson's urging to become "proactive," the group agreed to extend its life and expand its advisory role, by designing and coordinating special initiatives to address each of the four high-priority categories of policy issues. Each of these initiatives took a different approach to its goal of producing "policy options," each becoming a little ELSI experiment of its own. The stories of these initiatives are instructive:

1. *Clinical integration of new genetic tests.* The issues identified here were mainly issues of clinical policy and professional ethics: questions of when or for whom testing is "medically indicated," informed consent and confidentiality standards, pre-test education and post-test counseling practices, levels of professional skills and knowledge. In this sphere, the ELSI Working Group could take advantage of two time-honored approaches to professional policy development at NIH: contracting with the National Academy of Sciences/Institute of Medicine for a normative study by the professional leadership, and sponsoring clinical studies of the psychosocial impacts of genetic testing with an eye toward developing professional consensus statements from the results. The first approach produced a report containing a broad range of professional and public policy recommendations, which continue to percolate through the genetics community. In some cases, such as the recommendation that even routine newborn genetic screening (such as the testing for phenylketonuria that is performed in every state) be preceded by a clear informed-consent process, the report is generating controversy in its wake—while in others, such as its plea for increased health-professional education in genetics, it is not clear that anyone is listening.

The pursuit of the second approach fell to the NIH ELSI grant-making program, with a ready-made issue for its subject. The molecular mutations that cause cystic fibrosis were being elucidated, raising the prospect of direct heterozygote ("carrier") testing for the general population. Yet, against the backdrop of our history with mass carrier screening programs, most experts conceded that the health-care system was poorly prepared to provide such screening competently. Little was known about the public's interest in such testing, about the psychosocial consequences of such testing outside the context of specialized genetics clinics, or about the forms of education and counseling that best enable individuals and families to integrate such information into their health planning. In order to help develop the clinical standards for such testing, and to see whether, in fact, mass screening could feasibly be done in an ethically acceptable way, the NIH ELSI program solicited proposals for studies of these issues and created a consortium of clinical research projects from among the top-ranked applications. In the interim, the American Society for Human Genetics, the principal professional organization for medical genetics and a proponent of such preliminary clinical studies, endorsed this action by issuing a statement urging caution with respect to cystic fibrosis carrier testing until these studies were complete.[45]

The NIH cystic fibrosis studies consortium is now in the process of compiling, comparing, and drawing professional policy conclusions from its three-year studies. Meanwhile, an important science policy precedent has been set for the introduction of new genetic risk assessments: that new genetic services should be evaluated in terms of their psychosocial impact on individuals and families as well as in terms of their medical safety, reliability, and utility. One contextual point underscored repeatedly by the social scientists, clinicians, and patient advocates involved in the cystic fibrosis studies is the need to develop and use client-centered criteria in assessing new genetic technologies. The promise of genetic information lies in its ability to allow individuals and their families to name, understand, and sometimes control their inherited health risks. Thus, if genetic testing and counseling are to be judged successful, it must be from the recipients' point of view, in terms of the recipients' ability to use the results to enrich their lives.

The power of this precedent is visible in the speed with which the notion of conducting preliminary "social-impact assessments" of new genetic tests has already been adopted and applied in other areas of genetic technology development: ELSI is already sponsoring a second consortium with the National Cancer Institute to assess genetic testing for cancer risk, and similar psychosocial research initiatives have been undertaken by the Heart Institute, the National Institute of Mental Health, and the National Child Health Institute.

2. *Genetic privacy protections.* The issues contained in this category are almost exclusively legal and public policy issues concerning the management of stored genetic information about identifiable individuals—either in medical records or systems of personal identification, like the Army's "DNA Dog-tag project."[46] For this privacy initiative, the Department of Energy's ELSI grant-making program took the lead, by more or less directly commissioning a cohort of studies designed to review the current state of personal genetic information collection and storage, and to draft model legislation for protecting the privacy of such information. The researchers who conducted these studies presented their work in 1994, and the model law they produced was introduced as a bill in the Maryland legislature in the spring of 1995. It remains under discussion in the 1995–96 session.

[45] American Society for Human Genetics (ASHG), "Statement of the American Society for Human Genetics on Cystic Fibrosis Carrier Screening," *American Journal of Human Genetics*, vol. 51 (1992), pp. 1443–44.

[46] Nachama Wilker et al., "DNA Data Banking and the Public Interest," in Paul Billings, ed., *DNA on Trial: Genetic Identification and Criminal Justice* (Plainview, NY: Cold Spring Harbor Laboratory Press, 1992), pp. 141–51.

*3. Genetic discrimination prevention.* The issues involved in the exclusionary use of genetic test results by employers or insurers were also clearly public policy questions. On discrimination by employers, the ELSI Working Group was able to look to the recently passed Americans with Disabilities Act (ADA) for help, and to query the Equal Employment Opportunity Commission (EEOC) about that law's prospects for preventing exclusionary genetic screening by employers.[47] This relatively simple action provoked a three-year cascade of behind-the-scenes argument and political negotiation between the EEOC, ELSI grantees active on the issue, the Senate Committee on Disability Policy, and the Justice Department—negotiations which have only recently been concluded. The EEOC had initially responded negatively to the inquiry, arguing that because genetic risk assessments and carrier tests did not identify existing disabilities, only diagnostic genetic tests could legitimately be counted among the preemployment "medical exams" which the law forbids employers to use in selecting applicants. Now, the EEOC agrees that for the purposes of implementing the ADA, all forms of preemployment genetic testing fall under the law's protection.[48]

On the issues involved in the use of genetic risk information in insurance underwriting, the ELSI Working Group took yet another approach. These were issues that already involved clear stakeholders: the life and health insurance industries, consumer and public-interest groups, and the state government officials who are charged with regulating insurance practices. Under the leadership of two Working Group members, a separate group of consultants was created, composed of representatives from each of these constituencies and the set of ELSI grantees studying these issues. Leaning heavily on conceptual and empirical work from the grantees, the resulting report argued that the only secure way to prevent "genetic discrimination" in this context would be to reform the health-care system to do away with the need for individual risk underwriting altogether. Specifically, they recommended that:

> 1. Information about past, present, or future health status, including genetic information, should not be used to deny health care coverage to anyone. . . .
>
> 2. The U.S. health care system should ensure universal access to and participation by all in a program of basic health services that encompasses a continuum of services appropriate for the healthy to the seriously ill. . . .

[47] National Institutes of Health–Department of Energy (NIH-DOE) Joint Working Group on Ethical, Legal, and Social Implications of Human Genome Research, "Genetic Discrimination and the Americans with Disabilities Act," *Human Genome News*, vol. 3, no. 3 (1991), pp. 12–13.

[48] Rick Weiss, "Gene Discrimination Barred in Workplace," *Washington Post*, April 7, 1995, p. A3.

> 3. The program of basic health services should treat genetic services comparably to non-genetic services, and should encompass appropriate genetic counseling, testing, and treatment. . . .
>
> 4. [T]he cost of health care coverage borne by individuals and families for the program of basic health services should not be affected by information, including genetic information, about an individual's past, present or future health status. . . . [49]

This report was submitted to the White House Task Force on Health Care Reform in 1992, and Hillary Clinton, the chair of the task force, was subsequently briefed on its recommendations by the chair of the ELSI Working Group, Dr. Nancy Wexler (between courses at an awards dinner). The argument of the report became part of Mrs. Clinton's public case for health-care reform, and its specific recommendations were incorporated in the administration's health reform bill, the Health Care Security Act of 1993. Along the way, the ELSI Insurance Task Force dissolved and a committee of public-interest lobbyists and lay organizations was created in its place ("the Coalition of People with Genes") to press the task force's point with Congress. The rest (unfortunately) is history, in the wake of the Clinton administration's failure to realize its health-care reform proposals.

*4. Genetics literacy.* Even the best-crafted professional and public policies will not prevent the misuse of genetic information if those who collect and use it do not understand its significance correctly. One perennially and universally safe goal for the ELSI program to espouse has always been professional and public education. Skeptics at both ends of the spectrum agree that education is important—even though, in practice, one or the other camp is always upset by the content of any particular educational project.

Here, the focus of the Working Group's special initiative was to be a series of public forums on new advances in genetics, which could serve both to promote public awareness and discussion of the issues, and to solicit public input into the ELSI planning process. In fact, while twenty such local forums have now been sponsored by the ELSI program in almost as many states, only one was hosted by the ELSI Working Group itself, the one held in Iowa City in 1993. The rest have been sponsored through the extramural grant-making program, and organized by local hosts.

Two things about this group of four "high-priority" initiatives are worth noticing. First, all these initiatives really are focused downstream from the Human Genome Project itself. One of the interesting criticisms that

[49] NIH-DOE Joint Working Group, "Genetic Discrimination and the Americans with Disabilities Act," p. 2.

eventually started coming from the genome scientists was that the ELSI Working Group was "losing touch with genome science" and pursuing social problems for which the Human Genome Project had no reason to take responsibility. "If the Working Group wants to reform the health-care system, let Hillary pay for it," one frustrated scientist grumbled, in lobbying to add more scientists to the group in order to focus it (self-critically?) on the problems facing genome researchers themselves.

Secondly, none of these initiatives really depended on the active participation of the ELSI Working Group to be brought to conclusion. Unlike a grantee consortium, or even the expert panel brought together by the National Academy of Sciences, the ELSI Working Group as a corporate body does no work itself. It lacks the opportunity for sustained deliberations, and the common focus required for concerted action. Individual members of the group have been quite active in these initiatives, but usually while wearing other hats, as contractors or grantees of the ELSI program, members of the Institute of Medicine panel, or chairs of ELSI satellites like the Insurance Task Force. The driving forces in accomplishing what has been done across all of the program's "high-priority areas" have been the grantees who have gotten involved: people who have a stake in the specific issues because of their own professional and scholarly commitment to illuminating the contexts that create them.

Unfortunately, even this fact was not apparent at the midpoint of the ELSI program's first five years, when none of these initiatives had yet been brought to fruition. This was the point at which the House Committee on Government Operations convened a hearing on the federal management of genetic information as part of a series of hearings in support of an (ultimately unsuccessful) bill that would have established a Data Protection Board in the United States. NIH Director Dr. Bernadine Healy testified on behalf of her agency, reporting on the protections currently provided for genetic information gained through federally sponsored research and on the efforts of the U.S. Human Genome Project to anticipate and address such issues through its Ethical, Legal, and Social Implications (ELSI) programs.[50] Her description of the ELSI program focused on its mission of cultivating, through research, the information that would be necessary to address public policy issues involving genetics in a responsible way.

In response to these hearings, the Committee on Government Operations released a report on April 2, 1992. The report concluded that, while the existing ELSI programs were well designed to support extramural research and education, they "had no process" for developing or presenting policy recommendations to Congress in a timely, authoritative, and

[50] Bernadine Healy, "Testimony on the possible uses and misuses of genetic information," *Human Gene Therapy*, vol. 3 (1992), pp. 51–56.

independent fashion; and it recommended that a formal advisory commission be established jointly by the Secretary of Health and Human Services and the Secretary of Energy to provide that service.[51] The committee ignored the ongoing efforts of the ELSI Working Group entirely, but commented that, in any case, it would be too narrow a group to develop proposals with enough constituency support to be persuasive to policymakers.[52]

The ELSI program's lack of formal policy-development "processes" or "mechanisms" for getting the attention of policymakers quickly became a handle for other observers and science policy analysts unwilling "to wait until the extramural cows come home" for ELSI policy options. Citing the committee's report, the Office of Technology Assessment described the ELSI program a year later this way:

> The program operates on the model of peer review competition for grant funds. The ELSI Working Group, which advises both [the NIH and DOE ELSI grant-making programs], initially framed the agenda and establishes priority research areas. Nevertheless, the nature of the grant programs means the ultimate direction evolves from the bottom up—i.e., from the individual perspectives of researchers pursuing independent investigations—rather than from the top down—i.e., through policymakers or an overarching federal body. Furthermore, no formal mechanisms exist for ELSI-funded research findings to directly make their way back into the policy process.[53]

Two years later, a National Academy of Sciences/Institute of Medicine (NAS/IOM) background paper on the ELSI program still cites the committee's report, and concludes that

> [t]he basic flaw in the design of the ELSI program and its working group is that it has no authority to affect policy and no clear route for communicating the information it gathers to the policy arena. . . . There is no mechanism for ensuring that the results of these scholarly pursuits will make their way back to the policy arena unless one

[51] Committee on Government Operations, House of Representatives, U.S. Congress, *Designing Genetic Information Policy: The Need for an Independent Policy Review of the Ethical, Legal, and Social Implications of the Human Genome Project* (Washington, DC: U.S. Government Printing Office, 1992).

[52] It could have also pointed out that, in the eyes of the Federal Advisory Committee Act, the ELSI Working Group does not even exist between its meetings: strictly speaking, it is reconstituted for each meeting as a new "working group."

[53] Office of Technology Assessment, U.S. Congress, *Biomedical Ethics in U.S. Public Policy—Background Paper*, OTA-BP-BBS-105 (Washington, DC: U.S. Government Printing Office, June 1993), p. 8.

relies, in the words of one grantee's abstract, on absorption of the facts by "a general audience of intelligent readers."[54]

Against the backdrop of the policy initiatives described earlier in this section, the complaint that ELSI lacks "policy mechanisms" is quite mysterious. Granted, there is no single vehicle that ELSI always uses to deliver its findings "to the policy arena." But the issues that the ELSI program addresses span a number of policymaking spheres, from institutional to professional to public. In adapting its approach to each sphere, ELSI takes advantage of the "mechanisms" that seem most effective within that sphere. Thus, to speak authoritatively to health professionals, it combined the voice of the professional leadership (through the NAS/IOM) with a form of argument which that profession respects (peer-reviewed empirical research studies). To communicate public policy options, it can digest research into "reader-friendly" reports (like the Insurance Task Force Report), convey them freely to other government entities (like the White House Task Force or the EEOC), and use all of Washington's usual informal "mechanisms" (like personal contact) to get the attention of policymakers. To embarrass industry, it can make statements to the press (like the statement on recent efforts to commercialize genetic testing for breast-cancer risks). From the evidence, in fact, it appears that ELSI's repertoire of "policy mechanisms" is as robust as anybody else's inside the beltway. Certainly, for a program primarily designed to support academic research, ELSI has had a particularly active track record in the "policy arena."

Nevertheless, this running commentary on ELSI's policy potency did come at a particularly sensitive period in its history. By 1993, the program had disbursed over $10 million,[55] but its only visible "products" had been its initial round of introductory conferences and the first wave of academic publications on the "contextual studies" that had been born from those meetings. It was into this situation that Francis Collins stepped when he became director of the NCHGR after Watson resigned.

Collins came to NIH fresh from his experience as a clinician and researcher working on familial breast cancer, and, as he put it, he felt personally responsible for potentially "putting thousands of women at risk of discrimination" by helping to find the breast-cancer gene.[56] Against that frame, his own view was (and presumably remains) that the ELSI program should put practical matters first and reflect on the Genome

[54] Kathi E. Hanna, "The Ethical, Legal, and Social Implications Program of the National Center for Human Genome Research: A Missed Opportunity?" in Bulger, Bobby, and Fineberg, eds., *Society's Choices* (*supra* note 26), pp. 432–58.

[55] The same amount that went to one genome researcher, Eric Lander, that year alone—just to keep things in perspective!

[56] Cf. Barbara Biesecker et al., "Genetic Counseling for Families with Inherited Susceptibility to Breast and Ovarian Cancer," *Journal of the American Medical Association*, vol. 269 (1993), pp. 1970–74.

Project's "environmental interface" only when it has the luxury to do so. At an ELSI Working Group meeting in December 1993, he argued strongly that the program should reorient itself to allow the Working Group to function more effectively as a deliberative, policymaking body. According to the critics, this would require expanding the group to improve its representation of various stakeholders, finding for it a legitimate niche in the advisory-committee structure of the NIH and the DOE, providing it with its own research staff, giving it the resources to directly commission and contract for studies related to its policy initiatives, and, of course, providing it with a clear "policy mechanism" for delivering its conclusions.

To Collins's credit, instead of funding this new activity out of the "fat" in the ELSI portfolio, as some had proposed, he followed Watson's lead: he committed funds out of the budget for his new intramural genome laboratories to support two professional staff positions for the ELSI Working Group. The Working Group has also now been significantly expanded to include representatives from the clinical professions, lay constituencies, and genome scientists. It has settled on the "task force" model that produced its insurance report as its official "mechanism" for promulgating policy, and has already launched a new Task Force on Genetic Testing to explore the regulation of commercial DNA-based diagnostics. Its new mission statement reads: "The National Advisory Council for Human Genome Research (NIH) and the Health and Environment Research Advisory Council (DOE) delegate responsibility to the ELSI Working Group to explore and propose programmatic and policy options for the development of sound professional and public policies related to human genome research and its applications."[57]

One consequence of this shift, of course, has been a corresponding de-emphasis of the role of the extramural community in monitoring, shepherding, and nurturing ELSI's policy agenda. Plans to convene the subsets of grantees working on related issues in order to harvest their ideas have slipped to the back of the stove. Plans for a new extramural funding category to support interdisciplinary graduate training relevant to the study of ELSI's issues have been tabled. "Contextual" studies of the historical background, philosophical assumptions, and cultural underpinnings of the Genome Project's environmental interface require increasingly prolonged post-peer-review defense by staff in order to be awarded.

As I suggested above, ELSI's ability to weave together its community of researchers into a variety of policy initiatives tailored to specific spheres does give it the "mechanisms" to do exciting policy work. But to the extent that it is the program's extramural resources that make it special, redirecting the program's energy and the public's attention to the ELSI

[57] NIH-DOE Joint Working Group on the Ethical, Legal, and Social Implications of Human Genome Research, "Mission Statement," December 1, 1994.

Working Group is risky. By recasting itself in the image of a deliberative commission, the Working Group is preparing to play its critics' game, and that is a mistake. Fortunately, there is a vision for the program that makes sense of all its activities to date, and can be translated readily into a blueprint for future development. This is the vision of ELSI as supporting an ongoing community of scholars and professionals devoted to tracking, analyzing, and developing policy on new advances in human genetics.

## IV. Reinventing ELSI

### *A. The ELSI program's mission*

The ultimate purpose of the ELSI program is to help society and the scientific community successfully resolve the ethical, legal, and social issues that are raised by new advances in human genetics. But that is true only in the same way that the ultimate purpose of the Human Genome Project is to help science successfully answer the biological questions raised by the association of genes with DNA. Helping society resolve issues is the program's purpose, but its mission must be more focused than that if it is to be effective. The HGP focuses its helping mission on building the tools and infrastructure that will be required (by others beyond the HGP) to answer the fun biological questions. In the same way, the ELSI program should focus its helping mission on building the tools and infrastructure that will be required (by others beyond the ELSI program) to resolve the hard issues.

*Specifically, the ELSI program's mission should be to build two things that will be prerequisites for society's successful resolution of genetics issues: (1) the body of knowledge necessary to anticipate new issues and assess arguments for and against policy options, and (2) the community of informed and committed people, professional and lay, required to generate and use the body of knowledge in a sustained policy-development process.*

Just as the technical programs at the NCHGR support and facilitate the genomics community's autonomous efforts to achieve its members' scientific goals, the ELSI program should proceed on the assumption that effective social and professional policymaking is best pursued by researchers and policymakers in the field, working directly with their colleagues in the affected constituencies. In other words, the ELSI program's own involvement in policy development should be to serve as an "uncommission": an institutionalized source of support that sustains an evolving network of independent policymaking initiatives in different spheres.

The rationale for drawing ELSI's mission this way is fourfold:

1. It acknowledges the true complexity of the ELSI challenge. Resolving the ethical, legal, and social issues raised by new advances in human genetics means enacting new public policies, reforming professional practices, and influencing basic assumptions and beliefs in the public mind. These are not goals that any single program, commission, or initiative can

hope to accomplish on its own during a fifteen-year span, any more than the larger purpose of the HGP—understanding all the genes—could be so achieved. Building expectations on the part of Congress, the public, or the scientific community that ELSI can "make the world safe for genomocracy" in short order, only lays the basis for disappointment and frustration with the program.

2. On the other hand, cultivating a community and a body of knowledge is the most important contribution the HGP can make at this time to help society meet the larger challenge. The program could focus its resources on getting specific, high-profile tasks accomplished: e.g., a particular genetics privacy law or educational campaign. But without a growing knowledge base or a stable community of people who know how to use it, such achievements would be ephemeral and quickly outdated. If one looks at the ELSI challenge as analogous to a civil rights campaign, history suggests that before major legal changes will be possible, the growth of committed constituencies armed with knowledge will be necessary.

3. This vision plays to the strengths of the ELSI program. The ELSI program is not well positioned to directly resolve genetics issues. To that extent the program's critics are right: the ELSI program has no authority to directly formulate public policy, no resources to provide timely ethics consultations on professional practices, and no capacity to help members of the public with their individual problems. On the other hand, the ELSI program does have the authority, resources, and capacities to provide support for generating knowledge and cultivating a community that can apply that knowledge. This is, arguably, what the NIH does best.

4. Finally this mission reflects the advice of ELSI's most knowledgeable advisors. In preparing for the HGP's second five-year plan, the ELSI program undertook a five-step process of gathering advice about the program's mission and priorities from the ELSI research and education community, the public, and the scientific community. The resulting planning summary stresses the need for ongoing efforts in multiple areas of research and community building, not the need for ELSI to act as a commission or to pursue mass-education campaigns.[58]

### *B. The ELSI program's methods*

The ELSI program can best achieve its mission by using the grant-making and contract-letting authorities and mechanisms of the NIH to support six kinds of projects:

1. *Reconnaissance papers.* These are commissioned papers which survey current knowledge and forecast research and policy needs with respect to

[58] NIH-DOE Joint Working Group on Ethical, Legal, and Social Issues, *Five Year Planning Summary* (Bethesda, MD: NIH, April 15, 1993).

newly emergent ELSI issues. This has proven an efficient mechanism in several contexts: in the first year of the program, commissioned papers on cystic fibrosis screening, insurance issues, and employment-discrimination issues helped set the stage for subsequent programmatic initiatives; and the papers that were commissioned in 1992 on human-subjects issues in genetic family studies were instrumental in subsequent policy development at the NIH Office of Protection from Research Risk. The DOE privacy collaboration also involves a number of commissioned papers. However, this activity has never been regularized as a part of the program. If it were, it would provide the program with a vehicle for following up on new issues raised to its attention by the community and its advisory groups, and would further the program's knowledge-building mission. If $100,000 were devoted to supporting ten major commissioned papers a year, the program could respond quickly to almost all new needs, and would have an annual set of interim products to use in stimulating the community.

2. *Descriptive studies.* These are research projects that seek to discover information relevant to anticipating and addressing ELSI policy issues. One advocate of science education argued to me that "[p]eople will always ponder the ethical issues; but education projects just won't get done without ELSI support." But good pondering requires good facts, and good facts require research, which costs money. The research required for clear pondering includes not only psychosocial-impact and health-services studies performed to assess new genetic-testing modalities in the clinical setting, but also background studies of the economic, cultural, and historical context of new genetics services, public and professional attitudes and understandings of genetics concepts, and the philosophical assumptions underlying different policy approaches to genetics issues. These studies are not expected to yield particular policy recommendations, but aim at getting straight about the facts.

3. *Normative (policy) analyses.* These are research projects that seek to construct, compare, criticize, and defend arguments for and against particular policy positions on specific genetics issues. Pondering may be spontaneous, but actually developing a persuasive case for a particular public or professional course of action requires hard work. This work includes not only projects designed to produce recommendations for public policies, regulations, legislation, and standards governing professional or clinical practices, but also basic (e.g., theoretical) legal and ethical analyses of particular issues and basic background critiques of the value assumptions that underlie different positions on the issues. Without the latter, the former proceed in a vacuum.

4. *Policy conferences.* These are conferences that are designed to bring together researchers and policymakers to facilitate the development of sound policy options. Meetings, consultations, and workshops, as tiresome as they sometimes are, are necessary tools for synthesizing research results and achieving the critical mass of human resources to galvanize

policy development. In order to make a success of ELSI's initial goals, I would propose using these vehicles heavily over the coming year to flush out the policy lessons of the program's current research portfolio.

5. *Education projects.* These are education and public-participation projects designed to alert different communities to ELSI research findings and policy recommendations. In line with the program's basic mission and goals, the education projects ELSI supports should be primarily focused on efforts to build infrastructure for ongoing policymaking on genetics issues. As a result, efforts to enhance ELSI components of teacher training, health-professional education, and science-education policy should be emphasized, as should efforts to build stable forums for grassroots public participation in ELSI policy development. Less important are ephemeral (but expensive) public education efforts like television series and specific (quickly dated) educational tools. Science education per se is part and parcel of producing more informed understandings of ELSI issues; but the ELSI program should not be held responsible for ensuring the genetics literacy of the American public.

6. *Training grants.* These are training grants to help develop professionals with a commitment to ELSI research and policymaking. Part of the community-building mission of the ELSI program is to train professionals who are capable of moving easily between the scientific and policy worlds. ELSI currently supports only postdoctoral cross-disciplinary training, partly because there are no clear training sites that could support full-blown graduate programs. As research and education projects accumulate at particular institutions, however, centers of ELSI inquiry are emerging across the country—centers which could support interdisciplinary training programs. To ensure the future of the ELSI program's mission, the program could begin to support predoctoral graduate training grants as well. This would be a new category for ELSI, but one which fits its mission statement and which the community is ready to pioneer.

### C. *The role of the NIH-DOE ELSI Working Group*

The ELSI program has benefited tremendously from the advice and energy of the Working Group in helping NIH and DOE experiment with different visions of the program's mission. One vision that the program is not too well equipped to fulfill is the vision of the Working Group as an independent policymaking commission to which members of the community can submit their findings for analysis. By their nature, "working groups" have an episodic existence, which is a weakness for this vision (though a strength for others). If our society needs a policymaking commission that can cover genetics issues, the Working Group might lobby for its creation, but should not volunteer to take on its responsibilities.

On the other hand, the vision of ELSI's mission described above would allow the Working Group to take on a leadership role that can play to the program's strengths. In brief, the Working Group's job would be to help the ELSI program capture the body of knowledge and nurture the community that it was meant to create. It would do so by providing the main forum in which the ELSI program grantees are brought together with relevant policy people and the public to report and discuss their results. By providing the institutional memory that links the variety of "policy conferences" that will be needed to harvest the first round of work, the Working Group could be in an excellent position to highlight important recommendations for those who need to hear them, and to identify new information-gathering needs. These are tasks that the episodic nature of the group's existence can accommodate, and tasks which would actually help the larger program succeed in achieving its goals.

Again, the great opportunity for the Working Group is to function as the hub of the "un-commission" on ELSI matters and to be the midwife of a new field and its community.

## V. An ELSI Success Story

Is there any evidence from the annals of ELSI that the advice I have given in the previous section is sound? Yes. In fact, one of ELSI's most influential policy initiatives to date attests to its merits, because this initiative was also almost entirely a creature of the extramural community's "contextual" explorations.

Because research on isolating and identifying disease genes often involves extended, geographically dispersed families, researchers face questions which current regulations for research with human subjects simply do not address.[59] These include questions concerning strategies for recruiting extended-family members, the relevant risks to disclose during the consent process, and the subsequent research use of collected tissue samples; they also include questions of confidentiality—for example, questions about access to study data by subjects and their families, and about the publication of family pedigrees and research results. These questions, internal to the conduct of the Human Genome Project but relevant to much else besides, were never on the ELSI Working Group's list of "high-priority" areas for policymaking. They did not even make it onto the broad menu of topics on which the grant-making program solicits applications.

Questions about the research ethics of gene-hunting studies were originally raised for the ELSI program by scientists and genetic disease support-group members (e.g., research subjects) at one of the (much maligned) early agenda-setting conferences sponsored by the program in February 1991. This led to a second funded meeting, sponsored by the American Association for the Advancement of Science (AAAS) in June 1992, to

[59] Cf. Robert Levine, *The Ethics and Regulation of Clinical Research* (New York: Urban and Schwartzenberg, 1986).

assess the professional state of the art in this area. Genetic family studies, after all, have been conducted for at least as long as our twenty-year-old set of federal research rules has been around: surely by now institutions and research teams have developed policies and procedures for addressing these questions.

What emerged from the discussion at the AAAS meeting was that, indeed, research groups from across the field did have homegrown answers to these questions, of whose merits they were convinced. But no one seemed to have quite the same approach, and some of the differences left scientists in heartfelt disagreement. Should one routinely modify pedigree data in order to protect the confidentiality of one's subject family in publication? Is it appropriate to use a family member to recruit her relatives into a study, or is it better to contact extended-family members out of the blue to solicit their participation? What does it mean when a subject insists on his right to "withdraw" from a pedigree study? Are subject's entitled to your flaky early results, or only to solid (e.g., publishable) findings about themselves? Geneticists were reading from the same rule book, but with contradictory results. The AAAS recommended that perhaps this was a topic on which the NIH Office of Protection from Research Risk (OPRR), charged with interpreting the federal research regulations, should provide a reading.[60] In response, the NCHGR and the OPRR collaborated in October 1992 to bring to town a group of geneticists, ELSI grantees, and self-styled ethicists to develop improved guidance for investigators and research review boards considering genetic studies involving families. Within the year that followed, the deliberations and suggestions from that meeting were developed as a new chapter for the OPRR's *Institutional Review Board Guidebook*, a concordance of commentary and interpretation of the federal research regulations that is supplied to every institutional review board in the country.[61] Just the rumor that the OPRR was going to make suggestions in this area prompted some leading genetic research institutions (the University of Utah, Johns Hopkins, and even the NIH Clinical Center) to develop preemptive (and stricter) institutional policies of their own.

Moreover, that was not the end of the story. First, the major family and patient organization for people with genetic diseases, the Alliance of Genetic Support Groups, produced a brochure for its constituency that recasts the OPRR's points for institutional review boards to consider, in the form of questions for families to ask of investigators when approached about participating in genetic studies.[62] That brochure, distrib-

[60] Fred Li et al., "Recommendations on Predictive Testing for Germ-Line P53 Mutations among Cancer-Prone Individuals," *Journal of the National Cancer Institute*, vol. 84 (1992), pp. 1156–60.

[61] Office of Protection from Research Risk, *Protecting Human Subjects: Institutional Review Board Guidebook* (Bethesda, MD: OPRR, NIH, DHHS, 1993).

[62] Alliance of Genetic Support Groups, *Informed Consent: Participation in Genetic Research Studies* (Chevy Chase, MD: Alliance of Genetic Support Groups, 1993).

uted in bulk to the two hundred different organizations that make up the alliance, will help ensure that where institutional review boards neglect to ask these questions of investigators, their subjects are increasingly likely to do so themselves.

Next, the Council of Biology Editors, the professional organization for biomedical journal editors, became interested in the controversy over the appropriateness of "disguising" identifiable family pedigrees for publication in lieu of getting permission from subjects to publish clinical information about them. The council released a statement condemning the (widespread) practice, following closely the lines of argument elaborated by a philosopher grantee, Madison Powers, who wandered into this issue while thinking about what we could possibly mean by "genetic privacy."[63]

Next, researchers at the Centers for Disease Control (CDC) became interested in the questions involved in research with identifiable stored tissue samples, since they realized they had been transforming cell lines for genetic studies from identified blood samples collected as part of their national health survey, without ever having asked the donors to consent to genetic research. Two joint NIH/CDC workshops have now been held on this topic, and a lengthy position paper has been produced.[64] It is already being echoed by professional society statements as preferred policy in this area.[65]

Finally, into the midst of all this discussion fell the population geneticists' proposal for a sequel to the Human Genome Project: the Human Genome Diversity Project. This would involve the collection and genotyping of DNA samples from five hundred of the world's isolated indigenous populations, and the preservation of these samples as a research resource for studies of human migration, lineage, and evolution. At yet another workshop held in March 1993 to discuss the research-ethics issues involved in conducting such a project, Bill Schneider, a historian of science who received funding from ELSI and the National Endowment for the Humanities to trace the history of the genetics of "race" in prewar hematology, accurately forecast the negative political reaction of Third World interests to such a project.[66] This workshop led to the creation of an "ethics committee" for the project, whose main function has been to open lines of communication between the population scientists and the advocates for those whom they would study. Meanwhile, unlike the Human

[63] Madison Powers, "Publication-Related Risks to Privacy: Ethical Implications of Pedigree Studies," *IRB*, vol. 15 (1993), pp. 7–11; International Committee of Medical Journal Editors, "Altering Data for Publication," Statement to the Office of Protection from Research Risk, December 14, 1994.

[64] Ellen Clayton et al., "Informed Consent for Genetic Research on Stored Tissue Samples," *Journal of the American Medical Association*, vol. 274 (December 13, 1995), pp. 1786–92.

[65] American College of Medical Genetics, "Statement on Storage and Use of Genetic Materials," *American Journal of Human Genetics*, vol. 57 (1995), pp. 1499–1501.

[66] Margaret Locke, "Interrogating the Human Genome Diversity Project," *Social Science and Medicine*, vol. 39 (1994), pp. 603–6.

Genome Project, it is the ethical complexity of the Diversity Project which has become the primary challenge to its advancement: so far, only the National Science Foundation's physical anthropology program has expressed interest in having the Diversity Project proceed before its proponents establish better relations with its potential subjects, while both the DOE and the NIH have demurred.[67] Not that ELSI should be proud to stand in the way of progress, but here is a striking example of ELSI considerations being used self-critically by federal science to put the brakes on a juggernaut.

Notice that throughout the cascade of policymaking in this story the "mechanisms" that were key to its progress were the arguments, insights, and initiative of people whose participation in the "policy arena" was unplanned and unpredictable. Bring a historian to a population-genetics planning meeting? Ask a philosopher to consider biomedical publication practices? Invite lay support groups to help design a scholarly research agenda? It was the "un-commission" working at its best.

## VI. Conclusion: Time for the Un-Commission?

It is important to notice that almost all those who have criticized the ELSI program for lacking "policy mechanisms" have done so in pursuit of another agenda: building the case for the creation of some new federal body intended to develop policy on ethical, legal, and social issues in biomedicine. Part of making that case, of course, is demonstrating that no existing federal program, like the ELSI program, can meet the needs that the new entity would satisfy. To that extent, many of ELSI's troubles have been the result of "friendly fire" in the campaign to recreate a national forum in the U.S. for bioethical policymaking.[68]

It has been friendly fire because up until now, the Human Genome Project has been happy to lend its voice to that campaign. The HGP presents its own efforts to "upgrade" the ELSI Working Group as an admittedly stopgap measure, necessitated only by the absence of some overarching federal bioethical policymaking body to which ELSI grantees could report their research findings. Presumably, if a national commission were established, the ELSI program could relinquish its quest for policymaking mechanisms, and return to supporting a field of inquiry. Of course, that would mean scraping off again all the accoutrements of deliberative policy analysis that have been allowed to build up on the ELSI Working Group along with its policy promises. That might turn out to be more

[67] Francis Collins, "Statement on the Human Genome Diversity Project," Senate Committee on Government Affairs, Hearings on the Human Genome Diversity Project, April 26, 1993.

[68] For a history of the country's other efforts at national bioethical commissions, see Office of Technology Assessment, U.S. Congress, *Biomedical Ethics in U.S. Public Policy* (*supra* note 53), Appendix A.

difficult than it sounds, since a busy National Bioethics Commission could easily see ELSI as a useful place to delegate its responsibility to address genetics issues.

In the wake of the recent national political convulsions in the U.S., however, I wonder if even a National Bioethics Commission is as attractive a prospect as it once was for protecting the public interest in this area, compared with the un-commission model. For a while in the early 1990s, it looked as if the federal door was open again to establish an effective bioethics commission: health-care reform, the radiation research commission, and the Genome Project all seemed pointed in the same direction. But now that the White House Health Care Task Force Ethics Group and the NIH Embryo Research Panel have joined the Congressional Bioethics Board and the NIH Fetal Tissue Panel as frustrated efforts at national bioethical deliberations, it raises the question of whether a national body can really be much more successful than the ELSI program at "communicating its policy recommendations effectively." Commissions come and go, and while they are here they are captive to the political process. Grantees will devote their sustained energies to monitoring the issues (as long as the funding is there!), and are relatively better protected by the First Amendment from political compromise in articulating their views. Commissions have a scope beyond which unanticipated issues can fall unexamined. The ELSI research community has few bounds on its curiosity, and has proven itself capable of rewriting the ELSI program's agenda from the inside when unanticipated issues arise. Perhaps, in order to provide adequate "social-impact assessments" of other scientific innovations as they emerge, society and the scientific community should also look to the "un-commission" of their colleagues in the humanities, social sciences, the professions, and the public.[69]

In pursuing its goal of identifying and developing initial responses to the most urgent ethical, legal, and social issues posed by genome research, the ELSI program has been challenged to establish and direct a wide variety of policy-development vehicles, including grantee consortia, commissioned expert panel studies, advisory task forces, interagency workshops and working groups, public consultations, and conferences. The common hallmarks of these efforts have been their collaborative spirit and the diversity of the perspectives they have involved. Rather than settle on any one format for policy development, and thereby raise expectations which it will be difficult to fulfill, the ELSI program—and any others that seek to emulate it—should keep its options open, by concentrating on cultivating the contextual studies of science and technology

[69] The National Center for Human Genome Research has already been approached, for example, by representatives of the planned "Human Brain Project" at the National Institute of Mental Health about replicating an "ELSI" funding program within their efforts to compile and correlate all our knowledge of the brain.

that are its raison d'être. Taken collectively, these studies and the early policy products they have helped generate serve as strong preliminary evidence in favor of the "ELSI hypothesis": that combining scientific research funding with adequate support for complementary research and public deliberation on the uses of new knowledge will help our social policies about science evolve in a well-informed and robust way.

*Biomedical Ethics, Case Western Reserve University*

# WHEN POLITICS DRIVES SCIENCE: LYSENKO, GORE, AND U.S. BIOTECHNOLOGY POLICY

By Henry I. Miller

It has been said that those who do not remember the past are condemned to repeat it. It is important, therefore, to consider the parallels between the decimation of basic and applied biology by Trofim Denisovich Lysenko in the Soviet Union earlier in this century and the battering of present-day biotechnology by the Clinton administration. In both cases, we see the sacrifice of new science to old myth; heterodox, unscientific theories steering public policy; the abject failure of that public policy, with dire outcomes for research and commerce; and glib, condescending, and exclusionary attitudes toward policymaking.

## I. Lysenko, Oppressor of Science—and Scientists

Recall the case of Lysenko, the meagerly educated peasant agronomist and Soviet technocrat. In the decade following the collectivization of agriculture, which began in the late 1920s, the crisis in grain production had elicited in Soviet bureaucrats a yearning for a quick fix. Lysenko promised it, in the form of greater, more rapid, and less costly increases in crop yields than other scientists thought possible. As the incumbent in a series of posts and finally as director of the Institute of Genetics of the Academy of Sciences of the USSR and president of the then-powerful V. I. Lenin All-Union Academy of Agricultural Sciences, he challenged the dogma that genes conveyed hereditary traits, and despite the absence of experimental support, preached Lamarckian doctrine: that traits acquired by an organism during its lifetime could be passed on to its offspring. This theory had several advantages—superficial plausibility, resonance with bureaucrats' immediate needs, and political correctness.

There was, after all, a certain plausibility to the idea of giraffes stretching their necks to reach tender shoots on high tree limbs, and passing the trait of an elongated neck on to future generations. Lysenko also claimed that wheat plants cultivated in the appropriate environment produce seeds of rye, which is tantamount to saying that dogs living in the wild give birth to foxes. Always, Lysenkoite biology draped itself in self-righteousness. From its beginnings, Lysenkoism involved polemics and denunciations of "bourgeois science in the service of the capitalist class," and culminated in the removal of opponents from their positions, often leading to jail or the gulag. An example was Nicolai Vavilov, the great geneticist, who was arrested, tried as a spy, and condemned to a Siberian prison in 1940, where he died three years later.

Lysenko's attacks on a "mythical hereditary substance," as he called what would eventually be named DNA, were prodigious—and vicious. Eminent scientists Gregor Mendel (1822–1884) and Thomas Hunt Morgan (1866–1945), who had earlier laid some of the foundations of modern genetics, were vilified and referred to as racists, fascists, and advocates of something called "reactionary genetics." Repeated attempts, many successful, were made to destroy stocks of experimental fruit flies, just as today some would vandalize new-biotechnology-derived plants (that is, those manipulated with recombinant DNA, or gene-splicing, techniques) or prevent their field-testing. (It is particularly ironic that in 1944, while Lysenko was promulgating his theories and approaching the height of his power, Rockefeller University professor Oswald Avery and his collaborators were publishing evidence that DNA was the actual hereditary substance, or "transforming principle," as they called it.)

The political correctness of Lysenko's theories was of particular appeal to his masters: conventional evolution would not produce the desired results rapidly enough, but the inheritability of acquired characteristics provided a speedier path. This reasoning was applied both to the creation of the New Soviet Man and to agriculture: the new social order could even conquer Nature by expediting improvements. A paragon of Soviet science and political ideology, Lysenko received the full imprimatur of Stalin and the Party.

In the mid-1930s, Lysenko and his minions seized control of the institutional centers of Soviet agricultural science. Via persecution of dissenting scientists and political control of science, they wrought incalculable damage on biology and its application to agriculture. Soviet agricultural programs were a continuing embarrassment, with innovations and productivity lagging far behind other nations, many of which were rapidly improving crop varieties using orthodox genetics. It was decades until Lysenko's allies started to distance themselves from him, and only with the political demise of Nikita Khrushchev in 1964 were Lysenko's doctrines discredited. Thus began the end (see Section IV below) of three decades of Soviet biology's pursuit of bizarre and aberrant science.

Repeatedly, new science is denounced to save old myth. In the Soviet Union, the old myth resurrected by Lysenko was Lamarckian theory, but this was only one example of many. Less well publicized was V. R. Vilyams, an agricultural scientist who specialized in soil biology. Employing various mixtures of plants in crop rotation, he promised increases in fertility far in excess of what could be achieved by other techniques. His monomaniacal preoccupation was with the "texture" of the soil; he considered it the only truly important factor in agriculture, and thought that no degree of improvement in other parameters could compensate, in the absence of appropriate texture. According to Robert Conquest, no actual experimental data supported Vilyams's theories, but his "success was due to two factors: attractive promises and the branding of other views as Trotskyite."[1]

Many crackpot medical theories also thrived in the Soviet Union between about 1930 and the early 1960s. These ranged from questioning the existence of cells as components of organisms to quack cancer cures. As Conquest has observed, "[t]he addiction to miracle cures, a longing for quick results and dramatic short-cuts and solutions in every field, seems also to be a reflection of the revolutionary temperament."[2]

In the case of the new biotechnology in the United States today, the myth is of a childlike, "natural" world of purity and innocence that is corrupted by scientific advances, especially those that "tamper with Nature."

Elements common to the two cases include an ideology imposed on science and driving public policy, a lack of understanding of science (of either its method or phenomenology), and government officials' intolerance of dissenting views.

## II. Gore et al.: Lysenko's Heirs-Apparent?

Biotechnology, the use of living organisms or their parts for making commercial products, has been around for centuries. Examples include the use of yeast to make bread dough rise and the use of various microorganisms to produce cheese, yogurt, alcoholic beverages, and other fermentation products. Even sophisticated genetic engineering, in which organisms' traits have been modified by a variety of techniques, has long been applied quite safely to agriculture and to the production of pharmaceuticals, food, and beverages. In plants used for food, for example, genes have often been moved across species lines and even from one genus to another. This crossing of natural breeding boundaries—so-called "wide crosses"—has been carried out for decades by various techniques (such as "embryo rescue," where an embryo that would not survive in nature is "rescued" by nutritional or other supplementation). The plants that have been created by wide crosses have been widely tested, have entered the marketplace without special regulation or labeling, and are ubiquitous in the United States and Europe. They include corn, oats, black currants, pumpkins, tomatoes, potatoes, swede turnips, sugarbeets, and bread and durum wheat. Thus, the average consumer seldom gets through a day without ingesting these products of genetic engineering.

While "conventional" genetic engineering is a relatively blunt instrument, moving genes imprecisely and in large numbers, the techniques of the "new biotechnology" move or rearrange the genetic material—DNA—itself, in ways that are quite precise. The DNA is mixed or "recombined"

[1] Robert Conquest, *We and They* (London: Temple Smith, 1980), p. 78.
[2] *Ibid.*, p. 80.

and, in the process, cells are programmed to carry out useful functions or to manifest important traits. Examples of the application of this "recombinant DNA" technology include microorganisms that produce human proteins such as insulin or growth hormone (which can then be purified and used as drugs) or tomatoes that exhibit new resistance to disease or stress.

The new biotechnology, which uses recombinant DNA techniques ("gene-splicing") essentially to mimic and speed up nature's own movement of genes between organisms, should have been freed of much of its regulatory red tape years ago. In 1987, the United States National Academy of Sciences observed that "there is no evidence of the existence of unique hazards either in the use of rDNA [recombinant DNA] techniques or in the movement of genes between unrelated organisms"; and that "the risks associated with the introduction of rDNA-engineered organisms are the same in kind as those associated with the introduction of unmodified organisms and organisms modified by other methods."[3] Two years later, in a landmark comprehensive report, the United States National Research Council echoed the earlier findings and concluded that "no conceptual distinction exists between genetic modification of plants and microorganisms by classical methods or by molecular techniques that modify DNA and transfer genes."[4] The report noted that the precision of the newest recombinant DNA techniques ensures that the genetic changes made are likely to be better characterized and more predictable than those wrought by older techniques, such as hybridization or mutation. Numerous other prestigious national and international groups have echoed the view that the new biotechnology represents merely a refinement of older techniques and that it should be regulated no differently than other technology.[5]

The new biotechnology in the United States today finds itself in straitened circumstances. Budgets for ten biomedical institutes of the National Institutes of Health (NIH) were on the Clinton administration's cost-cutting block for fiscal year 1995 (FY95); and while research funding at the National Science Foundation (NSF) outpaced inflation, there was a worrisome shift away from fundamental research (which spawned the new biotechnology and still provides the substrate for advances). Overall, in FY95, as a percentage of the nation's gross domestic product (GDP), the White House's proposed science budget, at 2.6 percent, was the lowest since 1958. The funding picture is not likely to improve significantly. In

[3] National Research Council Committee on the Introduction of Genetically Engineered Organisms into the Environment, *Introduction of Recombinant DNA–Engineered Organisms into the Environment*: *Key Issues* (Washington, DC: National Academy Press, 1987), p. 22.

[4] *Field Testing Genetically Modified Organisms: Framework for Decisions* (Washington, DC: National Academy Press, 1989), p. 14.

[5] See Henry I. Miller, "Concepts of Risk Assessment: The 'Process versus Product' Controversy Put to Rest," in *Biotechnology*, ed. D. Brauer (Weinheim, Germany: VCH, 1995), pp. 39–62.

FY96, the National Institutes of Health, the main source of support for U.S. universities' biomedical research, will receive a hefty 5.7 percent increase over the previous year, $175 million more than the Clinton administration had requested. But in contrast to the Congress's liberal funding of biomedical research, other areas (whose appropriations had not been settled, at the time of this writing) are likely to suffer, especially those yielding high-quality research that is not particularly favored by the vice president. For example, in the president's budget, the request for the National Science Foundation barely keeps ahead of inflation (3.7 percent increase) and funding for nonmilitary research facilities takes a 7.6 percent cut, while the EPA's notoriously low-quality research receives a proposed increase of 15.8 percent, and the Department of Commerce, a proposed increase of 9.3 percent.

Basic research is not the only casualty; development has also been affected: investors have lost confidence that they can realize good return on investment (see below), and the flow of private capital to biotech companies has shrunk; companies' stocks were down more than 25 percent in the first two years of the Clinton administration; radical environmentalists continually beleaguer these companies' products; and unnecessary federal regulation of their products is endemic and growing. The Clinton administration bears much of the responsibility.

Biotechnology has become caught both directly and indirectly by Clinton administration policies. They include the White House health-care plan's assaults on drug prices and on physicians' ability to prescribe what they consider to be the best drugs, regardless of price; and they include the administration's insistence on discounts (and therefore lower profits) on pharmaceuticals paid for under government entitlement programs. Not surprisingly, small biotech firms, many of which do not yet have marketed products that yield revenues, have been more affected by the flight of potential investors than pharmaceutical giants. Small firms saw investment capital from public offerings drop more than 80 percent between 1991 and 1993, and biotechnology stocks have far underperformed other high-tech sectors. In theory, these data could simply be part of a normal business cycle that saw healthy companies spending in 1993 the capital they raised in earlier years. However, that interpretation is not consistent with biotech entrepreneurs' complaints that venture capitalists literally will no longer return their phone calls.

Bolstering the argument that administration policies are the culprit was a 1993 survey by the Biotechnology Industry Organization of companies involved in AIDS research, in which 40 percent of these companies cited the White House "cost containment" proposals as the cause of the industry-wide shortage of capital. Moreover, a survey by the Gordon Public Policy Center at Brandeis University found that of companies that planned to raise capital in 1993, 60 percent said they either fell short of their funding target or withdrew or postponed stock offerings.

However shocking these developments may be, they are no surprise to anyone familiar with the attitudes of America's own heirs-apparent to Lysenko: Vice President Al Gore, the administration's technology czar, and Greg C. Simon, his Chief Domestic Policy Advisor and point man for biotechnology.

Simon, a lawyer untrained in and unfamiliar with science, has long been a nemesis to the new biotechnology. While a staffer on the House Committee on Science, Space, and Technology, he was the author of the proposed Biotechnology Omnibus Act of 1990, H.R. 5232, the notorious proposal for comprehensive regulation of field research. Fortunately, the bill foundered in committee. H.R. 5232 would have established a vast regulatory infrastructure focused exclusively on organisms manipulated with recombinant DNA technology (that is, the most precise, state-of-the-art "gene-splicing" techniques). The bill, which was science-averse without even a pretense of sheltering consumers from genuine risks, would have created potent regulatory *dis*incentives to using the most precise and predictable genetic technology.

As the vice president's aide, Simon has delivered several speeches which show that he has not changed his position. In major speeches, Simon has said that the actual degree of biotechnology's risks is irrelevant, insisting that it must be subjected to a high degree of governmental control and regulation in order to calm a supposedly "hysterical" public. (Surveys have indicated repeatedly, however, that consumers are optimistic about the fruits of new biotechnology and surprisingly sanguine about its risks.)[6] In other forums, Simon has amplified his message, saying that for regulatory purposes, biotech products simply cannot be compared to traditional products and that "consumers will have to change their concept of how food is made" in order for the technology to be accepted by the public. It is difficult, however, to reconcile such assertions with consumers' actual behavior: new-biotech-produced chymosin, an enzyme approved by the FDA in 1990, is currently being used for the manufacture of more than 60 percent of cheese made in the U.S., with nary a complaint from consumers and without special labeling; and the newly approved long-shelf-life gene-spliced tomatoes have sold well, despite the much higher price.

Simon's views are shared by virtually no one in the scientific community and are diametrically opposite to the unequivocal conclusions and recommendations published by the National Academy of Sciences, the National Research Council (NRC), the American Medical Association, the Group of National Experts on Biotechnology of the Organization for Economic Cooperation and Development, the World Health Organization, and the United Nations' Food and Agriculture Organization, among others.[7] As I have

[6] Susanne L. Huttner, "Government, Researchers, and Activists: The Critical Public Policy Interface," in Brauer, ed., *Biotechnology*, pp. 459–94.

[7] See Miller, "Concepts of Risk Assessment," pp. 46–49.

noted, the scientific consensus holds, in the words of the NRC, that "no conceptual distinction exists between genetic modification of plants and microorganisms by classical methods or by molecular techniques that modify DNA and transfer genes."[8] Emphasizing the refinement of the new technology, the NRC states:

> Recombinant DNA methodology makes it possible to introduce pieces of DNA, consisting of either single or multiple genes, that can be defined in function and even in nucleotide sequence. With classical techniques of gene transfer, a variable number of genes can be transferred, the number depending on the mechanism of transfer; but predicting the precise number or the traits that have been transferred is difficult, and we cannot always predict the phenotypic expression that will result. With organisms modified by molecular methods, we are in a better, if not perfect, position to predict the phenotypic expression.[9]

In other words, the newer molecular techniques are vastly more precise and yield a better-characterized organism whose traits can be predicted with greater certainty.

In a recent speech, Simon cited the other members, aside from himself, of "the best team you could assemble on biotechnology"—including White House Science Advisor Jack Gibbons, FDA Commissioner David Kessler, and of course, its leader, Al Gore. The reality is that, given the robustness of U.S. biotechnology as recently as the early 1990s, it is difficult to imagine a sorrier outcome wrought by a less sagacious group of collaborators.

### *A. Al Gore: New Age philosopher, psychologist, environmentalist*

While a senator and self-styled expert on biotechnology issues, Al Gore praised *Algeny*,[10] Jeremy Rifkin's anti-biotechnology diatribe, and is quoted on its cover—praising it as "an important book" and an "insightful critique of the changing way in which mankind views nature." In a 1991 article in the *Harvard Journal of Law and Technology*,[11] Gore displayed a remarkable lack of insight into biotechnology's past, present, and future. For example, he described investors' eager reception of Genentech's stock offering in 1980 disdainfully as the first sellout of the "tree of knowledge to Wall Street."[12] He ignored biotechnology's pre-Genentech (and pre-gene-splicing) commercial successes: fermentation using microorganisms to produce antibiotics, enzymes, vaccines, foods, beverages, and other products was a $100 billion industry before gene-splicing! Gore observes

[8] *Field Testing Genetically Modified Organisms*, p. 14.

[9] *Ibid.*, p. 13.

[10] Jeremy Rifkin, *Algeny* (New York: Viking Press, 1983).

[11] Al Gore, "Planning a New Biotechnology Policy," *Harvard Journal of Law and Technology*, vol. 5 (Fall 1991), pp. 19–30.

[12] *Ibid.*, p. 22.

that companies' selection of products for research and development is driven by commercial motives like profit and patent protection, rather than "the public's interest"—an idea he finds distasteful. Gore disparages the principle of "let[ting] the marketplace decide," and thinks of minimal government oversight of negligible-risk experiments as a regulatory "vacuum." His rationale for unnecessary regulation: "If *you* don't do it, you know somebody else will."[13]

Gore goes on to observe that "the decisions to develop ice-minus [bacteria], herbicide-resistant plants, and bovine growth hormone ... *lent credibility to those who argued that biotechnology would make things worse before it made things better.*[14] Except for Gore's own bias against certain products (deriving from lack of understanding of either science or the free market), it is unfathomable how anyone could thus characterize the harmless and ubiquitous ice-minus bacterium used to prevent frost damage to crops, or the development of environmentally friendly herbicide-resistant plants that will reduce the use of chemicals and provide farmers with additional choices.

Gore's negative attitudes toward biotechnology are insupportable, but they seem to reflect his hostility toward science and technology, generally. His book *Earth in the Balance*[15] provides an extensive and disturbing insight into the thinking of America's technology potentate.

Gore's apocalyptic central thesis is that we need to take "bold and unequivocal action . . . [to] make the rescue of the environment the central organizing principle for civilization" (starting at p. 269). Throughout the book, he uses the metaphor that those who believe in technological progress are as sinister, and polluters are as evil, as the perpetrators of the World War II Holocaust (see, for example, pp. 177, 196, 232–33, 256–57, 272–75, 281–82, 285, 294, 298, 366).

> It is not merely in the service of analogy that I have referred so often to the struggles against Nazi and communist totalitarianism, because I believe that the emerging effort to save the environment is a continuation of these struggles, a crucial new phase of the long battle for true freedom and human dignity. (p. 275)

In *Earth in the Balance*, the vice president examines what he postulates are the political, "eco-nomic" (get it?), psychological, sociological, and religious roots of the pollution problem. His economic section posits that

> [c]lassical economics defines productivity narrowly and encourages us to equate gains in productivity with economic progress. But the

[13] *Ibid.*, p. 24 (emphasis added).

[14] *Ibid.*, pp. 24–25 (emphasis added).

[15] Al Gore, *Earth in the Balance* (New York: Plume, 1993); page references will be given parenthetically in the text.

> Holy Grail of progress is so alluring that economists tend to overlook the bad side effects that often accompany improvements. (p. 188)

This shortcoming of markets he considers "philosophically . . . similar in some ways to the moral blindness implicit in racism and anti-Semitism" (p. 189). Part of Gore's remedy is to redefine the relevant measures of a nation's economic activity—concepts like "growth," "productivity," "Gross National Product," and so forth—in order to enable the government to obscure the costs of environmental protection. The costs would be redefined as "benefits" and businesses would be forced to list as societal "costs" some wealth-creating activities that would normally be considered beneficial to society (p. 343).

Government intervention is a recurring Gore solution to the costs and shortcomings of market forces. Intervention by the wise and enlightened government is necessary to save us from ourselves because

> our civilization is, in effect, addicted to the consumption of the earth itself. This addictive relationship distracts us from the pain of what we have lost: a direct experience of our connection to the vividness, vibrancy, and aliveness of the rest of the natural world. The froth and frenzy of industrial civilization mask our deep loneliness for that communion with the world that can lift our spirits and fill our senses with the richness and immediacy of life itself. (pp. 220–21)

Gore's New Age philosophizing leaves few politically correct clichés unexplored. Even sexism gets a bashing, with Gore arguing that our approach to technological development has been shaped by aggressive male domination instead of by the nurturing instinct of women. "Ultimately, part of the solution for the environmental crisis may well lie in our ability to achieve a better balance between the sexes, leavening the dominant male perspective with a healthier respect for female ways of experiencing the world" (p. 213).

Gore the psychologist continues:

> The unprecedented assault on the natural world by our global civilization is also extremely complex, and many of its causes are related specifically to the geographic and historical context of its many points of attack. But in psychological terms, our rapid and aggressive expansion into what remains of the wildness of the earth represents an effort to plunder from outside civilization what we cannot find inside. Our insatiable drive to rummage deep beneath the surface of the earth, remove all the coal, petroleum, and other fossil fuels we can find, then burn them as quickly as they are found—in the process filling the atmosphere with carbon dioxide and other pollutants—is a willful expansion of our dysfunctional civilization into vulnerable parts of the natural world. And the destruction by industrial civilization of most of the rain forests and old-growth forests is a particu-

> larly frightening example of our aggressive expansion beyond proper boundaries, an insatiable drive to find outside solutions to problems arising from a dysfunctional pattern within. (p. 234)

Gore the philosopher disparages the Cartesian method, the heart of scientific inquiry, for disconnecting man from nature. He also expresses disdain for Francis Bacon, who "argued that not only were humans separate from nature" but

> science, he said, could safely be regarded as separate from religion. In his view, "facts" derived through the scientific method had no moral significance in and of themselves [and] . . . the new power derived from scientific knowledge could be used to dominate nature with moral impunity. (p. 252)

Gore concedes that this shift in thinking was essential for ending the Dark Ages and for the eventual launching of the Enlightenment. However, he thinks that Plato and then Descartes and Bacon broke an important "spiritual triangulation" in human thought that identified the natural world as sacred, because Gore believes that "each rock and tree was created by God" (p. 255). Gore argues that Bacon's "moral confusion . . . came from his assumption, echoing Plato, that human intellect could safely analyze and understand the natural world without reference to any moral principles defining our relationship and duties to both God and God's creation" (p. 256).

To this "error," which is the very essence of scientific objectivity, Gore attributes the responsibility for, among other evils, the atrocities of Hitler and Stalin:

> It is my view that the underlying moral schism that contributed to these extreme manifestations of evil has also conditioned our civilization to insulate its conscience from any responsibility for the collective endeavors that invisibly link millions of small, silent, banal acts and omissions together in a pattern of terrible cause and effect. . . . *But for the separation of science and religion, we might not be pumping so much gaseous chemical waste into the atmosphere and threatening the destruction of the earth's climate balance.* (p. 257; emphasis added)

(But for the separation of science and religion, we would likely still be saddled with the pre-Copernican notion that the sun and planets revolve around Earth.)

Gore, the vice president of the United States, the nation's technology czar and director of regulatory policy, conveys unmistakably that he doesn't much like or trust science, and that he believes it is more likely to generate societal problems than solutions or advances.

The guiding principle of Gore's environmental agenda is radical: "We must make the rescue of the environment the central organizing principle for civilization" (p. 269). He goes on to draw analogies between the effort needed for this mission and the mobilization of this country to defeat the Nazis and to win the cold war. He suggests an environmental "Marshall Plan" that might require $100 billion.

Gore suggests that massive government interventions, both direct and indirect, are necessary to avoid an environmental Armageddon. For example, he notes that the federal antitrust laws make it illegal for railroads to own trucking companies because of the potential for stifling beneficial competition between the two modes of transportation. By analogy, he proposes that government should have the right to "prevent such mergers" not only on antitrust grounds, but also on the basis of possible negative environmental effects. Particularly revealing is one of his examples of what government should intervene to prevent: chemical companies that produce agricultural chemicals "buying up seed companies and selecting and breeding seeds that maximize use of [the companies'] chemical products" (p. 343). If this provision had been incorporated into law a decade ago, it would have forced many of today's leaders in agricultural biotechnology, such as Dupont and Monsanto, from the field. Agricultural biotechnology research and development would be a small fraction of its current levels of activity.

Gore is not so intoxicated with his own rhetoric that he believes his views are currently centrist, but

> [i]n any effort to conceive of a plan to heal the global environment, the essence of realism is recognizing that public attitudes are still changing—and that proposals which are today considered too bold to be politically feasible will soon be derided as woefully inadequate to the task at hand. Yet while public acceptance of the magnitude of the threat is indeed curving upward—and will eventually rise almost vertically as awareness of the awful truth suddenly makes the search for remedies an all-consuming passion—it is just as important to recognize that at the present time, we are still in a period when the curve is just starting to bend. Ironically, at this stage, the maximum that is politically feasible still falls short of the minimum that is truly effective.... It seems to makes sense, therefore, to put in place a policy framework that will be ready to accommodate the worldwide demands for action when the magnitude of the threat becomes clear. And it is also essential to offer strong measures that are politically feasible now—even before the expected large shift in public opinion about the global environment—and that can be quickly scaled up as awareness of the crisis grows and even stronger action becomes possible. (pp. 304-5)

Thus, Gore's view is that he will initially have to settle for the partial measures that are politically possible, but that bold and dramatic measures are at the ready, awaiting the education and enlightenment of the public. This ethos is redolent of the vanguard of the proletariat working to raise the consciousness of man, a stratagem that Lysenko, Marx, and Engels would have understood.

### *B. The rest of the biotech team*

It seems tautological that a presidential science advisor should be an advocate for scientific and technological progress and for policies that promote research and development, but the biotechnology record of Jack Gibbons, President Clinton's science advisor, is tarnished. While the director of the congressional Office of Technology Assessment, Gibbons approved and endorsed a report, *Field Testing Engineered Organisms*, that served as a virtual L.L. Bean catalogue for anti-biotechnology sophistry.[16] It may be the least scholarly and least accurate analysis of biotechnology of the dozens produced by the U.S. government during the past two decades. Certainly, during his tenure as a senior advisor to the president, no one has accused Gibbons of being an advocate for science as the basis for biotechnology policy.

FDA Commissioner David Kessler's involvement with biotechnology has been more destructive: (1) He eliminated the two FDA policy offices with extensive involvement with the scientific community and industry (the Office of Biotechnology and the Office of Small Business, Scientific, and Trade Affairs). (2) He presided over an inexplicably prolonged, three-year review of a long-shelf-life tomato (by contrast, the reviews of the first new-biotech therapeutics in the early 1980s—human insulin and human growth hormone—required five and eleven *months*, respectively). (3) He directed the preparation of a notification scheme focused specifically on new-biotech foods, reversing fifteen years of risk-based policies.[17] (4) He instituted a vigorous FDA-wide search for reasons not to approve bST (bovine somatotropin, a protein that increases the productivity of dairy cows), on instructions from the White House (two completely unnecessary meetings of advisory committees were held during the final stages of bST's evaluation, as a kind of fishing expedition for arguments against approval). Moreover, now that bST has been approved (reluctantly), the FDA is permitting stores that sell dairy products to flaunt the agency's policy on labeling—that is, to label dairy products illegally (in a way that

[16] Office of Technology Assessment, U.S. Congress, *New Developments in Biotechnology—Field Testing Engineered Organisms: Genetic and Ecological Issues*, OTA-BA-350 (Washington, DC: U.S. Government Printing Office, May 1988).

[17] See Henry I. Miller, "The FDA's Fear of the Future," *New York Times*, May 20, 1995, p. 23.

implies inaccurately that there is a material difference between milk from bST-treated and untreated dairy cows); such labeling has the effect of "damaging" the acceptability of both bST and the milk from treated animals. (5) During congressional testimony, Kessler implicated the new biotechnology—inaccurately, as it turned out—in the creation of a high-nicotine tobacco plant. Dr. Kessler—a rare Bush-administration holdover—has been, let me put this delicately, unusually accommodating to the regulatory zeal of the Clinton administration.[18] The imprint of White House influence, over a supposedly independent regulatory agency, is evident to the FDA's long-term civil servants. It is exercised through political appointees with close ties to the vice president. Human nature, and politics, being what they are, it is inevitable that political considerations (and appointees) will influence the regulatory policies of federal agencies. But the Clinton administration has gone well beyond the politicization of policy to the micromanagement of decisions on the approval of specific products that the FDA regulates.[19]

In an executive order issued on September 30, 1993, President Clinton gave Al Gore what the *Washington Post* called "a potentially strong role in rule making by allowing him to set the administration's agenda of regulatory priorities." Gore, in other words, has been handed the power to make his regulatory *Weltanschauung* a reality.

## III. Biotech's Dire Straits

By all signs, Gore, Simon et al. are likely only to worsen the lot of the biotech industry even further. The new team has killed the Bush administration's Biotechnology Presidential Initiative, which would have provided additional research resources for areas that are underfunded.

Biotechnology regulation has become the bête noire of the administration's technology policy. On September 1, 1994, the EPA published a final regulation[20] for microbial pesticides that creates unwarranted barriers to research and innovation. It is squarely at odds with both the worldwide scientific consensus on safety and the widely perceived need for alternatives to chemical pesticides. In the regulation, the EPA targets research with microorganisms whose properties have been altered by "the introduction of genetic material that has been deliberately modified." With bureaucratic legerdemain, "deliberate" is defined as "directed," and finally "directed" is equated with the use of sophisticated and precise molecular techniques. What this EPA-speak means in lay terms is that microorganisms created with the most precise, state-of-the-art techniques

[18] See Henry I. Miller, "When Politics Drives Science," *Los Angeles Times*, December 12, 1994, p. B7.

[19] See *ibid.* and Peter Brimelow and Leslie Spencer, "Just Call Me 'Doc'," *Forbes*, November 22, 1993, p. 108.

[20] "Microbial Pesticides; Experimental Use Permits and Notifications; Final Rule," *Federal Register*, vol. 59 (September 1, 1994), pp. 45600–615.

have substantially greater regulatory burdens than others, regardless of risk; a corollary is that organisms with seemingly identical characteristics (that is, phenotypes) can be subject to very different degrees of regulation, if they are created with different genetic techniques. The EPA rationalizes that its circumlocution has identified a group of microorganisms that "have the greatest potential to pose risks to people or the environment."[21] The scientific community disagrees (as I noted in Section II).

What the EPA has circumscribed for regulation is research with organisms that are crafted with techniques that have an impressive and longstanding record of improving risk-assessment and *lowering* risk. The National Academy of Sciences confirmed the absence of unique hazards in either the use of the newest gene-splicing techniques or the movement of genes between unrelated organisms, and the National Research Council concluded that the precision of the newest recombinant DNA (gene-splicing) techniques ensures that the genetic changes made are likely to be better characterized and more predictable than those wrought by older techniques such as hybridization or mutation.[22] Numerous other prestigious national and international groups have echoed the view that the new biotechnology represents merely a refinement of older techniques and that it should be regulated no differently than other technology. A British expert advisory panel in 1993 characterized a regulatory approach like the EPA's as "excessively precautionary, obsolescent, and unscientific."[23]

The EPA has also announced plans to expand its regulatory dominion to another whole new category of biological pest-control products—plants that are made resistant to pests by using the new genetic techniques. American plant breeders have been creating improved plant varieties safely for more than a century without government regulation. However, common garden and crop plants could be regulated even *more stringently* than chemicals similar to DDT, if the EPA has its way.

As in the Soviet Union during the Lysenko period, the EPA's regulatory policies, crafted with the full approval and collaboration of the administration, represent not the result of scientific consensus, but ideology imposed on and debasing both scientific knowledge and common sense.

The combination of regulatory torpor and the forecasts of price controls on new drugs and biologics has inhibited investments in biotech firms. Some of the small, young firms that should be the backbone of the nation's biotech industry have already folded. Many others are perilously short of capital; for most, the time is still far off when their expensive

[21] "Final Rule on the Testing of Microbial Pesticides," EPA background document accompanying the biotechnology microbial pesticides rule (see note 20), EPA Office of Prevention, Pesticides, and Toxic Substances, August 1994.

[22] See *Introduction of Recombinant DNA-Engineered Organisms into the Environment* (*supra* note 3); and *Field Testing Genetically Modified Organisms* (*supra* note 4).

[23] Michael Ward, "Do U.K. Regulations of GMOs Hamper Industry?" *Bio/Technology*, vol. 11 (1993), p. 1213.

research and development will yield marketable goods. Analogous to Lysenkoism's devastating effects on Soviet agriculture, the Clinton administration's regulatory and other policies—born of heterodox ideology—have exerted a severe negative impact on biotechnology research and development.

## IV. The Gulag, American Style

There is no question that profound ignorance of scientific principles and the implementation of bad policy are hardly the moral equivalent of sending dissenters to the gulag. However, Simon and Gore have brooked no resistance to their view of policy or scientific rectitude and have gone to extremes to purge their "enemies." Between them, the vice president and his policy advisor, in their present capacities and in the past, have ended the careers of several scientists working in high positions in various agencies and departments. The issues have been various—differences over biotechnology policy, an unwelcome effectiveness in carrying out the policies of the previous Republican administration, or a refusal to bend scientific evidence to administration orthodoxy on ozone depletion and global warming. Prominent civil servants have, for ideological not scientific reasons, been moved to less visible positions, or forced to resign, and replaced with more politically acquiescent individuals.[24]

The legacy of the Clinton administration's scientific authoritarianism will likely be shorter-lived and less detrimental than the effects of Lysenkoism in the Soviet Union. The time of incumbency will be much less. Also, compared to the Soviet Union, the United States government's influence on scientific institutions—universities, academies, journals, learned societies—is weak. On the other hand, the far-reaching and lingering effects of perverse public policy should not be underestimated. Consider biologist Zhores Medvedev's observation, five years after Lysenko's fall from power:

> Lysenkoism is far from having been liquidated; nor has it lost its aggressiveness. Neither has it lost from its midst people capable of grasping and comprehending modern biology, biochemistry, and genetics, and capable of real education, yet unwilling to relinquish the primitive collection of dogmas they have so firmly mastered and held for so long. What is more to the point, they were also unwilling to relinquish the high posts they had occupied for so long (by no means because of their high qualifications).[25]

Analogously, by means of appointments to federal advisory committees, the hiring and promotion of tenured civil servants, the setting of

[24] See Henry I. Miller, ". . . Gore and His Minions Punish Civil Servants Who Dare to Disagree," *Washington Times*, June 2, 1994.

[25] Zhores A. Medvedev, *The Rise and Fall of T. D. Lysenko* (New York: Columbia University Press, 1969), p. 240.

funding priorities, the profusion of propaganda from federal agencies, the commitment of the United States to international agreements, and formal rule-making that establishes policies and crafts regulations, the Clinton administration will exert influence beyond its tenure.

## V. Summary

Certainly, the analogies between the two systems and eras can be overdrawn; for example, while Lysenko was semiliterate and charismatic, Gore is educated—one might even say "over-educated"—ponderous, and stilted in both his speeches and his writings. There are disturbing parallels, however, between the Lysenko era of Soviet genetics and current biotechnology regulatory policy in the United States. Lysenkoites preached and practiced discredited Lamarckian biology. The Clinton administration's approach to regulating the purported risks of the new biotechnology flies in the face of the worldwide scientific consensus that biotechnology oversight should be consistent with scientific principles and risk-based. In both cases, we see the adverse effects of flawed public policies on research, development, and the availability of important consumer products.

Both Lysenko and Gore can be characterized as doctrinaire, exclusionary, and condescending in their policymaking. The elaborate – albeit flawed – rationales employed to justify their approaches to public policy serve as a reminder that ignorance can be not a simple lack of knowledge but an active aversion to knowledge – the *refusal to know* – issuing from arrogance, zealotry, or laziness of mind.

More disturbing still, because of its practical implications and its parallels to the Soviet past, is Gore's approach to government, particularly to the federal oversight of new technology and of environmental protection. To paraphrase columnist George Will, Gore's views are paradigmatic of paternalistic liberalism, of government that is bullying because it is arrogant, and arrogant because it does not know what it does not know. Consider this excerpt—inserted against the U.S. Department of Agriculture's repeated objections—from President Clinton's January 1995 State of the Union speech: "For years, Congress has concealed in the budget scores of pet spending projects—and last year was no different: A million dollars to study stress in plants . . ." Did no one who vetted the speech understand that "stress in plants" refers not to lilies on Librium, but to the susceptibility of plants—especially crop plants—to disease, pests, and environmental extremes? Did none of "the best team you could assemble on biotechnology" know that genetic improvements in plants are essential to enhance productivity, decrease wastage in the field, and reduce the need for agricultural chemicals?

For decades, Lysenkoism savaged Soviet biological research and agriculture. In a relatively short time, Vice President Gore's influence, in particular, has damaged whole sectors of American research, development, and commercial application of the new biotechnology. Will the Clinton administration's mischief prove to be so pervasive and injurious that we have to wait decades for its effects to run their course, as in the Soviet Union? With U.S. industry currently competitive in most areas of biotechnology, how much will Americans have lost in jobs, industrial competitiveness, and new consumer products during that time? And what of the intangible effects of government policies that exhibit contempt toward rationality and science?

It is unlikely that our society will soon attain the desirable goal that decisions pertaining to science, technology, and risk should be independent of political ideology—for example, by systematically leaving these areas to nonpartisan experts and making them "off limits" to political operatives. But despite the president's repeated promises of a "leaner but not meaner" government, the Clinton administration's movement toward a highly ideological, exclusionary mentality reminiscent of the Lysenko excesses moves us farther from that ideal. It places citizens' interests increasingly at the mercy of activists and fosters inept political compromises. In the end, it argues for historian Barbara Tuchman's assertion that "[m]ankind, it seems, makes a poorer performance of government than of almost any other human activity."[26]

*Scientific Philosophy and Public Policy, Hoover Institution, Stanford University*

[26] Barbara W. Tuchman, *The March of Folly: From Troy to Vietnam* (New York: Knopf, 1984), p. 4.

# BIOTECHNOLOGY AND THE UTILITARIAN ARGUMENT FOR PATENTS*

By Michele Svatos

## I. Introduction

Biotechnology surpasses even computer technology in predictions of its potential for revolutionary effects on humankind. It includes agribusiness (genetically engineered plants, animals, hormones, etc.) and pharmaceuticals (diagnostics, genetic therapies, etc.). The U.S. government began investing heavily in biotechnology research in the 1980s, and by 1987 had spent approximately $2.7 billion to support research and development (R and D), including $150 million for agricultural biotechnology.[1] The approximately sixty U.S. biotechnology companies invested $3.2 billion in R and D in 1991 alone,[2] with a total of more than $10 billion spent since the industry began in the late 1970s.

Patenting the products and processes of biotechnology is a major legal, economic, and moral controversy. Patents grant the exclusive right to make, use, or sell an invention for a period of seventeen years. For an invention to be patentable, it must be novel, useful, and nonobvious to the average person skilled in the discipline. Ideas, theories, mathematical algorithms, laws of nature, and the like cannot be patented; processes (including production methods, special techniques, and diagnostic methods), products (such as microorganisms, enzymes, plasmids, cell lines, and DNA and RNA sequences), and new uses of an existing product can be patented.

Patents are already very common in biotechnology; for example, one source reports that Genentech, the company which developed the process to produce human insulin, has about fourteen hundred patent applications outstanding.[3] Many industry spokespersons have claimed that patents are essential for the growth of biotechnology. Andrew Hacking, author of *Economic Aspects of Biotechnology*, explains:

* I would like to thank the Social Philosophy and Policy Center at Bowling Green State University for a one-semester research leave and research support to work on this project.

[1] William B. Lacy, Lawrence Bush, and William D. Cole, "Biotechnology and Agricultural Cooperatives: Opportunities, Challenges, and Strategies for the Future," in *Biotechnology: Assessing Social Impacts and Policy Implications*, ed. David J. Webber (New York: Greenwood Press, 1990), p. 74.

[2] Fred Warshofsky, *The Patent Wars: The Battle to Own the World's Technology* (New York: John Wiley and Sons, 1994), p. 209.

[3] Andrew J. Hacking, *Economic Aspects of Biotechnology* (Cambridge and New York: Cambridge University Press, 1986), p. 46.

> Patenting is necessary to ensure that producers of new inventions or innovations receive a return on their investment in research and development. It is justified as being essential to induce innovation and to support research. Information may be expensive to produce but relatively cheap to copy. In biotechnology as elsewhere patents are an indispensable element in research and development, and much effort must be directed to ensure that work is patentable, otherwise it may have little commercial value.[4]

This is hardly a new argument; for several centuries patents have been claimed to be necessary for technological growth. In America, the first monopolies for inventions were granted by colonial governments, despite general distrust of monopolies; for example, in 1641, the "Body of Liberties" of the General Court of Massachusetts declared: "There shall be no monopolies granted or allowed among us, but of such new inventions as are profitable to the country, and that for a short time."[5] The U.S. Constitution gave Congress the power to grant patents and copyrights as privileges "[t]o promote the Progress of Science and useful Arts, by securing for limited Times to Authors and Inventors the exclusive Right to their respective Writings and Discoveries,"[6] and in 1790 the first patent act was approved. The basis of the current patent system is the 1836 Patent Act.

The utilitarian argument is the one most often given in attempting to justify the patent system or its extension to a new industry. Any welfare losses due to the restrictions in disseminating an invention are presumably far outweighed by the necessary incentive which such restrictions provide. Without the promise of being able to control an invention and thereby potentially recoup research and development costs, a company or individual would have little reason to invest in R and D. Since society benefits from the disclosure[7] and use of inventions as well as from the resulting increased economic activity, patents are justified. According to this argument, the rights granted are a matter of social convention, not natural law or distributive justice.[8]

[4] *Ibid.*, pp. 43–44.

[5] *Outline of the History of the United States Patent Office* (Patent Office Society, 1936); quoted in Warshofsky, *The Patent Wars*, p. 32.

[6] U.S. Constitution, section 8, para. 8.

[7] Some authors make a distinction between the argument that patents encourage R and D, and the argument that they encourage an inventor to disclose her invention rather than keeping it secret. Since in either case the patent is seen as an inducement for the inventor to benefit society, I will consider them two different parts of a utilitarian argument.

[8] J. S. Mill and Jeremy Bentham both argued for the patent system on grounds of distributive justice: it is only fair that the inventor receive a reward for his efforts, in proportion to the benefit he has given society. This seems to me to be closer to the argument that inventors have a natural right to their inventions. The argument that patents are justified as an incentive to inventors is more often identified as utilitarian, despite the positions of Mill and Bentham.

The biotech industry was founded on two inventions by collaborators Stanley Cohen of Stanford University and Herbert Boyer of the University of California, which were developed without thought as to their patentability. In fact, it was nearly too late to file when an administrator at Stanford read about the research and contacted Cohen. The Cohen-Boyer patents cover the recombinant DNA process—the process of making hybrid DNA from two different sources—in unicellular organisms, and products made by recombinant DNA techniques. (The product patent was granted in 1980; the more controversial process patent was not granted until 1984; both are still in effect.) A license to use the techniques for research leading to a commercial product costs $10,000 per annum, plus a royalty on sales of any product.[9]

Plants were the first living organisms to receive explicit patent-like protection. The Plant Patent Act of 1930 provided protection of asexually reproduced plants, and was mainly applied to flowers and certain fruits. The broader 1970 Plant Variety Protection Act (PVPA) provides patent-like protection for new varieties of plants, although it differs from a patent in that it lacks the utility requirement. Agricultural genetic engineers use both plant variety protection and patents for processes and other products. One company, Agracetus, now owns patents on all genetically engineered cotton and soybeans, regardless of the process used to engineer them or the traits engineered.[10]

Since the landmark 1980 Supreme Court decision in *Diamond v. Chakrabarty*, microorganisms and higher forms of life – "anything under the sun made by man"[11] – can be patented in the U.S. Explains one commentator: "There was no legal ... reason to differentiate animate and inanimate products of human manufacture. Biotechnology was recognized as a field of endeavor in which inventions could secure monopoly rewards."[12] Observers have claimed that the *Chakrabarty* case "opened the floodgates" of investment in biotechnology R and D, calling it "the driving force behind the commercial development of biotechnology."[13]

In 1988, the first transgenic animal—an animal containing a gene from another species—was patented: the "Harvard mouse" or "Oncomouse." Already a patent has been filed for germ-line genetic engineering, or rather "designer sperm."[14] The inventor intends to use the process on animals; however, he included humans in the patent application "for

[9] Hacking, *Economic Aspects of Biotechnology*, pp. 45–46.

[10] Rosie Mestel, "Bean Patent Sweeps the Field," *New Scientist*, vol. 142 (April 30, 1994), p. 7.

[11] *Diamond v. Chakrabarty*, 447 U.S. 303, 308–9 (1980).

[12] Martin Kenney, *Biotechnology: The University-Industrial Complex* (New Haven, CT: Yale University Press, 1986), p. 257.

[13] L. Christopher Plein, "Biotechnology: Issue Development and Evolution," in Webber, ed., *Biotechnology*, p. 158. Plein is himself describing the views of several observers.

[14] Somatic cell gene therapy affects only an individual's normal body cells, and is not passed on to offspring. Germ-line genetic engineering affects reproductive cells, and affects one's children as well as their offspring.

completeness."[15] Human cell lines and genes which each of us carry may already be patented.

What will be the effects of commercializing molecular biology? Biotechnology has greatly increased the relationship between universities and industry. Should universities (or government agencies) be allowed to patent? What once was controversial has now become commonplace. Will increasing industry involvement turn the free flow of scientific information into jealously guarded proprietary information? Will the benefits of biotechnology be fully exploited (in the good sense) by industry? Will biotechnology fulfill its promise of a better life for all humanity?

Since the most common argument for the patent system or its extension into a new area is utilitarian, this essay gives a critical analysis of the utilitarian argument for patents, particularly in the relatively new area of biotechnology. I argue that the patent system is not clearly justified on any roughly utilitarian grounds, as is often rather naively assumed. As one economist explains:

> The justification of the patent system is that by slowing down the diffusion of technical progress it ensures that there will be more progress to diffuse. . . . Since it is rooted in a contradiction, there can be no such thing as an ideally beneficial patent system, and it is bound to produce negative results in particular instances, impeding progress unnecessarily even if its general effect is favorable on balance.[16]

If our justification of intellectual property is the economic-incentive argument, then it makes more sense, particularly in the context of biotechnology, to address the issue as a straightforward question of whether we, as a society, want to encourage research to this extent and in this way. Should we include life-forms, including human genes, under patent law? What constitutes usefulness or nonobviousness? Should the mere fact of isolating a gene or purifying a substance found in nature make it fully appropriable? When patent law is extended into a new area, or interpreted in a particular way, policy decisions are made, implicitly or explicitly, about what sorts of research are to be encouraged and how and to what extent new technological knowledge will be disseminated. Justifying patents on utilitarian grounds should be seen as a problem of allocation of resources—a policy decision, like any other.

A utilitarian argument for the patent system, or for its extension to a new industry such as biotechnology, would have to show three things: (a) that the patent system makes a significant contribution to stimulating

[15] Andy Coghlan, "Outrage Greets Patent on Designer Sperm," *New Scientist*, vol. 142 (April 9, 1994).

[16] Joan Robinson, *The Accumulation of Capital* (London: Macmillan, 1956), p. 87; quoted in Dorothy Nelkin, *Science as Intellectual Property* (New York: Macmillan, 1984), p. 15.

invention; (b) that the patent system is the best way among the alternatives to stimulate invention; and (c) that, at a more basic level, stimulating technological invention in general—or in our case, stimulating biotechnological invention—is itself justified on utilitarian grounds. I will show that there are strong reasons to doubt each of these three necessary points, despite the fact that they are often simply assumed to be true and that the last point is seldom even mentioned. Although economists do not have the facts to completely support or reject (a) and (b), and are not particularly qualified to assess the truth of (c), I will show that there are many strong reasons to be dubious of the patent system's efficacy in maximizing utility. As a result, we must make a choice between either (1) rejecting or radically revising the patent system (or at least its extension to the products of biotechnology) on utilitarian grounds, or (2) looking to natural rights or distributive justice as the real foundation of the patent system.

## II. Problems with Patents as Incentives to Invent

There are numerous drawbacks to using patents as incentives to invent. They include the inefficient allocation of resources, encouragement of "work-arounds" or copycat inventions, changes in the allocation of research funds, increased secrecy, substantial legal and administrative costs, an arbitrary incentive to focus on the sorts of research which are patentable, and differential effects depending on the stage of industry development. This section explores these problems, particularly with regard to biotechnology. As we shall see, economists have been unable to determine empirically whether the economic benefits of the patent system outweigh its costs.

### *A. Underinvestment, overinvestment, and the inefficient allocation of resources*

The utilitarian argument recognizes that the benefits of the patent system are balanced against the disadvantage of granting a limited monopoly to inventors. Most obviously, a monopoly may (1) decrease competition and (2) allow the patent-holder to charge a higher price than the market would otherwise bear, resulting in deadweight loss—a reduction in utility due to inefficiency from the underutilization of the invention. Moreover, the patent-holder need not license her invention to anyone who might compete with her.

The development of the ballpoint pen is a clear historical example of a patent being used to charge prices vastly in excess of R and D costs, even given the risk involved in trying to invent and develop a new product. In 1945, Milton Reynolds charged $12.50—nearly $100 in 1995 dollars—for a pen whose average production cost was about 80 cents. His profits were as much as $500,000 a month, and his original investment only $26,000.[17] Without the government monopoly granted by a patent, Reynolds would have been unable to capture such high profits.

When someone patents an invention, there is certainly no guarantee that her profits will correspond to her investment costs, or that she will reinvest in more R and D with any additional profits. Naturally, it is the hope of huge profits like those made by Reynolds which provides an incentive to engage in risky R and D, or to simply bring forth a new idea. Even if the patent-holder herself chooses not to reinvest her profits in more R and D, other would-be inventors may be inspired by the example of people such as Reynolds, who were able to profit handsomely from an innovative idea. The incentive which patents offer must be considered within a dynamic rather than static system. Although, in the short run, patents decrease the dissemination of new inventions, in the long run they may do the opposite. Moreover, the monopoly is limited to a period of seventeen years, after which anyone may freely use the invention without licensing.

But are patents meant to (a) simply allow inventors to make a normal profit by internalizing positive externalities—that is, seeing that those who benefit from the invention pay for it—which might not happen (due to the special nature of intellectual property) without patent protection—or rather (b) allow inventors to make a supernormal profit on their investment, as a special inducement to innovation? Economists make a distinction between normal and economic profit. Profits are what is left over after explicit costs, such as the costs of production and R and D, are covered. Normal profit merely covers implicit costs—those things, such as opportunity costs, not normally counted in the company's financial reports as costs. In other words, normal profit "is the minimum payment to keep investment or entrepreneurial talent in a particular use. Normal profit, therefore, is really a cost."[18] Economic profit is anything beyond this; it goes beyond covering implicit opportunity costs. Long-term economic profits are fairly rare under competition. When a business reaps unusually high profits, the product may be underutilized, and consumers may complain that its price is unfair. This is one of the main allegations against monopolies, which prevent competition from driving the price down.

So, is the patent system designed to provide inventors with the incentive of normal or economic profits? Or, perhaps more to the point (especially in a utilitarian justification), what does it in fact do? Patents sometimes help the inventor to capture economic profits, sometimes normal profits, and sometimes neither. In fact, the majority of patents are probably net losses to the inventor, given the costs of patenting (and the majority of

[17] William P. Albrecht, Jr., *Economics*, 4th ed. (Englewood Cliffs, NJ: Prentice-Hall, 1974), p. 468.

[18] *Ibid.*, p. 102

patents are for minor inventions). Helping to capture normal profits versus economic profits may be the difference between preventing underinvestment in R and D versus promoting overinvestment. There is little agreement among economists as to which the patent system does, or is designed to do. It is important to note that the question of whether patents prevent underinvestment or promote overinvestment presumes that economics can tell us what the optimal level of investment in technology R and D is—a tendentious assumption which I shall discuss in more detail later.

It is sometimes argued, particularly on grounds of distributive justice, that the patent system is especially appropriate because it rewards the inventor in proportion to the benefit she confers on society. This might be relevant to a utilitarian justification if an individual could expect her returns (the inducement provided by the patent) to approximately equal the social rate of return, or utilitarian value, of her invention. However, leading patent economist Edwin Mansfield finds that "there is no significant correlation between an innovation's expected private rate of return and its social rate of return."[19] Just as there is no guarantee that patents will not allow "monopoly" profits, there is also no guarantee that a patent will help capture even normal profits, even if the invention is socially useful; this can result from a lack of marketing know-how, excessive litigation costs, etc.

In fact, patents are sometimes least effective where they would be most desirable, and businesses must look to alternatives to capture a profit. Exclusion costs are high for any self-reproducing organism; the "factory" is built-in. For example, while seed patents may be highly desirable to agribusiness, it is very difficult to keep farmers, cooperatives, or other plant breeders from regrowing and using and even selling proprietary seed (rather like the computer-software piracy problem). In fact, this is one of the main reasons why hybrids are so popular with seed companies; to maintain productivity—"hybrid vigor"—the farmer must buy newly hybridized seed each year rather than growing it out and saving some for next year. Thus, the farmer needs to keep buying seed each year, beyond any legal requirement which would be difficult to enforce.[20] The reason patents are so desirable often also makes them beside the point because of enforcement problems. Patent law does not ensure excludability or appropriability.

In summary, patents do sometimes work as an incentive by allowing inventors to capture a normal profit. However, sometimes they allow monopoly profit and underutilization of the invention. They scarcely

[19] Edwin Mansfield, J. Rapoport, J. Schnee, S. Wagner, and M. Hamburger, *The Production and Application of New Industrial Technology* (New York: W. W. Norton, 1977); quoted in Geoffrey Wyatt, *The Economics of Invention* (Brighton: Wheatsheaf, 1986), p. 215.

[20] See, for example, Jack Kloppenberg, *First the Seed: The Political Economy of Plant Biotechnology, 1492–2000* (New York: Cambridge University Press, 1988).

guarantee a profit, even for a useful invention; where they would be most desirable, they are often least effective. The correlation which is often naively assumed between the private rate of return and the social rate of return on an invention does not necessarily exist. Although patents stimulate invention to at least some degree, it is impossible to say on solely economic grounds whether the patent system does more to prevent underinvestment in R and D, or to promote overinvestment, or whether it is a net social benefit. This uncertainty is due in large part to the question of the social desirability of increased innovation in patentable areas, which I shall consider later.

### *B. Work-arounds*

Besides inefficient allocation of resources, there are other major drawbacks to the patent system from a utilitarian perspective. Patents encourage "work-arounds," the development of copycat inventions which differ only slightly from the original patented invention. This may be done in order to avoid licensing, although obtaining a license is not always possible because the inventor may prefer to retain exclusive license in order to avoid competition, sometimes in an attempt to dominate the industry. Even when a license is available, competitors may find it cheaper to either risk infringement and litigation, or else invent around the patent, with the advantage of knowing what they are working toward. Thus, work-arounds are quite common.

Many people have argued that this is wasteful; resources would be better channeled into nonduplicative efforts. One study found that "imitation cost averages about 65 percent of innovation cost, and imitation time averages about 70 percent of innovation time."[21] Why not actually try to build a better mousetrap rather than another variation on an old one? If licenses were not required, competitors would have no incentive to reinvent the wheel. It little benefits "the Progress of Science and the useful Arts" when companies try to duplicate, with very small differences, an invention which has already been made. Under competition, companies would still often be working on developing the same product at the same time; duplication of effort would not be entirely eliminated. However, once a product came out on the market, companies would have no incentive to invest the R and D funds to invent around the patent; they would simply copy it (which, however, might still involve some reverse engineering *if* the company were able to keep the details of the invention secret).

The patent system may encourage excessive duplication of effort in other ways. Several noted patent economists have argued that the system encourages a race to invent, particularly in the biotechnology industry

[21] Edwin Mansfield, "R&D and Innovation: Some Empirical Findings," in *R&D, Patents, and Productivity*, ed. Zvi Griliches (Chicago: University of Chicago Press, 1984), p. 142.

where, unlike the chemical industry, a large number of companies are often trying to develop the same one or two dozen interesting products. "This rush to invent before others make the prize inventions of the time, and to secure patent protection for their exclusive use, may result in overallocation of resources in inventive and innovative activities."[22] The race to invent promotes not only duplication of effort but also higher costs due to the need to complete the project before anyone else does; in the race to patent, there is no prize for second place.[23]

Without the patent system, a second independent inventor could still profit from her efforts. However, once a competitor is granted a patent, she may not be able to use her own research. Furthermore, since patent applications are not public, a firm can invest years of R and D in a product, only to find when their patent application is rejected—or worse, when the product is already on the market—that a patent application had already been filed on it by someone else. This happened with erythropoietin (EPO), a hormone which boosts the production of red blood cells. The biotech start-up company Amgen discovered only when its own patent claim was rejected that EPO had already been patented by another company, Genetics Institute.[24]

Of course, duplication of effort does introduce a certain amount of competition, somewhat counteracting the limited monopoly given by patents—but if there were no patents and hence no work-arounds, there would also be no monopoly and hence no worries about the lack of competition. In fact, imitation time is often the limiting factor in the useful life of a patent, rather than its limited duration by statute; once the invention has been successfully imitated, the patent is no longer very useful.

Copycat inventions are common in pharmaceuticals and plants. In the case of "me-too" drugs—drugs which are slightly different from a preexisting patented drug but designed to do the same job—or a plant variety which only differs from another in having a different color of flower, the patent acts as an incentive for a great deal of marketing and very little invention at all. In fact, according to the PVPA, utility does not even need to be demonstrated for the patent to issue. Therefore, irrelevant traits (in a cash crop) such as flower color are sufficient to legally justify a patent. The good name of the seed company, in conjunction with a massive marketing effort, then does the job of product differentiation. The farmer usually does not realize that what she is buying is, for all relevant purposes, the same as another company's seed.[25] Not only do patents en-

[22] Fritz Machlup, *Knowledge: Its Creation, Distribution and Economic Significance*, vol. 3, *The Economics of Information and Human Capital* (Princeton: Princeton University Press, 1984), p. 176.

[23] Wyatt, *The Economics of Invention*, p. 126.

[24] Warshofsky, *The Patent Wars*, pp. 214–30, 249.

[25] See, for example, Kloppenberg, *First the Seed*.

courage duplication of effort, they also may reward marketing rather than a truly new invention. Product differentiation can allow a higher price to be charged on the basis of a perceived difference in quality, and it is consumers who may lose out.

Economists and patent lawyers recognize the real difference between an invention and a marketing strategy by making a distinction between invention and innovation. One receives a patent for an invention, but the innovation is the final product which appears on the market. Without some kind of marketing strategy, the invention would not be utilized. Therefore, patents do not stimulate invention directly; rather, they stimulate some combination of invention and marketing skill. The proportion may vary greatly from one product to the next; in the case of work-arounds, the inventive component may be very small. This is not to say that marketing is not useful and even necessary to inform consumers. However, since the patent system (and especially the PVPA) rewards even very minor and not particularly useful inventions, it sometimes acts as an incentive to invent around other patents and to launch a massive marketing campaign, rather than as an incentive to do socially useful R and D. In fact, with the increasing use of commercial success as a criterion for demonstrating nonobviousness in court cases (rather than an examination of the methods used, which demands more scientific expertise on the part of the court system), the focus on marketing innovation rather than scientific invention becomes more intense.[26]

The patent system may encourage invention, but in the race to be first or in an effort to avoid licensing (licensing, of course, may not even be an option if the inventor retains exclusive license), it also encourages work-arounds and the duplication of effort rather than real technological advancement. Furthermore, it sometimes rewards marketing skill more than inventive ability, and may help prevent consumers from recognizing functionally equivalent products.

### C. *Allocation of research funds*

Patents provide an incentive to work on applied rather than basic research, and can skew which areas within a particular science receive funding. Molecular biology is the foundation of biotechnology, and, as a consequence, biology departments have seen explosive growth of that area of their discipline. Funding may be diverted from areas of biology, such as ecology and evolution, which are not so amenable to commercialization at any stage—and not only funding, but professorships and graduate students as well. "Indeed, graduate students at some universities have complained that their research options are limited as they are

[26] Robert P. Merges, "Commercial Success and Patent Standards: Economic Perspectives on Innovation," *California Law Review*, vol. 76 (July 1988).

diverted to those areas of commercial potential of interest to their advisors."[27] With only a small percentage of science funds devoted to basic research, how will biotechnology (and patents within the university system in general) affect the allocation of those funds?

Moreover, as commercially oriented research and partnerships with industry increase within the university, a considerable number of prominent university researchers, some Nobel laureates, have been lured into industry by higher salaries, and more graduate students are inclined to go into industry after graduation.[28] The result is a sort of "brain drain" away from the university, which jeopardizes the training of future scientists; industry may well be slowly killing the goose that laid the golden egg. Furthermore, economist Fritz Machlup argued decades ago that increasing demand for inventors eventually leads to lower-quality personnel, fewer inventions per input unit, and more rejected inventions.[29] His point is likely to still be valid; as we encourage increased research, we may reap diminishing marginal returns, and we must realize that scientific talent may be diverted from other valuable areas such as education.

Patents do more than reallocate funds from basic research to applied research, or from one area of biology to another, and lure researchers from academia to industry; they also reallocate resources from nonpatentable disciplines or commercial ventures, to patentable ones. Within the university, more funds may go to science and engineering fields which can bring in needed funds, rather than to social sciences which cost more than they generate; one might well argue that this pushes the university more toward overinvestment in the hard sciences compared to other disciplines where patents are not available. In utilitarian terms, it is not obvious that this increased emphasis on scientific research rather than social sciences and humanities research is justified. In commercial endeavors, patents may encourage investors toward R and D of patentable inventions and away from unpatentable ones. Moreover, it may encourage them to simply overinvest in R and D, at the expense of other forms of investment. Geoffrey Wyatt argues in his 1986 book *The Economics of Invention* that the patent system

> has the effect of drawing socially excessive resources into inventive activity as a whole, and directing too much within the total towards patentable inventions. . . . [I]nduced inventions will typically be of minor importance, representing improvements to existing technologies perhaps, rather than fundamental changes.
>
> It can be predicted that changes in the rewards for invention will imply an elastic response in terms of inventive activity or the number

[27] Nelkin, *Science as Intellectual Property*, p. 26.
[28] *Ibid.*, p. 28.
[29] Machlup, "The Supply of Inventors and Inventions"; quoted in Wyatt, *The Economics of Invention*, p. 205.

> of inventions produced. Thus if new categories of technology become patentable, researchers will redirect their energies accordingly. Recent corroboration of this has been seen in the responses to the change in United States patent law that allows new hybrid species of plants to be patented. But it may reasonably be doubted whether such changes are important for the production of socially valuable technological change. Most induced inventions will be of minor importance.[30]

Wyatt concludes that "the supply of technological improvements, as opposed to numbers of inventions, responds rather inelastically to demand inducements."[31] Not only do attempts at stimulating invention lure scientists from one area of research to another, or from academia into industry, but such attempts may have little marginal utility.

Encouraging patentable research encourages certain types of solutions to the problems of humanity over others. Scientist Martha Crouch argues that the focus on molecular biology leads to ways of thinking about problems which may not best serve utility. For example, in less developed countries (LDCs), lack of complete protein sources is often a problem. Biotechnology suggests genetically engineered rice with the missing amino acids as the solution. However, genetically engineered crops often require chemical and other inputs (not to mention the genetically engineered seed itself) which farmers in LDCs can ill afford. A better and more environmentally sustainable solution to the problem might be found by studying crop rotation cycles, biocontrol of pests, intercropping, traditional farming practices, etc. Crouch argues that such areas are more deserving of funding than biotechnology.[32] Patents channel research funds into areas with patent potential, without regard for maximizing utility.

### *D. The legal and administrative costs of the patent system*

The patent system requires that considerable resources be devoted to filing for patents and trying infringement cases. In biotechnology, patent costs and agent fees begin at around \$1,000 to file an application and at least \$1,000 per country, plus maintenance fees. Coverage in twenty countries costs around \$50,000 over the life of the patent.[33]

Patent fees and the threat of litigation can have a chilling effect on research. In one case, separate research groups at Children's Hospital in Boston and the Toronto Hospital for Sick Children were working on different sections of the gene which causes Duchenne muscular dystro-

[30] Wyatt, *The Economics of Invention*, pp. 15–16.

[31] *Ibid.*, p. 17.

[32] Martha Crouch, "The Very Structure of Scientific Research Mitigates against Developing Products to Help the Environment, the Poor, and the Hungry," *Journal of Agricultural and Environmental Ethics*, vol. 4, no. 2 (1991).

[33] Hacking, *Economic Aspects of Biotechnology*, p. 45.

phy. Each group filed for a patent on its respective sections of the gene, but the Toronto group "had to drop its application because it could not afford the $20,000-plus cost of pursuing the patent."[34] Nonetheless, they continued to work with the gene and with their patients. Genica, the pharmaceutical company to which the Boston group licensed its patent rights, threatened to file suit, claiming that the Toronto group's use of antibodies corresponding to patented sections of the gene in order to diagnose dystrophin dysfunction constituted a commercial use. The Toronto doctors could either stop work, pay royalties, or await a lawsuit.[35]

In addition to filing and maintenance fees, a considerable percentage of the millions spent on biotechnology R and D must often be spent in patent court. For example, one biotech company's legal costs in its battle over one patent were at least $10 million—10 percent of the R and D costs for that product.[36] A 1992 article in the *Financial Times* reports that total worldwide spending on biotechnology patent costs probably exceeds $100 million annually.[37] Moreover:

> Firms are often forced to take out patents of uncertain validity and fight off challenges to them in the courts because competitors are doing the same. . . . However, patent battles are usually won by the company with the greatest financial resources for legal costs. The necessity of litigation and the uncertainty about biotechnology firms' ability to enforce proprietary rights has added to the uncertainty faced by investors, making the biotechnology industry less attractive, at least in the short run. Industry analysts expect the patent scramble to contribute to a trend over the next few years of great consolidation in the biotechnology industry.[38]

One commentator argues that the patent system has become a patent "arms race," where "everyone must run harder and incur significant additional costs just to stay even. The effect has been to increase quite dramatically the cost of innovation," and researchers must now spend considerable time assisting patent attorneys.[39] From 1980 to 1990, patent litigation increased by 52 percent, and in biotechnology "legal briefs out-

[34] Bernice Wuethrich, "All Rights Reserved: How the Gene-Patenting Race Is Affecting Science," *Science News*, vol. 144 (September 4, 1993), p. 154.

[35] *Ibid.*

[36] Brian C. Cannon, "Toward a Clear Standard of Obviousness for Biotechnology Patents," *Cornell Law Review*, vol. 79 (1994), p. 761.

[37] Clive Cookson and Julie Clayton, "Of Mice, Men, and Money: Legal Action over Patent Disputes Threatens to Stifle Investment in Biotechnology," *Financial Times*, June 3, 1992, p. 18; cited in Cannon, "Toward a Clear Standard," p. 761 n. 169.

[38] Beverly Fleisher, "Who Will Benefit from Agricultural Biotechnology: An Analysis of Economic and Legal Influences," in Webber, ed., *Biotechnology* (*supra* note 1), pp. 104–5.

[39] Cecil D. Quillen, Jr., "Innovation and the United States Patent System Today" (paper presented to the Antitrust and Patent Sections of the American Bar Association meeting, October 19, 1992); quoted in Warshofsky, *The Patent Wars*, p. 246.

weigh scientific papers by orders of magnitude, and lawyers are as eagerly sought as Ph.D.s."[40]

Individual inventors and small companies may well not be able to take advantage of the patent system simply because they cannot afford the legal costs and do not have as much experience with the patent system. "For the highly innovative and usually underfunded companies that make up much of the biotech industry, the mere threat of patent litigation is enough to force them to shut down a production or shutter the business itself" when faced with a choice between that or possible sales of $500,000 per year with a couple million dollars spent fighting a lawsuit of uncertain outcome.[41] Large companies can intimidate small ones out of business or out of the field, regardless of the merit of their infringement case, simply because the costs of litigation are so astronomical. One victim of patent litigation complains: "You have companies using old patents to go after younger, more entrepreneurial companies. They are demanding what amounts to protection money. They are saying, 'Pay me or I'll sue.'"[42] The agribusiness and pharmaceutical industries already tend to be rather oligopolistic. The high costs of patenting may further this tendency, certainly not always to the advantage of consumers.

On the other hand, (a) it is not clear that larger firms do not better promote utility, and (b) patents can also work in favor of small companies or individual entrepreneurs, who do not have some of the other advantages of large companies, such as an established reputation and distribution system. A small company with a patent on a successful product may be bought out by a larger corporation, at a considerable profit to its owners. The patent system does not always work against smaller companies, although there is that tendency. However, it may work against the biotechnology industry in general, because the uncertainty associated with patenting the products of biotechnology increases risks and thereby increases the cost of capital; the industry as a whole becomes less attractive to investors.

Not only can small companies ill afford high patent costs, but such costs are wasteful of potential research funds. If we want to stimulate invention, then diverting millions from biotechnology R and D into the legal system is hardly productive. One officer of a large company claimed that he might cut R and D expenditures by half if patent protection were removed. However, approximately half of the R and D budget of the company was spent on securing and enforcing patents. Thus, half the amount of money might buy just as much research.[43] Furthermore, if each company did not have to pay licenses and royalties to other companies

[40] Warshofsky, *The Patent Wars*, p. 247.

[41] *Ibid.*, pp. 247–48.

[42] Michael Rostoker, quoted in *ibid.*, p. 251.

[43] Fritz Machlup, *The Production and Distribution of Knowledge in the United States* (Princeton: Princeton University Press, 1962), p. 169.

for the use of their patents, R and D costs would be further reduced. Choosing in favor of the patent system, rather than other ways of encouraging research (or other, nonresearch allocations of resources), constitutes a choice to allocate very considerable resources to the legal system. Good news for lawyers, perhaps, but certainly a utilitarian cost of the patent system which cannot be ignored.

### *E. Secrecy and disclosure*

Although the patent system is supposed to have the advantage of encouraging inventors to disclose their inventions, thus promoting the free flow of information, the requirements of patenting may have the opposite effect, especially in the short run. Before a patent application is made, inventors must be careful *not* to disclose information about their inventions. Someone else may develop their ideas into a patentable invention first: "Patent first, publish later." At scientific meetings, scientists now sometimes refuse to divulge details of their technique or the organism they are working on because they consider them to be proprietary information.

The increasing presence of patents in scientific research has made many scientists—even in universities, much less in industry—more wary of sharing information, reagents, tissue samples, and so on with other researchers. In 1977, a man dying of leukemia donated a sample of his blood-forming cells for scientific research. Researchers at the University of California succeeded in growing the cells, thus producing a new cell line for leukemia research. They sent the cell line to a researcher at the National Cancer Institute, who sent a sample to another researcher at an institute funded by the pharmaceutical company Hoffman-LaRoche. This researcher was able to manipulate it for the production of interferon, a natural human antiviral protein, and devise a technique for producing substantial quantities. Hoffman-LaRoche filed patent applications for both the interferon and the manufacturing process. A court case between the company and the University of California over the cell line was finally settled out of court in 1983.[44] The lesson many scientists learned from this was to keep basic research materials to themselves.

Ownership and priority disputes have become more common since the early 1980s. Said one scientist at the University of California at San Diego (UCSD): "There used to be a good, healthy exchange of ideas and information among researchers at UCSD, the Salk Institute, and the Scripps Clinic. Now we are locking our doors."[45] Former Stanford President Donald Kennedy claimed: "Scientists who once shared prepublication information freely and exchanged cell lines without hesitation are now much more reluctant to do so. . . . The fragile network of informal communica-

[44] For an account of this, see, for example, Nelkin, *Science as Intellectual Property*, pp. 9–10.
[45] Russell Doolittle, quoted in Nelkin, *Science as Intellectual Property*, p. 11.

tion . . . is likely to rupture."[46] Secrecy in science "precludes replication and weakens the system of peer review. It may also cause conflicts for graduate students, postdoctoral researchers, and younger faculty who need to further their academic careers through publication."[47] In one 1985 study, 25 percent of industrially supported biotechnology faculty reported that they have conducted proprietary research which belongs to the firm and cannot be published without prior consent, and 40 percent reported that their collaboration resulted in unreasonable publication delays.[48]

Patenting is changing the social structure of scientific research, even in university and government labs, as well as on an international level.[49] Many scientists consider the changes to be for the worse. The incentive which patents provide must be balanced against losses in the open structure of scientific discovery. "Balancing secrecy against the open exchange of ideas has always been part of the culture of science, but the economic incentives now at stake have upset the traditional equilibrium by further encouraging protection of data and ideas."[50]

Of course, some proprietary information is in the form of trade secrets rather than patents. The formula for Coca-Cola, for example, has been a trade secret for decades. Trade-secrecy law protects companies from misappropriation of a company's valuable, secret information (by theft, industrial espionage, etc.). Trade-secrecy protection lasts indefinitely (unlike the limited term of a patent), and unlike patent law, it does not require—in fact, it does not permit—disclosure of the invention. It also does not involve a costly registration process, although the company may have to take security measures to protect its secret. (There can be no misappropriation of information which the company makes public, or does not make an effort to keep secret.) The drawback, from industry's point of view, is that it is virtually impossible to keep some sorts of information secret once the product has been released. For example, one could hardly

[46] Donald Kennedy, "Health Research: Can Utility and Quality Co-exist?" (lecture given at the University of Pennsylvania, December 6, 1980), quoted in Nelkin, *Science as Intellectual Property*, p. 12.

[47] Nelkin, *Science as Intellectual Property*, p. 25.

[48] David Blumenthal, Michael Gluck, Karen Seashore Louis, Michael A. Stoto, and David Wise, "University-Industry Research Relationships in Biotechnology: Implications for the University," *Science*, vol. 232 (June 13, 1986), pp. 1361–66; and Blumenthal, Gluck, Louis, and Wise, "Industrial Support of University Research in Biotechnology," *Science*, vol. 231 (January 17, 1986), pp. 242–46—both cited in Lacy, Bush, and Cole, "Biotechnology and Agricultural Cooperatives" (*supra* note 1), p. 79.

[49] For example, see Michael Mackenzie, Peter Keating, and Alberto Cambrosio, "Patents and Free Scientific Information: Making Monoclonal Antibodies Property," *Science, Technology, and Human Values*, vol. 15, no. 1 (Winter 1990), pp. 65-83. The authors conclude that "[t]here has been a shift in the boundaries—an extension of the territory of proprietary information into that of free information—which has profound implications for the way scientific research is done. This shift, taking place under pressure of economic interests, amounts to nothing less than a subtle but significant realignment in the political economy of science and technology."

[50] Nelkin, *Science as Intellectual Property*, p. 98.

keep the design for a paper clip a secret once it had been released on the market. Many of the products of biotechnology are rather like paper clips in this sense. From the point of view of society, trade secrets have the disadvantage of keeping scientific or technical advances secret, so that others cannot build upon them—they prevent the spread of information.

In a 1980 Senate hearing on biotechnology, "every business representative explicitly underlined the importance of patenting for the growth of the industry. The explicit threat was that the lack of patent protection would result in all biotechnical knowledge being treated as trade secrets."[51] Although it is no doubt true that industry would use trade-secrecy law more if patents were not available, it is an exaggeration to say that "all biotechnical knowledge" would be treated as trade secrets. Certainly the Cohen-Boyer recombinant DNA patents which founded the biotechnology industry would not have been, since the researchers published their data without any thought for making their inventions proprietary. Most university research, which forms much of the basic research for the biotech industry, would not be treated as trade secrets.

Furthermore, trade secrets are often not effective in biotechnology because it is difficult to keep the secret once the product is on the market and can be examined and analyzed by competitors. One noted economist claims: "The patent system cannot be said to serve the purpose of eliciting any secrets that would not in any event become known in the near future. People patent only what they cannot hope to keep secret."[52] Perhaps without patents the research would not have been done to create the secret which is to be disclosed. Nonetheless, there is good reason to question whether patents succeed to any great extent in their task of encouraging the spread of information.

## *F. Patents and stages of industry development*

The question of whether or not patents encourage innovation may depend on an industry's stage of development. Patents in an early stage of development may slow the industry down and make it difficult for latecomers to enter. Patenting of the basic components of the human genome has created a great deal of controversy. In 1992, a former National Institutes of Health (NIH) scientist working on the Human Genome Project tried to patent 6,122 gene fragments useful only in tagging a gene for which no function is known, on the chance that the gene's function might eventually be discovered and prove useful. Sequencing is done by machine, hundreds a day. As usual, the patent application was written as broadly as possible, claiming not only the gene fragment but also the

[51] Kenney, *Biotechnology* (*supra* note 12), p. 256.

[52] Fritz Machlup, *The Political Economy of Monopoly* (Baltimore: Johns Hopkins University Press, 1952), p. 281; quoted in Tom G. Palmer, "Intellectual Property: A Non-Posnerian Law and Economics Approach," *Hamline Law Review*, vol. 12, no. 2 (Spring 1989), p. 293.

unknown gene it would point to, and whatever protein the gene codes for (although the last part of the claim was eventually dropped). The entire human genome of some 100,000 genes could have been patented this way, in bits and pieces, with a small number of corporations, universities, and governments owning humanity's genetic code—even though scientists understand the function of less than 1,500 human genes.

The NIH's thousands of patent applications (filed in three batches) were eventually rejected. However, had they been upheld on appeal, these patents would have slowed research, discouraged cooperation among scientists and nations, and further slowed the development of therapies once the genes' functions were discovered. A company which wished to work on developing a diagnostic kit or therapy using a gene which had been tagged and thereby patented would have to obtain a license to do so, if the patent owner even offered such a license. Some companies were already working on genes which the NIH had filed patents for. Even *applying* for the patents slowed research and discouraged cooperation, as other companies and nations scrambled to file for patents on the sequences they had found, in case the NIH bid were to be successful. Britain postponed release of its researchers' findings of more than a thousand gene fragments for a year while battling the U.S. and European patent systems.[53]

Patenting can also cause problems in a well-developed industry. The more patents have been granted in an industry, the more difficult it can be to discover relevant patents and avoid infringement. A patent-heavy industry may discourage research, cause additional funds to be diverted to legal costs (including not only court costs but also simple patent searches), encourage work-arounds, and again leave the way open for a large corporation to gain control of strategic patents and thereby dominate the industry.

### G. Economic assessments of the patent system

Finally, economists are far from decisive about the actual influence of the patent system on innovation. Fritz Machlup, in his classic 1958 economic study of the patent system, admitted that "[n]o economist, on the basis of present knowledge, could possibly state with certainty that the patent system, as it now operates, confers a net benefit or a net loss upon society."[54] Although more work has been done in this area since that study, some patent lawyers and economists still consider the data completely unreliable. George Priest calls it "one of the least productive lines

[53] Wuethrich, "All Rights Reserved," pp. 154–57. See also the continued discussion of the issue over the past several years in *Science* and *Nature*.

[54] Fritz Machlup, "An Economic Review of the Patent System," *Patent Studies*, no. 1 (Subcommittee on Patents, Trademarks, and Copyrights of the Committee on the Judiciary, U.S. Senate, Eighty-fifth Congress, Second Session, 1958), p. 15; quoted in Palmer, "Intellectual Property," p. 300.

of inquiry in all economic thought."[55] There are so many variables that it is virtually impossible to know how well the patent system accomplishes its goal.

The patent system has considerable disadvantages. When taken together, it is far from obvious that they are offset by the benefits provided by the stimulation of innovation, even in simple economic terms. The benefit of the patent system is not the sum total of inventions patented; rather, it is only that portion of inventions which would not have been made, or made so quickly, in the absence of the system, and it is difficult to tell what that portion is. Although industry often claims that patents are utterly essential, this is not necessarily so. For more than a century, economists have been unable to agree whether the system is a net social benefit, whether it prevents underinvestment or promotes overinvestment in R and D, or even whether the patent system or its absence is most consistent with a capitalist economic system. This must give the utilitarian hoping to justify the patent system considerable pause. In the next section, I shall briefly consider some alternatives to the patent system, before going on in the final section to consider whether the patent system, or its extension to biotechnology, is in the end justified.

## III. Alternatives to the Patent System

If one compares the utility of having the patent system with the utility of simply abolishing it, perhaps it would be justified. However, this presents a false dichotomy. Patent policy is hardly the only incentive affecting biotechnology. A 1984 Office of Technology Assessment (OTA) report identifies nine other important factors: financing and tax climate, health and environmental regulation, university-industry relations, government funding for research, availability of trained personnel, antitrust law, international market and trade arrangements, government policies relating directly to biotechnology, and public opinion.[56] "Some of the high risk associated with biotechnology is now being reduced by government policies, subsidies, grants, capital allowances, the U.S. capital gains tax and so on."[57]

Tax policy plays a very important role in influencing corporate R and D decisions, and may be more effective than patent law at encouraging corporations to reinvest profits in more R and D. For one thing, a tax break for R and D is a sure bet, whereas relying on R and D to produce a profitable, patentable invention is risky. Low-interest loans may also be useful. Moreover, tax breaks and special loan programs are more easily targeted to industries where increased R and D efforts would be most socially useful,

[55] George L. Priest, "What Economists Can Tell Lawyers about Intellectual Property," *Research in Law and Economics*, vol. 8 (1986), p. 19.

[56] Office of Technology Assessment, U.S. Congress, *Commercial Biotechnology: An International Analysis* (Washington, DC: U.S. Government Printing Office, 1984).

[57] Hacking, *Economic Aspects of Biotechnology*, p. 281.

and could even promote R and D in areas where profits, even with patents, would be otherwise insufficient to justify the investment (perhaps because of excludability problems or a limited market). Of course, to be effective, tax policy must be intelligently designed, which has not always been a feature of U.S. tax breaks aimed at encouraging R and D. Corporations will ignore alleged incentives or make unintended uses of them if policy is not carefully designed to further the interests of corporations in engaging in useful R and D.

If we see patent law as a policy to promote R and D by helping companies to make economic profits on new products, then we must ask whether a policy with such aims would better take a different form—whether the increased prices consumers pay would better come in the form of a tax (perhaps even a sales tax, which would be like patent law in that it would only charge those who use the new technology) to be spent in ways that are likely to be socially useful, rather than simply at the discretion of the patent-holder. Redistribution of the tax monies would then differ little from existing methods of government spending, allocating a certain amount to agricultural research, health research, and so on—or, alternatively, offering tax breaks for research in these areas. If the research is done by a private firm, that firm still has every reason to try to make its research successful and to market a successful, useful product; it is simply that part of the returns from the firm's invention will not include licensing fees and royalties. While government allocations of resources would undoubtedly suffer from certain inefficiencies, a utilitarian must consider whether the drawbacks of such government decision-making outweigh the utilitarian drawbacks of the patent system.

Much scientific research is conducted at universities, usually under grants from government agencies such as the National Science Foundation and the NIH. Patents play less of a role in this environment, although as university budgets shrink and grant money becomes more scarce, the pressure to patent increases. However, if our justification for the patent system is utilitarian, we must consider whether the grant system, suitably expanded, might instead be more efficient at promoting utility. Although not without its problems, the grant system has advantages.

First of all, the inventor receives the money (which, we must recall, is supposed to serve as an incentive rather than, or more fundamentally than, a reward) *before* the product is finished and on the market. In an age where R and D costs are often substantial, this seems to make sense. It would perhaps serve to partially counteract the tendency for only large, well-established firms to have adequate funds to devote to years of R and D on a product. Although the biotechnology industry began as a number of small firms funded by venture capitalists, the vast majority of them soon either went bankrupt or were bought out by large companies—simply because the small companies could not continue to fund the years of research necessary to develop enough successful products to make the company viable. The patent system provides an *ex post facto* incentive only for those with the capital to hold out until research yields a profitable product.

Secondly, the grant system allows for review (usually peer review) of research projects to determine their merit. Of course, research ideas are also reviewed in the private sector, but the primary consideration there is the potential for profit, which certainly need not be identical with social utility. A case in point is the development by Monsanto of bGH, or bovine growth hormone, a genetically engineered product designed to increase milk production by 10 percent or more, which went on the market in 1994. It would hardly have been a top pick on utilitarian grounds for the millions devoted to its R and D, given the oversupply of milk and the existence of price supports and government subsidies to dairy farmers in the U.S. It is, however, an economically successful product; even though many dairy farmers lobbied against it, since it has become available they nonetheless feel economically pressured to use it in order to remain competitive.[58] Or, to give another example, large chemical companies which have acquired seed companies often try to genetically engineer their seeds to be specially compatible with or dependent upon the particular insecticides, pesticides, and so on which they market. Research may be geared more toward increasing demand for the company's chemical products than producing the sorts of seeds farmers would most like to see.[59]

> Biotechnology offers new opportunities to tailor crops to specific needs, a reduction in the use of purchased inputs, an emphasis on nutritional quality, and fewer environmental problems in agriculture. Alternatively, biotechnology could induce further concentration in farm structure and further industrialization of agriculture, with the highly monopolized input and output sectors of the agribusiness community capturing the bulk of the benefit.[60]

Government grants have the potential to target research which is most likely to be socially useful.[61] The grant system is not without its drawbacks,[62] and it is idealistic to assume that grant committees are unbiased

[58] David Suzuki and Joseph Levine, *The Secret of Life* (Boston: WGBH, 1993).

[59] See, for example, Kloppenberg, *First the Seed*; and Lacy, Bush, and Cole, "Biotechnology and Agricultural Cooperatives," p. 77.

[60] Lacy, Bush, and Cole, "Biotechnology and Agricultural Cooperatives," p. 82.

[61] They also have the potential for funding pure research, as they often do now. Social utility need not be the only criterion for awarding research grants; or, a certain level of funding for pure research may best promote long-run utility.

[62] One might worry about the established scientific community's resistance to really innovative ideas. This is already a topic of concern within the grant system. One proposed solution is to set aside money specifically for very new avenues of research which challenge established ideas, and in fact the NIH is now funding research on "alternative" medicine as a result of this concern. Moreover, even if the patent system were eliminated, the grant system might be combined with some other way(s) of encouraging innovation.

or that they have special insight about what research is most likely to be socially useful. However, the grant system is not so tied to economic profitability and can be used to promote utility more overtly than the patent system.

Of course, government research grants are already available, even to industry. Government grants to small businesses have been particularly successful. It is important to note that a great deal of research for biotechnology is already conducted with government funds. University research (much of which is publicly funded even at private institutions) contributes basic research for biotechnology. Furthermore, the U.S. government is funding the Human Genome Project (which actually extends to other species as well) to the tune of $3 billion. Its goal is to decode our genes by mapping each gene on its chromosome and sequencing the entire stretch of human DNA. Accomplishing this will provide industry researchers with a head start in their research on specific genes. Certainly this is a significant contribution to the biotechnology industry, especially in conjunction with other government agency (particularly NIH) funding of research projects in biotechnology. Is social welfare really best served by both extending the patent system to biotechnology as a research incentive, *and* funding research to this level? We need to recognize that the patent system, applied to biotechnology, is a tool for promoting research much in the way that direct government research funding is; they are two means to the same end.

There are, moreover, less expensive alternatives to research grants: "In tight fiscal times, incentives may, for example, be offered more frequently in the form of technology transfer activities and less restrictive legislation and regulation."[63] Food and Drug Administration (FDA) policy and lag-time adds considerable time and expense to the drug approval process; in agricultural biotechnology, the Environmental Protection Agency (EPA) or other agencies can play a similar role. If the abolition of patents would tend to greatly reduce R and D, other policies which might benefit the public even more could compensate. Apart from government grants or tax incentives, some of the resources currently devoted to patent fees could instead be paid to the FDA to speed up the approval process.[64] One of the costliest factors in drug research is the number of years it takes to get FDA approval. Not only is this costly to the company, it also has social-welfare costs to those individuals who await the new drug. While

[63] Morris Bosin, "Policymakers Address Biotechnology: Issues and Responsibilities," in Webber, ed., *Biotechnology* (*supra* note 1), p. 172.

[64] The patent office, with a budget of $520 million in 1994, is entirely funded by its own income from patent applications; that money could, for example, be paid by companies to the FDA instead, to help fund the additional staff needed to speed up approvals. On the other hand, reducing the responsibilities of the FDA in approving new drugs would also speed the process and might (or might not) promote overall utility.

abolition of patents alone may not be justified, we must consider whether abolition in conjunction with other methods of encouraging innovation might better promote utility.

One might argue that companies need some sort of *ex post facto* reward as an incentive to make sure that their R and D investments are fruitful. Yet R and D often continues even when it is uncertain whether an industry's products will receive patent protection. Uncertainty is the hallmark of biotechnology patenting. There are often profits to be made, even without a limited monopoly, from being first to bring a product to market or being able to make investment decisions based on the new invention before others know about it. Biotechnology shortens the product cycle of new drugs by making it likely that another firm will soon find a better or cheaper product. "The shorter the life cycle, the less the point in getting patents. . . . The rewards for invention for drug firms will increasingly come from being first to market."[65]

It is questionable just how necessary patents are to the majority of inventions once the costs of patenting are factored in. New industries may argue that they need them as an incentive, but this is often an exaggeration. Plant breeding and biotechnology certainly existed before patents were widely available in those industries. Developed countries do now generally recognize patents, but that may be more of an effect than a cause of increased technological development.

If *more* of an incentive *is* needed than that provided by the free market without patents, there are alternatives to the patent system—even *ex post facto*. The grant system could be combined with governmental or private monetary awards for especially useful inventions. In fact, the Nobel prize combines social recognition with a considerable monetary award (and, of the two, the former may well be more valuable). Again, this improves on the patent system by allowing a conscious decision to be made about which inventions best promote utility.

Without patents, inventors would have greater incentive to find ways of increasing excludability themselves. Lighthouses are the paradigmatic example of a nonexcludable good, yet as Ronald Coase points out, lighthouse owners figured out a way around this by charging fees for using ports served by them.[66] As Kenneth Goldin writes, "[l]ighthouses are a favorite textbook example of public goods, because most economists cannot imagine a method of exclusion. (All this proves is that economists are less imaginative than lighthousekeepers.)"[67] Tom Palmer argues that in-

[65] "Patently Outdated: Changes in the Way Drugs Are Invented Are Making Patents Unworkable," *The Economist*, July 18, 1987, pp. 17–18.

[66] Ronald Coase, "The Lighthouse in Economics," *Journal of Law and Economics*, vol. 17 (1974), p. 357; quoted in Palmer, *ibid.*, p. 286.

[67] Kenneth Goldin, "Equal Access vs. Selective Access: A Critique of Public Goods Theory," *Public Choice*, vol. 29 (1977), p. 62; quoted in Palmer, "Intellectual Property," p. 286.

ventors should be left to their own devices in protecting and profiting from their intellectual property. From advertising to fund radio and television, to VCR tapes which foil would-be bootleggers, inventors have and will continue to find ways to capture profits on "nonexcludable" goods. In the absence of the patent system, they will have an even greater incentive to do so—even if economists and philosophers cannot imagine how.

Of course, if inventors do build "fences" around their own intellectual property, we must question whether this would better serve utility. After all, we would not need police if we locked ourselves up behind barbed wire and expensive security systems, but that would hardly maximize utility. Despite police and patents, we do use fences to some extent already. Where intellectual property laws do not deter many would-be copiers, as with videotapes, the "fences" exist alongside patents and copyrights. In the computer-software industry, where copyright and patent laws are largely ineffective against individual copiers, there has been considerable consumer resistance to software which cannot be copied.[68] Arguably, an optimal level of copying is emerging—a point at which some copiers are deterred and the company can make a reasonable profit, but beyond which more fencing efforts would not be cost-effective. As an alternative or in addition to fences, some companies approach the problem with a carrot rather than a stick: buy a registered copy of our software, and we'll provide you with manuals and technical support. A lack of patent laws (or a lack of *effective* patent laws) encourages companies to innovate. Of course, diverting research funds into creating locks and fences may be roughly equivalent to diverting the funds into legal costs. Although right now it is impossible to say whether greater reliance on innovative ideas for excluding free-riders would best promote utility, in the absence of patents, more industries would come to think of it as a problem in finding the optimal level of copying.

Apart from increasing "fencing," there are other ways in which inventors may recoup costs on their own, without the patent system or government assistance. Eli Whitney was granted a patent on his cotton gin, and he and his partners planned to retain control of all ginning, buying the raw product and selling the ginned cotton. They invested considerable resources in enforcing their patent, to very little effect. Economist Jack Hirshleifer points out in his article on the reward to inventive activity that Whitney had other opportunities to profit from his invention. He could have exploited the speculative implications of the invention of the

[68] Strictly speaking, virtually any software can be copied, regardless of copy-proofing, by a sufficiently determined and knowledgeable person. Technological "locks" in particular are susceptible to technological lock-picks. Some software developers have realized that hackers are only a step behind them with each new anti-copying device, and have given up copy-proofing as a wasteful, never-ending effort to outsmart the hackers.

cotton gin. As the inventor, he could predict likely changes that would result in the price of cotton, cotton farms, cotton warehouses, competitive and complementary industries, and so on.[69] Hirshleifer argues that "[t]he fundamental argument for patent protection is gravely weakened when it is recognized that the pecuniary effects of the invention are a potentially enormous source of return to the inventor."[70] Government policy can somewhat affect the degree to which inventors can make use of speculative information from new inventions through more relaxed antitrust policy.

In summary, there are numerous ways to encourage R and D besides the patent system. Tax policy, government-funded research, government regulation, and innovative "fencing" strategies can all help to encourage development in a field such as biotechnology. However, we must next consider whether encouraging research is the best way to maximize utility.

## IV. The Utility of Promoting Technological Innovation

Even supposing that the patent system is the best means for stimulating innovation, such a system may still not be justified on utilitarian grounds. As George Priest points out in his article "What Economists Can Tell Lawyers about Intellectual Property,"

> [a]n economist can tell a lawyer whether a particular rule will lead to more or less inventive activity, but this analysis does not provide a basis for a conclusion by the lawyer as to whether the new level of inventive activity at the new level of costs enhances or diminishes social welfare. . . .
>
> [T]here is much less consensus about the welfare implications of inventive activity than there is about the welfare implications of criminal activity or pollution. As a consequence, the role of economic analysis diminishes. Virtually every question in patent law that is not purely procedural is a question, ultimately, of whether one wants to enlarge or restrict the patent grant. . . . Since economists cannot define for us the appropriate scope of the patent grant, economists cannot provide clear guidance to lawyers about appropriate patent enforcement. The more general point is that the utility of economic analysis to lawyers . . . is a direct function of the level of underlying normative consensus about the particular area of law in question. . . .
>
> Economists, of course, have completed very considerable work analyzing the effect of patent license practices. These analyses,

[69] Jack Hirshleifer, "The Private and Social Value of Information and the Reward to Inventive Activity," *American Economic Review*, vol. 61 (September 1971), pp. 570–71.
[70] *Ibid.*, p. 572.

> however, must derive from some basic assumptions—necessarily insupportable—about the appropriate scope of the patent grant.[71]

Priest concludes that lawyers must look beyond economics for guidance. The justification of the patent system, even in utilitarian terms, cannot rest solely on judgments of economic efficiency, or on the bare fact that the patent system does stimulate innovation. There is a further question of how much innovation, and what sort, is desirable, and at what cost; and the costs of the patent system are not solely of an economic nature.

First of all, resources might be better devoted to, say, social programs. The government already makes policy decisions about spending, including spending on various forms of research. It is naive to assume that general technological progress will most effectively bring about an increase in the general happiness. The technocratic view, that social progress will follow automatically on the heels of technological progress, became common during the nineteenth century. Romantics such as Henry David Thoreau questioned this, and in the second half of the twentieth century the drawbacks and limitations of technology have become increasingly obvious. While technology has no doubt increased the standard of living, it has also created its own ills. Moreover, it is not clear that the standard of living as it is usually measured can be simply equated with quality of life, or with any utilitarian conception of happiness. The point is not that we should throw our *sabots*[72] into the machines and go live next to Walden Pond. Rather, we need to question whether the most effective way to promote the general good is by continuing to promote technological development through granting monopolies to inventors—especially if that system promotes any profitable technologies at all, without regard for their social (as opposed to economic) value. Social value or utility is certainly difficult to define and more difficult to measure; however, as I argue below, philosophical utilitarians are not justified in equating overall utility with economic utility. If technology is progress, we must ask: "Progress toward what?"[73]

Secondly, even if many inventions, particularly medical ones, are effective in promoting the general good, other economically valuable inventions may actually work against it. Although an invention must be useful to be patentable, there is no stipulation on what the invention may or may not be useful *for*. Genetically engineered crops that are able to withstand more chemical inputs at the expense of the environment and

[71] Priest, "What Economists Can Tell Lawyers about Intellectual Property," pp. 22-23.

[72] Wooden shoes, or *sabots*, the French root of "saboteur." There are various stories about this. According to one story, workers in the early Industrial Revolution threw their *sabots* into machinery to stop it, probably in a protest against mechanization. Another story has it that workers would *saboter*—work clumsily, clattering their wooden shoes as they walked.

[73] Leo Marx, "Does Improved Technology Mean Progress?" *Technology Review*, January 1987.

the health of farmers and rural people are real examples of inventions which may well work against the general good.[74]

Even more likely, economically valuable inventions may fail to promote utility to the extent that less economically viable inventions would—even apart from copycat inventions. This often seems to be the case in agricultural biotechnology. Industry, particularly agribusiness, has spent decades objecting to land-grant universities' releasing finished products through their extension offices, and has finally largely succeeded in stopping this practice. Publicly produced seeds were often either superior to, or the source of, seed company seeds, and were widely used by farmers. The introduction of the Plant Variety Protection Act and the withdrawal of the universities from seed distribution allowed seed companies to differentiate seeds primarily by marketing rather than any real differences in quality. Making private industry the sole disseminator of the end product gives industry control over the sort of research that is done in the universities; if university scientists want their research to be useful, they must research things which industry wishes to exploit, rather than other things which farmers might prefer to see developed. In an age when seed companies have mostly been bought out by large chemical corporations, it is unlikely that biotechnology will be allowed to achieve its full potential for reducing chemical inputs and providing other benefits.[75]

> Much of the evidence . . . suggests that just the reverse is happening. An associate dean of a U.S. college of agriculture illustrated this conflict when he related the following, "In speaking to a group of state agribusiness leaders recently, I observed that in the distant future I could foresee a perennial corn crop which fixes nitrogen, performs photosynthesis more efficiently and is weed and pest resistant." With that one statement he alienated nearly every sector of the agribusiness community.[76]

Blind encouragement of research in agricultural biotechnology is likely not justified, because overproduction is already a major problem for U.S. agriculture, involving government subsidies and price supports. Genetically engineered crops designed for higher yields, or designed to withstand more fertilizers or pesticides and thereby also increase yields, are hardly the sorts of research we need to encourage while overproduction remains such a huge problem. On the other hand, research which would reduce chemical inputs and thereby cut costs for farmers and benefit the environment should be encouraged. However, seed companies owned by chemical companies have little incentive to conduct research to reduce the

[74] See Kloppenberg, *First the Seed* (*supra* note 20).
[75] See *ibid.*
[76] Lacy, Bush, and Cole, "Biotechnology and Agricultural Cooperatives," p. 80. The authors cite an anonymous personal interview.

use of their stock-in-trade. The patent system does not provide a vehicle whereby decisions can be made regarding which areas of research might be most socially beneficial, and in fact it skews the sorts of research which are funded. It is the blind promotion of technological innovation in general, with the mere hope that the outcome will maximize utility.

If the putative justification for the patent system is utilitarian, surely there are ways of encouraging research which would better maximize utility. In the absence of the patent system, the market would still give individuals and companies an incentive to innovate. If a social decision were made—perhaps by elected representatives, or even by popular vote—to further encourage certain types of socially valuable research, then funding for that research could be budgeted (from sales taxes on technological products, income taxes, etc). Grants, tax incentives, and so on might then be given (probably after a process of peer review) for research in those areas. If, however, encouraging more research turned out not to be a high priority, given other alternatives and given tax and deficit levels which most congresspersons would like to reduce, then additional research would not be funded. While public funding decisions and government allocation of funds certainly suffer from many faults, utilitarians must seriously consider the possibility that such a system would better maximize utility—or that additional research inducements of any sort do not serve to maximize utility.

It may be argued that patents promote the general good not so much because of the inventions themselves, which may or may not be especially conducive to utility, but because innovation stimulates the economy. New products mean new jobs, new spending, and so on, so that even if the invention is simply a new form of toy gun, everyone in general benefits from a more robust economy. However, economists have been unable to prove that such benefits outweigh the economic costs of the patent system. Furthermore, the benefits of stimulating the economy must be balanced against technological unemployment, displacement of workers, a high obsolescence rate, increasing distance between rich and poor, and so on.

Regardless of whether patents allow or prevent the most economically efficient allocation of resources to research, certainly a utilitarian must question the identification of economic efficiency with any robust definition of utility. My assumption throughout this essay has been that utility is not best defined in solely economic terms.[77] Although defining utility in terms of efficiency or wealth-maximization may be a useful simplifying move for economists, this is surely not an adequate philosophical definition. Cigarette smoking may be good for wealth-maximization—think

[77] And, if utility is to be defined in terms of preference-satisfaction, I assume that an individual's preferences are incompletely described by her actions in the economic realm.

of the increased spending not only on cigarettes, but also on health care—but it is unquestionably still something a utilitarian should condemn. The mere fact that patents might be wealth-maximizing does not imply that they would therefore be justified on utilitarian grounds, unless we confine ourselves to a simplified and philosophically implausible definition of utility. And even at that, economists have not been able to prove that patents *are* wealth-maximizing.

Even if the patent system were shown to maximize utility (whether defined in economic terms or not), this finding might be applicable simply to the U.S., or to Western nations in general. Patents often work to the disadvantage of LDCs, as their resistance to recognizing Western patents or adopting intellectual property laws within their own legal systems demonstrates. Underutilization of inventions can become a very dramatic problem in a country with great need and little money to spend on technology.

Furthermore, the recognition of international intellectual property laws may be shortsighted. Countries such as the U.S. have been known to appropriate what intellectual wealth exists in LDCs for their own use. Western botanists travel to LDCs to collect the seeds of crops, in order to deposit them in the international seed banks which are supposed to benefit everyone. The germ plasm from these seeds, developed over generations within the LDCs, can then be used by Western genetic engineers looking for genes which provide, say, resistance to a certain pest. In some instances, genetic engineers have made slight cosmetic changes to a seed from an LDC, patented it as their own, and then (adding insult to injury) have sold the seed back to the LDC.[78] When the genetically engineered seed is then used in the LDC, it may replace native varieties developed over generations—the germ plasm the biotech industry needs and freely uses.

When Western intellectual property is recognized internationally, while the genetic heritage of the LDCs is considered a free resource, the LDCs suffer. In the long run we all may suffer. Biotechnology companies may portray the situation as one in which the LDCs steal their intellectual property, but there is a substantial transfer of wealth (the germ plasm of plant varieties developed over centuries by native peoples) from LDCs to Western countries—a transfer which intellectual property law does not recognize. LDCs consider both Western seeds and native varieties to be the "common heritage of humankind" which "should be available without restriction"; Western countries want only their own seeds to be pro-

[78] See Cary Fowler and Pat Mooney, *Shattering: Food, Politics, and the Loss of Genetic Diversity* (Tucson: University of Arizona Press, 1990); and Hope Shand, "There Is a Conflict between Intellectual Property Rights and the Rights of Farmers in Developing Countries," *Journal of Agricultural and Environmental Ethics*, vol. 4, no. 2 (1991).

prietary. LDC ambassadors to the United Nations' Food and Agricultural Organization (FAO) have spoken out against this inequity.[79]

As noted above, patents have been awarded for all genetically engineered cotton and soybeans, regardless of the method of genetic engineering or the traits engineered. Other crops will surely follow. Allowing such broad patents can hardly be in the best interests of developing nations, some of which already depend upon genetically engineered rice or other crops to feed their growing populations and perhaps produce a small amount for export.

In another appalling example, the U.S. government has applied for patents on cell lines from indigenous people in LDCs, with neither their knowledge nor consent—and, later, in the face of their governments' protests.[80] An individual cannot own a cell line derived from her body and must donate it to science; however, industry or even the government of a different nation can patent it and profit from it. Again, it is highly developed Western countries which benefit from the genetic wealth of LDCs. If any medical treatment resulted from this cell line, LDCs would probably be the last countries to see it.

In fact, although medical and other inventions often do "trickle down" to LDCs and thereby benefit them to a certain extent, LDCs probably need medical and agricultural biotechnology the most, and will receive the fewest benefits from them. For example, simple and inexpensive vaccinations have greatly helped LDCs. However, vaccination rates remain in the range of 40 to 80 percent in developing countries, and are as low as 25 percent in the poorest countries.[81] New advances in biotechnology are likely to be more expensive and more complicated than vaccines, and thus are likely to have even lower penetration rates. Furthermore, diseases such as leprosy, river blindness, hookworms, and sleeping sickness, which still ravage millions of people in LDCs, enjoy little attention from researchers when they do not threaten Western countries.[82] Although millions of lives might be saved, and millions of people might be saved from suffering—certainly important utilitarian considerations—the patent system helps encourage research on *other*, less needed treatments (in terms of the number of people suffering, severity of the disease, and age of onset) for Westerners who can better afford them. If utilitarianism justifies a policy to encourage research, surely it would not be the patent system.

[79] Shand, "There Is a Conflict between Intellectual Property Rights and the Rights of Farmers in Developing Countries," p. 133.

[80] Chris Bright, "Who Owns Indigenous Peoples' DNA?" *World Watch*, November/December 1994. The application was later dropped in the face of protests and because the product turned out not to be commercially valuable.

[81] Søren Holm, "Genetic Engineering and the North-South Divide," in *Ethics and Biotechnology*, ed. Anthony Dyson and John Harris (New York: Routledge, 1994), p. 51.

[82] *Ibid.*, p. 54.

When patents are assessed on utilitarian grounds, the version of utilitarianism used is usually (a) limited to the economic realm, and (b) limited to the U.S., or at least to technologically advanced nations. Given the vast number of people living in LDCs, it is doubtful that the patent system can be justified on truly universalist utilitarian grounds if it fails to work to their advantage. Economists may justifiably work with a more limited utilitarianism, but we can hardly say as philosophical utilitarians that the patent system is really justified without considering its effects on well-being internationally. If the system does not work to the advantage of the majority of the world's population, this is certainly a major barrier to a true universalist utilitarian justification. And the reluctance of LDCs to adopt or recognize patent laws suggests that the patent system *does*, in fact, fail to work to their advantage. Although Western agricultural technology and medicine often do "trickle down" to LDCs and thereby benefit them, the Western patent system certainly was not designed (and does not act) to protect their interests and maximize utility on a global scale. At any rate, it is misleading to assert that the patent system is justified on utilitarian grounds if one does not carefully consider its effects on a large portion of the world's population. Although utilitarian-style reasoning is popular with lawmakers and economists, I fear that utilitarianism itself, as a moral theory, is not.

## V. Conclusion

Agricultural and medical biotechnology have enormous potential to affect human welfare. Medical biotechnology has the potential to diagnose, treat, or even eradicate major inherited diseases. It may help millions of people, but it also may become a powerful weapon in the hands of corporations, insurance companies, and employers. As for agricultural biotechnology:

> The processes by which these products are developed will affect the structure of the public and private agricultural research communities, changing the nature of their agendas and who they serve. The way in which these products are developed and marketed will likely favor the large-scale companies and producers and significantly affect the cooperatives. The products themselves may affect the structure of agriculture and the nature of the food system in this country and around the world.[83]

To what extent should patent law be applied to biotechnology? Definitions of terms in patent law are often quite ambiguous or arbitrary. What constitutes nonobviousness or usefulness, and is commercial success a reliable indicator of either? How minor may an improvement on, or

[83] Lacy, Bush, and Cole, "Biotechnology and Agricultural Cooperatives," p. 75.

deviation from, an existing product or process be in order to be patentable? Should the mere fact of isolating a gene or purifying a substance found in nature make it fully appropriable? Should a company which finds one way to genetically engineer cotton, be given a patent for *all* genetically engineered cotton, even if it is engineered by a completely different method and for a completely different trait? Should a company which works on a gene in the human immune system be given a patent over all possible medical uses of that gene? Should a company be allowed to own a patent on all germ-line genetic engineering, which has the potential to permanently alter the genetic makeup of one's descendants *in perpetuity*? If an individual does not own her own genetic code, should insurance companies and employers be able to make use of it without her consent?

When patent law is extended to a new area, or interpreted in a particular way, decisions are made about what research is to be encouraged, and to what extent. If the putative justification of the patent system is utilitarian, we should see the encouragement of inventive activity as a problem of allocation of resources—a policy issue, like any other. Utilitarians should explore alternatives and encourage innovation only in needed, underdeveloped areas, rather than across the board; they need to recognize that the patent system is probably not a good vehicle for promoting utility, and that the alternatives need to be considered more seriously. Furthermore, we must pause to consider, especially in this age of environmental crises and tight government funding, the role of technology in promoting human welfare. Encouraging technology in general, and at the expense of other possible uses of resources, will not necessarily maximize utility.

The economic, quasi-utilitarian justification of the patent system is inconclusive. The claim that patents are essential for technological innovation is more truism than proven fact. Machlup states that if we do not know the net effect of the patent system, we should just muddle along as we are. However, the philosophical utilitarian justification of the patent system, which does not interpret utility in terms of wealth-maximization, is worse than inconclusive. Given the dubious economic basis of the patent system and the numerous serious problems it creates, it cannot be justified on utilitarian grounds. We must either consider the alternatives to the patent system and reassess our commitment to encouraging technological innovation, or else look to natural rights or distributive justice as its foundation.[84]

*Philosophy, Iowa State University*

[84] Although I think that the patent system is unjustified on utilitarian grounds, I am not a utilitarian. I would favor a natural rights approach to justifying intellectual property. However, I suspect that such an approach might not justify the current American patent system, and it also might not justify the patenting of, e.g., genetically engineered life-forms.

# PROPERTY RIGHTS THEORY AND THE COMMONS: THE CASE OF SCIENTIFIC RESEARCH

By Robert P. Merges

## I. Introduction

For some time now, commentators in and out of the scientific community have been expressing concern over the direction of scientific research. Cogent critics have labeled it excessively commercial, out of touch with its "pure," public-spirited roots, and generally too much a creature of its entrepreneurial, self-interested times. In most if not all of this hand-wringing, the scientific community's growing reliance on intellectual property rights, especially patents, looms large. Indeed, for many the pursuit of patents is emblematic of just what is rotten in the republic of science today.

These concerns with property rights, and commercialization of science in general, spring from a number of motivations. For some, the issue is strictly utilitarian. Under this view of things, the traditional division of labor between the public and private spheres has proven so effective—contributing as it has to the development of such modern indispensables as semiconductors, penicillin, and jet transportation—that to change our approach now is sheer madness.[1] For these observers of the latest trends in science, the changes currently afoot are a threat to kill (or at least cripple) the goose that has laid before us, like so many golden eggs, many of the conveniences we take for granted.

Others are concerned for different reasons. They express a more fundamental objection: that commercializing the heretofore noble, pure, and otherwise *untainted* field of science is not just poor policy, but intrinsically bad.[2] They are consumed with the notion that current trends threaten to undermine not simply an effective set of institutions, but ultimately a successful part of our shared public life—what they might characterize as

[1] See Donald Kennedy, "Research in the Universities: How Much Utility?" in *The Positive Sum Strategy: Harnessing Technology for Economic Growth*, ed. Ralph Landau and Nathan Rosenberg (Washington, DC: National Academy Press, 1986); and Leonard G. Boonin, "The University, Scientific Research, and the Ownership of Knowledge," in *Owning Scientific and Technical Information: Value and Ethical Issues*, ed. Vivian Weil and John W. Snapper (New Brunswick, NJ: Rutgers University Press, 1989), p. 253.

[2] See, e.g., Martin Kenney, *Biotechnology: The University-Industry Complex* (New Haven: Yale University Press, 1986); and *Commercialization of Academic Biomedical Research* (Hearings before the Subcommittee on Investigations and Oversight and the Subcommittee on Science, Research, and Technology of the House Committee on Science and Technology, Ninety-

an important cultural achievement of post–World War II democracy. To some extent, this view finds expression in the recently renewed interest in eliminating patents for scientific research directed toward isolating and characterizing human genes.[3] Even those who would shy away from this grand form of the argument contend that regardless of the greater significance of scientific institutions and their historical achievements, those institutions have a uniquely appropriate place in our social setup. And that place, all on this side agree, is the *public sphere*.

As with so many issues, divergent vocabularies conceal similarities. Both the high-principle defenders of traditional public science and their utilitarian/economist fellow travelers share a sense that current trends pose a threat. For purposes of this essay, that is enough to provide a starting-point. Although as I proceed I will try to keep in mind the two very different motivations that lead to attacks on current trends in the direction of scientific research and the institutions that conduct it, the essay must ultimately reflect my sense both that the two sets of concerns motivate very similar policy arguments, and that at some level they are in fact closely intertwined.

In any event, with this quick summary of the current discontents of science behind us, we can turn to a statement of the burden I wish to carry in this essay. Simply put, the burden has two parts: first, to show that the public sphere spoken of respectfully in traditional science is less than it appears, being in fact more analogous in some ways to a limited-membership, shared-access common area than a truly wide-open, *unclaimed* space; and second, to argue that even under such a revised view of the public sphere, some current practices—broadly cognizable under the heading of privatization or (less accurately) commercialization—do indeed threaten to undermine certain cornerstones of our scientific infrastructure. In short, although the shape of the worry is different from the one commonly supposed, it is a real worry nevertheless. To some extent, I argue, the scientific community has begun to address these concerns itself, primarily through a host of voluntary practices that, in effect, water down patent rights. Yet enough of a threat remains that, toward the end of the essay, I propose some policy directions that might alleviate the

seventh Congress, First Session, 1981), pp. 62–63 (testimony of Dr. Jonathan King, Professor of Biology, Massachusetts Institute of Technology):

> The openness, the free exchange of ideas and information, the free exchange of strains, of protein, of techniques, have been a critical component in the creativity and productivity of the biomedical research community. . . .
>
> This freedom of communication stemmed from the fact that all of the investigators shared the same professional canon: the increase of knowledge of health and disease for the general benefit of the citizenry. . . .

[3] See Sally Lehrman, "Broad Coalition Adds Voice to Religious Protest on Gene Patents," *Biotechnology Newswatch*, June 19, 1995, p. 1, in which Lehrman quotes Richard Levins, Professor of Population Science at the Harvard School of Public Health, as stating that gene patenting is a means of "subordinating a common intellectual heritage for private gain."

*creeping propertization* that characterizes science today. Perhaps not surprisingly, given my understanding that even traditional "pure" science includes de facto (though skeletal) property rights, I do not recommend the complete elimination of all property rights, formal and informal, from basic scientific research. Instead, I argue for a more carefully crafted set of property rights, including (1) a generally available exemption from patent-infringement liability in the case of pure research conducted with federal funds (a broad form of the so-called "research exemption"), and (2) an occasional decision by senior science officials to exclude particular research areas from patentability altogether, when the direct and indirect costs of establishing, enforcing, and administering property rights is deemed excessive in comparison to the benefits of access under the "normal" rules of basic science. The recent decision by the director of the National Institutes of Health (NIH) to drop a series of patent applications on aspects of the Human Genome Project serves as an example of reasoned policy in this regard.

## II. The Public Sphere, the Scientific Commons, and Formal Property Rights

For most people, the description of science as an innately public enterprise comes quite naturally. This is most likely a function of two attributes widely associated with scientific research: government funding and open dissemination. These are closely related, of course; but a moment's reflection ought to show that they are not coextensive. After all, there are activities that are funded by the government that are not publicized (e.g., intelligence work), and the private sector funds a fair amount of scientific research that is published in peer-reviewed journals and otherwise bears the earmarks of public availability. In other words, the implicit pairings "public/open" and "private/closed" are misleading.

The large volume of privately funded basic research apparently does not undercut the view of science as an inherently public undertaking. Because of this, it might even be argued that the open dissemination of research results—which is, of course, common to most basic science, whoever funds it—is thought by most to be the key indicator of basic or pure science.

The point here is not to quibble with this, but to unpack it. That is, I am concerned in this section with a brief description of how and under what circumstances basic research results are shared with the world. As we shall see, it is a much more limited, and closely regulated, form of disclosure than is usually imagined. The many limitations on truly public dissemination lead, in fact, to the conclusion that science is not so much given freely to the public as shared under a largely implicit code of conduct among a more or less well-identified circle of similarly situated scientists. In other words, we will come to see that science is more like a limited-access commons than a truly open public domain. Later we will see how this revised understanding of the traditional degree of scientific openness contributes to our understanding of what policies should be adopted to stem the tide of current abuses.

### *A. The nature of scientific research*

Science is a highly competitive enterprise regulated by a complex set of professional norms. Indeed, because of the elegant elaboration of those norms—especially at the hands of sociologists of science, particularly Robert Merton—they are sometimes confused with science itself.

Merton[4] described four norms that define the scientific culture: universalism, communism, disinterestedness, and organized skepticism. Briefly, "universalism" means that impersonal criteria, independent of the identity and characteristics of the individual scientist(s) who does the research, are employed to judge the soundness of scientific work. "Communism" means that scientific findings are made open to all, immediately, with no sense that they are or should be proprietary in any way. "Disinterestedness" means that scientists pursue truth rather than self-interest, that they are ideally indifferent to the success of an experiment or the reception of a research finding. "Organized skepticism" means that the scientific community should rigorously test research results before accepting them as true, and that all research is in some sense "born in doubt," false until dispositively proven true.

Of course, norms (in the sense in which Merton used the term) are aspirational; they have—to notice the linguistic clue—a normative dimension. Consequently, it is not surprising that sociologists of science have documented a set of practices that deviate in many respects from the norms Merton identified. Of most interest to us here is a set of observations made by the sociologist Warren O. Hagstrom[5] on what might be called proprietary practices in science. Hagstrom states:

> Scientists who are concerned about the possibility of being anticipated as a result of the theft of their ideas tend to be secretive. An organic chemist [in an interview] said that he only communicated with persons he was friendly with and could trust. . . .
>
> To the extent that scientists can establish property rights over work in progress, they need not fear anticipation. Such property rights may be more or less explicit and formal. . . . When it becomes evident to two [scientists in the same field] that their research will probably produce the same results, they may informally agree on a division of labor. . . . [Another way scientists treat their work as proprietary is by

[4] Robert K. Merton, *The Sociology of Science* (Chicago: University of Chicago Press, 1973).
[5] Warren O. Hagstrom, *The Scientific Community* (New York: Basic Books, 1965).

> publishing a preliminary version of research in an abstract.] The latent function of publishing abstracts is to permit individuals to "stake a claim," establish property rights on research in progress.[6]

Hagstrom concludes with the observation that "[s]cientific knowledge is community property. Discoverers have limited rights, but among them are rights to be recognized for their discoveries." Thus, we can summarize Hagstrom's findings by saying that he found certain proprietary impulses at work beneath the surface of the otherwise Mertonian world of shared, or public, science.

More recently, the practice of asserting informal property rights appears to have become even more prominent.[7] In cutting-edge biotechnology research, for example, pre- and even post-publication practices with respect to biological materials useful to fellow researchers (such as genetically engineered mice, or particularly useful cell lines) reflect greater reluctance to share widely. While it is difficult to trace the contours of a practice that few scientists admit to, and that few even seem willing to discuss openly, several operational principles can be traced, if somewhat speculatively. First, the more expensive and difficult it is to create a given biological material, the less likely it is that it will be shared widely and quickly.[8] Second, the creator of a biological material is more likely to share quickly with those in fields unrelated to the creator's central interests; property rights are asserted most forcefully, in other words, with direct competitors.[9] Third, despite the increased assertion of informal property rights, these rights still fall far short of absolute exclusivity. A recent investigation of sharing practices in the field of recombinant DNA research "reveals that while no makers of [mice] simply refuse to share them, some researchers substitute their own policies for those of [the National Institutes of Health, which mandates free access after publication]: not sharing mice until long after publication, or sharing mice selectively."[10] In practice, then, this example suggests that scientists fall short of the ideal of instantaneous, widespread disclosure.

Of course, the most obvious illustration of creeping propertization is the now widespread practice of seeking *formal* property rights—in the

[6] *Ibid.*, pp. 87, 91.

[7] Jon Cohen, "Share and Share Alike Isn't Always the Rule in Science; Many Researchers Fail to Share Materials," *Science*, vol. 268 (June 23, 1995), pp. 1715–18.

[8] *Ibid.*, p. 1715: "A National Research Council (NRC) report last year on problems with sharing genetically engineered mice such as knockouts [i.e., mice genetically engineered to have immune systems lacking a defense against a disease, used to test drugs aimed at treating that disease] concluded that 'increased cost and competition . . . appear to be challenging the tradition of sharing in some branches of biological research.'"

[9] See *ibid.*, p. 1717, where Cohen recounts the story of the creator of a research mouse who directed his graduate student to "initially [turn] down [a] request because [the requestor] was a direct competitor; that researcher was later given the mouse for a specific experiment in an area unrelated to [the creator's work or that of his graduate student]."

[10] *Ibid.*, p. 1716.

form of patents—over research results. Nothing could be further from the aspirational norm of openness. Indeed, the absolute exclusivity of a patent would seem entirely inconsistent with the earlier observation that science is characterized by *informal* property rights. Yet the truth is that in general, within the community of researchers, potentially patentable and even patented research results are often shared, though on a more limited basis. Surely it would be stretching quite a bit to argue that the presence of patents does not make a difference in the conduct of science. Yet just as surely it would be wrong to say that patents lead researchers to completely shut off the exchange of research results. Nor are patents universally enforced to the hilt among researchers; far from it.

As the studies cited earlier reveal, patents have affected the way science is done. Even so, in many cases scientist-patentees assert far less than the full exclusionary force bestowed by the legal system via their patents. A limited set of rights is asserted against the community, even though the patentee holds a greater set of rights. Indeed, it is not stretching too far to argue that conduct in today's scientific community in many cases approximates the effect achieved under the older practice of establishing "informal" property rights. The difference is that, now, the "informalness" of the rights is achieved by relinquishing (or at least not asserting) some of the scientist's formal rights. It is as if the old practice of establishing minimal property out of a background of zero formal rights has been replaced by relinquishing some rights against a background of a strong, formal entitlement.

Several recent uproars in the science world illustrate the community's continued practice of costless sharing, even in the presence of patents. Arguments over conflict-of-interest policies,[11] the appropriateness of university patent-licensing policies,[12] and the licensing of patents for certain foundational research technologies reveal that the creeping propertization identified earlier has not yet reached into every aspect of community practice.

Like the internal tensions identified by sociologists of science in the pre-patent era, contemporary arguments are almost always a matter of degree. Very rarely is it argued that a member in good standing of the public research community is simply shutting the community out entirely. The debate centers on the terms of access, and on whether the restrictions some researcher seeks to impose are in keeping with the operational content of the norm of shared knowledge as currently practiced, even in the presence of patents. Again, the point is that few scientists see the debate in polar terms—as a simple choice between the total

[11] See, e.g., Student Note, "Ties That Bind: Conflicts of Interest in University-Industry Links," *U.C. Davis Law Review*, vol. 17 (January 1984), p. 895.

[12] See, e.g., Carl Djerassi, "The Gray Zone: Academic Researchers and Private Enterprise," *Science*, vol. 261 (August 20, 1993), p. 972.

absence of property rights (or their equivalent) and the wholesale adoption of strong, formal property rights (in the form of patents). Most scientists seem to think that the optimal policy entails maintaining some of the traditional practices that sociologists have identified with an informal set of property rights in research results, even in an era when *formal* property rights have been widely adopted.

For example, a number of brushfires have broken out in recent years regarding the extent to which a researcher must make his or her results available to other members of the community prior to, or even after, publication. Since major research results—finding a gene, or identifying the active portion of a protein coded for by a gene of interest, for example—are usually published very quickly, they are not usually at issue. Instead, the arguments are over another issue: the dissemination of assays, reagents, and other research tools of the trade, which have come to be known generically as *biological materials*. Very often these are developed as an interim step on the way to the final goal of obtaining the gene or protein subunit or whatever. Since most of the basic research funding that goes into the creation of these tools is public money, the question arises: When must they be shared?

Often the discussion takes the form of back-channel gossip regarding a certain lab's unwillingness to share a research tool.[13] Interestingly, for our purposes, the point of this gossip-induced social pressure is *not* that the tool must be described in a formal, printed publication. It is simply that the tool be provided, on a reasonable basis, to other interested labs so that they can use it in the course of their research. Indeed, other labs understand that they will almost always be required to use the biological material under a duty not to disclose it to others, and certainly not to disclose it to the public generally, until its originator has published a full account of it.[14]

[13] See, e.g., Cohen, "Share and Share Alike Isn't Always the Rule in Science," p. 1715:

> [P]roblems in materials sharing . . . crop up in cell-line repositories, crystallographic databases—indeed wherever competitors would like to share research materials. And these problems stir passions in the scientific community. "Typically, over coffee or beer at night, this is what our colleagues are talking about," says one researcher at the University of California, Berkeley, who insisted on anonymity.

*Science*'s investigation, however, reveals that, e.g., "while no makers of [the genetically engineered mice known as "knockouts"] simply refuse to share them, some researchers substitute their own policies for those of NIH: not sharing mice until long after publication, or sharing mice selectively. Insiders in the field—none of whom would allow themselves to be named—repeatedly mentioned Nobel prize–winning immunologist Susumu Tonegawa as someone whose mice are not freely available immediately after publication."

[14] See Dan L. Burk, "Misappropriation of Trade Secrets in Biotechnology Licensing," *Albany Law Journal of Science and Technology*, vol. 4 (1994), pp. 141–42:

> The professional norms of the scientific community have long required that scientists share data and materials with one another, both to allow repetition and validation of reported results and to facilitate new discoveries. . . . These exchange practices have to

Insider criticism of other contemporary practices is aimed at the same goal of limited access. Thus, the controversy over inadequate disclosure of research tools employed in the discovery of published research results subsided when certain benchmark publications such as *Science* agreed to require researchers to simply make the tools available with a reasonable set of restrictions.[15]

The same pattern holds when the patenting of research results is at issue. Normally, the criticism of excessive patenting activity or inappropriate licensing practices does not start from the assumption that complete public access should be the norm. For example, the outcry over certain large-scale research funding arrangements between private industry and prominent research institutions does not assume that the research output of the institutions would be freely available to all in the absence of the funding agreement. Implicit is the notion that the agreements exceed standard limits on the *degree* of privatization that is acceptable in science. No one assumes that a modest degree of privatization is against the working norms of the community.

This makes an interesting backdrop to our consideration of a historical moment when it appeared that policymakers might adopt formal, statutory property rights for scientific research.

### *B. History of explicit proposals for formal property rights in scientific discoveries*

Traditionally, the findings of pure scientific research have been excluded from patent protection.[16] Some have proposed that it is a mistake to exclude such things, however. The history of these attempts to extend formal rights to the products of scientific research bears recounting for two reasons. First, it shows once again that despite the norm of openness (or "communism," to use Merton's term), property rights—even of the formal variety—have not been a complete stranger to the world of science. Second, certain objections to these earlier proposals seem just as valid now as when they were first made. The upshot is that this older debate holds some useful lessons for the current discussion.

The movement for formal property rights in scientific discoveries took shape in France just after World War I, when scientists were suffering greatly from the national devastation (and destitution) brought on by the

---

some extent been constrained by an unwritten and often unspoken agreement among researchers that the materials shared will not be used for commercial gain and will not be passed on without permission from the original owner.

[15] *Ibid.*, p. 142.

[16] See Robert P. Merges, *Patent Law and Policy* (Charlottesville, VA: Michie Co., 1992), ch. 2.

war.[17] The movement received formal recognition in 1922, when a detailed legislative proposal was introduced into the French Chamber of Deputies by J. Barthelemy, a French law professor and Member of the Chamber. Professor Barthelemy's proposal would have overturned a provision of the French Patent Law of 1844 which declared null and void all patents concerning "principles, methods, systems, discoveries and theoretical or purely scientific conceptions of which no industrial applications are indicated."[18] Barthelemy's proposal contained two essential provisions. First, it stipulated that a scientist who has made a discovery may take no action so long as no one tries to apply the discovery. As soon as a practical application of the theoretical discovery is made, however, the scientist may present a claim for a part of the profits. Second, a scientist may obtain a "patent of principle." This would not confer on the patentee an exclusive right to make or use the discovery, but only the right to grant licenses for those utilizing the practical applications of the discovery. Anyone would be free to utilize the invention or discovery, so long as he or she paid royalties to the scientist who had discovered it. The duration of protection would have been more akin to copyright: the life of the discoverer plus fifty years. As intellectual-property scholar Stephen Ladas points out, the Barthelemy proposal was part of a larger post-World War I movement in France in favor of a "Droit de Suite" or set of "moral rights" for authors and creators.[19]

Also in 1922, the League of Nations' Committee on Intellectual Cooperation took up the question of scientific property at the insistence of its chairman, Professor Bergson. The committee eventually approved a plan drafted by Senator Ruffini of Italy.[20] Ruffini's proposal began by dismissing the theoretical objections to the patenting of scientific discoveries. After reciting the various objections to protecting "discoveries" rather than inventions, Ruffini concludes: "The whole question is dominated by crudest utilitarianism, empiricism unhappily disguised in scientific nebulosity, and, finally, the most disconcerting arbitrariness."[21] Ruffini also pointed out that one objection to the proposal of Barthelemy in France was that French industry would be handicapped by being forced to recognize an intellectual property right not recognized throughout the world. Ruffini's solution was to propose an international treaty which would

[17] This and other details of the early movement for property rights in science are drawn from C. J. Hamson, *Patent Rights for Scientific Discoveries* (Indianapolis: Bobbs-Merrill Co., 1930).

[18] Quoted in Stephen P. Ladas, *Patents, Trademarks, and Related Rights: National and International Protection* (Cambridge: Harvard University Press, 1975), vol. 3, p. 1856.

[19] Ladas, *Patents, Trademarks, and Related Rights*, vol. 3, section 1012, p. 1856.

[20] F. Ruffini, *Report on Scientific Property* (Committee on Intellectual Cooperation, League of Nations, Document A. 38, 1923), XII, 10; quoted in Ladas, *Patents, Trademarks, and Related Rights*, section 1012, p. 1856.

[21] *Ibid.*

create such a right in all signatory nations, thus eliminating the possibility that companies in one country would carry the extra financial burden of paying royalties to scientists.

Ruffini's substantive proposals were straightforward. He proposed a term of protection identical to that of Barthelemy's plan: life plus fifty years. He called for the exclusion of discoveries which merely presented a scientific explanation of obvious facts or practices of human life. (This point was made in response to a memorandum from Dean Henry Wigmore of Northwestern Law School, who objected to the proposal on this basis.) In addition, the plan provided for four possible means of establishing priority in an idea, including publication, self-authentication, "patents of principle," and ordinary patents.

While these proposals drew criticism, they also found defenders. One view had it that the industries that used a scientific discovery in particular applications had a "quasi-contractual obligation" to remunerate the discoverer of the principle.[22] In fact, the plan went so far as to be made the subject of a draft convention prepared by a committee of experts at the League of Nations.[23] However, the project lost momentum in 1930, and was never revitalized, except in France. There the government adopted a decree creating a Medal of Scientific Research with prizes, which took the place of the discovery patent. This decree, and certain legislated principles in the socialist countries, are the only actual legislative products of the scientific-discovery patent movement.[24]

A number of authors familiar with these proposals from the 1930s have raised or reviewed objections to them.[25] First, it is very often difficult to trace the scientific origins of a particular industrial application. Second, there is a significant lag time between the disclosure of a scientific discovery and the development of the first application; the argument that fairness dictates compensation for the scientist who makes a discovery would seem to be mitigated by the length of time between his or her discovery and its application. Third, very often it can be assumed that a scientific disclosure will be missed by industrialists; they will thus end up paying royalties for a scientific discovery which in fact was not relied upon in creating their industrial application. And finally, the very significant burdens on scientific communication that a system of property rights would create represent perhaps the most severe problem. Since science was (and still is) thought to depend on free and open communication, and since property rights are presumed to be at odds with such free

[22] See Ladas, *Patents, Trademarks, and Related Rights*, section 1017, p. 1862.

[23] *Ibid.*

[24] See *ibid.*, sections 1021–26, pp. 1868–75. It should be noted that Article 2(viii) of the convention establishing the World Intellectual Property Organization (WIPO) includes, in the definition of "intellectual property," rights relating to "scientific discoveries" and "all other rights resulting from intellectual activity in the . . . scientific . . . fields."

[25] See Hamson, *Patent Rights for Scientific Discoveries*; and Ladas, *Patents, Trademarks, and Related Rights*.

communication, property rights and science were thought to be an ill-fated combination.

An additional objection to patents in scientific discoveries is that they are not necessary to spur scientific research. As Judge Jerome Frank put it:

> Epoch-making "discoveries" or "mere" general scientific "laws," without more, cannot be patented. . . . So the great "discoveries" of Newton or Faraday could not have been rewarded with such a grant of monopoly. Interestingly enough, apparently many scientists like Faraday care little for monetary rewards; generally the motives of such outstanding geniuses are not pecuniary. . . . Perhaps (although no one really knows) the same cannot be said of those lesser geniuses who put such discoveries to practical uses.[26]

On this view, granting patents for discoveries that scientists *would have made anyway* would be socially wasteful.

For many, this latter assumption would be far less defensible in today's environment of tight federal budgets. Regardless of what *motivates* a scientist, the argument would surely run, he or she cannot make any progress in the vast majority of scientific disciplines without a great deal of money. Equipment, personnel, and the like—all essential to the performance of modern science—are very expensive. Thus, since adequate funding is essential to science, society will not receive the results of scientific research without either extensive public support or some other revenue source. It follows that if property rights can secure this alternative revenue source, they may well provide a necessary impetus for the performance of research. Far from being redundant—an unnecessary reward, heaped on a researcher who would have done the same work without it—they may well be essential. This of course moots Judge Frank's objection to the granting of rights for pure scientific findings.

If it is true that property rights are increasingly essential to the research endeavor, it is no less true that these rights will bring with them a host of problems. It is these problems—which I would describe as an entire family of new *transaction costs*—which drive the discussion in Section IV concerning policy solutions to the imposition of property rights in science.

### *C. The rise of patents for the results of "pure" science*

Proposals to explicitly allow patents for the results of basic scientific research eventually faced a resounding defeat. Given that the only occasion on which the appropriateness of these patents was discussed in detail yielded such negative results, it is perhaps surprising that basic research is now considered an entirely proper source of patentable subject matter. Although broad statements of scientific truth—such as $E = mc^2$—

[26] *Katz v. Horni Signal Mfg. Corp.*, 145 F.2d 961, 63 U.S.P.Q. (BNA) 190 (2d Cir. 1944).

are still considered unpatentable,[27] many of the fruits of contemporary basic science find their way into patent claims of one variety or another these days. To some extent, this is a result of growing sophistication by patent lawyers, who have learned to state a scientific finding in terms of an at least nominally useful application.[28] Apart from this, however, what happened to produce this de facto change in policy?

For the most part, the answer lies with changes in the relationship between science and technology since the 1930s.[29] In the 1930s, the important science-based industries were centered around the electrical and chemical fields. Because electrical engineering and modern, analytic chemistry were still very young, the findings of basic science were very basic indeed. The conceptual distance between basic research and applied technology, in other words, was very large. As a consequence, huge investments were required to translate the findings of the basic research laboratory into viable commercial products.

By the 1970s and 1980s, however, the relationship between science and technology had grown a good deal closer in many fields. In important fields such as biotechnology and certain branches of physics, the jump from lab result to commercial product was much shorter than it had been in the past.[30] Thus, for example, the basic Cohen-Boyer research on gene-splicing led to a commercial product (genetically engineered insulin) in only a few short years. The early work on lasers, to take another example, yielded commercial results after a relatively short time as well.

In addition, a host of subsidiary factors contributed to the hastening rate of commercial application. One important factor—often overlooked—is the change in the ease of capital formation for science-intensive industries.[31] In the 1930s, it was widely thought that only large, integrated companies could afford the "luxury" of long-term-oriented basic scientific research. By the 1970s, however, with the advent of the venture-capital industry and related support institutions, start-up companies based on new scientific findings often found a ready supply of capital from firms specializing in such speculative investments. Genentech, founded in the mid-1970s, is of course the paradigm. It is also an example of a technology-intensive start-up that was later highly touted by investment analysts when it made the jump from "private" to public financing, via an initial public offering of stock.

[27] See Merges, *Patent Law and Policy*, ch. 2.

[28] This is the legal test used to determine patentability in close cases involving a putative "scientific principle." See *ibid.*, ch. 2.

[29] See Robert Teitelman, *Profits of Science: The American Marriage of Business and Technology* (New York: Basic Books, 1994).

[30] See *ibid.*, p. 8, where Teitelman contrasts the 1953 elucidation of the structure of the DNA molecule by James Watson and Francis Crick, which had no commercial impact until decades later, with the 1973 Cohen-Boyer work on recombinant DNA, which led to the founding of Genentech in 1976.

[31] See *ibid.*, ch. 1.

As the Genentech story illustrates, capital markets—together with the changing interplay between science and technology—played a crucial role in the commercialization of basic science. It is important to recognize that extensive university involvement in technology licensing—another recent development often said to be at the heart of the commercialization process—is in fact closely related to the growing sophistication of capital markets with regard to basic science. For it is quite clear that without a prospective market, fueled by the idea of significant returns on investments in the basic findings of science, the university licensing offices founded with such frequency in the 1980s and 1990s would have no one to sell to.

These licensing offices demonstrate the extent of the changes that have taken place within many areas of basic science since the 1930s. Far from needing special legislation to create a new branch of patent law, the laboratory findings of certain branches of modern science fit comfortably within the contours of traditional patent law. Once the science/technology interface grew closer, and capital was attracted, obstacles to patentability largely dropped away.

### *D. Incentives to seek property rights despite community norms*

Despite the fact that, for a variety of reasons, patents are now available for an increasing proportion of the results of basic research, the community norm of open access remains strong. Thus, it is perhaps not clear why, even though the operative legal standard has changed vis-à-vis modern science, scientists and the institutions that employ them today are seeking so many patents for their research. In other words, just because they *can* obtain patents, it does not follow that all of them *will*. Why then is everyone, in fact, making more and more use of the patent system?

The answer as I see it is fairly simple. The increasing value of patents makes adherence to the traditional community norm of nonproprietary open access implicitly more expensive. Thus, even if a particular scientist believes strongly in adherence to the norm, he or she knows that others will be tempted to ignore it because of the higher payoff that stems from seeking a patent. Since many scientists believe that although the norm is still the "correct" mode of behavior, many of their colleagues will abandon it, even those scientists who believe in the norm may well abandon it. Only a scientist who would revel in the thought that he or she was the last one remaining who adheres to the norm would continue to adhere to it.

Those familiar with the logic of game theory will recognize the basic structure of this situation. Although most players attribute the greatest value to continued shared access—to "cooperation," in game theory lingo—even many of these, fearing the inevitable abandonment of the shared norm in light of the higher individual payoffs from "defecting," will themselves defect from the prior cooperative arrangement. Others, anticipating this, will also defect. In this way, even though everyone would be better off if the cooperative behavior continued, the "equilibrium strategy" will be to defect. The problem, to put it simply, is that there is no way to enforce the norm of shared access, and no way to bind other members of the community to the cooperative arrangement. The players must rely on each other to continue to do the right thing without formal sanctions for doing otherwise. Once the payoffs from defecting increase, however, there is less assurance that the other players will continue to do the right thing. One way of stating this is that the implicit costs of the informal sanctions brought to bear on defectors—negative gossip, loss of reputation, etc.—are outweighed by the benefits, in the form of greater payoffs due to the enhanced returns provided by the formal property rights. As one highly astute observer of these matters put it recently:

> For years biomedical research has flourished while investigators have drawn heavily upon discoveries that their predecessors left in the public domain. Even if exclusive rights enhance private incentives to develop further research tools, they could do considerable damage to the research enterprise by inhibiting the effective utilization of existing ones.[32]

There is already evidence that this dynamic has begun to set in.[33]

Since scientists may well conclude that it is in each scientist's self-interest to patent his or her research tools, each will expect the others to avail themselves of patents. This expectation that others will defect leads even those who rue the demise of the norm of cooperation to defect, since the very worst position of all is to continue to cooperate while all those around you are defecting. In the case of patents on pure science, this would take the form of a scientist refusing to patent her results despite the fact that all her colleagues are patenting theirs. She would have to pay royalties to all the others to use their results, while her own work went completely uncompensated. Indeed, if royalty income were a substitute for research funding from the government or the like, she might even be

[32] Rebecca Eisenberg, "A Technology Policy Perspective on the NIH Gene Patenting Controversy," *University of Pittsburgh Law Review*, vol. 55 (Spring 1994), p. 646.

[33] Jim Carlton, "Roche Brings Leading Institutions into Lawsuit over Patent Rights," *Wall Street Journal*, May 25, 1995, p. B4:

> At a conference here this week, scientists reacted with dismay [to a suit brought by Roche against Promega, another biotechnology company, in which Roche accused Promega of "contributory infringement" by supplying scientists with a key component that allows them to use Roche's patented polymerase chain reaction (PCR) technology], saying they could be prevented from using patented products—such as for computers and biotechnology—in their scientific research. They say they have done research virtually unfettered by patent constraints for some 200 years.

Note that many of these scientists—or at least the institutions where they work—are actively seeking patents on the results of *their* research. In other words, they are dismayed that their own strategy of defecting from the cooperative arrangement is becoming the norm!

driven out of science altogether. Thus, she might well adopt the approach of patenting her research despite deep misgivings about abandoning the traditional norm of openness in science.

Even if this account of the motivations of individual scientists is correct (and it is admittedly highly stylized), some important questions remain. Just because patent law has in effect dropped its objections to patenting what comes out of certain basic-research labs, and just because scientists might have an incentive to patent, does that mean that the science community, or society at large, should encourage widespread patenting of these results? Are there policy concerns that extend beyond the domain of what patent law considers appropriate subject matter? I take up these questions in Section IV.

A recent development illustrates how scientists and research labs are responding to the incentives they face. In March 1995, a group called the Association of University Technology Managers (AUTM) announced a new, standardized form for the transfer of biological materials between nonprofit (i.e., government-funded) research labs.[34] The Uniform Biotechnology Materials Transfer Agreement, or UBMTA, embodies the research community's current sense of the best practices with respect to the sorts of limitations that can appropriately be placed on the transfer of research tools created with public funding.[35] For our purposes, two features of the UBMTA scheme are of paramount importance. First, there are two versions, one styled "nonprofit to nonprofit," and the other "nonprofit to for-profit." (I explore this two-tier property rights regime in Section III.) Second, the UBMTA recognizes a number of serious restrictions on use—incursions into the pure public domain, if you will.

For example, in the "nonprofit to nonprofit" form, free use is given of the research tool in its original form, but adaptations, modifications, and alterations are not covered. Indeed, modifications intended for ultimate commercialization are to be the subject of negotiations with the original provider of the material. And, perhaps most relevant here, the relatively permissive treatment of transfers applies only if the transferee does not intend a subsequent transfer to a private, for-profit firm. These private firms, being outside the common in some sense, must negotiate formal, commercial licenses.

[34] On lab transfer agreements, see Charles E. Lipsey et al., "Protecting Trade Secrets in Biotechnology," in *Protecting Trade Secrets* (PLI Patent, Copyright, Trademarks, and Literary Property Course Handbook Series No. 224, 1986), Exhibit K.

[35] This uniform MTA suggests that standard contractual terms—a form of transaction-cost-reducing industry coordination—are beginning to emerge. (My source here is a personal interview with Sandy Shotwell—an AUTM member and a participant in the project to draft the Uniform Biotechnology Material Transfer Agreement (UBMTA)—conducted in Washington, D.C., in February 1994.) On the evolution of transaction-cost-reducing institutions and practices in intellectual property-intensive industries, see Robert P. Merges, "Of Coase, Property Rules, and Intellectual Property," *Columbia Law Review*, 1994, p. 2655; and Robert P. Merges, "Intellectual Property and the Costs of Commercial Exchange: A Review Essay," *Michigan Law Review*, vol. 93 (1995), p. 1570.

*E. Contemporary research on common-property regimes*

This description of contemporary trends and understandings in science should give some hint of why I have come to see science as a limited-access commons, rather than a truly open public domain. In this subsection, I shall briefly review some contemporary scholarship on common-access property rights regimes, both to get a deeper sense of how the analogy works and to frame the discussion in Section IV concerning proper policy toward scientific research.

Throughout the 1970s and into the 1980s, much of the research in political economy, the economics of the public sector, and economics in general led to a great deal of skepticism toward the workability not just of government, but of collective institutions in general. At the formation stage, institutions were faced with formidable problems, most notably the difficulty of overcoming self-interest; the problem of collective action, we were told, was pervasive. And if by some miracle of cooperation or coercion collective institutions took shape, they were immediately besieged by rent-seeking interest groups concerned exclusively with turning the institution to private advantage. The forces at work during the operative stage of an institution—which we might generally refer to as public-choice concerns—were thus just as corrosive as the original conditions of collective action.

Partly in response to the deep skepticism engendered by the collective-action and public-choice literatures, a number of social scientists set out to study real-world institutions to see how they worked. Some started inductively, arriving at the threshold of the theory of institutions only after having accumulated a mass of facts. Others began with a sense that the received wisdom was somehow deficient; they seemed to have in mind the old adage that sure, it worked in practice, but would it work in theory?

Whatever their starting point, however, these social scientists soon began to assemble an intricate factual basis for some major revisions to the received view of institutions. In sociology, economics, and even legal studies (with the work of scholars such as Robert Ellickson at Yale Law School), detailed studies of institutions took shape.[36] Collectively, they form the basis for a much more nuanced theory of institutional formation, administration, and change. As if to ratify the trend, the Nobel economics committee last year awarded its prize to the granddaddy of institutional theorists, economic historian Douglass North.

Many of the trends that culminated with the award of the Nobel to North are on display in Eleanor Ostrom's pioneering book, *Governing the*

[36] See Robert Ellickson, *Order without Law* (Cambridge: Harvard University Press, 1989); and Thrainn Eggertsson, *Economic Behavior and Institutions* (Cambridge: Cambridge University Press, 1990).

*Commons*.[37] The thrust of Ostrom's work is a description of how voluntary institutions arise to allocate scarce, commonly shared resources such as water, without formal property rights or significant government oversight. Her cases reveal a rich pattern of adaptive, consensual responses to the "tragedy of the commons." Each case describes who organized the institution and why. Then Ostrom details the complex rules governing who can join, how informal "rights" to resources are determined, how compliance is monitored, how rules are enforced (e.g., how violators are sanctioned), and whether (and to what extent) "external" governmental authorities are called on to structure, ratify, oversee, or enforce any aspects of the institution.

Because they mirror the operation of scientific research institutions in some ways, I will consider the example of water basin authorities in Southern California, a set of institutions Ostrom studies in detail. These institutions emerged out of a classic tragedy of the commons: an open-access resource combined with minimal (almost nonexistent) property rights. Municipalities that shared these water basins—which are large, permanent subsurface water sources—formed water authorities in response to repeated litigation over how much water each city could appropriate under state law. This law was based on the notion of capture; it provided that a municipality had the right to use as much water as it could make beneficial use of, subject to the caveat that the total usage could not exceed the sustainable yield of the water basin. In the shadow of this minimal set of first-comer entitlements, and under the threat of continuous litigation under the just-mentioned caveat, the municipalities formed voluntary organizations such as the Raymond Basin water district and the West Basin Water Association. After initially implementing proportional water-pumping cutbacks, to comply with the sustainable-yield requirement, these institutions assumed their current operational role. They now provide for fixed water allocations, neutral monitors (so-called watermasters, whose salaries are paid mostly by member cities but partly by the state of California), and even systematic investments in groundwater-enhancement technologies, paid for by proportional contributions of the member cities. Although the influence of government can be seen in the formation and operation of these institutions, Ostrom stresses the essentially private nature of the collective action behind these institutions: "The solutions to the pumping race . . . were not imposed on the participants by external authorities. Rather, the participants used public arenas to *impose constraints on themselves*." Ostrom's study of water authorities and the other common-pool organizations culminates in eight design principles, which Ostrom lays out as a checklist for institutional designers. These are her answers to the deficiencies of the received theory of institutions, especially collective-action theory and public choice. For our

[37] Eleanor Ostrom, *Governing the Commons* (Cambridge: Cambridge University Press, 1990).

purposes, what is important is that she demonstrates the operation of voluntary common-property resource allocation institutions based on shared rules and norms. (A host of other studies in the same vein reach quite similar conclusions.)[38]

### *F. Scientific research as a common-property resource*

One could agree that the baseline in science is not complete openness, and still resist the analogy between common-property regimes and contemporary norms of science. After all, unlike water or common pasture land, scientific research is not a product of nature, waiting to be exploited. It has to be created. Thus, the thought might be that the institutions that operate in the realm of science cannot be legitimately compared to those that allocate access to preexisting natural resources such as water.

This is no doubt true; the analogy is incomplete in many respects, perhaps fatally so. There is, however, one similarity so important as to make it worth pursuing (in my mind, at any rate): the notion that both in the common-resource institutions studied by social scientists such as Ostrom and in the case of scientific research, the members of the community act as if some intermediate form of social organization—neither purely private nor completely nonprivate, i.e., public—is in force.

This shared assumption stems, at least in part, from the fact that although science itself is not a freely given asset, such as water or pasture land, it is based on a resource that the members of the relevant community treat as a given: public money. Thus, public funding produces science, which therefore carries with it some of the attributes of a public (or, I would argue, common) resource. True, unlike with a physical resource, where the only issue is allocation, science must first be produced by participants. And true, once it is produced, it must be disclosed in order for other members of the community to use it. Nevertheless, in many ways the practice of science makes these distinctions less important than they might at first appear. First, the production of science is a highly cooperative venture. Those who produce it understand that the community always has extensive claims on it, because without shared knowledge, research techniques, and even biological materials, there would often be no results, no progress, and hence nothing to argue about. Second, and most importantly, in the absence of shared norms, science, like water, would be subject to highly deleterious forms of self-serving behavior. A lab that always "takes" research results, but that never "gives" in return, for example, is like a municipality that pumps water as fast as it can, at the expense both of its neighbors and ultimately of rational

[38] See, e.g, Glenn Stevenson, *Common Property Economics: A General Theory and Land Use Applications* (Cambridge: Cambridge University Press, 1991), which presents empirical studies of grazing rights in common pastures. (The Ostrom quote earlier in this paragraph is from *Governing the Commons*, p. 110.)

water use. Thus, in science, as with open-access water resources, cooperation produces very large gains.

## III. The New Norms of Science: Two-Tiered Property Rights

In science, as we have seen, emerging pro-commercialization practices coexist (sometimes uneasily) with traditional "Mertonian" norms. The resulting set of practices, although still in the formative stage, suggests a basic structure that is quite compatible with Ostrom's institutional analysis. It is worthwhile to take a moment to reconsider these practices, then, with an eye to understanding them as an example of collective-action institutions in formation.

In essence, the new practices can be explained—roughly and preliminarily—in the following terms. They seek to preserve the old norms while recognizing a fundamentally changed landscape.[39] They do this by dividing potential transactions into two classes: those with other pure scientists, in which efforts are made to preserve the old rules of scientific discourse; and those with commercial entities, in which more-explicit insistence on property rights, and the attendant element of immediate compensation, are both expected. Consistent with the earlier explanation, it is important to notice that the former set of transactions are not in any sense *devoid* of property rights. Instead, they rely on *informal* property rights. The latter transactions, by contrast, depend on formal property rights, and are conducted "in the shadow of" these rights. This explains, for example, why transfers of as-yet-unpatented materials to commercial labs come with greater restrictions. The possibility that a patent might be sought leads to greater safeguards, such as an insistence that any commercialization, publication, or property right claims growing out of the commercial recipient's use of the materials come only after the sender has received notice and has time to respond. (This can preserve the sender's right to file his or her own patent, for instance, a right that might be endangered if the recipient makes the sender's invention public before the sender acts, e.g., by filing a patent application.)

Although I believe the two-tiered property right concept properly captures an important feature of contemporary science, I would add some warnings about its continued relevance. In general, science is in such a rapid state of flux that the differential treatment of pure and commercial science may only be a way station on the road toward a totally new set of

[39] In this respect, they bring to mind some intriguing observations of my colleague Bob Cooter regarding the formation of formal markets for property rights in Papua New Guinea, a country currently undergoing a transition from a traditional, clan-based system of real-property ownership to a more modern system. See Robert Cooter, "Inventing Market Property: The Land Courts of Papua New Guinea," *Law and Society Review*, vol. 25 (1991), p. 760, where Cooter argues that the best approach to modernizing is for courts to encourage "novel forms of market property that are more congenial to tradition."

practices. Perhaps the destination will be the complete specification and enforcement of property rights, against all comers, pure and commercial. Perhaps it will be a return to the old patterns of interaction, fueled by a declining interest in funding from commercial entities. The point here is that the two-tiered system I observe currently is only one possible configuration in the long term. Before extensive policy formation is undertaken in response to it, we should make sure it has some degree of permanence.

## IV. Some Tentative Policy Ideas

What policy recommendations flow from the fact of "creeping propertization" of science, and the emergence of a two-tiered system? And what do we gain, in formulating policies, by seeing scientific research both as a common asset shared under strict rules by a close-knit community, and as a marketable product? I present the answers to these questions in two parts: first, a pair of formal policy proposals, and second, an admonition on implementation.

### *A. Specific policy proposals*

First, we ought to consider adjusting some of the rules of the formal intellectual-property system to better reflect the fact that science originates as a product of the commons. As is well recognized, the bold individual is the darling of our system, and of patent law especially. Yet the origin of scientific research is with the group, and its use and dissemination, in the first instance at least, ought to be a group affair. Thus, the common-property approach would lead us to consider very seriously proposals to formalize a line of legal decisions hinting at a *pure research exemption* to patent infringement.[40] While none of these proposals to date would explicitly allow fellow scientists to use research results notwith-

[40] See Rebecca Eisenberg, "Patents and the Progress of Science: Exclusive Rights and Experimental Use," *University of Chicago Law Review*, vol. 56 (1989), p. 1017, where Eisenberg describes the interaction between the scientific research ethos and intellectual property rules.

The pure research exemption to patent infringement, known as the experimental-use doctrine, had its origins in Justice Joseph Story's opinion in *Whittemore v. Cutter*, 29 F. Cas. 1120 (C.C.D.Mass. 1813) (No. 17,600). In this case, the defendant appealed a jury instruction which stated, in effect, that the "making of a machine . . . with a design to use it for profit" constituted infringement. Justice Story upheld the trial judge's instruction, and stated that "it could never have been the intention of the legislature to punish a man, who constructed such a machine merely for philosophical experiments, or for the purpose of ascertaining the sufficiency of the machine to produce its described effects" (29 F. Cas. at 555). Other cases followed, generally limiting the exception to these quite narrow grounds. See Note, "Experimental Use as Patent Infringement: The Impropriety of a Broad Exception," *Yale Law Journal*, vol. 100 (1991), p. 2169, which states that the experimental-use exception "should be applied as it has been in the past: in a very restrictive manner, consistent with the purpose and function of the patent system."

In *Roche Products, Inc. v. Bolar Pharmaceutical Co.*, 733 F.2d 858, 221 U.S.P.Q. (BNA) 937 (Fed. Cir.), cert. denied, 469 U.S. 856 (1984), the Federal Circuit Court of Appeals considered

standing the presence of formal patent rights,[41] the "experimental-use doctrine" seems precisely the right sort of accommodation between the needs of the scientific community and the requirements of a formal property rights system. Whereas under current norms scientists in effect scale back their property rights when dealing with each other, the experimental-use doctrine as typically described[42] scales back the rights that any patentee—commercial entity or pure scientist—can assert against a pure researcher. The doctrine could thus be described as having two primary effects: codifying current practices within the scientific community, and extending those practices to dealings between commercial entities and pure scientists.

The second proposal worth considering is to explicitly reevaluate the patent system's rule regarding how early in a research project a researcher can file a viable patent application. This rule, called the "utility requirement" by patent lawyers, plays a crucial role in mediating the boundary between academic (or pure) science and applied, commercially valuable science. Although there are some decided cases that show an appreciation that the requirement serves this role, there is as yet no thoroughgoing conceptualization along these lines. What is needed is an appreciation of the fact that pure researchers, long before it is clear whether they are actually infringing any patent, change their behavior upon the mere filing of a patent application by some other researcher or lab. They may shy away from the area covered by the patent application, in fear of eventual patent litigation; they may file a competing application, "defensively" as it were, to counter the incipient threat with a property right of their own; or they may be seduced wholeheartedly into the speculative game, and thus file a patent with potential commercial gain in mind—that is, an "offensive" patent.

The utility requirement does not prevent these results, it merely delays them. By requiring that an invention must reach a significant degree of practical promise before a patent application is filed, it at least prevents the kind of "race to the patent office" that is both theoretically predictable and actually observed in some cases.[43]

the experimental-use defense for the first time. Here, the defendant, Bolar Pharmaceuticals, engaged in infringing acts prior to the expiration of the plaintiff's patent in order to facilitate Food and Drug Administration testing, so as to be ready to market the drug as soon as the patent expired. The Federal Circuit Court overruled the district court's finding of noninfringement, holding that the experimental-use exception did not include "the limited use of a patented drug for testing and investigation strictly related to FDA drug approval requirements . . ." (733 F.2d at 861).

[41] In fact, in "Patents and the Progress of Science," Eisenberg explicitly recommends that "[r]esearch use of a patented invention with a primary or significant market among research users should not be exempt from infringement liability when the research user is an ordinary consumer of the patented invention."

[42] See Eisenberg, "Patents and the Progress of Science."

[43] The most notorious recent case involves patents on short snippets of genetic material, which, it is hoped, will one day be identified as portions of larger, whole genes having commercial applications. See Rebecca Eisenberg, "Genes, Patents, and Product Develop-

### B. "Open-access absolutism": A policy to avoid

In pursuing the policy goals outlined above (as well as others intended to address the same problem), I propose that we keep one important thought in mind: we must show respect for the internal rules of the scientific community. This will take the form, primarily, of *refusing* to adopt flat requirements that all federal scientific research, or even some portion of it, be made instantaneously available to the general public, or even to all other scientists. In other words, we must show an understanding that even if formal property rights are prohibited, a set of norms in the scientific community will continue to regulate access and related issues in ways that might be described as the imposition of certain *informal* property rights. Where this is so, we must respect it. Instead of conceiving of science as innately public, and therefore viewing any and all restrictions on public availability as inherently wrong, we should ask why the community does things the way it does. Some restrictions on dissemination—such as the prohibition on commercial use of shared biological materials—may well be designed to add to the amount and quality of science that is ultimately available to the public. Some practices, such as less-than-total disclosure of research tools upon publication, might have important roots in the incentive structure of individual scientists working in the context of the scientific community. (That is, in order to develop a new tool in the first place, scientists might need an extra advantage of exclusive use of a new research tool for some period beyond the first publication generated by use of that tool.) In any case, we ought to see how the practice under scrutiny evolved in the community, and how it affects the overall functioning of the community, instead of bluntly requiring that science adhere to the naive baseline of total and immediate public dissemination.

## V. Conclusion

I have attempted to describe the emergence of a new set of practices, or norms, in the scientific community. This community, which is undergoing a process of "creeping propertization," has responded by adapting the informal norms that served it in the past to a new regime, one characterized by the presence of strong, formal property rights. I have argued that while science was never completely "open," and while "informal" property rights were asserted and recognized even in the older, precommercial era, the advent of formal rights has resulted in an uneasy, shifting con-

ment," *Science*, vol. 257, p. 903; Reid Adler, "Genome Research: Fulfilling the Public's Expectations for Knowledge and Commercialization," *Science*, vol. 257 (1992), p. 908; Thomas Kiley, "Patents on Random Complementary DNA Fragments?" *Science*, vol. 257 (1992), p. 915; and Bernadine Healy, "Special Report on Gene Patenting," *New England Journal of Medicine*, vol. 327 (1992), p. 664.

figuration best described as a two-tiered system of rights. In the realm of "pure" research, the older practices involving "informal" property rights are still ascendant, though certain accommodations have been made, based on the shared understanding that what is pure today may have commercial potential tomorrow. In the main, in other words, there are signs that the scientific commons has been defended from the onslaught of propertization, at least for the time being. Dealings between pure researchers and those in the realm of commercial research are conducted on a different basis, however. They are based more on formal rights, and financial compensation (present or future) is an expected component of the relationship. In this case, when members of the commons deal with outsiders,[44] informal rights give way to formal rights. It is an interesting feature of the scientific community that its members can simultaneously maintain informal internal institutions for conducting exchange, and also conduct market transactions with those who are not members of the community.

I have also argued that the current accommodation may prove to be unstable, and that in any event it would be wise to consider certain policies that reflect the dual nature of contemporary science. In particular, I suggest giving some thought to proposals to formalize an "experimental-use" defense against charges of patent infringement, for pure research scientists, and I suggest reconceiving the utility requirement in patent law to hold the line on early patenting, and thus preserve the two-tiered structure scientists seem to be converging on. These and other policy ideas are well worth considering when one takes into account the enormous contributions made by science to social welfare in the past several hundred years. It is also worth considering that the institutional and legal foundation on which science rests plays an important part in bringing about these welfare gains, and that any policy or practice that affects this foundation deserves as much attention as the content of the scientific research itself.

*Law, University of California, Berkeley*

[44] The "outsiders" may also be members of the commons, only acting in a commercial capacity. It is typical in university research circles for academic researchers to have commercial affiliations. I assume here that community members "role differentiate" in their dealings with each other, that is, behave differently in a transaction with the same partner when that partner is acting in a different role (e.g., commercial entity rather than academic colleague).

# PROPERTY RIGHTS AND TECHNOLOGICAL INNOVATION*

By Svetozar Pejovich

## I. Economic Development, Innovation, and Property Rights

The economist Armen Alchian said once that ever since the fiasco in the Garden of Eden, we have been living in a world in which what we want exceeds what is available. The desire for more satisfaction is a predictable behavioral implication of the fact of scarcity. In fact, it might have helped mankind to survive against competition from other forms of life. Man's desire for more utility gives rise to two interdependent issues that each and every society has to face: (i) how to increase the value of the community's wealth,[1] and (ii) how to allocate the increment in wealth. We generalize those issues as the demand for economic development.[2]

Innovation means doing something that has not been done before. It could be the production of a new good, the opening up of a new market, the discovery of a new source of supply, the development of a new method of production, or changes in the rules of the game. Whichever is the case, by injecting a novelty into the flow of economic life, innovation offers the community a new choice. Innovation is the engine of economic progress.

Most innovations that affect the economy are technological (scientific) innovations.[3] Technology, broadly defined, embodies the prevailing knowledge. The growth of knowledge then creates new technological possi-

* An earlier version of this paper was presented at the Conference on the Process of Transition in Eastern Europe in Trento, Italy, in March 1995. I am grateful to the Earhart Foundation for support of my research on the economics of property rights.

[1] Wealth is the value of all pecuniary and nonpecuniary goods that yield income to a person. In addition to assets that yield money (pecuniary) incomes, people derive nonpecuniary income from a number of specific "goods" such as leisure, a pleasant environment, clean air, a good football team in town, friendly neighbors, and so on. The value of satisfaction from nonpecuniary goods is subjective and has its monetary equivalent.

[2] Economic development and economic growth are not identical concepts. Economic development means changes in the value of people's total wealth. Economic growth measures changes in the value of goods and services included in various accounting categories such as gross national product (GNP). The former is all-inclusive and subjective. The latter is easier to quantify. However, it leaves out of the calculation many of the (nonpecuniary) goods that determine the value of people's wealth.

[3] This essay is about technological innovations by business firms. I prefer to use the term "technological innovation"; the term "scientific innovation" might fail to convey a clear distinction between invention and innovation—that is, between creating new knowledge (which is generally but not exclusively done by scientists) and using it (which is done by nonscientists as well). Examples of technological innovation are modern airplanes, computers, the Internet, etc. For all practical purposes, the two terms ("technological innovation" and "scientific innovation") could be used interchangeably.

bilities. Since both the growth and the direction of new knowledge are unpredictable, the flow of innovations is also unpredictable and their impact on the economy uncertain. The innovator translates new technological possibilities into new choices. That is, innovation is a consequence of the *individual's* perceptions about the applicability of technology, willingness to accept the risk and uncertainty associated with doing something new, and ability to see the innovation through. Thus, the innovator must possess traits such as ingenuity, optimism, stubbornness, perseverance, and imagination. Boards of directors, governments, agencies, organizations, and other groups cannot innovate. A member of one of those entities has to perceive an opportunity to innovate and sell it to his colleagues. Potential innovators are difficult to identify *ex ante*, and innovation is not an activity that we can plan for. We cannot decide to have two innovations each month.

Innovation represents an addition to the community's set of opportunity choices. The implementation of a novelty requires that resources be withdrawn from other uses. By implication, innovation is a trade-off between (1) the value of output which the resources used by the innovator were producing before and (2) the use of those resources to make an addition to the community's set of choices. Voluntary acceptance of an innovation by the community means that the community is better off. Otherwise, innovation would have failed.

The innovator is, then, much more than a passive agent who directs production in accordance with the consumers' preferences. He is a mover and shaker of the system, while the consumers get to judge the innovator's entrepreneurial decisions. This means that we have no way of telling whether innovations that are not voluntarily accepted by interacting individuals benefit the community. Consider, for example, the influence of state authorities such as the Food and Drug Administration (FDA), which have the power to impose and *enforce* policies regarding innovation. Such policies, as Karl Brunner notes, can have unexpected and adverse consequences:

> The traumatic impact on public impressions made by the tragically crippled and deformed babies resulting from the use of thalidomide by pregnant women influenced new legislation and tougher regulatory policies. . . . The measures implemented [to reduce the risk of such a tragedy being repeated] raised the costs of development for new products by a large factor. . . . Innovation consequently declined by a wide margin and the appearance of new drugs sharply contracted. . . . A policy addressed to minimize the probability of bad [pharmaceutical] products maximized at the same time the probability of *not* having useful drugs.[4]

[4] Karl Brunner, "The Limits of Economic Policy," in *Socialism: Institutional, Philosophical, and Economic Issues*, ed. Svetozar Pejovich (Dordrecht: Kluwer Academic Publishers, 1987), pp. 41–42.

We can say that technological innovation unfolds the meaning of economic development as the expansion of choices *voluntarily* accepted by the community. That is, economic development is neither about more of the same nor about new choices imposed on the community from without.

Thus, economic analysis of economic development must identify the factors that affect the flow of innovation in the community and the circumstances upon which those factors depend. Research and empirical evidence have shown that property-rights structures are one such critical factor.[5] The purpose of this essay is to analyze the impact of three types of property rights in business firms[6] on the flow of technological innovation. I focus on the three types of firms that have been implemented over a reasonably long period: the privately owned firm under capitalism,[7] the labor-managed firm in a decentralized socialist state (former Yugoslavia and, to a lesser degree, Hungary),[8] and the state-owned firm in a centrally planned economy (former USSR and most Eastern European countries). The last two types of business firms, the only two which were fully implemented in the pre-1989 socialist world, were entirely consistent with the basic philosophical and economic premises of the socialist doctrine as it had evolved since the eighteenth century.

## II. Property Rights and the Flow of Innovation

This essay analyzes the effects of alternative types of property rights on the flow of innovation under several subheadings: freedom to innovate, incentives to innovate, the power to innovate, and the integration of innovation into the economy.

[5] For example, Douglass North has demonstrated a strong link between different types of property rights and economic development (and has received a Nobel prize for his research).

[6] Most innovations, especially technological innovations, are likely to take place within business organizations. For example, an independent innovator has incentives to create a firm before carrying out his or her innovation, in order to reduce the costs of negotiating contracts across markets, to limit liabilities to creditors, and to exploit tax advantages.

[7] The bundle of property rights that define the privately owned firm includes the owner's right to appropriate the residual after all cooperating inputs are paid their contractual prices, the owner's right to hire and fire cooperating inputs, and the owner's right to sell those two rights in competitive markets.

[8] The bundle of rights that define the labor-managed firm includes the state's ownership of capital assets held by the firm, the employees' right to appropriate (and distribute among themselves) the return from those assets, and the employees' right to govern the firm. The employees' rights specified above are not transferable; they are contingent on their employment by that firm. It is important not to confuse the labor-managed economy with producers' cooperatives in capitalism. In a free-market, private-property society, producers' cooperatives emerge spontaneously and have to survive competition from other types of firms. The fact that producers' cooperatives have not happened on any significant scale in capitalism is evidence of their relative inefficiency. I am always puzzled when some colleagues say that I have tried, in some of my works, to show that the labor-managed firm is inefficient. Nothing could be further from the truth. Competitive markets have done that. All that an economist can do is to try to determine why the labor-managed firm is inefficient.

*A. Alternative types of property rights and freedom to innovate*

Potential innovators do not emerge from a specific social class. We observe that they come from all social groups. Thus, the larger the number of people who have the freedom to innovate, the higher the probability of increasing the flow of innovation.

In a private-property, free-market economy, everyone has the right to acquire resources and use them to pursue any lawful activity, including innovation. However, private property rights are often attenuated in free societies. For example, codetermination laws[9] raise the cost of equity capital, license requirements reduce the number of people who can pursue specific activities, monopoly privileges (including protectionism) limit one's right choose how to use one's own resources, FDA rules delay and perhaps discourage some innovators.[10] While it would be wrong to argue that restrictions on the right of ownership have no benefits, the attenuation of private property has to affect the flow of innovation by placing restrictions on the freedom to innovate.

In a centrally planned economy, entry into decision making is attained through membership in the ruling elite. Individuals (including members of the ruling group) have no right to acquire productive resources. Members of the ruling group, managers of enterprises, and all other individuals who perceive an opportunity for an innovation must sell the idea to their colleagues or superiors, who in turn have to sell it to their superiors, and so on.

In a labor-managed economy,[11] the pool of those who have the right to acquire and use resources is restricted to the working collective. The term "working collective" is important here. Only a working collective, either directly or through its governing board, can decide to carry out innovations. An employee who perceives an opportunity to innovate must sell the idea to other employees (or to the board). That is, he must sell it to a group of people with limited business experience, diverse attitudes toward risk, and short time horizons.[12]

[9] Codetermination means that employees join shareholders on the boards of directors of corporate firms and take an active role in decision making. Germany has been a leader in promoting codetermination in the West. For example, the Codetermination Act of 1976 requires that in business firms employing more than two thousand employees, one-half of the members of the board of directors (in Germany it is called the "supervisory board") must be labor representatives.

[10] See Brunner, "The Limits of Economic Policy."

[11] The labor-managed firm is a socialist version of codetermination: labor participation in decision making without private property rights. Former Yugoslavia is the only socialist country that has tried this type of firm on a large scale and over a long period of time. A major academic advocate of this method for organizing production in the West has been professor Jaroslav Vanek of Cornell University; see, e.g., Jaroslav Vanek, *The General Theory of Labor-Managed Market Economies* (Ithaca, NY: Cornell University Press, 1970). See also note 8 above.

[12] The shortness of time horizons is due to the nontransferability of assets held by the group. In the context of the labor-managed firm, the nontransferability means that workers have the right to use assets held by their firm and to appropriate returns (earnings) from

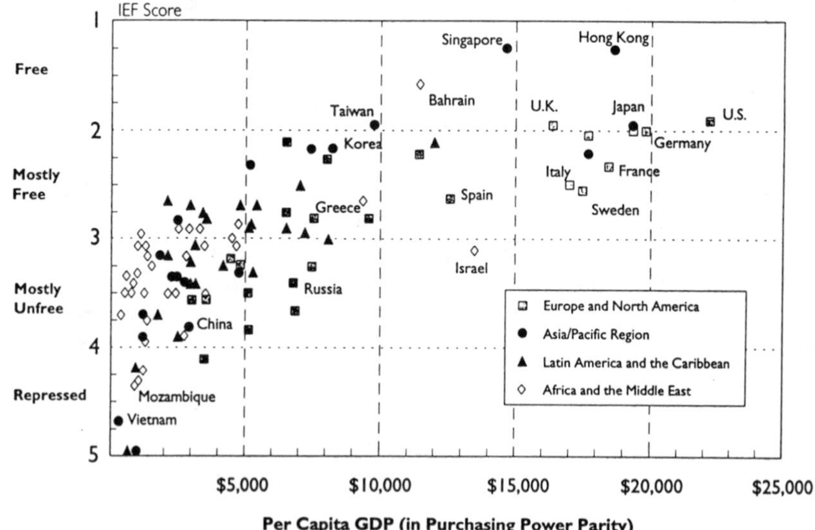


FIGURE 1. A comparison of economic freedom and wealth in various countries.

In a carefully researched study, Bryan Johnson and Thomas Sheehy set out to find a method for measuring the relationship between economic freedom and wealth, as well as the relationship between economic freedom and the rate of growth. To this end they developed an index of economic freedom.[13] The index is based on several factors including private property rights. Using their index, Johnson and Sheehy examined 101 countries and ranked them as *free* (7 countries), *mostly free* (36), *mostly unfree* (50), and *repressed* (8).[14] The study provides compelling evidence of a strong relationship between economic freedom and economic prosperity. Figures 1 and 2 summarize Johnson and Sheehy's major findings.[15]

The study is a rich source of observations about the link between economic freedom and prosperity. Hong Kong and Singapore, classified as free economies, have enjoyed a high rate of economic development over

those assets, but not to sell the assets or change their value (i.e., workers must reinvest each year an amount approximately equal to the assets' wear and tear).

[13] Bryan Johnson and Thomas Sheehy, *The Index of Economic Freedom* (Washington, DC: Heritage Foundation, 1995). The study does not discuss political and civic freedoms.

[14] Johnson and Sheehy classify Eastern European countries along with all other countries and do so on the basis of their institutional arrangements prevailing in the early 1990s.

[15] Both tables are reproduced from Johnson and Sheehy, *The Index of Economic Freedom*, by permission of the Heritage Foundation. In Figure 2, the 1965 figures are from the Agency for International Development and first appeared in Edward Hudgins and Bryan Johnson, "Why Asia Grows and Africa Doesn't," Heritage Foundation Backgrounder No. 756 (March 2, 1990); the 1991 figures are from the United Nations Development Programme's *Human Development Report 1994*; the figures for Taiwan are for per-capita GNP.

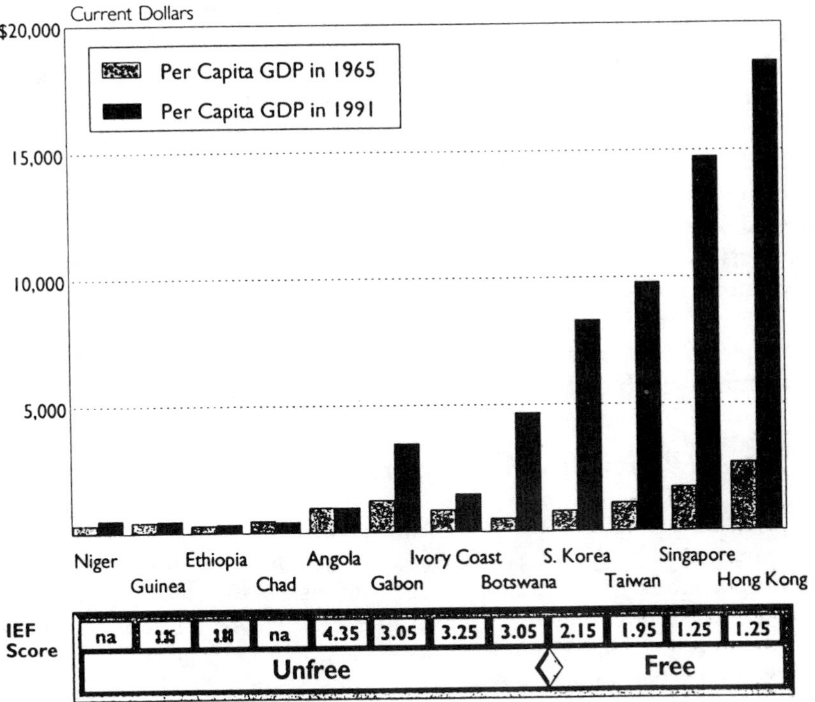


FIGURE 2. Per-capita GDP growth in developing countries: 1965 and 1991.

the last twenty-five years. By contrast, the repressed economies of Vietnam and North Korea are among the world's poorest.

In 1965, mostly unfree Gabon had a per-capita gross domestic product (GDP) of $1,286. Since that year Gabon has been flooded with hundreds of millions of dollars of foreign aid and other nonmarket grants. Yet, by 1991, Gabon's per-capita GDP had risen to only $3,448. By contrast, per-capita GDP in free Taiwan rose from $1,133 in 1965 to $9,805 in 1991. And Taiwan received a relatively insignificant amount of nonmarket funds during that period.

In the early 1970s, Chile was the world's second largest recipient of foreign aid, had a stagnating economy and, under Salvador Allende, had a shrinking GDP. By 1990, Chile's economy had changed dramatically. Augusto Pinochet's market reforms drastically reduced government intervention in the economy, maximized economic freedoms, and helped transform Chile into one of the fastest-growing economies of the world.

Among former communist countries, mostly free Estonia and the Czech Republic have provided credible guarantees of property rights, adopted low rates of taxation, and seriously reduced government regulations. And the economies of these two countries are performing better than any other former socialist state.

In an interesting article, Keith Richburg discusses the issue of why African development has lagged so far behind that of East Asia, which suffered from a similar set of initial obstacles. Why has East Asia become a model of economic success, while Africa, since independence, has seen increasing poverty and hunger? Richburg offers two major explanations for those differences in economic development. First, after independence, which for most of them occurred in the first two decades after the end of World War II, the majority of African countries opted for government ownership of enterprises, due to a distrust of private property rights and foreign investment. Asians chose a brand of capitalism. Second, the prevailing informal institutions in Africa turned out to be less adaptable (relative to the prevailing informal institutions in East Asia) to the requirements of efficiency in production and exchange.[16]

### *B. Alternative types of property rights and incentives to innovate*

A successful innovation yields benefits in excess of what the bundle of resources used by the innovator was earning before. However, innovation is a nonroutine activity, and the level of risk associated with it is not known. The innovator has to choose, in effect, between investing a bundle of resources in a project whose outcome is unpredictable, or in one of the routine activities for which the level of risk is known. The latter is the cost of innovation. The innovator's decision must then depend on his or her incentives (i.e., the penalty-reward system) to accept the uncertainty associated with the outcome of the innovation.

In a private-property capitalist economy, the innovator can capture the present value of the flow of benefits from a successful innovation either in one lump sum (by selling it to another person or company) or as a stream of payments. Also, a private-property, free-market economy provides incentives to innovate even for those who do not own resources. For example, the manager of a privately owned firm benefits from a successful innovation through the labor market for managers, in which the current profitability of the enterprise operated by that manager affects his salary via competing offers by other firms.

The gains from a successful innovation are only temporary, however. In a private-property, free-market economy, the gains attract duplications and imitations. Thus, the present value of the benefits from a successful innovation depends on how long the benefits are expected to last. That is, the innovator's choice between routine investments and

[16] Keith Richburg, "Why Is Black Africa Overwhelmed while East Asia Overcomes?" *International Herald Tribune*, July 14, 1992, pp. 1 and 6. Informal institutions in a community are parts of its heritage which have passed the test of time. They stem from the experiences, traditional values, religious beliefs, and all other factors that influence the subjective perceptions that individuals form about survival requirements in the world in which they live. Those informal rules are frequently referred to as the ethos, the hand-of-the-past, or the carriers of history.

innovation has to be influenced by the expected length of the imitation lag.[17] In fact, if all potential rivals were able to imitate successful innovations quickly, incentives to innovate would be seriously impaired. The gap between the novelty and the routine use of resources, which is the source of the innovator's gain, endures because it takes time, effort, and resources for potential rivals to learn, evaluate, and implement new technology.

The prevailing property rights in a labor-managed economy (i.e., in the absence of transferable claims on the returns from capital goods) have two consequences that tend to dampen the collective's incentives to innovate. First, the absence of the right to capitalize the expected future benefits into their present market price means that the working collective cannot appropriate the expected benefits of a successful innovation in one lump sum. Relative to a free-market, private-property economy, the innovator has fewer options for appropriating the benefits of a successful innovation. Second, since the collective can capture the benefits only as they occur, some of its members (e.g., those who expect to retire soon or change jobs) must have a bias against innovations that are expected to yield benefits over a long period of time.

In a planned economy, any individual (e.g., the manager of a firm) is free to propose an innovation to his superiors. However, there is a world of difference between the right to make suggestions and the right to do things. For at least two reasons, a member of the ruling group has reduced incentives to push an innovation through the decision-making channels. First, decisions to innovate are not made by individuals. They are reviewed and debated by layers of various committees, whose members are likely to have incentives not to rock the boat. Second, the private costs of pushing a specific innovation through the channels are substantial.[18] If the innovation is a success, the innovator will share the benefits with colleagues and superiors. If it is a failure, colleagues and superiors will blame the innovator. Socialist states did attempt to alleviate the absence of incentives to innovate via various awards (Lenin prizes, Stakhanovite rewards for performance, free vacations, etc.), but those attempts avoided granting more property rights to potential innovators. Thus, they were not strong enough to offset the effects of the absence of credible and stable incentive structures on the flow of scientific innovation. In a very interesting study, Leszek Balcerowicz, the first Minister of Finance of post-communist Poland, argued that the then-prevailing institutional structures in a Soviet-type economy were totally incapable of either producing scientific innovations or imitating technological developments abroad. Balcerowicz's point was that information about Western

[17] The purpose of copyrights, patents, etc., is to extend this lag over a long enough period not to discourage innovations.

[18] In addition to a potential loss of income due to demotion, the innovator's private costs in a Soviet-type economy also include potential loss of nonpecuniary benefits such as better housing, subsidized vacation, access to special stores, etc.

technological innovations, which the Soviets used to steal at high costs, was generally useless to them.[19]

### C. Alternative types of property rights and the power to innovate

Having the freedom to acquire and use resources is not the same thing as actually having the power to get them. And not all potential innovators have resources of their own. By evaluating and pricing our perceptions of opportunity choices, financial markets in a capitalist economy match the quantity of venture capital demanded with the quantity supplied to reflect contractual agreements on various issues, including risks. In fact, a major issue facing successful firms in a capitalist economy is how to preserve creativity as they grow in size. Pat Haggerty, a founder of Texas Instruments, has remarked that the firm's top management spent many months trying to find a way to institutionalize the process of proposing, approving, and implementing innovations. We can say that private property rights provide an institutional framework within which new firms with humble beginnings (e.g., Apple, Microsoft, etc.) can acquire the power to innovate, while such rights give mature firms like Texas Instruments an opportunity to regain their initial vigor.

In a labor-managed economy, the nontransferability of the employees' claims on the firm's cash flow, and the fact that those nontransferable claims have to be contingent on people's employment with that firm,[20] reduce the collective ability to acquire the power to innovate. The absence of financial markets leaves the labor-managed firm with two major sources of investable funds: retained earnings and bank credit. The former is not a likely source of funds for innovation. A loss of retained earnings is borne by the entire working collective now, while the benefits of a successful innovation have to be shared with new employees. The power of the labor-managed firm to innovate, then, depends on the banking system. But a study I conducted recently in this area suggests that the incentive effects of the prevailing property rights in a labor-managed economy rule out bank credit as a reliable source of funds to innovate.[21]

In a planned economy, the ability to innovate is limited to those inno-

[19] Leszek Balcerowicz, "The Soviet-Type Economic System and Innovativeness," Institute for Economic Development, Warsaw, 1988, paper no. 19.

[20] To alleviate the effects of these conditions, some writers have proposed various immunizing stratagems (e.g., giving workers who leave the firm some future rights in the residual) which either ignore the costs of those stratagems, or ignore transaction costs *specific* to the labor-managed economy, or tend to privatize labor-managed firms, or all of the above. See Henryk Flakierski, *The Economic System and Income Distribution in Yugoslavia* (New York: M. E. Sharpe, 1989), pp. 67–70.

[21] See Svetozar Pejovich, "Why Has the Labor-Managed Firm Failed?" *Cato Journal*, vol. 6, no. 2 (Fall 1992), pp. 461–73. The study shows that the employees of the labor-managed firm have incentives to make investments that would shift the firm's profits forward (benefiting current employees), and to negotiate investment loans with repayment schedules that are as lengthy as the banks are willing to provide (shifting costs to future workers).

vations that are approved by the ruling group, and it usually requires a miracle to get the state bureaucracy to go along with a risky novelty. A remarkable 1957 book by Vladimir Dudintsev, which has not aged with the passage of time, describes the frustration of an engineer in the USSR who has an idea for an important technical innovation but is faced with an entrenched bureaucracy which would rather destroy him than approve a risky venture.[22]

The importance of the transferability of claims (a critical feature of the private-property economy) for the flow of innovation is difficult to exaggerate. Transferable claims allow for specialization in risk-bearing across individuals with different degrees of risk-aversion. (For example: Being risk-averse I sell an oil field I have inherited and put my money in government bonds. My colleague Maurice, who is a risk-preferrer, cashes in his inheritance of government bonds and invests the proceeds in a Broadway show.) That is, people can choose a portfolio of claims consistent with their attitudes toward risk. Moreover, the absence of transferable claims (that is, the absence of, or restrictions on, private property rights) makes it all but impossible to compare the future consequences of the alternative decisions one is currently faced with.

### *D. Alternative types of property rights and the integration of innovation into the economy*

A novelty does not necessarily make people better off. It has to be voluntarily accepted and integrated into the economy. Once again the question is: How do different types of property rights integrate innovations into the economy?

In a private-property economy, competitive markets evaluate the novelty. As German philosopher Hans Albert writes:

> The power of the consumer . . . does not consist of giving orders for the solutions of problems in the sphere of production, but in testing the solutions adopted by the entrepreneurs and in influencing the future activities in the sphere of production indirectly by accepting or refuting these solutions.[23]

Freedom of exchange reveals the costs and benefits of the novelty as perceived by interacting individuals. And those costs and benefits, via relative prices, tell us whether or not the innovation has enriched the community. By internalizing the gains from a successful innovation,[24]

[22] Vladimir Dudintsev, *Not by Bread Alone* (New York: E. P. Dutton and Co., 1957).

[23] Hans Albert, "Is Socialism Inevitable? Historical Prophecy and the Possibility of Reason," in Pejovich, ed., *Socialism (supra* note 4), p. 69.

[24] That is, by making the innovator and those who choose to imitate his or her innovation bear the costs and capture the benefits of their actions.

TABLE 1. *Money incomes of families in various income groups in the U.S. (as a percentage of total national income).*

| | 1950 | 1960 | 1970 | 1980 | 1990 |
|---|---|---|---|---|---|
| Lowest fifth | 4.5 | 4.8 | 5.4 | 5.1 | 4.6 |
| Second fifth | 12.0 | 12.2 | 12.2 | 11.6 | 10.8 |
| Middle fifth | 17.4 | 17.8 | 17.6 | 17.5 | 16.6 |
| Fourth fifth | 23.4 | 24.0 | 23.8 | 24.3 | 23.8 |
| Top fifth | 42.7 | 41.3 | 40.9 | 41.6 | 44.3 |

private property rights encourage a greater flow of innovation[25] than collective or state property rights under socialism.

A greater flow of innovations has two important consequences. First, it raises the average income in the community.[26] Second, a greater flow of innovations increases the mobility of individuals between income classes without any appreciable effect on the distribution of income. Initially, successful innovators earn more money than before. However, the resulting increase in income inequalities is only a temporary phenomenon. Large incomes of successful innovators are eventually whittled away through market competition via (i) lower prices paid by consumers, and (ii) higher prices of resources (used to imitate innovations) received by their owners. For example, the distribution of income in the United States has remained relatively stable over several decades in spite of different growth rates during those years (see Table 1). The income share of the poorest 20 percent of families (and unattached individuals) in the United States was about 4.5 percent of the total national income in 1950 and 4.6 percent in 1990; the income share of the wealthiest 20 percent was 42.7 percent of the total in 1950 and 44.3 percent in 1990.[27]

In the 1970s, Lowell Gallaway estimated the income shares by quintile in the United States, Sweden, and the former Soviet Union.[28] He found

[25] Governments have tried to capture a share of profits from innovations via various devices such as progressive taxes on profit, windfall taxes, etc. The (observable) effect of those profit-sharing schemes is to reduce incentives to innovate.

[26] I am assuming here that a larger flow of innovations tends to produce a larger flow of successful innovations.

[27] Imagine the list of all families and unattached individuals ranked in terms of their income in a given year. Then, separate them into five equal groups, add incomes within each group, and divide them by the total income for the country. The numbers in Table 1 are the percentages of total national income in current prices captured by each of those five groups. The reader should bear in mind that a relative stability of income shares by five income groups does not affect the flow of people between income groups from one period to another. (The figures in Table 1 are from U.S. Bureau of the Census, *Current Population Report*, Series P-60, No. 174, 1993.)

[28] Lowell Gallaway, "The Folklore of Unemployment and Poverty," in *Government Controls and the Free Market*, ed. Svetozar Pejovich (College Station: Texas A&M University Press, 1976), pp. 41-69.

the differences in the degree of inequality in the respective distributions to be minor. Thus, the important factor is the effect of property rights on the average income, as shown in Figure 1 (see Section IIA above).[29]

Integration of innovation in a labor-managed economy has three limitations, all of which can be attributed to the prevailing property rights. First, although a successful innovation creates larger earnings for the collective which implements it, it is less likely to spread to other firms than would be the case under a capitalist system: the absence of financial markets raises the cost of information to potential rivals. Second, when information about larger profits does become available, only existing firms enter into competition with the innovating firm. The entry of new firms in a labor-managed economy has to be slow because it requires a group and/or state decision to create a new firm. Third, suppose that rival firms have to hire additional workers in order to compete with the innovating firm. Given the prevailing property rights, new workers are new policy-makers as well. This means that the current collective has incentives to trade off some pecuniary income that could be had by hiring additional workers in order to ensure the security of its common interests.

Thus, the labor-managed economy provides signals regarding whether the community has or has not accepted an innovation only at a significant cost. First, the labor-managed economy has no built-in incentives to reduce the costs of identifying the mix of outputs reflecting consumers' preferences. Second, the labor-managed economy does not have a built-in mechanism (like a private-property, free-market economy, discussed above) to reestablish the initial distribution of income. An implication of this is that the process of imitating successful technological innovations in a labor-managed economy has a predictable tendency to increase money-income inequalities.

In a planned economy, the absence of private property rights and contractual freedom makes the costs of knowing whether the community has or has not accepted an innovation staggeringly high. Why? The acceptance of an innovation requires its evaluation in terms of the value which resources used by the innovator would have if they were employed differently. But the only source of value can be the individual interacting

[29] There is no economic theory that says that more equality in the distribution of money income is better than less equality. All that economists can do is try to identify and analyze the factors that account for income differences between individuals and groups and the circumstances upon which those factors depend. For example, in the early 1990s, median income for Asian Americans, whose work ethic and entrepreneurship are exemplary, was $36,784, and median income for whites was $31,435 (*New York Times*, July 24, 1992, p. A16). Also, any attempt at income redistribution creates at least two problems. First, a society in which incomes are not related to performance is going to be a poor society. This is so because adverse incentives reduce the production of *future* wealth. Second, the administrative costs of redistribution eat up *current* incomes. As Richard Posner writes: "Involuntary redistribution is a coerced transfer not justified by high market-transaction costs; it is, in efficiency terms, a form of theft. Its justification must be sought in ethics rather than in economics" (Richard Posner, *Economic Analysis of Law*, 4th ed. [Boston: Little, Brown, and Company, 1992], p. 461).

with other individuals in free markets. To paraphrase James Buchanan: economic activities can only be conceived in terms of values; but how are values determined? They are determined by prices which emerge in competitive markets. That is, prices have no meaning (other than being accounting devices for the state) in a nonmarket context, where the choice-influenced opportunity costs (the value of goods and services in their best alternative uses) are not identifiable.[30]

## III. Conclusion

This essay has two conclusions. First, alternative types of property rights have specific and predictable (i.e., observable) effects on the flow of technological innovation. Second, the rights of ownership and contractual freedom are more conducive to enhancing the flow of technological innovation than other institutional arrangements. I conjecture that the failure of socialist states and the slow rate of economic development in countries of the so-called Third World[31] are predictable consequences of their inability or unwillingness to adopt and enforce the basic institutions of capitalism: the right of private ownership, the freedom of contract, and the constitutional state.

*Economics, Texas A&M University*

[30] James Buchanan, "General Implications of Subjectivism in Economics," paper presented at the Conference on Subjectivism in Economics, Dallas, Texas, 1976, p. 8.

[31] Many countries, especially developing countries, tend to attribute their low rate of economic development to a variety of causes, such as exploitation by former colonial rulers, an inadequate resource base, shortage of capital, and/or poor planning. None of these alleged causes of "poverty" makes much sense. After several decades of political sovereignty, the exploitation argument is increasingly becoming an embarrassing one for developing countries to offer as an excuse for economic stagnation. If an inadequate resource base is responsible for poverty in India, why is a resource-poor country like Japan doing well? If overpopulation is a problem in China, why are people in Hong Kong so much better off? A shortage of capital is not holding back economic development in Eastern Europe, Africa, South America, etc. The flow of capital is held back by political instabilities, currency controls, restrictions on the right of ownership, discriminatory taxes, and corrupt governments. Compare the level of capital flowing into Japan with that flowing into India, or the level in East Asia with that in Africa, or the level in the Czech Republic with that in Romania.

# MEDICINE, ANIMAL EXPERIMENTATION, AND THE MORAL PROBLEM OF UNFORTUNATE HUMANS

By R. G. Frey

## I. Introduction: The Use of Animals for Human Benefit in Medicine

We live in an age of great scientific and technological innovation, and what seemed out of the question or at least very doubtful only a few years ago, today lies almost within our grasp. In no area is this more true than that of human health care, where lifesaving and life-enhancing technologies have given, or have the enormous potential in the not so distant future to give, relief from some of the most terrible human illnesses. On two fronts in particular, xenograft or cross-species transplantation[1] and genetic engineering of animals on behalf of gene therapy in humans,[2] such relief appears very promising, if not actually on the horizon. Certainly, extensive research work on both fronts is underway both in the United States and abroad.

These uses of animals for human benefit occur, however, in an intellectual and ethical environment in which scientists and technicians engaged in animal research are increasingly on notice, both from within and

[1] For an overview of some of the work in this area, see Rebecca Malouin, "Surgeons' Quest for Life: The History and the Future of Xenotransplantation," *Perspectives in Biology and Medicine*, vol. 37 (1994), pp. 416–28; Jerold M. Lowenstein, "The Transplant Gap," *Discover*, vol. 14, no. 6 (June 1993), pp. 26–30; and Thomas E. Mandel, "Future Directions in Transplantation," *Medical Journal of Australia*, vol. 158 (1993), pp. 269–73. See also my "Animal Parts, Human Wholes: On the Use of Animals as a Source of Organs for Human Transplants," in J. M. Humber and R. F. Almeder, eds., *Biomedical Ethics Reviews 1987* (Clifton, NJ: Humana Press, 1987), pp. 89–107.

[2] For a discussion of some of the work in this area, see Andrew Kimbrell, "Facing the Future: Genetic Engineering," *The Animals' Agenda*, vol. 15 (1995), pp. 24–28; and Kimbrell, *The Human Body Shop* (San Francisco: Harper, 1993). For some very recent developments, see "Doctors Transplant Pig Tissue into a Man with Parkinson's," *New York Times*, April 21, 1995, p. A15; and Philip J. Hilts, "Success in Temporary Transplants of Pigs' Hearts in Baboons," *New York Times*, April 30, 1995. Two books that give a broad overview of the array of genetic work being done in animals as well as some preliminary assessments of it are N. First and F. P. Haseltine, eds., *Transgenic Animals* (Boston: Butterworth-Heinemann, 1991); and J. Warren Evans and Alexander Hollaender, eds., *Genetic Engineering of Animals: An Agricultural Perspective* (New York: Plenum Press, 1986). For a discussion of some of the philosophical and ethical issues involved in the genetic engineering of animals, see S. Donnelley et al., "The Brave New World of Animal Biotechnology," *Hastings Center Report*, vol. 24, Supplementary Report (1994), pp. 1–32; and B. E. Rollin, *The Frankenstein Syndrome: Ethical and Social Issues in the Genetic Engineering of Animals* (New York: Cambridge University Press, 1995). I do not accept the moral framework within which these last two items locate their discussions.

 

without their ranks,[3] that the very trade-off upon which their work depends, namely, animal sacrifice for human gain, is once again under moral scrutiny. As moral beings, the rest of us, who accept the benefits that animal research confers, have an interest in what this moral scrutiny uncovers. This is especially true of those, such as myself, who support (much of) animal research and wish to see its benefits for humans continue. For if it turns out that those benefits are obtained by immoral practices, then they seem tainted. This is not to say that we would not still continue to make use of them;[4] we might simply judge that the price of living up to our moral convictions would be too costly. But the high calling that medical research is usually taken to represent would have been compromised; after all, most of us as moral beings do not boast of the ends we achieve through immoral means.

Today, most of us are aware that, unless full replacement of animals with artificial means (tissue cultures, computer models, etc.) is achieved—something I suspect will never occur completely[5]—we in part purchase our health and lives at the expense of animals. We intentionally, deliberately, and systematically use them to these ends, and we need at the broadest level to justify this use of them. This is as true of those who think any and all medical research involving animals is justified as of those who think otherwise; for we need to have some idea of what makes it right for us to use them at all.

Two developments give added incentive to this search for a justification of animal research. First, it can seem that health care is of unique importance to human beings,[6] since virtually all conceptions of the good life, or conceptions of how one wants to live, depend upon or assume reasonably good health. Certainly, it is hard to imagine any substantive discussion of human quality of life without reference at some point to the health of the subject, even if only to explain that (and why) the subject is prepared to

[3] Works in this area by scientists include W. M. S. Russell and R. L. Burch, *The Principles of Humane Experimental Technique* (London: Methuen, 1959); H. B. W. M. Köeter and C. F. M. Hendriksen, eds., *Animals in Biomedical Research: Replacement, Reduction, and Refinement* (Amsterdam: Elsevier Science Publishers, 1991); Patrick Bateson, "When to Experiment upon Animals," *New Scientist*, February 20, 1986, pp. 30–32; and M. S. Dawkins, *Animal Suffering*, 2d ed. (London: Chapman and Hall, 1992).

[4] That we might not be deterred is, I think, a real possibility. If the Nazi doctors in the camps of the Second World War had developed a cure for pancreatic cancer as a result of their horrific experiments, would we refuse to make use of that cure, since we condemn the way it was obtained? Or if a treatment for Batten's disease (a brain disorder in juveniles) emerged from genetic work that involved the mistreatment of infants, would we forgo it?

[5] My reason for thinking this stems from the vast number of uses we make of animals in medical research and the varying likelihoods of our being able to replace them all. In this regard, see the white paper of the American Medical Association *Uses of Animals in Biomedical Research: The Challenge and Response*, rev. ed. (Chicago: AMA, 1992). For a very detailed discussion of many of these uses in science, see F. B. Orlans, *In the Name of Science: Issues in Responsible Animal Experimentation* (New York: Oxford University Press, 1993).

[6] This is why, in so many discussions of the macroallocation of resources, health care can seem to demand, if not the biggest, then one of the biggest shares.

sacrifice this important good. It can seem, then, I think, that the unique status of health care shows very clearly the benefit that animal research either does confer or has the potential to confer. As a result, it might be held that there are clear differences between medical contexts and other contexts in which we use animals to our ends.[7]

For example, someone might argue that we do not need further toxicity testing for cosmetics and floor polish; there are enough of these products already on the market. We do not need further use of fur, leather, and other animal skins; there are enough synthetic materials available to clothe and warm us. We do not need to eat meat in order to survive; a properly supplemented vegetarian diet, indeed, even a vegan one, can enable us to survive. I can imagine someone endorsing all these views, yet still having reservations about dispensing with the use of animals in the case of health care. For the removal of illness and the prolongation of life, given the unique status of health and the role health plays in our quality of life, are both obvious and important benefits, and if animal experimentation is required in order to produce them, then I can imagine even some strong animal-welfare supporters wavering in their opposition to this use of animals.[8] Of course, animal welfarists will hope for a new dawn, when such experimentation is no longer required to achieve human health benefits (in my judgment, a vain hope). Until that new dawn is upon us, however, what do we do? How many of us are prepared to forgo all current health benefits produced by animal experimentation, together with all the benefits that xenograft on the one hand and genetic engineering and gene therapy on the other increasingly promise? In fact, I think, the very status of health care in society, which reflects the role of health in the quality of our individual lives, exerts pressure on us not merely to tolerate animal experimentation but also substantially to increase its use. In a word, the more pressing the illnesses that ravage our individual lives, such as AIDS and other scourges, the more pressing the societal case to increase animal research.

Second, it may be thought by many that the use of animals in medicine, from research to teaching, is declining, owing to a number of (well-publicized) factors. Among these, I include such things as (i) continuing doubts about the reliability of animal models for humans (with regard to

[7] One does not want, however, to be too hasty here. In the case of some people, especially the elderly, a pet adds immeasurably to the quality of their lives, while it may only be at the very end of their lives that they require serious health treatment, and then only for a relatively brief additional period of life. If they had to choose, they might well choose the earlier higher quality of life and thus the pet over the later brief extension of life and health care.

[8] The point here, obviously is that an animal liberationist might think that important health benefits are worth the harm to the animal. That this could on occasion be true is obvious. But I am suspicious of a purported animal defender for whom it turns out that any health benefit whatever justifies, say, sacrifice of the animal. In order to be a genuine animal liberationist, I think, there have to be cases where the concern for the animal(s) trumps concern for human benefit.

some human illnesses),[9] (ii) the search for replacements and alternatives, including increasing reliance upon computer models and simulations,[10] (iii) the greatly increased scrutiny by animal-research review committees in hospitals and research facilities of research protocols that involve the infliction of pain and suffering,[11] (iv) increased doubts about using primates, our nearest relatives, at all,[12] and (v) the zany, sometimes violent antics of some members of the animal-liberation lobby. In fact, the number of animals used in medical research continues to number in the countless millions each year,[13] and it would be a foolish person who, should xenograft and gene therapy prove successful on even a moderate basis, would not predict a rush to use (and to raise) research animals on an even more extensive scale than at present.

In genetic engineering, we create "new" creatures by inserting a new gene, from another animal and/or species, into an animal's DNA, and one of the main goals that motivates this engineering is to enable researchers to study the progress and pathology of illnesses in living creatures with a reasonably close genetic and physiological structure to our own. In such engineering, what we are often doing by the insertion of a human gene into a mouse's DNA is attempting to develop a creature that will now be able to contract and be subject to an illness or condition to which it would otherwise not be subject in its original state. Such is the case, for example, with the mouse recently engineered to be subject to amyotrophic lateral sclerosis or Lou Gehrig's disease,[14] an incurable, neurodegenerative disorder that, in time, paralyzes and kills its victim.

[9] For a detailed discussion of this issue, see Robert Sharpe, "Animal Experiments: A Failed Technology," in Gill Langley, ed., *Animal Experimentation: The Consensus Changes* (New York: Chapman and Hall, 1989), pp. 88–117; F. B. Orlans, "Data on Animal Experimentation in the United States: What They Do and Do Not Show," *Perspectives in Biology and Medicine*, vol. 37 (1994), pp. 217–31; H. LaFollette and N. Shanks, "Animal Models in Biomedical Research: Some Epistemological Worries," *Public Affairs Quarterly*, vol. 7 (1993), pp. 113–20.

[10] See, e.g., Michael Balls et al., eds., *Animals and Alternatives in Toxicity Testing* (London: Academic Press, 1983); J. A. Smith and K. M. Boyd, eds., *Lives in the Balance: The Ethics of Using Animals in Biomedical Research* (Oxford: Oxford University Press, 1991), ch. 6; and Martin Stephens, "Replacing Animal Experiments," in Langley, ed., *Animal Experimentation*, pp. 144–68.

[11] See R. A. Whitney, Jr., "Animal Care and Use Committees: History and Current National Policies in the United States," *Laboratory Animal Science*, vol. 37 (January 1987), pp. 18–21; R. Dresser, "Developing Standards in Animal Research Review," *Journal of American Veterinary Medical Association*, vol. 194 (1989), pp. 1184–91; and American Psychological Association, *Guidelines for Ethical Conduct in the Care and Use of Animals* (Washington, DC: American Psychological Association, 1993).

[12] In fact, the protection of primates may be said to be one of the main aims of the animal-rights/animal-liberation lobby. In this regard, see Paola Cavalieri and Peter Singer, eds., *The Great Ape Project* (New York: St. Martin's Press, 1994). For a philosophical discussion of Darwinian-inspired claims that show our closeness to primates, see James Rachels, *Created from Animals* (Oxford: Oxford University Press, 1990).

[13] See Orlans, *In the Name of Science* (*supra* note 5), ch. 5. Her estimate of the number of animals used in the United States alone is 25 to 30 million annually.

[14] "New Mice Are Created to Battle a Disease," *New York Times*, June 21, 1994, p. C6.

Elimination of this dreadful disease—and elimination of Huntington's, Parkinson's, Tay-Sachs, Alzheimer's, AIDS, and all those other diseases and illnesses that genetic engineering might help us to understand and gene therapy to treat[15]—would be an enormous benefit to us in terms of both life expectancy and, perhaps even more importantly, the condition or quality of life lived. It is likely, then, that animal use in the search for such obvious benefits, far from diminishing, is going to increase substantially.

It is fear of just such an increase that appears to be a significant reason behind the worry about allowing these "new" life-forms to be patented, a practice which the United States has permitted since 1988[16] but which the countries of the European Union still do not allow.[17] The worry is that extension of private property rights over the intellectual property that biotechnology and its creation of "designer" animals represents will encourage even more genetic engineering of animals, as the uses to which these "new" animals can be put, medically, begin to reap an economic reward. Of course, this worry may well assume that there is something wrong with genetically engineering animals in the first place, if more of it is to be considered a bad thing as well. Thus, it may be that some will want to claim that *ownership* is an inappropriate relation in which we should stand to these "new" parts of the animal kingdom. Yet, as the Office of Technology Assessment's report *New Developments in Biotechnology* rightly observes,[18] we already stand in this relation to present members of the animal kingdom, as in the cases of pets, farm and zoo animals, and so on. Clearly, a much wider change in society's stance on the ownership of animals will be needed, if ownership of "new" creatures is to be quite the objection that some take it to be.

To alter a mouse and thereby to expose it to illnesses and complaints that are not natural to it, and to which it would otherwise not be exposed, is to make it worse off—in some cases, much worse off—than it would otherwise be. This way of putting the matter need not obscure a distinction that in some contexts it might be important to observe, namely, the

[15] In fact, organizations that cater to certain groups now report genetic advances to their members. E.g., on Alzheimer's disease, see B. Baker, "Of Mice and Men," *Bulletin of the American Association of Retired Persons*, vol. 36, no. 4 (1995), p. 2.

[16] Office of Technology Assessment, U.S. Congress, *New Developments in Biotechnology: Patenting Life—Special Report* (Washington: U.S. Government Printing Office, 1989), p. 12.

[17] I should perhaps qualify what I say here. Restrictions apply both in the European Union and Canada on patenting any new life-form whose complexity *exceeds* that of microorganisms. How much longer these countries will hold out, given the commercial rewards that biotech firms seem destined to make, remains to be seen.

[18] The section of the report that deals with ethics is Baruch A. Brody, "Ethical Issues Related to the Patenting of Animals," in Office of Technology Assessment, *New Developments in Biotechnology*, pp. 127–38. For a general discussion of the ethical issues involved in patenting animals, see R. Dresser, "Ethical and Legal Issues in Patenting Animal Life," *Jurimetrics Journal*, Summer 1988, pp. 399–435.

distinction between already-existent animals taken and used for research[19] and animals brought into existence specifically for the purpose of experimentation. This latter group of animals would not exist apart from experimentation and thus have no lives at all, it may be said, to which their lives under the control of the experimenter could be compared. My point, however, is about comparing the mouse with and without the illness or complaint in question. A mouse whose legs are cut off or whose eyes are blinded or whose body is severely burned seems worse off than it would be if these things were not done to it, whether the mouse already exists or whether it was bred specifically to have these things done to it. The point, a general one, is about the quality of life lived, not about reasons for creating lives in the first place.

Now in medicine, to envisage a fate similar to that of the mouse for a human being, to genetically engineer humans in order to "improve" them, let alone to make them subject to illnesses and complaints, is absolutely forbidden.[20] The word "eugenics" and the specter of the Nazi camps haunt us still, even to the point, for some people, of casting doubt upon the whole Human Genome Project.[21] Yet, it is a version of this hell, it might be said, that we envisage for animals. What brings this ethical question about engineering humans directly into view, therefore, is whether we can distinguish the human case from the animal case sufficiently to justify using the latter but never the former in experiments. Anyone who has followed the animal-rights debates—indeed, anyone who has followed the abortion debate in the United States—will know how difficult it is to find that characteristic or set of characteristics which all and only (existing) humans possess. I return to this matter below.

Another development that is likely to boost our use of animals in medicine is our growing awareness of them as repositories of organs for human transplant. Xenograft, or cross-species transplantation, is an issue, I believe, that is going to play an increasingly important part in debates in medicine about our uses of animals. From Dr. Leonard Bailey's attempt to transplant a baboon heart into an infant ("Baby Fae") at the Loma

[19] One worry here, of course, especially in the case of primates, is depletion of animals in the wild; at another level, however, the worry is over the use of domesticated pets. See Orlans, *In the Name of Science*, ch. 13 ("The Source of Laboratory Dogs and Cats").

[20] But what if one genetically engineers humans, not to make them *subject* to illness, but to make them *resistant* to disease? Can we "improve" people in this way? E.g., can we resort to genetic testing to determine susceptibility to Huntington's disease and use gene therapy to replace the defective gene? If so, then if we were to find a gene correlated with violence, could we use gene therapy on the person carrying the gene as well, even against his or her will?

[21] This is why, increasingly, many people want explicit guidelines governing what may and may not be done to humans. See, e.g., *Draft Convention for the Protection of Human Rights and Dignity of the Human Being, with Regard to the Application of Biology and Medicine* (Strasbourg: Council of Europe, Directorate of Legal Affairs, July 1994).

Linda Hospital,[22] to Dr. Thomas Starzl's recent attempt to transplant a baboon liver into an adult at the University of Pittsburgh Hospital,[23] to the recent decision by an advisory committee of the Food and Drug Administration (FDA) to approve a bone-marrow transplant from a baboon to an adult dying of AIDS in a project directed by Dr. Suzanne Ildstad of the University of Pittsburgh,[24] xenograft has come to seem an important transplant option. The reason is obvious: there is what is sometimes called a transplant gap, i.e., a gap between the number of organs available to transplant and the ever-growing number of persons requiring transplants.[25] Explanations of the shortfall of donors are legion: many people are indifferent to the needs of others for organs; some people are squeamish about having loved ones "cut up" or "mutilated" after death; many cite religious convictions having to do with the person and the body after death as a reason against donation; and many, I suspect, in spite of increased publicity, are simply unaware of the gap between organ need and organ availability. Whatever the full or complete explanation, animals provide a solution to the problem. If enough human donors are not forthcoming for whatever reasons, then why not use, and also breed, types (and strains of types) of animals to make good the shortfall?[26] Genetic engineering could then be employed to assist in getting just the "right sort" of donor we want, and we should be able to produce such donors at will.

To date, while there are some cases of xenograft that are reasonably standard, such as the transplantation of pigs' heart valves into human hearts, the history of xenograft on a rather broad scale, involving organs such as hearts, livers, and kidneys, is a checkered one.[27] A major problem has been the ultimate rejection by the recipient's body of the transplanted organ, a problem presently being addressed by the development of additional and more powerful immunosuppressant drugs. Once this and other problems are overcome, however, I suspect it is only going to take one successful effort by Dr. Starzl or others to put this checkered past

[22] For a very clear discussion of this case, see G. E. Pence, *Classic Cases in Medical Ethics* (New York: McGraw-Hill, 1995), ch. 13. See also my paper "Animal Parts, Human Wholes" (*supra* note 1).

[23] T. E. Starzl et al., "Baboon-to-Human Liver Transplantation," *Lancet*, vol. 341 (January 1993), pp. 65–71.

[24] Pat Griffith, "Panel Blesses Marrow Transplant from Baboon to Man with AIDS," *Toledo Blade*, July 16, 1995, p. A15.

[25] See Lowenstein, "The Transplant Gap" (*supra* note 1). In passing, Lowenstein discusses the transplants by Bailey and Starzl.

[26] Obviously, this is one of the serious motives behind xenografts. It makes animals pay the price of our failure to donate organs. Should xenografts prove successful, I expect the level of donations to fall even further.

[27] See Hilts, "Success in Temporary Transplants of Pigs' Hearts in Baboons" (*supra* note 2); and Philip J. Hilts, "Advances Reported in Using Animal Organs," *New York Times*, May 5, 1995.

behind us and to produce an immense pressure to harvest animal organs for human use.

Here, too, the fact that it is our health and that health is an important and substantial component of our quality of life seems to matter to our view of the ethics of the situation. For example, many of us frown upon the harvesting of animal organs for aphrodisiacs, and numerous animal-welfare groups, together with many governments around the world, have tried to put in place a ban on trafficking in animal parts for this purpose. Again, many people frown upon the use of animal parts, or, indeed, whole animals, in tribal, cultural, or religious ceremonies, whether for the purpose of animal sacrifice or for the purpose of healing through the allegedly magical properties of animals or their parts. When it is a matter of our health, however, the same frowns are not apparent: as I have indicated, far from being deterred in further animal use, we seem to feel the urgency to achieve health-care benefits to a degree sufficient to ensure not merely continued but also increased animal use.

Here, too, the fact that, say, baboons could be specifically bred for the purpose of transplants, so that there would be from this cause no further diminution of baboons in the wild, does not address the central issue. That issue is how research animals are treated and what happens to their lives once they exist, not why we brought them into existence in the first place. If they were not brought into existence, then there could be no adverse treatment of them, whether with respect to pain and suffering or to killing. (I leave aside here philosophical issues having to do with whether existence is a good and whether a case exists for bestowing that good systematically throughout the world.)

The view of animals as repositories of organs for transplant raises immediately the human question: Why may we not regard humans as repositories in the same way? How do the two cases differ? Suppose I offer financial incentives to women with seriously deformed/defective fetuses to bring those fetuses to term for the purpose of harvesting organs: I assume there would be widespread objection. Certainly, in the United States, many people object to envisaging markets in body parts,[28] whatever the practice elsewhere and despite the fact that we have allowed people to sell their (renewable resource of) blood. Ruth Macklin puts her objection very graphically:

[28] They do so, moreover, without regard to spares. That is, one could sell a kidney without dying, but not, of course, a heart. An interesting moral issue can arise. Because there would seem to be a market of sorts in organs in portions of India and China, would it be wrong, if one had the money, to buy an organ abroad and thus by purchase avoid the waiting list in the United States that has built up because of a policy of donation? Discussion of the matter with Michael McDonald, Arthur Caplan, and others has not yet convinced me that it would be wrong.

> Medical and other health services are a special sort of social good, one that should not be subject to the same market forces that govern the sale of pork bellies. The human body, its parts, and its reproductive products are not "mere meat." The United States Congress wisely enacted a law prohibiting commercial arrangements for procuring and distributing organs for transplantation.[29]

Notice that her complaint over markets in body parts is not the usual one, namely, that the poor will be encouraged to sell their organs for money, though doubtless she believes this as well. Rather, it seems to be her view that, somehow, the presence of money taints certain activities or life functions, that buying and selling the human organs involved reduces them to the level of commercial transactions in animal parts. This view of *our* body parts is almost certainly part of a religious vision of the body as God's possession, with an integrity and value that forms part of and flows through this vision, a vision, rather conveniently, that does not cover animal body parts. So far as I can see, the net effect of this vision and Macklin's position at the moment is to sentence countless individuals to death through organ shortages. (I have more to say about this vision and the ethic that underlies it below.)

Moreover, organ shortages substantially increase the pressure to say exactly what the difference is between the human and animal case. For all informed persons are aware today of the existence of humans, e.g., anencephalic infants and those judged brain dead, whose quality of life is so low that we would not wish their lives on anyone, yet where many, perfectly healthy organs could be harvested.[30] Even here, in medical experimentation, we use perfectly healthy animals in preference to those humans. Why? What do we seize upon as the crucial differences between the two, differences that have the convenient and important result not only of protecting us and exposing animals but also of protecting us even when our lives have fallen to a level of abysmal quality, a level that is readily exceeded by the quality of life of a healthy baboon?

This mention of a primate invites a pause. For if the lobby that seeks the abolition of all animal experimentation in medicine is active anywhere, it is over our use of our nearest relatives. Indeed, part of what has come to

[29] Ruth Macklin, "Is There Anything Wrong with Surrogate Motherhood? An Ethical Analysis," in W. H. Shaw, ed., *Social and Personal Ethics* (Belmont, CA: Wadsworth Publishing Co., 1993), p. 286. For a general discussion of the body parts issue, see Arthur Caplan, *If I Were a Rich Man, Could I Buy a Pancreas?* (Bloomington: Indiana University Press, 1993); and Kimbrell, *The Human Body Shop* (*supra* note 2).

[30] See, e.g., A. Capron, "Anencephalic Donors: Separate the Dead from the Dying," *Hastings Center Report*, vol. 17 (1987), pp. 5–9; D. A. Shermon et al., "The Use of Anencephalic Infants as Organ Donors: A Critique," *Journal of the American Medical Association*, vol. 261 (1989), pp. 1773–81.

be known as the Great Ape Project[31] consists in seeking virtually a complete ban on their use in medical/scientific research, including AIDS research. Yet, in the United States, genetic engineering already takes place in primates, and the amount is almost certain to increase. The reason is plain: their very similarities to ourselves genetically, physiologically, pathologically, metabolically, neurologically, etc., make them the model of choice for research into human medical conditions. (I do not here prejudge the case that some might want to make, namely, that primate models are not all that reliable for certain human ailments.)[32] When I speak of an increase in use for this reason, it should be understood that I am referring primarily to the United States. For it is already true, e.g., in Britain, that restrictions on the use of primates in medical/scientific research are significantly more pronounced than they are in the U.S.[33] and that some or a good deal of present research involving them here could not be done there.

In 1994, researchers at the University of Wisconsin primate center successfully isolated stem cells from rhesus monkeys and marmosets.[34] These cells are the parent cells of all tissue in the body, and, with these cells isolated, we could then, through inserting into monkeys the gene that was correlated with a certain disorder, produce monkeys that had that disorder. With this work, the prospect for genetically engineering monkeys that have amyotrophic lateral sclerosis, multiple sclerosis, AIDS, Huntington's disease, cystic fibrosis, etc., took a major step forward. The assistant director of the primate center of the University of California at Davis was quoted as greeting the news of this breakthrough with the remark that "the possibility of transgenic work in primates would be tremendous."[35] It is precisely because of their similarities to ourselves in the ways I have indicated that the ability to produce primates that have human illnesses is so exciting, medically. Just exactly how close to us they are can surprise one: it is estimated, for example, that chimpanzees and humans share almost 99 percent of their DNA, an extraordinarily slight difference, genetically speaking.[36]

So, although genetic engineering in medicine may focus initially upon mice and rodents generally, the whole thrust of the enterprise, if we are to find models similar to ourselves in the relevant respects, in order to study and understand the progression and pathology of illnesses, is to

[31] See note 12.

[32] This is why the choice of animal as experimental subject can be so crucial. See Smith and Boyd, eds., *Lives in the Balance* (*supra* note 10), ch. 5 ("Animals as Experimental Subjects").

[33] See *ibid.*, ch. 10 ("From Theory to Practice"); and J. Hampton, "Legislation and the Changing Consensus," in Langley, ed., *Animal Experimentation* (*supra* note 9), pp. 219–51.

[34] Jeffrey Roberts, "Scientists Take Big Step Toward New Gene Therapy," *Toledo Blade*, November 4, 1994, p. 22.

[35] *Ibid.*

[36] An example of how this estimate figures in an animal-liberationist challenge to the uniqueness of humans can be found in Peter Singer, *Rethinking Life and Death* (New York: St. Martin's Press, 1995), pp. 172–80.

take this research into primates. Yet, it is precisely because of their similarities to ourselves in the ways researchers find useful for their models that a number of people object to the use of primates in medical research, such as the use of baboons in AIDS research. This is the trend in Britain.[37] No one can possibly think, however, that the more stringent British regulations governing the use of primates stem from the fact that the public, the Parliament, and the medical/scientific community have all become hostages of the animal-liberation front. Rather, the greater protections accorded primates there have grown out of the very similarities that make primates the models of choice for the study of human illnesses. An obvious tension is thus apparent: similarity to ourselves is both the reason to use and not to use primates in medical research. The more animal studies reveal both the depth and extent of primates' similarities to ourselves, the more likely this tension will increasingly surface as a reason against primate experimentation—particularly, I suspect, if these matters reach the general public through the media.

Of course, primates may be thought to constitute a special case, in view of the number and degree of similarities to ourselves; but mice and rodents generally are similar to us in being able to feel pain and to suffer, and in having experiences that, as it were, make up the content of their lives. It is *these* similarities that, as we shall see, ultimately matter; for, just as in our case, they are important parts of an experiential being's quality of life.

## II. Animal Experimentation and the Moral Status of Animals

Before turning to these issues, let me be explicit with respect to one position on animal research, namely, abolitionism. In a series of public debates that Tom Regan and I have had around the country, he has come out in favor of complete cessation of animal experiments now, in all regards, at whatever stage, however promising. Abolition is doubtless the view of other animal liberationists, provided, perhaps, that due allowance is made for a more gradual, progressive cessation. As readers will now realize, however, abolitionism is too extreme a position for me, and, I believe, for most other people, for whom the removal of illnesses and the enhancement and prolongation of human lives are clear benefits and thus are judged very much worth having. (I am not concerned here with cases of the prolongation of life to an extent beyond which the person in question wants to live, cases which are today a staple of the euthanasia/physician-assisted suicide debate.) I also think, however, that if any claim of human benefit is to be at all plausible as a justification for animal experimentation, a further argument is needed in order to explain why

[37] See Hampton, "Legislation and the Changing Consensus."

we may not achieve the very same benefits by experiments upon (some) humans. Put differently, if there is a sharp divide between humans and animals, such that, in our laboratories, we may never do to the former what we regularly do to the latter, in what does that divide consist?

I doubt that this dividing line can be found in the areas in which it has traditionally been sought, some of which I consider below. In fact, my view is that there is no sharp dividing line but that a justification nevertheless exists for using animals in preference to normal adult humans in experiments.

### *A. Pain and suffering and the "anything goes" position*

If the abolition of all animal experimentation, including xenograft and genetic engineering, and the forgoing of all benefits in terms of the removal of illnesses and prolongation of human life that animal research confers or promises, is an extreme position, so, too, in my opinion, is the position at the other end of the spectrum, viz., the "anything goes" position. On it, we may do anything we please to research animals (but not, of course, to humans).

If it was ever true that research scientists and others thought to support the "anything goes" position with the claim that research animals, whether primates or rodents, do not feel pain and suffer,[38] it is true no longer. Certainly, those who think that human benefit justifies the infliction of pain and suffering on animals believe that those animals feel pain and suffer. That humans may suffer more and in different ways from animals may be true, but does not affect the point.

Some obvious facts of present-day research practice also bear out the truth of animal suffering. Hospital and research facilities now routinely have ethics review committees that oversee the institutional use and care of animals;[39] they routinely have in place guidelines governing the infliction of pain and suffering upon animals. Medical journals have instituted peer review policies that focus in part on what was done to animals in the course of research and just what in the experiment is supposed to justify the infliction of pain and suffering. Research facilities and medical societies have instituted guidelines that demand that animal suffering be

[38] I put the matter this way because I am unclear just how influential Descartes's claim that animals are not conscious has been in research science. (My suggestion elsewhere that animals are not self-conscious is to be sharply distinguished from Descartes's claim; see my *Interests and Rights* [Oxford: Clarendon Press, 1980].) Recently, the philosopher Peter Carruthers has put forward the claim that animals do not feel pain in a morally significant sense; see Carruthers, *The Animals Issue* (Cambridge: Cambridge University Press, 1992). While his argument is interesting, I do not think it succeeds.

[39] Institutional Animal Care and Use Committees (IACUC), which are concerned with the care and treatment of animals, are a standard part of research facilities in the United States. For a discussion of these and how they arose, see Gary L. Francione, *Animals, Property, and the Law* (Philadelphia: Temple University Press, 1995), ch. 9.

controlled, limited, mitigated where feasible, and justified in the course of research.[40] Where these guidelines are not properly observed, government and/or institutional oversight committees have the power to deny further funding for the research and thereby, effectively, to terminate it. In fact, some scientists today endorse the "three R's" approach to animal research: *reduction* in the number of animals used and the suffering inflicted; *refinement* of the experiment to eliminate, e.g., repetitive uses of animals, continual duplication of results, and, perhaps, the use of animals at all; and *replacement* of animals with nonanimal models.[41]

As is well-known, the mere presence of the capacity to feel pain and to suffer was enough for Bentham to confer moral standing upon animals.[42] Pain is pain, an evil in as well as a blight upon the lives of all who experience it, whether human or animal, and adaptive behavior in both humans and animals is directed toward its avoidance. Pain and suffering matter morally, then, because they are evils in themselves which, additionally, blight the lives of those who experience them.

### *B. The moral significance of animal pain and suffering*

Why cannot one agree, however, that animals feel pain and suffer but deny that these things are morally significant in their case? That is, these things are morally significant if felt by a human but not if felt by an animal. There are a number of different responses to this line of argument, some of which I notice in other remarks below. But one obvious problem seems to be that fewer and fewer people, scientist or layman, give any indication of believing what this response implies. Suppose a child dips the family cat into gasoline and sets it alight: it rings hollow to say that what is morally wrong with this act has nothing essentially to do with the pain and suffering the cat feels. To hold that the act was wrong because it might encourage the child to set fire to his sister, because it might help to induce in the child a character trait that is socially disadvantageous, because it failed to exemplify some virtue or other, because it violated some human duty to be kind to animals, because it was upsetting to and disapproved by other family members or society generally—to hold these views strains credulity, if they are taken in any way to imply that the cat's pain and suffering are not central data bearing upon the morality/immorality of what was done to it. Pain and suffering are moral-bearing characteristics for us, so that, whether one pours scalding water on a child

[40] See, e.g., Smith and Boyd, eds., *Lives in the Balance*, ch. 8.

[41] The three R's stem from the work of Russell and Burch, *The Principles of Humane Experimental Technique* (*supra* note 3). They are much discussed in animal research today and are often portrayed as eventual goals of such research. But they are not endorsed by all scientists; see, e.g., H. Lansdell, "The Three R's: A Restrictive and Refutable Rigmarole," *Ethics and Behavior*, vol. 3 (1993), pp. 177–85.

[42] Jeremy Bentham, *The Principles of Morals and Legislation* (1789), ch. 17, section 1.

or a cat, the morality/immorality of what was done is determined (at least in part) by the pain and suffering of the creature in question. This does not mean that other people may not be more outraged by the scalding of the child (though it would be interesting to know why they were). Nor does it mean that one cannot also point to other moral-bearing characteristics that one may think relevant to the child's (or the cat's) case. It means only that one cannot ignore, morally, the cat's pain and suffering.

### *C. Animal research and animals' quality of life*

What is it about animals that does not warrant our moral attention? The two obvious replies are their pain and suffering and their lives. But pain and suffering are moral-bearing characteristics for us, and, as I have indicated, everywhere in medical research in the United States today there are guidelines that insist that animal suffering be controlled, limited, mitigated where feasible, and justified in the research protocol and/or the actual experiment. Some research-oriented journals in medicine actually require that their editors be satisfied on these counts before agreeing to publish results. Besides, the meticulous care that researchers bestow upon their animals reveals how seriously they take animal suffering, as, indeed, does their frequent insistence that experimental animals be euthanized before they recover from anesthetic.

To suggest, however, that animal suffering counts but that animal lives do not seems implausible, since much of the worry over suffering, in their case as well as our own, is because of the way it can blight and impair a life. If animal lives had absolutely no value whatever, then why, in medical research, do we go to such lengths to try to justify animal sacrifice? Why would we even bother to try to use human benefit to justify the infliction of pain and suffering and the systematic destruction of animal lives? If, however, animal lives have *some* value, then we need to justify their intentional destruction, the destruction of things of value, and the deliberate diminution of their quality of life.

What makes animal lives of value is the same thing that makes human lives of value. The fact that mice, cats, and humans have experiential lives, have unfolding series of experiences, some painful, others not, makes human lives of value and so, too, makes animal lives of value.[43] Certainly, no one can doubt the presence of such experiences in the case of the "higher" animals, especially primates. With experiential lives, the quality of life of an animal can be affected favorably or unfavorably by what is done to it; thus, it has a welfare or well-being that can increase or decrease

[43] Creatures who have experiential lives can have the *value* of their lives adversely affected in different ways. See my "Moral Standing, the Value of Lives, and Speciesism," *Between the Species*, vol. 4 (1988), pp. 191–201; and my "Vivisection, Morals, and Medicine," in Tom Regan and Peter Singer, eds., *Animal Rights and Human Obligations* (Englewood Cliffs, NJ: Prentice-Hall, 1989), pp. 223–36.

according to what is done to it. And it has this welfare or well-being whether or not it was brought into existence specifically for the purpose of experimentation.

What matters in the case of the value of animal life is what matters in our case: it is not life but quality of life that determines the value of a life, and different lives can have different qualities and thus different values.[44] (Indeed, in our case, an important part of contemporary medical ethics turns precisely upon the cases of some unfortunate humans, whose quality of life has so plummeted that even they themselves no longer wish to live those lives.) Once animals have lives of even some value, however, not only the intentional diminution of their quality of life but also the deliberate destruction of those lives must be justified. Nor will it seem quite so obvious that these things *are* justified, by the claim, for instance, that the saving of even a single human life is worth the slaughter of innumerable animals. Such a claim, without further argument, seems to place far too high a value on one part of the moral community as opposed to and at the expense of the value of other parts, something which is especially true, as we shall see, when the favored part has a very low quality of life.

To focus exclusively upon pain and suffering, then, can be misleading. It makes it appear that moral standing is an all-or-nothing affair, that the mere presence of the capacity to feel pain and to suffer, because pain and suffering are moral-bearing characteristics, not only includes one within the community of morally considerable beings but also confers upon one a status equal to that of all other members of the community. In this regard, scalding a cat and scalding a human come out the same way. But in the case of the *value* of the lives of experiential beings, while the value of those lives turns upon the content of their experiences, that content is not the same for all such lives; because of varying content, the lives of experiential beings can have a variable quality and thus a variable value. In *this* regard, the more valuable the life, the greater the moral status, and thereby the greater the moral protections accorded the life. Here, there are different degrees of moral status. Thus, while the presence of pain and suffering in the life of any experiential being is an evil, it is not true that those lives have necessarily the same value. With respect to the different values of lives, moral status is a matter of degree; some lives can have a higher moral status than others. (What is coming may be evident: I do not think that animal life is as valuable as normal adult human life, but I also do not think that all human lives are equally as valuable as normal adult human life.)

[44] My endorsement of a quality-of-life view of the value of a life is compatible with, but does not issue from, my utilitarianism. For a discussion and criticism of my version of it, see, e.g., Tom L. Beauchamp, "The Moral Standing of Animals in Medical Research," *Journal of Law, Medicine, and Ethics*, vol. 20 (1992), pp. 7–16.

*D. Searching for the moral difference between humans and animals*

Defenders of the "anything goes" position must hold that there is a genuine moral difference between the animal and human cases, where pain and suffering or the destruction of valuable lives is concerned. But what is the genuine moral difference between scalding a man and scalding a baboon, between infecting a man with a nervous disorder and genetically engineering a baboon to be subject to that disorder, between killing a man and killing a baboon? The point is not that someone may feel that it is worse to do these things to the man; it is that, on the "anything goes" position, doing these things to the baboon is of no moral concern whatever, even though, as in the man's case, suffering occurs, the quality of life is drastically lowered, and killing takes place. Done to a man, these things are wrong; done to a baboon, they are not. We need to be told how species membership can make this moral difference. For it is not easy, in the case of killing, to see how species membership can constitute a moral difference between two relevantly similar acts of killing (or drastic lowering of quality of life). In the case of pain and suffering, I can see no moral difference at all.

Defenders of the "anything goes" position seem required to come up with the magical characteristic that separates the human from the animal case, that characteristic whose presence, morally, picks out all and only humans and thus prevents our using (some) humans in some of the ways in medicine that we use animals. The search for this magical ingredient has been with us a long time, and the more we learn about animals the more doubts seem to arise about any particular characteristic. Toolmaking, problem solving, rationality, intention, choice, etc.—the list has by now grown lengthy. (Arguably, the Ape Language experiments in part address the characteristic of language use,[45] though I myself remain far from clear about what these experiments show about, e.g., a grasp of the syntactical and semantic components of language.) It is clear that cognitive characteristics have been the preferred ones, since, initially, it might seem that they give us the best chance for showing a marked difference between humans and animals.[46] And one can always go in for ever-finer

[45] Whether chimps can use language creatively, whether they have a grasp of syntax and semantics, etc., are issues that are the object of ingenious learning experiments that might shed some light on the matter, e.g., of whether chimps possess a concept of self. For a discussion of some of these experiments, see Judith de Luce and Hugh T. Wilder, eds., *Language in Primates: Perspectives and Implications* (New York: Springer-Verlag, 1983); E. Sue Savage-Rumbaugh, *Ape Language: From Conditioned Response to Symbol* (Oxford: Oxford University Press, 1986); and D. Premack and A. J. Premack, *The Mind of an Ape* (New York: Norton, 1983). For a recent critical discussion of some of the central issues involved in the claim that apes possess language, see Derek Bickerton, *Language and Species* (Chicago: University of Chicago Press, 1990).

[46] See Beauchamp, "The Moral Standing of Animals in Medical Research." This is the path I have partially followed; see my "Autonomy and the Value of Animal Life," *The Monist*, vol.

distinctions: it is not, e.g., making choices that matters but making choices of a particular kind in a particular way; it is not rationality that matters but being able to reason in a particular way in a particular set of circumstances. Or one can go down the path of greater complexity: what matters for moral standing is being able to envisage oneself as standing in an interlocking set of relationships, where reciprocal behavior is the touchstone of functioning relationships; what matters is that one be possessed of rational autonomy, according to a highly specific, specialized conception of that expression; or what matters, though this can often seem very implausible to all but fervent contractualists, is the capacity to make certain sorts of contracts to do and/or to forbear from doing certain sorts of things to fellow contractees.

Of course, a difficulty with this whole search is to see quite how the preferred characteristic has moral relevance. Thus, what has the absence of choice got to do with moral considerability? Our hospitals, nursing homes, and hospices contain all manner of people who are incapable of choice; those in the final stages of senile dementia, for example, often cannot perform certain (cognitive) tasks even to the level of a baboon. Most of us would doubt, however, that these unfortunate people had ceased to be part of the moral community. (Nor, on my view, *have* they ceased to be part of that community; but the value of their lives has been adversely affected, in the way I indicated above.)

But the major difficulty with this search for the magical characteristic that separates humans from animals is not, as is sometimes claimed, that we can find animals with the preferred characteristic, though increasingly this can appear to be the case. Rather, it is that we can find humans without it. Why, it might be asked, should this matter? Why should we use the cases of unfortunate humans in order to discuss the issue of moral standing at all? The answer, I think, is clear: the argument from benefit does not differentiate among creatures from whom the benefit may be obtained, so that all humans who lack the preferred characteristic potentially fall into that important class. They actually fall into that class unless (i) they can be included in the preferred class through, for example, the interests of those already in that class, or (ii) some other characteristic can be found that, at the last hurdle, rescues all humans that lack the preferred characteristic but no animals. But (ii) merely takes us back to the starting-point of our discussion of moral standing, and (i) makes the inclusion of unfortunate humans in the moral community a contingent affair. The fact of the matter is that we show no inclination to use such humans in medicine as we presently use animals, yet the logic of the

---

70 (1987), pp. 50–63; "The Significance of Agency and Marginal Cases," *Philosophica*, vol. 39 (1987), pp. 39–46; "Animals, Science, and Morality," *Behavioral and Brain Sciences*, vol. 13 (1990), p. 22; and "Moral Standing, the Value of Lives, and Speciesism."

position seems to make this the consistent path. Obviously, there would be one other way of being consistent here: we could refrain from doing to animals what we will not do to those humans who lack the preferred characteristic. This is antivivisectionism and the equivalent of abolition, however, and all of us who are extremely reluctant to give up medical benefits of the sort that animal use has produced and promises to produce will not accept this. Experiments on some humans, then, must be envisaged.

Accordingly, it should be apparent that I regard it as a mistake to think that agency is a necessary condition for inclusion into the moral community. Plenty of humans lack it, yet are held by us to be part of that community anyway and thus beyond the hand of the medical experimenter. Consistency requires that we address the animal case in a similar fashion.[47]

### *E. The "partiality position"*

Another version of the "anything goes" position is possible and sometimes, today, takes on a life of its own. We might think of this as the "partiality position." What this position effectively does is to move away from any search for the characteristic or set of characteristics that separates the human and animal cases and to concede that it is not in terms of any such demarcation that we try to puzzle out how the very same act is wrong if done to a man but right if done to a chimp. Rather, it simply asks why we cannot prefer our own kind and then uses this preference to anchor a moral difference between men and chimps.

There are (at least) three difficulties with the "partiality position." First, to cite a preference for our own kind requires us to say how we determine that kind. Were I to identify my "kind" as male, then as white male, then as heterosexual white male, I take it that many would not think that, if I were to show preference in my moral thinking for this kind, I was on the right moral track. Second, as this example shows, we do not really escape, by citing a preference for our own kind, from the hard work of determining the characteristic or sets of characteristics that will be deemed both factually and morally relevant. Thus, though I cite a preference for a kind, the characteristics I select to determine that kind—male, white, heterosexual—are where all the interesting action occurs, including argument, as it were, both to defend my selection of those characteristics as the relevant ones and to rebut your claims that they are not. Third, in the absence of argument to these ends, my choice of characteristics can look arbitrary (as having no inherently moral dimension more pronounced

[47] I do consider a kind of trustee argument by which to include humans who lack agency in the moral community; see "The Significance of Agency and Marginal Cases."

than the characteristics female, black, and homosexual have) or even biased.

Several years ago, I read a newspaper article about a yacht sinking off the coast of Florida. The owner and his wife managed to escape and to cling to a rubber dingy. They then faced a choice of whether to bring their dog or the surviving member of their crew on board; they chose the dog and tossed a rope to the man. Unfortunately, before they reached land, sharks ate most of the man. Did the couple choose rightly? They cited the dog's years with them, his faithful service, his status as a member of the family, and so on; the man they hardly knew and had taken on only for this cruise. I think the couple made the wrong decision, but not because of anything having to do with species and with failing to prefer their own kind. I think they were wrong because the man's life, all other things being equal, was more valuable than the dog's life.

If a parent can favor her child and have that count as moral, however, why cannot we favor our species and have that count as moral? I think at least part of the answer is this: while a parent stands in a special moral relationship to a child, we do not all stand in a special relationship to each other. Typically, we do not stand to each other, to each and every other, in any special moral relationship whatever; mere membership in the moral community is not, for instance, usually taken to constitute a special moral relationship. (Besides, if it did, since animals are part of the moral community, as I have suggested, there would still be no basis for distinguishing the human case from the animal case.)

Suppose, however, that one insists that being members of the same species forms a special moral relationship: we need now to go further in saying precisely what constitutes a special moral relationship, something that would carry us beyond the scope of this essay. But it seems obvious that there are characteristics of some moral relationships that species membership does not meet. For example, it lies beyond our control whether to be in that special moral relationship, whether to choose to be in it in the first place, whether to denounce, reject, or step outside it, whether to see it as binding upon us, and so on. To stand in a moral relationship where these things are true, as in the case of species membership, can thus seem an unusual view of moral relations generally, so that more must be said in order to show that membership in the species *Homo sapiens* in and of itself does constitute a special moral relationship. I recognize that there is a certain sentimental or romantic view that it does constitute such a relationship, as when the poet John Donne remarks that "each man's death diminishes me"; but the continued plight of the starving poor abroad would seem to indicate that the vast majority of people do not see themselves as seriously diminished by the deaths of such people, at least to an extent sufficient to motivate them to do something about that plight. If our wives and children starve, however, matters look very different.

Perhaps this is only to note that our sentiments of benevolence are limited in their extent, as Hume observed long ago, but it may provide some evidence for the view that we take our wives and children to stand to us in a way morally that others, through merely being members of our species, do not.

Nor must we confuse any such view of species membership with the claim that, to the extent that we are able, we all stand under a duty to render assistance or aid to each other. (I am not here concerned with whether there is such a duty.) I have never seen a defense of this claim that seeks to ground it in species membership. To be sure, it may be that only humans can be under such a duty, but that is not the same thing as to say that the ground of the duty lies in membership in the same species.

### *F. Justifying animal research by appeal to tradition*

Instead of outright appeal to partiality for our own kind, one might seek to achieve the same thing indirectly by locating this appeal in and identifying it as fundamental to our "tradition." Thus, in our tradition, it might be said, humans have been and are regarded differently from animals. Certain things done to research animals have not been done to humans, and the moral and legal protections accorded the latter, whether or not with regard to research purposes, far outstrip the protections accorded the former.

I am skeptical of the invocation of tradition as a justificatory device; for I can see no inherent connection between a practice's being part of one's cultural tradition and its being morally justified. The fact that some traditions include practices of casting wives on the funeral pyres of their husbands, or of mutilating the genitalia of girls, or of killing female newborns does not settle the matter of the morality of those practices. The response that all my complaint is doing is registering that (i) these practices are not part of my tradition, and (ii) there is no accepted way of deciding between different traditions as to the morality of practices, is supposed to generate a justificatory standoff. But what this response ignores, I think, is that public, rational debate of issues can actually erode or change a tradition from within, by the very people who actually have been living under it. It is something of this sort that is occurring in Anglo-American society today.

A religious view of human beings has underlain much of the discussion of what can be done to them. The Judeo-Christian ethic has been with us a long time, and it has served us well. It continues to underlie Anglo-American medical and medical-research practice, and departures from it are often still condemned because they are departures from it. Plainly, it would be foolish to replace it wholesale, without something equally as good to put in its place. But the problem we face is that individual planks of that ethic are coming under increasing attack, quite apart from those involved in the abortion controversies, and the challengers are no longer content to be silenced by the claim that what they propose would be at odds with the ethic. Indeed, the very fact that they are at odds with a part of it is often the reason the challenges are aired in public in the first place.

To give but a single instance, the dictum "Do no harm" has certainly been a fundamental part of the Judeo-Christian ethic, so far as medicine is concerned. There have always been difficult or borderline cases, of course, where disagreement exists on whether this or that constitutes harming. But if the dictum has meant anything at all, it has certainly meant that doctors may not intentionally kill their patients. Yet, today, intentional killing by doctors is a serious option before the public, not in cultures utterly alien to us but in our own culture, informed, as it is, by the Judeo-Christian ethic. I have in mind here, not only such things as, say, killing defective newborns, but also, and perhaps more topically, cases of euthanasia and physician-assisted suicide. Some people presently beg for death and for release from lives that they themselves very much want terminated, and I suspect before much longer a number of states in the United States will have assisted-suicide statutes that survive legal scrutiny,[48] and thus will follow the Netherlands and the Northern Territory in Australia in permitting doctors in certain conditions intentionally to kill their patients. This challenge to the Judeo-Christian ethic is posed not (or not only) by those from an alien culture but by those who otherwise may be sympathetic to much of that ethic. These latter people have simply come, e.g., to rethink the juxtaposition and weight of the values of preservation of human life (out of religious reasons) and of individual autonomy or choice over ending a life. It is not obvious that they are wrong. Of course, one can now retreat into ever-narrower delineations of who counts as an adherent of one's culture or tradition, so as to bar such people; but the appeal to culture or tradition is far less attractive if it is now confined to some very narrowly defined group, say, to those living in the southeast corner of Bowling Green, Ohio, between Campbell Hill Road and Interstate 75. It becomes more difficult to believe in the justificatory role of culture or tradition the narrower that culture or tradition is circumscribed, since such an appeal begins to look much more overtly like the claim "If we practice it, then it is morally right."

The position I am defending on animal experimentation runs up against another plank of the Judeo-Christian ethic: while my position affirms, with an important qualification, that (1) human life is more valuable than animal life, it denies that (2) all human lives are of equal value or worth. It is largely as a result of (2), for example, that discussing human lives in terms of their social worth has distressed so many adherents to the Judeo-

[48] The assisted-suicide statutes of Oregon and Washington have not thus far survived legal scrutiny. For an excellent discussion of challenges out of medicine to the Judeo-Christian ethic, see Peter Singer, *Rethinking Life and Death* (*supra* note 36).

Christian ethic, whereas it is largely as a result of (1) that adherents have set the safeguards for protecting human life at a far higher pitch than those for protecting animal life. If we think of (1) as the *greater-value thesis* and (2) as the *equal-value thesis*, then, as readers may already appreciate, I think that, on quality-of-life considerations, which strike me as the most plausible defense of (1), the greater-value thesis is true but that, on these same considerations, the equal-value thesis is false. And its falsity has dramatic implications for animal experimentation and the use of unfortunate humans in medicine.

## III. Comparing the Value of Human Life and Animal Life

I reject, then, both the abolitionist and the "anything goes" positions on animal experimentation: both are too extreme, though for different reasons. The position I favor, as I have indicated, is a middle or moderate one: it justifies (many but not all) experiments upon animals, while accepting and taking into account the fact that animals are members of the moral community and that, as a result, what we do to them is of moral concern. I have defended parts of this position elsewhere;[49] here, I want to use a discussion of the greater-value thesis to cast doubt upon the equal-value thesis, in order to show how the falsity of this latter claim about humans seriously affects the case for animal experimentation.

### A. The greater-value thesis

My position permits experimentation but treats chimps and mice as morally considerable. Because, as shown earlier, there is no difference between the human case and the animal case where pain and suffering are concerned, if we confine ourselves to experimentation involving killing, then the justificatory parameters to our discussion seem apparent. I require a defense of our using and destroying valuable animal lives that must include not only an account of what makes a life valuable but also, because of our refusal to use and destroy human lives in similar ways, a non-speciesist account of why human life is more valuable than animal life. (This latter point is important, for I have denied that species can be the determining factor in why an act of killing is wrong.) I believe such a defense is readily available to us.

I remarked above that, if a baboon or a man could be killed and the benefits of the experiment obtained, then many might well want to say, all

[49] In addition to the essays referred to in notes 1, 43, and 46, see my "The Ethics of Using Animals for Human Benefit," in T. B. Mepham, G. A. Tucker, and J. Wiseman, eds., *Issues in Agricultural Bioethics* (Nottingham: Nottingham University Press, 1995), pp. 335–44; and my "Moral Community and Animal Research in Medicine," which has been submitted in symposium form together with essays by Carl Cohen, Tom Regan, and Tom L. Beauchamp to *The American Psychologist*.

other things being equal, that it is worse to kill the man. What makes it worse is not species membership but our widely shared view that human life is more valuable than animal life. While the baboon's life has value, it does not have the same value as the man's life, and it is worse to destroy lives of greater rather than lesser value. (This is why I think the yacht owner was wrong, all other things being equal, to save his dog instead of his crew member.) This comparative view of the value of a life will itself be speciesist, however, unless something other than species membership confers greater value on the man's life. If something else *does* confer greater value on his life, then we can point to a genuine moral difference between killing a baboon and killing a man, which can then be incorporated into the argument from benefit in order to justify (some) animal experimentation.

The view that I think best captures this "something else" is a quality-of-life account of the value of a life. I see no reason to give an account of the value of animal life different from that of human life, given that animals and humans are experiential creatures; quality-of-life views give the same account of both. Moreover, such views are widely familiar today: they figure centrally in discussions of the value of life in medical ethics and allied areas, and they even figure prominently in the views of medical researchers about the comparative value of human and animal life, or so I have found in discussion.

The central datum of what matters is not life but, as the furor over euthanasia and physician-assisted suicide shows, the quality of the life lived. Such a view, I think, makes the value of a life turn upon its content or experiences, and this in turn raises the philosophically and scientifically fascinating issue of the nature of, and of the nature of our access to, the subjective lives and inner experiences of animals. Today, very few informed people doubt that animals—certainly, the "higher" animals, most certainly, primates—have such experiences. It is these unfolding experiences that, in part, make up their inner lives and, as a result, make them psychological beings. As we have seen, however, with an experiential life, an animal's quality of life can be affected favorably or unfavorably by what is done to it; it has a welfare or well-being that can be positively or negatively affected by how it is treated.

On my view, the value of a life is a function of its quality; its quality is a function of its richness of content; and its richness of content is a function of its capacities and scope for enrichment. With respect to the value of any experiential creature's life, then, it is of the utmost significance exactly how pronounced a creature's capacities for a rich life are, and, in this, everything that observation and science teaches us indicates that the human case and the animal case differ. I agree that the lives of mice and monkeys have value: both can suffer; both have unfolding series of experiences and thus have experiential lives that can go well or badly; both can live out lives appropriate to their species. The issue is whether the life of the mouse or monkey approaches our own in richness, quality, and value, given its capacities and the life that is appropriate to its species; and observation and the behavioral sciences give us no reason to think so. The capacities for enrichment of, e.g., the mouse are just too limited in number, scope, and variety to lead us to think differently.

Much here is difficult (though fascinating) precisely because of the difficulty of gaining access to animals' inner lives. It will not do, however, to claim that we can know nothing whatever of the richness of animal lives, so that I am barred from making use of that notion. Animal behaviorists sympathetic to the "animal-rights" cause, such as Marian Dawkins, Marc Bekoff, Rosemary Rodd, and Donald Griffin, certainly think we can know something of the richness and quality of the lives of "higher" animals.[50] (Indeed, laymen sympathetic to "animal rights" think the same thing, when they point out that pain and suffering, boredom, inability to scratch or peck, etc., affect a creature's quality of life.) That we cannot know everything about an animal's inner life does not mean that we cannot now know a good deal and learn more in the future. What we do know, however, leads us to believe that the capacities associated with normal adult human life exceed anything associated with the lives of mice, pigs, or even chimps. This difference in capacities for enrichment affects the content of a life and thus affects its quality and value, but nothing here smacks of speciesism or discrimination on the basis of species. Normal adult human life is more valuable than animal life, not because of species membership, but because of richness of content.

The upshot is clear: the greater value of normal adult human life explains why it is worse to kill the man. It amounts to the destruction of something of greater value, and this difference can be placed into the argument from benefit, in order to justify (some) animal experimentation.

With respect to the comparative value of human life and animal life, then, much turns upon the richness of content. Anyone familiar with hospital settings or with medical ethics today knows that difficulties abound with judgments of quality of life even within our own species, when we try, e.g., to judge and compare the quality of life of two patients. But such comparisons are not entirely beyond us: in our hospitals everywhere, decisions are made routinely on all manner of issues, including which patient to invest resources in, which patient to deem one for whom further treatment would be futile, which patient from whom feeding tubes should be withheld or withdrawn, based on quality-of-life judgments. I do not deny, of course, that different factors can be taken into account to affect our judgment. Perhaps the most pressing is how we factor into

[50] Dawkins, *Animal Suffering* (*supra* note 3); M. S. Dawkins, *Through Our Eyes Only: The Search for Animal Consciousness* (New York: W. H. Freeman, 1993); Marc Bekoff, "Cognitive Ethology and the Treatment of Non-Human Animals," *Animal Welfare*, vol. 3 (1994), pp. 75–96; Rosemary Rodd, *Biology, Ethics and Animals* (Oxford: Clarendon Press, 1990); Donald Griffin, *Animal Minds* (Chicago: University of Chicago Press, 1992).

quality-of-life judgments the subjective perception of the patient of how well his or her life is going, even when it is, by all objective criteria deemed relevant by medical people informed as to the patient's illness and condition, going very badly indeed. One area where promising work is occurring in this direction is in the quality-adjusted-life-year (QALY) literature,[51] wherein the scales of measurement of the quality of life—in order to assign a quality-adjusted-life-year ranking and thus to be able to compare and contrast different lives—weave together objective and subjective criteria of richness of content. The point is that such a weaving together is not entirely beyond us.

Interspecies comparisons of richness and quality of life are likely to be even more difficult, though not again impossible. To be sure, as we descend from the "higher" animals, we are likely to lose all behavioral correlates that we use to gain access to the interior lives of animals. Yet more and more scientific work in the animal sciences, including the Ape Language experiments, gives us a glimpse into these interior lives; and the detailed observations of animals in the wild, such as those carried on by Jane Goodall and others, have come to assist us mightily in this enterprise. I suppose that, while the purport of this work is that animal lives are far richer than we have supposed, that in no way amounts to saying that they are as rich as normal adult human lives. (On this count, ethologists are usually cautious.) Several further points are worth noting about comparative assessments of richness.

1. We must not use in some unreflective manner criteria for assessing the richness of human lives as if they applied straightforwardly to animals. I am also not a speciesist in this second-order sense. We must use all that we know about animals, especially primates, in order to try to gauge the quality of their lives in terms appropriate to their species. We must then try to assess the differences we allude to when we say, first of a mouse, then of a human, that each has led a rich, full life. It would be hard to find any scientifically informed person, I think, who would claim that the richest, fullest life of a mouse (or, for that matter, a chimp) approached what we would mean when we used such expressions of a normal adult human being. Once more, this in no way denies that the lives of the mouse and the chimp have a richness, quality, and value; it is rather a comparative judgment based upon the extensive, varied, and active capacities of normal adult humans vis-à-vis mice and chimps.

2. Can I say for *certain*, however, that the mouse's life is not as rich as the lives of normal adult humans? This, I think, is to misconstrue the

[51] For a discussion of QALYs and the QALY literature, see Gavin Mooney, *Economics, Medicine, and Health Care* (Atlantic Highlands: Humanities Press International, 1986); Paul Menzel, *Strong Medicine: The Ethical Rationing of Health Care* (Oxford: Oxford University Press, 1990), ch. 5; and the essays on QALYs by Michael Lockwood, John Broome, and John Harris in J. M. Bell and Susan Mendus, eds., *Philosophy and Medical Welfare* (Cambridge: Cambridge University Press, 1988), pp. 33–96.

issue. What one needs to supply, if one wants to maintain that the two lives are equally valuable, is a reason to believe that, whatever the capacities of the mouse and however limited in number and variety these may be, they suffice to confer a richness upon its life that, if it does not equal, at least approximates the richness of life of a normal adult human. The problem is that it is hard to see how a mouse's keener sense of smell or a dog's keener sense of hearing or an eagle's keener sense of sight can transform the richness of its life to approximate ours. We need evidence and thus a reason to believe this, since by its behavior alone we will not ordinarily think this of, say, a mouse. Nor will the challenge of richness be met by supposing that, e.g., a mouse's keener sense of smell produces in it a delirium so vast that it more than compensates for the difference in extent and variety of capacities in the human case; for it is difficult to see how extensiveness in a single dimension can make up for variety, depth, and extensiveness in numerous dimensions. In judging what counts as a rich, full life for us, we can in no way ignore the variety, depth, and extensiveness of experiences, as if experience along a single dimension constituted richness. To make the claim believable in the animal case, then, we need to see the measure or table of compensation, in order to be able to see how the amount or total of single-dimensional experience can "compensate" for the multi-dimensional experiences.

3. I do not think one can mute the claim of reduced richness in the animal case by retaining a quality-of-life view of the value of a life but dropping any account of the richness of life. For if quality of life is not to be determined by richness—by, that is, the extent, variety, depth, and quality of experiences—I do not know what else is to determine it. Thus, to retain a quality-of-life view of the value of a life requires, in the animal case, that some account of the richness of experience be given that makes us believe that this richness, irrespective of the differences in capacities for enrichment between normal adult humans and animals, equals or approximates our own.

4. One might try to block this requirement by suggesting that, since both human and animal have but one life to live, we should judge each life by its respective capacities. Then, so judged, we could maintain that each creature leads a rich, full, but different (kind of) life. I think this line of argument misses the mark, though in an interesting way. For it seems to imply that these lives, and thus the components that go to make up these lives, are in some sense incommensurable, when in fact the central components, experiences and the unfolding of experiences in a life, appear remarkably alike. (Indeed, it is this fact that helps give us access to the animal case.) We can know somewhat, to a greater or lesser extent, what it is like to be a horse or a dog; that is why we believe that taking the former for runs and playing fetch with the latter enriches their lives. Suppose now that one asks whether we can know exactly how much

running and fetching enriches these lives: the answer seems to be that, while I do not know the precise degree of enrichment in these cases, we also sometimes do not know the degree of enrichment in humans. Based on what we know, we have no reason to believe that the horse's or dog's life possesses anything like the extent, variety, and depth of ways of enrichment that normal adult human life possesses, and we need evidence to make us believe otherwise. Once again, the eagle can see farther and deeper than I can, but we need to be given some reason to believe that this fact transforms the richness of its life to approximate the richness that all the extent, variety, and depth of my capacities confer upon me. What I am seeking to deny, then, is that there are incommensurabilities here, which have the effect of denying me access *in principle* to the richness and quality of animal life. This is an important point to establish, obviously, in order to pursue and to have any hope of resolving the comparative-value question; for it would tend to support the view that the difficulties in fully addressing the richness and quality of life of at least the "higher" animals are ones of degree and not of kind.

5. To give anything remotely resembling an adequate account of the richness of a human life, we must move beyond a picture that is sometimes associated with earlier, utilitarian writers. In this picture—in which the body was, as it were, the container of experiences—in order to have a valuable life, one had to cram as many, e.g., pleasurable experiences as one could into the container.[52] The picture, in other words, was one in which valuable experiences were added on top of one another, so that the value of a life became a function of the total value of the experiences added together. This means that a life can have no more value than the sum total of the value of its experiences, and this is misleading.

While we share many activities with animals, such as eating, sleeping, and reproducing, no combination of such activities comes anywhere near exhausting the richness of normal adult human life, where love, family, friends, art, music, literature, science, and the further products of reason and reflection add immeasurably to our lives. Moreover, and this is the point, we can mold and shape our lives in ways that are themselves additional sources of value; we can live out the lives of academic, artist, or ballplayer. Put differently, we can school our desires in ways appropriate to conceptions of how we want to live, thereby enabling ourselves to fashion a life that is rewarding in the ways we prefer.[53] Even if all this is ultimately cashed out in terms of experiences, it shows that we are creatures that can fashion our lives in order best to suit how we want to live. In this sense, we are not mere receptacles of the experiences we

[52] I discuss the container view in "Utilitarianism and Persons," in R. G. Frey, ed., *Utility and Rights* (Oxford: Blackwell, 1985), pp. 3–19.

[53] One way we can add value to our lives is through the use of our autonomy; see my "Autonomy and the Value of Animal Life" (*supra* note 46).

have; we are not condemned to a life "appropriate to our species," though, to be sure, there are limits to the sorts of lives that we can devise for ourselves.

Here, we reach an important difference with the animal case: it is not *just* a matter of our capacities for enrichment being more extensive than those of animals. We have the prospect of integrating our lives into wholes whose value is thereby enhanced. This integrative task is partly an intellectual one, governed not only by some conception of the good life or how we want to live, but also by psychological awareness of how we are as people—awareness of not only how similar we are to others, including other creatures, but also how different we are as well. This integration of our lives, and the molding and shaping of them, is a central part of the value of our lives and what makes them worth living, a part that we do not share with animals. The receptacle picture of merely adding experiences together can fail to notice this integrative feature of ourselves.

Plainly, a good deal more needs to be said about the richness of life and about the comparative richness of human life and animal life, in order even to begin to pronounce with any certainty in this area. Yet even with the account we presently have, the implications for the equal-value thesis are dire.

### *B. The equal-value thesis*

Normal adult human life is more valuable than animal life and for a non-speciesist reason. Not all human lives, however, have the same richness or scope for enrichment as normal adult human lives; therefore, not all human lives have the same value. As we all know, the quality of human life can plummet to such a degree that not only would *we* not want to live that life but also the very people living it do not want to continue living it. Tragic lives abound, from infants with hypoplastic left-heart syndrome and AIDS to adults who are severely brain damaged or who are dying from amyotrophic lateral sclerosis or from cardiomyopathy. It strikes me as absurd to pretend that lives of these sorts, lives that no one would wish to live or wish others to live, are as valuable as normal adult human lives. I reject, then, what is sometimes called the argument from marginal cases (a rather tasteless expression for tragic human lives), under which all human life, including massively impaired human life, is ceded equal value, with the implication that animal life of a similarly reduced richness and scope for enrichment should be ceded equal value with normal adult human life as well. The equal-value thesis is false, and, what is more, we know that it is.

Of course, this will not stop some, as it were, from continuing to postulate that all human life has equal value, as they seek to reinvoke their view that we are all equal in the eyes of God or, if they no longer wish to go down the path of religion, that we all have equal inherent worth separate from the value of our lives. This latter move, which Tom Regan has adopted,[54] is simply a move toward an abstraction that can hopefully be used to do battle with the fact that not all of our lives are of equal value. Regan is unconvincing over the ground of this abstraction, let alone how we recognize its presence or absence and how we unpack in what it consists. But he has recourse to it because he finds it distasteful to think that, somehow, the breaks of life that produce tragic lives should be able to affect the value of a human life. I agree that it may be distasteful, but it is the case.

### C. *The argument from benefit*

There are, then, human lives that massively deviate from the quality of normal adult human life, and this carries a serious implication, *if* we appeal to the argument from benefit in order to justify animal experimentation. Since the benefit may be obtained from either a human or an animal, what justifies our using an animal with a high quality of life rather than a human with a low quality of life? What we need is a cast-iron guarantee that, without exception, a human life of any quality, however low, exceeds in value an animal life of any quality, however high. I see nothing that can provide that guarantee, and therefore I see nothing that enables us to avoid having to face the issue of experiments upon humans.

This is where the logic of the argument leads. If the argument from benefit justifies animal experimentation, and if one appeals to the comparative value of human life and animal life in order to justify not using humans in order to obtain the benefit, then human experiments confront us. This, I submit, is the situation in which most people in favor of animal research find themselves today: human benefit drives the research, and the greater value of human life is the philosophical undergirding of the refusal to use humans. This undergirding is not up to the task, and it can only be brought up to the task by providing that which perpetually ensures that the quality of a human life will always exceed the quality of any animal life.

This conclusion in no way underwrites a plank of the form that the stronger may use or exploit the weaker for their own ends. For I do not here pronounce upon the merits of the argument from benefit, which determines whether animal experimentation is justified. Rather, the conclusion enters at a different level: *if* the argument from benefit is employed in order to justify experimentation, then we face the question of which creatures to use. The answer is that we use those of lower quality of life. There is nothing exploitative about this answer. The case of lifetaking is simply on a par with lifesaving. If we can save a life of higher

[54] Tom Regan, "The Case for Animal Rights," in Peter Singer, ed., *In Defense of Animals* (Oxford: Blackwell, 1985), pp. 13–26.

quality, we select it over one of lower quality; if we take life, and we can choose to take one of lower quality, then we select it over one of higher quality.

Now I am in no doubt that most people will want to resist any prospect of using some humans as we presently use animals; but then how do they, as morally serious people, persist with animal experimentation? Down this path lies abolitionism. But then how likely are we to give up further medical benefits that medical research on animals holds out for us? Down this path lies human illnesses and deaths, terrible things that animal research may well continue to do something about. On balance, will not most of us decide in favor of continued research? But the cost, experiments on some humans, is very heavy. I recognize, obviously, that many people will want to appeal to the side effects of any prospect of experiments on humans, such as outrage, destruction of the doctor/patient relation, and so on. Side effects, however, often have a way of disappearing, as a case is argued rationally in public for why a particular change in past practice should be envisaged. Against this, devotees of slippery-slope arguments rise up when it appears that such public debate might actually have an effect: any change in practice of the sort envisaged, and we will slide into the abyss. Permit one abortion, and we shall soon be killing normal adult humans; permit one case of physician-assisted suicide, and doctors will soon be killing off more and more healthy persons. I do not deny that slippery-slope arguments are sometimes important and germane to the permissibility of what is envisaged; but I cannot see any reason whatever to treat the fear of a slippery slope as if it were an indication that, inevitably, we shall slide down the slope. My grandmother told me that, if I took a drink, I should end up a drunkard. She was wrong. To be sure, if I never took a drink, I could never end up a drunkard; but then I should have missed one of the glories of France and the pleasures of life.

It is, I think, important that in 1995 the American Medical Association (AMA) took a positive stance on the permissibility of using anencephalic infants as organ donors.[55] On my view, infants without a brain lack the capacities for enrichment that could confer any quality of life upon their lives, yet they have organs that could be harvested for transplant. Even here, we have used perfectly healthy animals in their stead. Why? Notice that one cannot use in this case an argument of the form that this being has had a rich life but simply has fallen into a catastrophic condition:

[55] See Gina Kolata, "Doomed Babies Are Seen as the Donors of Organs," *New York Times*, May 24, 1995; and Council on Ethical and Judicial Affairs, American Medical Association, "The Use of Anencephalic Neonates as Organ Donors," *Journal of the American Medical Association*, vol. 273 (May 24/31, 1995), pp. 1614–18. In January 1996, the AMA temporarily suspended its approval of anencephalic donors. One reason for the suspension was that some wanted to argue that such infants, born with a brain stem, had not been shown to be legally dead, i.e., without brain function at all. See "AMA Opposes Taking Organs from Brain-Abnormal Babies," *New York Times*, January 7, 1996, p. A11.

anencephalic infants have never had a rich life and, because of incapacity, never will. What could possibly justify harvesting a perfectly healthy baboon's organs in place of the organs of these infants? Again, notice how several ways of thinking of such infants cohere with my argument. One could argue that, without a brain (though some may have a brain stem), they are not human at all. But then they would not enjoy the protections of humans, and harvesting could be envisaged at once. Again, one could argue that, in spite of the presence of a brain stem, they are brain dead.[56] But then why would that not again make them candidates for harvesting? One can always appeal to the fact that such infants are the children of someone and that these individuals might well have their quality of life adversely affected if harvesting of organs took place. But then we could at least begin to appeal to the nobility of donating organs to save or assist other infants in order to reduce the adverse impact upon them of harvesting, much the way, in fact, that the AMA envisages.

As I see it, then, we either endorse abolitionism or envisage the use of humans in medical experiments, if we employ the argument from benefit to justify animal research and if we appeal to the comparative value of human life and animal life to justify our using animals but never humans. The only way out of this terrible dilemma, so far as I can see, is if one can cite that which makes it always, without exception, the case that a human life of any quality, however low, is more valuable than an animal life of any quality, however high. I know of nothing to cite.

Finally, why cannot one, if I am right about this dilemma, simply switch to a different view of the value of a life? I think we are now aware, however, what that view will conveniently look like: even though we know that there are human lives that deviate massively from the quality of normal adult human life, lives that no one would want to live or want anyone else to live—lives, in fact, that we would move heaven and earth not to live or to have a member of our family live—we will find some way to allow even those lives to trump the lives of animals, always and in every case. This strikes me as a little *too* convenient for moral comfort.

*Philosophy, Bowling Green State University*

[56] This is the position Robert M. Veatch adopted during a presentation at a recent conference on animal experimentation, sponsored by the Kennedy Institute of Ethics of Georgetown University.

# A WORLD OF STRONG PRIVACY: PROMISES AND PERILS OF ENCRYPTION

By David Friedman

A major theme in discussions of the influence of technology on society has been the computer as a threat to privacy. It now appears that the truth is precisely the opposite. Three technologies associated with computers—public-key encryption, networking, and virtual reality—are in the process of giving us a level of privacy never known before. The U.S. government is currently intervening in an attempt, not to protect privacy, but to prevent it.

Section I of this essay is an explanation of the technologies, intended to demonstrate that current developments, if they continue, will produce a world of strong privacy, a world in which large parts of our lives are technologically protected from the observation of others. Section II is a discussion of the likely consequences, attractive and unattractive, of that change. Section III is a brief account of attempts by the U.S. government to prevent or control the rise of strong privacy.

## I. The Technologies

One way to keep your communications private is to make sure that nobody can intercept them. If you are worried about eavesdroppers, check under the eaves—or hold your confidential conversations in the middle of large open spaces. Send letters only by trusted messengers.

This approach has become more difficult over time, and in some contexts, such as cellular phone calls, very nearly impossible. Broadcast signals can be intercepted. A complicated switching network, such as the phone system, can be tapped. E-mail goes from one computer to another through a series of intermediates; someone controlling any of the intermediate machines can intercept the message. How, in such a world, can we preserve privacy?

One approach is by legal restrictions on the interception of messages and the use of information. Tapping phone lines is, under most circumstances, illegal. The use of even legally obtained information is restricted by legislation such as the Fair Credit Reporting Act (1970).

An alternative, and in many contexts superior, approach is to encrypt the message, so that even if it is intercepted it cannot be read. Parents spell out messages they do not want their small children to understand; when the children learn to spell, the parents switch to using a foreign language. The military and intelligence services rely on more sophisticated applications of the same principle to protect sensitive communications.

Until quite recently, encryption suffered from two serious handicaps. Encrypting and decrypting were slow and laborious processes, making encryption of any save highly sensitive information more trouble than it was worth. And in order for B to decrypt the message received from A, B had to get from A the information necessary for decryption: the key. If the key was intercepted or stolen, the encrypted message could be read.[1]

Both problems have been solved. With modern computers, written messages can be encrypted and decrypted faster than they can be typed. It is becoming possible to encrypt and decrypt even spoken messages as fast as they are spoken.[2]

The problem of transmitting keys was solved by the invention of public-key cryptography.[3] A public-key encryption scheme involves two keys, each of which functions as an inverse of the other: if key 1 is used to encrypt a message, key 2 is required to decrypt it, and vice versa.

This sounds puzzling; how can someone have the information necessary to encrypt a message yet be unable to decrypt it? A description of how actual public-key algorithms work would require a level of mathematics unsuited to this volume, so I will instead describe a form of public-key encryption designed for a world more mathematically primitive than our own.

### *A. Public-key encryption: A very elementary example*

Imagine a world in which people know how to multiply numbers but not how to divide them. Further imagine that there exists some mathematical procedure capable of generating pairs of numbers that are inverses of each other: X and 1/X. Finally, assume that the messages we wish to encrypt are simply numbers.

[1] For the history of cryptography, see David Kahn, *The Codebreakers* (New York: Macmillan, 1967).

[2] In addition to the Clipper Chip, discussed below, there are now two public-domain programs which allow someone equipped with an ordinary personal computer and a modem to decrypt and encrypt speech in real time: PGPfone (released for the Macintosh, with a DOS/Windows version coming) and Nautilus (released for DOS/Windows).

[3] The idea of public-key cryptography is due to Martin Helman and Whitfield Diffie. The first successful implementation is due to Ronald Rivest, Adi Shamir, and Leonard Adelman, who patented their algorithms and formed a company, RSA Data Security. See Whitfield Diffie, "The First Ten Years of Public-Key Cryptography," *Proceedings of the IEEE*, vol. 76 (1988), pp. 560–77. A good summary for the lay reader is Paul Fahn, "Answers to Frequently Asked Questions about Today's Cryptography"; the current version is available by anonymous FTP from RSA.com. Information is also available from RSA's home page on the World Wide Web at: http://www.rsa.com/.

I generate a pair X, 1/X. To encrypt the number M using the key X, I multiply X times M. We might write:

$$E(M,X) = MX$$

—meaning "Message M encrypted using the key X is M times X."

Suppose someone has the encrypted message MX and the key X. Since he does not know how to divide, he cannot decrypt the message and find out what the number M is. If, however, he has the other key 1/X, he can multiply it by the encrypted message to get back the original M:

$$(1/X)MX = (X/X)M = M$$

Alternatively, someone who knows only 1/X could encrypt a message by multiplying it by 1/X, giving us:

$$E(M,1/X) = M/X$$

Someone else who knows 1/X but does not know X has no way of decrypting the message and finding out what M is. But someone with X can multiply it by the encrypted messages and get back M:

$$X(M/X) = M$$

So in this world, multiplication provides a primitive form of public-key encryption: a message encrypted by multiplying it with one key can only be decrypted with the other.

Public-key encryption depends on mathematical operations which, like multiplication and division in my example, are very much easier to do in one direction than the other. In the real world, we know how to divide and our computers can divide large numbers rapidly, so we must find other operations to base public-key encryption on. The RSA algorithm, for example, depends on the fact that it is easy to generate a large number by multiplying together several large primes,[4] but much harder to start with a large number and find its prime factors.[5] The keys in such a system are not literally inverses of each other, like X and 1/X, but they are functional inverses, since either can undo (decrypt) what the other does (encrypts).

[4] A prime is an integer divisible only by itself and 1. The number 7 is a prime, 15 is not (its prime factors are 1, 3, and 5). (The RSA algorithm is named for its inventors: Rivest, Shamir, and Adelman [see note 3].)

[5] Modern encryption involves very large numbers. A 128-bit key, for example, would be represented by about a thirty-eight digit number—say:

27,602,185,284,285,729,509,372,650,983,276,043,748.

*B. Using public-key encryption*

Suppose I wish to make it possible for other people to send me messages that only I can read. I publish one of my two keys, called my "public key," where anyone can read it—in the phone book or its future equivalent. The other key, my private key, I keep secret. Anyone who wishes to send me a message encrypts it using my public key. Decrypting it requires my private key, which only I have. The private key cannot be deduced from the public key at any reasonable cost in computing time.[6]

Suppose I wish to send someone a message and prove that it comes from me. I encrypt the message with my private key. The recipient decrypts it with my public key. The fact that he ends up with a message and not gibberish implies that it was encrypted with my private key—which only I have.

Public-key encryption thus solves two problems at once. It provides secure communications—messages that can only be read by the intended recipient. And it provides the digital equivalent of a signature, a way of proving the origin of a message. By encrypting a message with both the intended recipient's public key and the author's private key, one can produce a message that is both secure and signed.[7] Only the author could have created it, since it was encrypted with the author's private key; only the intended recipient can read it, since it must be decrypted with the intended recipient's private key.

Public-key encryption as it now exists, implemented in readily available computer programs such as PGP,[8] provides a secure and verifiable

[6] This statement, like other statements about the security of encryption schemes, depends in part on the length of the key. The longer the string of numbers making up the key, the more difficult it is to break the encryption.

[7] I am describing simpler implementations of public-key encryption than those in common use, in order to keep the explanations in the text from becoming too complicated. Public-key encryption is slower than some equally secure single-key encryption schemes, so in practice the message is encrypted with a single-key system such as DES (Data Encryption Standard), the DES key is encrypted with the recipient's public key, and both are sent. The recipient uses his private key to decrypt the DES key, then uses that to decrypt the message.

Digital signature protocols in current use, such as those supported by Verisign, Inc., are also more complicated than the one I have described. The sender applies a hash function to his message to create a message digest, encrypts that with his private key, and sends the message and the encrypted digest. (A hash function takes a long string of characters, such as a message, and produces a number from it, called the message digest; the number, although large, is much shorter than the string. The important characteristic of a good hash function is that it is easy to calculate the digest from a message, but very difficult, given a digest, to create a message that will hash to that number.) The recipient calculates the digest for himself by hashing the message, decrypts the digest attached to the message using the sender's public key, and checks that the two digests match. Since it is impractical to change a message without changing its digest (i.e., to find another message that hashes to the same value), a digital signature not only guarantees the sender's identity, it also guarantees that the message has not been altered since it was signed. Since the digest is much shorter than the message, encryption and decryption are faster with this protocol than with the simpler one described in the text.

[8] PGP (for Pretty Good Privacy) is a public-domain encryption computer program in widespread use, available for both DOS and Macintosh computers. It allows a user to create

way of transmitting E-mail. It thus provides strong privacy, privacy that depends neither on secure communication channels nor on legal protection, for a small but increasingly important class of communications. It permits individuals to send messages across the Internet with reasonable confidence that if intercepted, even by the Federal Bureau of Investigation (FBI) or the National Security Agency, they cannot be read.

Several technological developments already in progress will greatly increase the importance of encryption. One is the availability of more and more powerful computers, which make it possible to encrypt more and more complicated signals. Currently it is easy to encrypt text, and possible to encrypt speech, in real time (as fast as it is typed or spoken); in the near future it should be possible to do the same for speech plus video.

Increasing computer power not only makes it easier to encrypt, it also makes it easier to break encrypted messages. As computers become more powerful, users must lengthen their keys if they do not wish their messages to become easier to crack. With the encryption algorithms and the approaches to cracking them currently in use, increasing the key length increases the time needed to crack an encrypted message by more than it increases the time needed to encrypt it, so increases in computing power favor encryption over cracking.[9]

A related development is the increased use and bandwidth[10] of computer networks. At present, a few tens of millions of people have access to the Internet. The number is growing rapidly; it seems likely that in another decade or so, a majority of the population of the developed world will have access to the Internet or something similar. At present, Internet connections go through channels of varying bandwidth, from modems up to fiber-optic cables. The result is a transmission rate adequate for text messages for essentially all users, for transmission of still pictures for many users, and for transmission of real-time audio-video signals for very few. Changes currently in progress should result, over a decade or two, in a network with sufficient bandwidth to support real-time audio-video for most users.

One reason such a capacity is important is another technology: virtual reality. The year is 2010. From the viewpoint of an observer, I am alone in my office, wearing goggles and earphones. From my viewpoint, I am at a table in a conference room with a dozen other people. The other people

his own pair of keys, keep track of other people's public keys, and encrypt and decrypt messages. The latest released version can be found at the MIT distribution site for PGP, located on the Web at: http://web.mit.edu/network/pgp.

[9] If one wishes current messages to stay private for the next ten years, one should use encryption adequate to defend against the computers of ten years from now—otherwise someone can intercept and record your messages now, then decrypt them when sufficiently powerful computers become available.

[10] The bandwidth of a communications channel is a measure of how much information it can carry—the wider the bandwidth, the more information can be transmitted per second.

are real—seated in offices scattered around the world. The table and the room exist only in the mind of a computer. The scene is being drawn, at a rate of sixty frames a second, on my goggles—a little differently for each eye, to give three-dimensional vision. The meeting is virtual, but, to my sight and hearing, it might as well be real. It is sufficiently real for the purposes of a large fraction of human interactions—consulting, teaching, meeting. There is little point to shuttling people around the world when you can achieve the same effect by shuttling signals instead. As wideband networks and sufficiently powerful computers become generally available, a large part of our communication will shift to cyberspace.

Encryption makes the content of messages private. Even if the content is private, however, the mere fact that A is communicating, or doing business, with B provides information to observers—especially if B is a criminal or a supporter of unpopular political positions. That raises two problems for a technology of privacy: how to make cash transactions private and how to prevent monitoring of who is talking to whom. There are solutions to both.

### *C. Digital cash*

The solution to the first problem is digital cash, invented by cryptographer David Chaum.[11] It is a way of using encryption to permit payments in which neither payer nor payee can identify the other, and the creator of the private money they are transferring can identify neither. A less sophisticated equivalent would be transactions using discrete banks in a trustworthy jurisdiction—perhaps a nation that makes its living in part through banking privacy. With digital cash, payments can be made by simply sending messages—without either party knowing the identity or physical location of the other. The cash can pass from one person to another through a long and anonymous chain, before the final recipient returns it to the issuing bank to be redeemed for (say) dollars.

### *D. Anonymous remailers*

One solution to the second problem already exists: anonymous remailers. An anonymous remailer is a site on the Internet which receives messages, each with the address of its destination attached, and then resends them to that address. An observer sees a thousand messages come into the remailer and a thousand come out, but even if he knows the source of

[11] Extensive information on Chaumian digital cash can be found on the World Wide Web at: http://www.digicash.com/publish/pu_fr_dc.html. See also David Chaum, "Security without Identification: Transaction Systems to Make Big Brother Obsolete," *Communications of the ACM*, vol. 28, no. 10 (October 1985), pp. 1030–44. The Mark Twain Bank of St. Louis recently announced that it is implementing digital cash in partnership with Digicash.

each incoming message and the destination of each outgoing one, he does not know which sender is communicating with which recipient.

Anonymous remailers can use encryption to prevent a spy from either reading destination addresses on intercepted incoming messages or matching incoming and outgoing messages by comparing them. The original sender encrypts the message with the recipient's public key, then encrypts both that encrypted message and the destination using the remailer's public key. The remailer uses his private key to decrypt, leaving him with a message that he cannot read and a destination that he can.

What if the remailer is secretly working for the observer? The solution is to relay a message through multiple remailers. As long as at least one is honest, the observer cannot match up sender and receiver. With sufficiently high speed networks and computers, the whole process occurs fast enough to introduce no noticeable lag. Using digital cash, anonymous remailers can function as private businesses, selling privacy at a few cents an hour.

A more sophisticated solution to the problem of concealing who is talking with whom has been proposed by David Chaum. It is a procedure by which a group of individuals jointly generate a signal in such a way that no subgroup can identify the contribution of any single member. If all save one member of the group has nothing to say, that one member is the source of the message—but no member or group of members (short of everyone else in the group) can tell which one it is.[12]

## II. A World of Strong Privacy

Consider a world in which the technologies I have described exist and are widely available. What will it look like?

In that world, any transaction that can be carried out in virtual reality over a network is secure—it cannot be observed by private snoops, the FBI, or the Internal Revenue Service (IRS).[13] Not only is the content of the transaction private, so is the identity of the parties. I can plot a crime, or address a mass meeting, anonymously.

[12] The procedure is described in David Chaum, "The Dining Cryptographers Problem," *Journal of Cryptology*, vol. 1 (1988), pp. 65–75; and David Chaum, "Achieving Electronic Privacy," *Scientific American*, August 1992.

[13] The statement that a transaction cannot be observed must be qualified in three ways. The sorts of encryption I have been discussing are all vulnerable to an observer with a big enough computer and enough time. A transaction is secure if no such observer exists who wants to crack it. And even transactions that are cryptographically secure may be vulnerable to attacks that do not depend on encryption, such as secretly searching your house for the piece of paper on which you have imprudently written down your private key. Even in a world of strong privacy, one must still be careful. Finally, even encryption schemes that are believed to be secure are not, in most cases, provably secure—there is always the possibility that a sufficiently ingenious attack, or some future development in the relevant branches of mathematics, could dramatically reduce the time needed to crack them. For a discussion of recent experience with the vulnerability of encryption schemes, see E. F. Brickell and A. M. Odlyzko, "Cryptanalysis: A Survey of Recent Results," *Proceedings of the IEEE*, vol. 76 (1988), pp. 578–93.

One disadvantage of anonymity at present is that an anonymous agent has no reputation to protect and therefore cannot be trusted. Digital signatures solve that problem. A firm can go into business by publishing its public key. Thereafter, anyone who sends messages encrypted with that public key knows he is dealing with that firm, since nobody else can read them. Anyone who receives messages that make sense when decrypted with that key knows they are from the firm. Thus, a firm or an individual can have an identity and a reputation, despite the fact that nobody outside the firm knows where it is located or who controls it.

This world has both advantages and disadvantages in comparison with ours. One obvious advantage is freedom of speech that does not depend on Congress or the courts. What cannot be observed cannot be controlled.

A more ambiguous consequence will be a severe restriction on the ability of governments to tax. In a world of strong privacy, I can sell my services as teacher, lawyer, or business consultant without anyone, even my customers, knowing who I am. My business name and attached reputation are defined by my public key. A large and growing part of the economy will no longer be taxable.

The IRS has the alternative of deducing income from expenditures, a traditional approach to dealing with those whose income is hard to observe. In a world of strong privacy, however, a substantial part of my expenditures will also be invisible, spent as digital cash to buy information and services over the net. In such a world, taxes, whether of production or consumption, will shift away from information goods and services and toward goods that can be physically observed: food, housing, fuel.

Another consequence of strong privacy will be to make certain sorts of legal regulation impractical. In many ways, this will be a good thing. Political censorship, for example, will become enormously more difficult. Many professions, such as medicine, will no longer be able to use professional licensing or trade barriers to restrict competition.

Other consequences are less obviously attractive. In a world of strong privacy, violation of copyright becomes easy. A pirate publisher, operating anonymously, will be able to set up a commercial archive of copyrighted books, music, or programs and sell them over the net just like a legitimate dealer. His customers will be able to communicate with him and he with them, but neither party to the transaction need know the physical location or true identity of the other.

Privacy might also be used to protect other illegal enterprises. Buying and selling of trade secrets, purchasing embarrassing information for purposes of blackmail, even hiring a contract killer, become easier in a world where businesses can operate, and establish reputations, without revealing their physical location or proprietors.

One way to prevent these threats is by preventing the world I have described from coming into existence; in Section III, I discuss that possibility. A more interesting approach is to find ways of using the technologies that create the problems to solve them, or at least to reduce their costs.

Consider the case of copyright. In a world of strong privacy, intellectual property law is unenforceable. Contract law, however, is still enforceable because parties choose whom to contract with. I can insist on contractual partners providing adequate guarantees of performance, whether by revealing their identity (in a jurisdiction that enforces contracts), posting a bond with a reputable bonding agency, or simply having a reputation in cyberspace (attached to their public key—which is what defines their identity in cyberspace) that they do not want to lose. This suggests the possibility of using (enforceable) contracts to substitute for (unenforceable) intellectual property law.

Suppose I have created an item of intellectual property, say a book. Imagine that there is a way to label each separate copy of the book, so that if a pirated copy appears I can prove which original it is from. I protect my intellectual property by requiring purchasers to agree to be liable for substantial damages if a pirated copy made from their original is offered for sale.

There are two obvious problems with this approach: ability to label and willingness of purchasers to assume liability. Let us start with the first.

Suppose I am writing a book. From time to time I come to a sentence that I could write in either of two equally good ways. Instead of choosing one, I record both. When I am done, I have a book with a hundred such pairs of variant sentences. Every time I sell a copy, my computer chooses at random which variant of each sentence to use, creates a copy using those choices, and records the copy and the buyer. With a hundred variant sentences, there are $2^{100}$ possible versions of the book—roughly a thousand billion billion billion. If a pirated copy appears, I compare it with the record of the copies sold and sue the purchaser of the copy on which it was based.

Unfortunately, a clever pirate can defeat this form of labeling. The pirate buys ten copies instead of one. His computer compares the ten versions in order to identify the variant sentences, then randomly chooses one sentence from each pair to create an eleventh version—which he offers for sale.

While this form of labeling does not work on something as simple as a book, it can work for more complicated forms of intellectual property. For a simple example of why it can work, consider an arithmetic text in which both questions and answers exist in variant versions. A pirate who buys ten copies and picks alternatives at random will produce a copy in which questions and answers no longer match.

That particular example is too simple; the pirate would recognize the problem and vary questions and answers together. For a workable example, consider a computer program. A program can be varied in a multitude of ways that are irrelevant to how it works—provided that everything varies together. It does not matter whether a particular variable is located at memory location 2,000 or 3,000—provided that every reference to that variable points to the right location. To produce labeled copies, the programmer writes the program in his preferred source language, then uses a variant compiler to produce ten thousand different machine language versions, all functionally equivalent. A pirate can, if he wishes, buy ten versions and combine them to make an eleventh—but its probability of running will be very close to zero.[14]

Thus, the problem of labeling copies is solvable for complicated forms of intellectual property, such as computer programs, although not for simple forms, such as books. For complicated property, it should be possible to prove which purchaser is responsible for letting his copy be pirated. We are left with the problem of persuading purchasers to agree to be liable if pirated copies are made from their original.

Whether they are willing to agree to accept such liability depends on how likely it is that their copy will get out without their permission. In our world, where my master copies of programs are located on disks in an unlocked drawer of my office, I would be reluctant to agree to be liable for thousands, perhaps hundreds of thousands, of dollars of damages if they were stolen. But we are considering a world where strong encryption is in common use. In such a world, my copy of a program exists inside my computer system, encrypted with a key that only I have, and therefore is unlikely to get out without my cooperation. While there is some risk, it should be less than the risk I now take, every time I drive, of getting in an accident and finding myself liable for a large damage payment.

My conclusion is that contract law will provide an effective way of protecting some intellectual property. Other intellectual property will be protected by other technological means.[15] Producers of intellectual property that cannot be protected will have to make money from their work in less direct ways.

There are many different indirect ways to get paid for intellectual property—although they are not perfect substitutes for legal protection. A

[14] This is the case because a computer program is a set of instructions that go together precisely. If one instruction tells the computer to fetch a number from a particular memory location, the instruction that put the number there has to have put it in the same location. If version one of the program stores the number in location 358,273, and version two stores it in location 527,203, then a program that gets its "put" instruction from version 1 and its "fetch" instruction from version two is not going to work. Multiply that problem by ten thousand instructions, and the chance that a program assembled from several different versions will run becomes essentially zero.

An alternative way for a would-be pirate to proceed is to try to decompile the program—deduce the source code from the machine language version—and then recompile, producing his own different but functionally equivalent version of the program. Decompiling is a hard problem—just how hard is a matter of controversy. It can be made harder by the use of compilers designed to produce machine code whose detailed working is hard to deduce.

The approach I am describing does not protect against copying observable features of a program; whether and when such copying violates present U.S. copyright law is a complicated question, the answer to which is not yet entirely clear.

[15] Another way of protecting a computer program is to keep it on the owner's computer, and sell, not the program itself, but the right to access it over the network.

children's movie might, as some do, collect large revenues from the sale of toys based on it—even in a world of strong privacy, intellectual property law is still enforceable when what is being sold is a physical object (a toy) rather than information (the text of a book). Programmers sometimes ask for—and sometimes get—payments for the use of their shareware programs, based on moral suasion or tie-ins with less easily pirated goods, such as support. Philip Zimmermann received no royalties for writing the encryption program PGP, but the effect on his reputation may have greatly increased his future earning power.

The new technology produces both new problems for intellectual property protection and new solutions. The same should be true in other contexts, such as the problem of criminal firms with brand-name reputations. Law will provide less protection than before, since it will be harder to enforce, but potential victims will be more able than before to defend themselves through privacy. It is hard to have a competitor killed, or even to steal his trade secrets, if you have no idea what he looks like or where on the globe he lives.[16] The larger the fraction of one's activities that take place in cyberspace, the more practical protection through anonymity will be.

As the example of intellectual property suggests, while strong privacy makes more difficult the enforcement of laws imposed on unwilling parties, it permits enforcement of agreed-upon rules and greatly facilitates freedom of association. One implication is the possibility of replacing, for a considerable range of human activities, politically generated law with market generated law.

Consider a simple, and real, example: a mail-group. Individuals with E-mail access wish to hold a conversation on some topic of mutual interest. One of them creates an E-mail address for the group and sets up his computer so that E-mail incoming to that address is relayed back to everyone on the list.

Such a mail-group is, among other things, a proprietary community. The list administrator controls the list of addresses from which E-mail is accepted for the group and to which E-mail is echoed. He can make any rules he likes about what other members must do to remain in the group. In practice, this often means rules defining the level of courtesy required and excluding conversations on subjects unrelated to the purpose of the group. Thus, such a group exhibits a simple form of private law.[17]

[16] This is one of the central ideas of "True Names," a science fiction story by a computer scientist who was one of the early writers to recognize the social implications of computer networks and associated technologies. In this story, individuals know each other in cyberspace, but their true names, their actual physical identities, are closely guarded secrets. See Vernor Vinge, "True Names," originally published in 1981 and available in Vernor Vinge, *True Names and Other Dangers* (New York: Baen Books, 1987).

[17] This point was first brought to my attention on the Extropians E-mail list. The idea of competitive private production of law in the physical world is explored in David Friedman, *The Machinery of Freedom: Guide to a Radical Capitalism* (La Salle, IL: Open Court, 1989), part III. For a more recent discussion, see David Friedman, "Law as a Private Good," *Economics and Philosophy*, vol. 10 (1994), pp. 319–27.

The list administrator is a dictator, but not a monopolist. If others find his rules unsatisfactory, they are free to set up their own groups. The list administrator, like the proprietor of a firm in a competitive market, can do whatever he pleases—but if he does not please his customers, he will soon have none.

I have been describing mail-groups as they now exist, private communities held together by a very narrow bandwidth communication: occasional text messages. Consider the same institution as it would exist in a world of virtual reality and high bandwidth networks. In this world, the mail-group becomes a virtual community, whose members can see and hear each other, gather in (virtual) living rooms, interact in many of the ways possible to real communities.[18]

In part III of *Anarchy, State, and Utopia*, Robert Nozick described a utopian vision—a world of communities, each set up under its own rules, with members free to move among communities or start their own.[19] Within the limits of cyberspace, that vision already exists in the form of mail-groups and will exist, within a few decades, in the form of full-fledged virtual communities. Each community will have its own rules, enforced by a single sanction: expulsion. The result will be a world defined by a single rule: freedom of association. Encryption is the essential defensive technology for such a world, the technology that gives individuals the power to set up and maintain virtual communities inhabited by willing citizens, whether or not other individuals, or governments, approve. Think of it as crypto anarchy.[20]

This is an attractive vision, at least to those committed to the idea of individual freedom. The problems occur on the interface between cyberspace and physical space—when, for example, the anonymity of crypto anarchy is used to protect a firm that assassinates real bodies.

## III. Can Strong Privacy Be Stopped?

So far, I have presented strong privacy as an inevitable result of current technological developments. This raises an obvious question: Can it be stopped?

[18] Throughout this discussion, I have been assuming a virtual-reality technology that is only a modestly improved version of what we already have—sight and sound. A more radical alternative would be to bypass the sense organs and feed information directly to the brain—a controlled dream. With that technology, a virtual community would appear to its participants exactly like a real community; the only difference is that they can produce only virtual objects. Virtual food, however tasty, provides no nutrition, so real food must still be produced somewhere in the real world.

[19] Robert Nozick, *Anarchy, State, and Utopia* (New York: Basic Books, 1974), part III.

[20] The term was originated by Timothy C. May, author of the "Crypto Anarchist Manifesto," which may be found on the Web at: http://www.quadralay.com/www/Crypt/Crypto-Anarchist/crypto-anarchist.html. For a more extensive exploration of May's thoughtful and unconventional views, see his "Cyphernomicon" at: http://www.swiss.ai.mit.edu/6095/articles/cyphernomicon/CP-FAQ.

In one sense, the answer is obviously yes. If, for example, a thermonuclear war returns us to the technological level of the Stone Age, the problems and promises of strong privacy will cease to be of much concern. If, to take a less extreme case, governments decide to entirely prohibit private use of computer networks, one of the key technologies will be eliminated.

I do not think it likely that many developed countries will ban computer networks. The advantages of networks are too enormous to be forgone, even if they bring with them long-term risks.[21] It is particularly unlikely given that governments tend to make their decisions primarily in terms of short-term costs and benefits.[22]

A more plausible strategy is to permit networks but forbid encryption. This restriction is also costly, although less costly than banning networks entirely, since encryption is important for many uses of networks that governments have no wish to prevent, such as banking services. Even for activities in which security is not essential, it is still of considerable value in contexts where messages are easy to intercept.[23] It therefore seems unlikely that attempts to ban encryption will be successful. Attempts to prevent the developments discussed here are more likely to take the form of policies designed either to slow the spread of encryption or to control it. That has in fact been the pattern so far in the U.S.

The government of the U.S. has tried to impede the development and spread of encryption by the use of export controls. The International Traffic in Arms Regulations (ITAR) define cryptographic devices, including software, as munitions; exporting them requires permission from the State Department, and such permission is generally not available for software embodying strong protection.

This policy makes little sense as a way of keeping foreign governments from learning how to protect their secrets and steal ours, since it does not prevent the domestic sale of such products; it is easy enough to smuggle floppy disks out in a diplomatic pouch. It makes more sense as a way of slowing the spread of encryption into general use. An American

[21] It is worth noting that the Clinton administration, despite its support for controlling encryption via the Clipper Chip, has been outspoken in its support of the idea of developing computer networks.

[22] The reason we can expect governments to behave in this way is twofold. Individuals with political power, such as governors and congressmen, have very insecure property rights in their offices and thus little incentive to make long-term investments – to bear political costs now in order to produce benefits for the holders of those offices twenty years hence. Individual voters have secure property rights in both their citizenship and their franchise, but because of rational ignorance they are unlikely to have the information necessary to evaluate the long-term consequences of the policies followed by their government.

[23] Consider the example of cordless phones, whose signals can be easily intercepted by anyone with a scanner. The more expensive models now include encryption, although it is unlikely that drug dealers, terrorists, or bankers make up a significant fraction of the relevant market. Most people prefer to be able to have at least some of their conversations in private.

company that wishes to include strong encryption capabilities in its software products must create and maintain a different version for its foreign customers. Netscape, the most popular of the browsers used to read documents on the World Wide Web, for example, provides encryption with 128-bit keys in its domestic version, but with only 40-bit keys in its export version.

Several recent legal controversies have centered on export controls of encryption. One involved Philip Zimmermann, whose program PGP is widely used, here and abroad, for the public-key encryption and decryption of E-mail. He was widely reported to be under investigation by a grand jury for violating export controls by making PGP available on servers from which it was possible for foreigners to download it;[24] the grand jury did not end up filing any charges against him. A second legal controversy is a recent lawsuit by Dan Bernstein, a graduate student in mathematics at the University of California at Berkeley, supported by the Electronic Freedom Foundation, seeking to have the present system of export controls declared unconstitutional, chiefly on First Amendment grounds.[25]

The outcome of such cases may affect how rapidly encryption comes into use. But even if the government's position prevails, that will only delay these developments, not prevent them. Since encryption software is useful, reasonably easy to write, and, like any software, easy to copy and transmit, it is hard to see how such restrictions can permanently prevent its spread.[26]

A second approach is the Clipper initiative, an attempt to establish an encryption standard designed to be vulnerable to a law-enforcement agent with a court order. The Clipper Chip was announced under the Clinton administration, but represents the outcome of a National Security Agency research program going back many years.[27] The essential features of the chip and the proposed policy are:

[24] Via a procedure known as anonymous file transfer protocol—anonymous because the user does not require a password to access the server.

[25] The case is *Bernstein v. U.S. Department of State, et al.* Information can be found on the World Wide Web at: http://www.eff.org/pub/Privacy/ITAR_export/Bernstein_case/. A second case has just been filed by Philip R. Karn, Jr., against the U.S. Department of State and Thomas E. McNamara, the Assistant Secretary of the State Department's Bureau of Political-Military Affairs, challenging the Arms Export Control Act, 22 U.S.C. 2778 *et seq.*, and the International Traffic in Arms Regulations (ITAR). Information on that case can be found at: http://www.qualcomm.com/people/pkarn/export/index.html.

[26] When Nautilus, a public-domain program for encrypting telephone conversations, was released, it was placed only on servers that had restrictions preventing transmission abroad, in order to avoid any possible violation of the ITAR. Shortly thereafter a posting appeared on one of the Usenet newsgroups from an Australian, asking for someone to download Nautilus and transmit it, via a remailer, to his favorite software archive in Australia. It was immediately followed by a second posting, apologizing for the first; the poster had checked the Australian archive and Nautilus was already there. The incident demonstrates the difficulty of enforcing regulations designed to prevent the spread of software.

[27] A good history of the agency, which has played an important role in both the development of encryption and the attempt to limit its general availability, is J. Bamford, *The Puzzle Palace* (Boston: Houghton Mifflin, 1982).

1. Every Clipper Chip has a key built into it which is separated into two parts, two separate keys, when the chip is programmed, in such a way that both parts are required to deduce the chip's key. Two escrow agencies will be established, one to hold a database containing the first key for every chip produced, one to hold a database containing the second key for every chip produced. A law-enforcement agent with a court order for a wiretap takes the court order and the serial number of the chip to be tapped to the escrow agencies and obtains the keys.

2. The government asserts that the Clipper Chip provides secure encryption against anyone not possessing the keys. The encryption algorithm, however, will not be made public, and the chip has been designed to prevent discovery of the algorithm by reverse engineering.

3. The government is not at present either requiring telephone companies to use the Clipper Chip or forbidding the use of other forms of encryption, although the original announcement implied that the latter possibility had not been ruled out.[28] The intention is to get Clipper voluntarily adopted as a standard. AT&T has announced that it will use the Clipper Chip in forthcoming encryption devices.

4. The government will use the Clipper Chip itself for sensitive but not for classified communications. It is hoped that government use will encourage its adoption by private parties who wish to be able to hold encrypted conversations with government agencies, and therefore help make it a standard.

The Clipper Chip was announced by the Clinton administration as a way of preventing terrorists, drug dealers, and foreign spies from using modern technology to make themselves impervious to wire taps, while providing ordinary citizens with the benefit of electronic privacy. This raises an obvious problem. It hardly seems likely that a malefactor sophisticated enough to use encryption would deliberately choose a form of encryption specifically designed to be vulnerable to a law-enforcement agent with a court order. So achieving the declared purpose of the Clipper Chip seems to require that other forms of encryption be prevented.

It is not clear whether this is either desirable or practical. Even if every telephone in the country is equipped with a Clipper Chip, a criminal may still be able to use his own hardware to pre-encrypt a message before it gets to the phone—in which case the law-enforcement agent listening to the conversation, after decrypting the Clipper encryption, will still hear gibberish. Thus, the effect of widespread adoption of the standard may be to permit law enforcement to tap the phones of everyone except the sophisticated criminals whose deeds the Clipper is supposed to prevent.

[28] "Q: If the Administration were unable to find a technological solution like the one proposed, would the Administration be willing to use legal remedies to restrict access to more powerful encryption devices? A: This is a fundamental policy question which will be considered during the broad policy review" (White House Press Release on the Clipper, April 16, 1993).

This suggests that the supporters of the Clipper Chip may be doing a poor job of describing what it is good for. It is of limited usefulness as a way of maintaining the ability of law-enforcement agents to intercept communications between sophisticated criminals, both because sophisticated criminals can evade it and because wiretaps represent only a small part of law-enforcement efforts.[29] If Clipper can be established as a standard, however, it might be very useful as a way of preventing unsophisticated customers from dealing with sophisticated criminal firms—from hiring assassins, for example. It might also be useful for monitoring sophisticated criminals in their communications with people other than their confederates.

The information available about the Clipper leaves considerable doubt as to how good the protection it provides will be—a particularly serious issue if alternative forms of encryption are forbidden or discouraged. The general view of the cryptographic community is that the only practical way of testing the security of a new algorithm is for lots of clever people to spend lots of time trying to see if they can find a way of breaking it. By refusing to make the Clipper's algorithm public, the government prevents such a test.

This raises further questions concerning the reason for keeping the algorithm secret. One much-discussed possibility is that it contains a back door, a deliberate weakness that can be exploited, presumably by the NSA, to decrypt messages. A second possibility is that the algorithm is being kept secret not because it is known to have a back door but because it might have one. Keeping the algorithm secret makes it harder for cryptographers to figure out how to break it. Of course, the NSA itself knows the algorithm and employs able cryptographers. So if this explanation is correct, the NSA may eventually be able to read conversations encrypted by the Clipper Chip without the formality of a court order.[30]

Even if the Clipper Chip provides adequate security against anyone who does not have the key, there remain two problems inherent in the

[29] "In 1993, 976 U.S. police wiretaps were authorized, 17 were never installed, and 55 were electronic bugs [which are unaffected by encryption], leaving 904 nonbug wiretaps installed. They cost an average of $57,256 each, for a total of $51.7 million spent on legal police wiretaps in 1993. . . . (I will neglect the possibility that police spent much more than this on illegal taps.) This is less than one part in 600 of the $31.8 billion spent by U.S. police in 1990, and most of it was spent on time the police sat and listened to 1.7 million conversations (at $32 per conversation). . . . Wiretaps cost an average of $14,300 per arrest aided in 1993 . . . or almost five times the $3,000 average spent per non-traffic arrest by U.S. police in 1991 . . ." (Robin Hanson, "Can Wiretaps Remain Cost Effective?" *Communications of the ACM*, vol. 37, no. 12 [December 1994], pp. 13–15; also available on the Web at: http://www.hss.caltech.edu/~hanson/wiretap-cacm.html).

[30] A third explanation for secrecy, and the one favored by the supporters of the Clipper initiative, is that Skipjack (the algorithm used in the Clipper Chip) incorporates new and valuable methods of encryption which the NSA wishes to keep out of the hands of foreign governments. For a discussion of the Clipper proposal from a generally friendly viewpoint, see Dorothy E. Denning, "The Clipper Encryption System," *American Scientist*, vol. 81, no. 4 (July–August 1993), pp. 319–23.

idea of key-escrow encryption. The first is the security of the agencies controlling the keys. It does no good to have a technologically secure system if it is vulnerable to any private detective with the right contacts. The second is that foreign countries are unlikely to trust and adopt an encryption system created, kept secret, and controlled by the U.S. government. So even if Clipper could be established as a standard within the U.S., it is unlikely to be established as a standard for the world—which, in a worldwide network, defeats much of the point of having a standard.

For these reasons and others, the Clipper Chip proposal has met heavy opposition from large parts of the computer and communications industries.[31] While it is possible that this administration or the next will push the proposal through despite that opposition, it will probably not be able to convert the Clipper into a mandatory standard by banning alternative forms of encryption. It therefore seems unlikely that the Clipper will be adopted sufficiently widely to prevent the spread of other forms of encryption, here and abroad.[32] It follows that the future I have been describing, a future of strong privacy, is, although not certain, probable.

*Law, Santa Clara University*

[31] "Common objections include: the Skipjack algorithm is not public . . . and may not be secure; the key escrow agencies will be vulnerable to attack; there are not enough key escrow agencies; the keys on the Clipper chips are not generated in a sufficiently secure fashion; there will not be sufficient competition among implementers, resulting in expensive and slow chips; software implementations are not possible; and the key size is fixed and cannot be increased if necessary" (Fahn, "Answers to Frequently Asked Questions" [*supra* note 3]).

[32] The same conclusion applies to other forms of mandatory escrowed encryption that have been suggested in response to criticisms of the Clipper proposal. See, for example, Stephen T. Walker, "Software Key Escrow: A Better Solution for Law Enforcement's Needs?" in *Building in Big Brother*, ed. Lance J. Hoffman (New York: Springer-Verlag, 1995), pp. 174–79; and David M. Balenson, Carl M. Ellison, Steven B. Lipner, and Stephen T. Walker, "A New Approach to Software Key Encryption," in *ibid.*, pp. 180–207.

# COMPUTER RELIABILITY AND PUBLIC POLICY: LIMITS OF KNOWLEDGE OF COMPUTER-BASED SYSTEMS*

By James H. Fetzer

## I. Introduction

Perhaps no technological innovation has so dominated the second half of the twentieth century as has the introduction of the programmable computer. It is quite difficult if not impossible to imagine how contemporary affairs—in business and science, communications and transportation, governmental and military activities, for example—could be conducted without the use of computing machines, whose principal contribution has been to relieve us of the necessity for certain kinds of mental exertion. The computer revolution has reduced our mental labors by means of these machines, just as the Industrial Revolution reduced our physical labor by means of other machines.

The public policy problems that accompany this technology are diverse—ranging from matters of liability when safety-critical systems malfunction to issues of patent and copyright protection for software and on to questions of propriety relative to the transmission of pornography via electronic bulletin-boards. Some of these, such as matters of patent and copyright protection, may represent old problems in a new guise, while others, such as those of liability when safety-critical systems malfunction, may go beyond the scope of previous technology and create difficulties that require innovative solutions. The available remedies may simply not be adequate.

Discovering adequate solutions to novel problems presupposes that those problems themselves are well-understood. The purpose of this essay is to contribute toward better understanding the dimensions of these problems by an exploration of the limits of our knowledge about computer systems as *knowledge-based systems*. This notion is typically applied to a branch of computer science known as *expert systems*, which uses the knowledge of experts in producing programs, but it can also be applied to *artificial intelligence*, which incorporates procedures intended to model human minds. Even ordinary computers, however, are knowledge-based in a broad sense.

During the course of this study, distinctions will be drawn between the software and hardware components of computers, on the one hand, and between computers and computer systems, on the other. The first of these

* I am grateful to Tim Colburn, M. M. Lehman, and the editors of this volume for critical comments and valuable suggestions regarding this essay.

is no doubt familiar, but becomes especially important in attempting to elaborate different senses in which computer systems qualify as "knowledge-based." The software component of an expert system, for example, crucially depends upon information provided by an "expert" and transmitted by a "knowledge engineer," where the person who writes the program typically uses the "knowledge" thus supplied at the direction of his project manager.

The function of the program, of course, is to control the performance of a computer when it executes that program. The intended effects that may be brought about thereby, however, extend far beyond symbol processing and number crunching to treating cancer and operating aircraft. Studies of reliability, therefore, need to distinguish between techniques and methods that can be applied to software, to hardware, and to entire "computer systems," where computer systems consist of computers and associated equipment situated in the world. For the approaches that are available for evaluating the reliability of some of these may differ from those available for evaluating the reliability of the others.

The discussion that follows will consider the most general features that distinguish computers and computer systems in order to isolate what seem to be their most important features with respect to issues of public policy: (1) their epistemic origins as various kinds of knowledge-based systems; (2) their ontic character relative to models of three distinct varieties; and (3) the limits of the extent to which their performance can be guaranteed. The considerations that follow suggest that the reliability of these systems—including their correctness—cannot be guaranteed, and that our increasing dependence on computer technology in various dimensions of our personal and social lives raises fundamental ethical questions and related problems of public policy which need to be addressed and may no longer be ignored.

## II. Expert Systems

### *A. Computers as data-processing machines*

Computing machines are often described as *data-processing* mechanisms, which take "data" as input and produce "information" as output. One author, for example, has distinguished between Tycho Brahe's observations of the positions of the planets as *data* in relation to Johannes Kepler's calculations of the orbits of the planets as *information*.[1] From a theoretical perspective, however, Brahe's "data" appears to be informative about some issues (such as the locations of certain heavenly bodies at certain dates and times), while Kepler's laws have functioned as "data"

[1] William S. Davis, *Fundamental Computer Concepts* (Reading, MA: Addison-Wesley, 1986), p. 2.

relative to other inquiries (such as Isaac Newton's calculation of the laws of motion and universal gravitation).

These reflections suggest that the difference between "data" and "information" must be *pragmatic* in character and determined by what we want to learn ("information") in relation to what we already know ("data"). An alternative conception would place computing machines within a pragmatic context by viewing them as *problem-solving* mechanisms, where the (general purpose) computer becomes a special-purpose problem-solver when it has been provided with suitable software. The point of computer science thus becomes that of providing the means to create hardware that can run various kinds of software and software that can solve various kinds of problems.

The kinds of problems that might be solved depend upon the kinds of solutions that are available for solving them. Software commonly comes into existence when *programs* are composed that implement algorithms in specific computer languages (Pascal, Prolog, and so on), where *algorithms* formulate "step-by-step" procedures that provide solutions to specific kinds of problems in a finite number of steps.[2] In those cases in which no algorithm happens to exist or can exist, partial solutions may be available in the form of *asymmetrical procedures* (which provide acceptable solutions, when they provide a solution), or of *heuristics* (as "solutions" that have exceptions).[3]

Programs are thus properly understood as sets of instructions for computers, where the adequacy of those instructions tends to depend on and vary with the sources from which they were derived. A program for processing U.S. income-tax returns, for example, could be based upon current (or dated) information provided by the Internal Revenue Service (or by some other source), where its utility for generating acceptable returns could be enormously variable. Those who compose such programs ("programmers") might or might not be highly competent problem-solvers with respect to the problem-domain (of tax policy, for example) and may depend on guidance provided by others.

Those who are highly competent in devising or in evaluating solutions to problems within a specific problem-domain are usually called "experts." In order for the knowledge possessed by an expert to be available to the programmer, however, it must be secured from that expert in a form that makes it accessible to the programmer, a responsibility that is carried by persons known as "knowledge engineers." The process of obtaining knowledge from an expert and recasting that knowledge into

[2] Stephen C. Kleene, *Mathematical Logic* (New York: John Wiley and Sons, 1967), ch. 5.

[3] Douglas Downing and Michael Covington, *Dictionary of Computer Terms* (Woodbury, NY: Barron's, 1986), p. 117. On the use of the term "heuristics" in the field of artificial intelligence, see Avron Barr and Edward A. Feigenbaum, *The Handbook of Artificial Intelligence*, vol. I (Reading, MA: Addison-Wesley, 1981), pp. 28–30, 58, 109.

the form of a program yields an "expert system."[4] There are various kinds of expert systems, whose properties are by and large well-understood.[5]

*B. Expert systems as "knowledge-based"*

Expert systems thus reflect one familiar sense in which a computer system can qualify as a "knowledge-based" system. An expert system for the diagnosis of blood diseases known as MYCIN, for example, has been studied extensively.[6] MYCIN employs over five hundred rules that relate the results of tests to diagnose diseases and recommend treatments, where the reliability of the system obviously depends upon the adequacy of the knowledge upon which that system is based. The system of rules that MYCIN employs represents a combination of current scientific knowledge about diseases of the blood with heuristic methods to produce a system that approximates human expertise.

The inference rules that expert systems like MYCIN employ include not only "forward-chaining" rules that permit ordinary deductive inferences to be drawn, but also rules that allow other kinds of inferences to be drawn. MYCIN obtains data about patients through interviews with their doctors; information from these interviews is used to assign values to variables relevant to rendering diagnoses of patients' diseases and prescriptions of recommended treatments. That data in turn is processed by applying conditional rules like the following:

*RULE 156*

IF: 1) the site of the culture is blood, and
2) the gram stain of the organism is gramneg, and
3) the morphology of the organism is rod, and
4) the portal entry of the organism is urine, and
5) the patient has not had a genito-urinary manipulative procedure, and
6) cystitis is not a problem for which the patient has been treated,

THEN: There is suggestive evidence (.6) that the identity of the organism is *E. coli*.[7]

[4] Examples of expert systems may be found in Avron Barr and Edward A. Feigenbaum, *The Handbook of Artificial Intelligence*, vol. II (Reading, MA: Addison-Wesley, 1982).

[5] A discussion of various kinds of expert systems may be found in James H. Fetzer, *Artificial Intelligence: Its Scope and Limits* (Dordrecht, The Netherlands: Kluwer Academic Publishers, 1990), pp. 180–91.

[6] Bruce G. Buchanan and Edward H. Shortliffe, eds., *Rule-based Expert Systems: The MYCIN Experiments of the Stanford Heuristic Programming Project* (Reading, MA: Addison-Wesley, 1984).

[7] *Ibid.*, p. 74. The number ".6" represents a "certainty factor" which, on a scale from –1 to 1, indicates how strongly the claim has been confirmed (CF > 0) or disconfirmed (CF < 0); see also note 34 below.

This specific rule exemplifies "backward chaining," which involves drawing an inference from test results (interpreted as "symptoms") to their most likely causes (as "infections" or as "diseases"). It therefore represents a type of inductive inference from effects to their causes that might best be understood as "inference to the best explanation." An inference of this kind presupposes the availability of a set of alternative possible explanations, some of which may provide more adequate (or "preferable") explanations of the evidence (or "data") than do others. When the available evidence is sufficient, then the most adequate explanation ought to be tentatively adopted.[8]

Because more than one cause (infection or disease) might produce some of the same effects (or symptoms), rules of inference of this kind in MYCIN are qualified by "certainty factors" (or CFs), such as .6 in Rule 156. Thus,

> experience with clinicians had shown that clinicians do not use the information comparable to implemented standard statistical methods [such as ordinary "probabilities" and "likelihoods"]. However, the concept of CFs did appear to fit the clinicians' reasoning patterns—their judgments of how they weighted factors, strong or weak, in decision making.[9]

The domain-specific expertise needed to construct a knowledge-based system such as MYCIN thus extends beyond mere descriptions of symptoms (effects) to the capacity to derive inferences to their causes (infections or diseases).

Thus, in providing a characterization of "expert systems" generally, a distinction is commonly drawn between the *knowledge base* and the *inference engine*. In the case of MYCIN, for example, the knowledge base includes information about causal relations and statistical correlations between the occurrence of infections and diseases and the occurrence of various symptoms, including rules such as Rule 156, while the inference engine applies them to specific cases. When data about a new case is provided as input to a system via its user interface, the application of the inference engine produces the information that is desired as output, as shown in Figure 1.[10]

[8] Inference to the best explanation is also known as "abductive inference." See, for example, James H. Fetzer and Robert Almeder, *Glossary of Epistemology/Philosophy of Science* (New York: Paragon House, 1993); and especially Yun Peng and James Reggia, *Abductive Inference Models for Diagnostic Problem-Solving* (New York: Springer-Verlag, 1990).

[9] Barr and Feigenbaum, *The Handbook of Artificial Intelligence*, vol. II, p. 189. The tendency has been toward the use of measures of subjective probability in lieu of CFs; see note 34 below.

[10] Buchanan and Shortliffe, eds., *Rule-based Expert Systems*, p. 4.

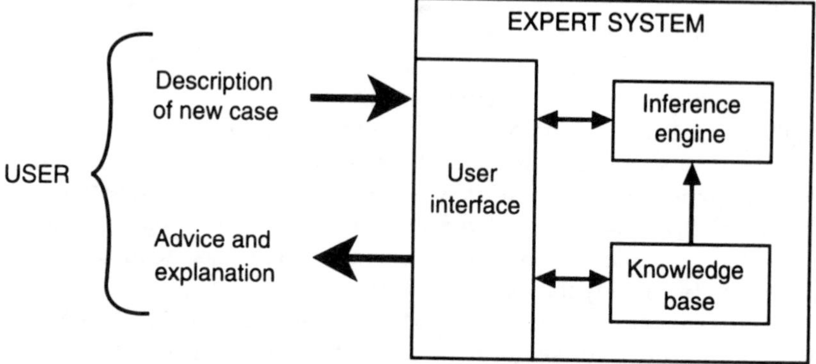


FIGURE 1. Components of an expert system.

*C. Expert systems as performance systems*

Because MYCIN offers recommendations to doctors with respect to how they should treat their patients, it has sometimes been described as a "performance system" in the sense that it is employed to perform a task.[11] Whether or not this conception successfully differentiates systems such as this one from other systems, however, is not entirely obvious. An income-tax processing system, for example, appears to be employed to perform a task in that very same sense. Indeed, even a pocket calculator might be characterized as a "performance system" insofar as we employ it to perform various arithmetic tasks (of addition, subtraction, division, multiplication, etc.).

Such an approach merely reinforces the notion that programmable computers are best envisioned not simply as "data-processing" devices but rather as "problem-solving" mechanisms. To the extent to which their problem-solving abilities depend upon domain-specific knowledge, however, it should be apparent that computer scientists *as* computer scientists are typically not sources of the domain-specific knowledge which knowledge-based systems require. Sometimes it might happen that an expert on diseases of the blood, for example, happens to program a computer to enable it to diagnose blood diseases, but such circumstances are quite uncommon.

The programmer and the knowledge engineer may sometimes coincide, when both tasks are fulfilled by the same person. This makes individuals who can assume both roles especially valuable, since they not only can interact with experts to acquire domain-specific knowledge but also can codify that knowledge in the form of a program. When this happens, the risk of the introduction of distortion or of the loss of information in going from the expert to the programmer is drastically reduced.

[11] *Ibid.*, p. 5.

Whether or not the knowledge engineer wholly succeeds in understanding the expert, the programmer at least does not risk misunderstanding the knowledge engineer.

As a theoretical possibility, of course, a programmer might become an expert within a specific problem-domain (such as income-tax preparation or blood-disease diagnosis) and thereby position himself to evaluate the information provided to him by knowledge engineers. As a practical necessity, however, this alternative is virtually never available, for all of the obvious reasons motivating divisions of labor. Thus, computer programmers *as* computer programmers are typically not only not the sources of the domain-specific knowledge that expert systems require but also are not appropriately positioned to evaluate the adequacy of that knowledge.

This implies that computer programmers who program expert systems are dependent upon their expert sources in two different ways. First, they must accept those *sources* as appropriate for providing information in the construction of expert systems. Second, they must accept *that information* as suitable for the purpose of programming these systems. Computer programmers are therefore typically dependent upon sources whose competence lies beyond their control, for information the reliability of which they are unable to evaluate. They thus have no alternative but to rely upon "experts" as authorities and cannot assess the quality of the knowledge they are given.

## III. Knowledge and Reasoning

### A. *"Information" versus "knowledge"*

Not all "appeals to authority" are fallacious, of course. When a person who is an authority in one field is cited in another field in which he is *not* an authority, a fallacious appeal to authority occurs. When a person who is an authority is cited in a field in which he *is* an authority, a nonfallacious appeal to authority occurs. (Citing Einstein's views on problems in physics, for example, is clearly nonfallacious, but citing Einstein on world peace is.) The problem is not that knowledge engineers commonly commit fallacious appeals to authority in selecting sources of information for expert systems, but rather that programmers are usually not qualified to tell the difference between fallacious and nonfallacious appeals.

The situation might be alleviated if knowledge engineers were suitably positioned to select appropriate sources of knowledge in their endeavor to secure information for the construction of expert systems. But knowledge engineers are ordinarily directed to rely upon the information provided by specific sources designated by *project managers*, who in turn are responsible to those who have commissioned these systems. It should not be surprising if those who finance the construction of such systems—typically, as products that are intended for military, industrial, or commercial consumption—reserve the right to specify those sources of information to be used.[12]

The appropriate source, of course, depends upon the kind of system under development. An expert system for tax preparation would require an expert on tax preparation; an expert system for the diagnosis of diseases of the blood would require an expert on blood diseases; and an expert system on the behavior of a specific person—such as Joseph Stalin, Adolf Hitler, or Saddam Hussein—would require an expert on Stalin, Hitler, or Hussein. The kind of knowledge required would differ accordingly from case to case: in some cases, it may be easily available, but in other cases, it may be harder to acquire—and in certain other special cases, it may be relatively esoteric.[13]

Perhaps the most important consequence of this is that computer scientists as hardware and software specialists are not well positioned to evaluate whether the information they are provided properly qualifies as "knowledge." They are typically participants in group projects supervised by project managers, and the selection of experts as sources is usually a matter that lies beyond their control. While programmers may be responsible for their programming, responsibility for the construction of the software component of an expert system must be *distributed* between the project manager, the authority selected, the knowledge engineer, and the programmer.

Even when the assumptions are made (a) that no information has been lost in the process of the transmission of information from its source to the programmer by the knowledge engineer, and (b) that no mistakes have been made by the programmer in translating that information into a program by means of a suitable language, it remains possible (c) that the expert system so derived might fail because the information on which it is based is either inaccurate or incomplete. When problems arise with the use of an "expert system" that derive from the content of the program itself, therefore, one possible explanation is that the information provided was not "knowledge."

### B. The nature of knowledge

The situation is compounded by the consideration that computer programmers *as* computer programmers need not understand the nature of knowledge itself. The theory of knowledge is a philosophical subject that aims at defining the nature and the scope of human knowledge. Since the theory of knowledge is not a subject in the computer science curriculum,

[12] On the project manager, see, for example, Neal Whitten, *Managing Software Development Projects* (New York: John Wiley and Sons, 1989).

[13] Criteria for the selection of domain experts are discussed by D. A. Waterman, *A Guide to Expert Systems* (Reading, MA: Addison-Wesley, 1986).

it is clear that if a computer programmer happened to be familiar with problems in the theory of knowledge, it would not be by virtue of the background and training which he had acquired in the study of computer science but rather by virtue of the background and training which he had acquired in the study of philosophy.

The traditional conception of knowledge defines "knowledge" within the context of sentences of the form "$x$ knows that $p$" as warranted true belief.[14] That is, a person $x$ possesses knowledge described by the sentence $p$ when $x$ believes that $p$, $x$ is warranted in that belief, and $p$ is the case (that is, the sentence $p$ is true). Thus, $p$ might describe information for processing tax returns (or information about diseases and infections of the blood, etc.). A person $x$ who was especially knowledgeable about processing tax returns (diseases and infections of the blood, etc.) thus might seem to be an "expert" by virtue of possessing numerous warranted true beliefs about that domain.

What may be most important about "experts" and "knowledge," however, is the presumption that the evidence available that warrants beliefs within this domain is presumed to be warranted in turn. In other words, "experts" are not merely persons who possess *true beliefs* in relation to some problem domain; they are persons who *know how* those beliefs themselves are warranted by means of other beliefs, and, in turn, how those other beliefs are warranted. Thus, the conception of knowledge that characterizes "experts" is not only that their beliefs about problems within their domain are warranted but that the evidence on the basis of which they are warranted is also warranted to the maximum possible extent.

From this perspective, a domain expert is someone who not only possesses knowledge of the *know-that* variety with respect to true beliefs within his domain of expertise, but also possesses knowledge of the *know-how* variety with respect to how those beliefs came to be accepted within that domain.[15] The study of expert systems, however, has had the intriguing side-effect of displaying the difficulty that experts can have in articulating that expertise. There appear to be stages in the acquisition of expertise, where procedures that were initially explicitly rule-governed and self-conscious become habitual. It can be hard for experts to find words that describe what they do.

The knowledge possessed by experts includes (possibly implicit) knowledge of the methods by which that knowledge itself is acquired. Those who pose as "experts" but lack this form of "expertise" may be able to deceive others about themselves but could be exposed by the real thing.

[14] The term "traditional" occurs here in contrast to the (far weaker) "artificial intelligence" conception of knowledge, in particular. On the traditional conception, see, for example, Israel Scheffler, *Conditions of Knowledge* (Chicago, IL: University of Chicago Press, 1965). On the use of this term in AI, see especially Fetzer, *Artificial Intelligence*, ch. 5, pp. 127–32.

[15] See James H. Fetzer, *Scientific Knowledge* (Dordrecht, The Netherlands: D. Reidel, 1981), ch. 1.

The principal difference between experts and nonexperts (quacks, frauds, and so on) in relation to a specific problem-domain thus seems to be that while quacks or frauds, especially, may appear to possess domain-specific knowledge, they lack an understanding of the corresponding methods that yield those warrants without which there is no domain-specific knowledge.

### C. *The analytic-synthetic distinction*

The kinds of warrants that are appropriate, however, depend upon and vary with the content of the object of belief. Person $x$ is entitled to believe in the truth of a sentence $p$ whose truth or falsity merely depends upon the language in which it is expressed by appropriate reference to that language. In relation to English, for example, beliefs that bachelors are unmarried, that triangles have three sides, and so on are warranted by *dictionary definitions*, which record the established usage of words within a community. Since their truth follows from definitions, beliefs of this kind are often called "definitional truths," and the sentences that express them are called "analytic."

Sentences whose truth does not follow from definitions alone, however, require other kinds of warrants. The belief that there is a beer in the refrigerator, for example, might be warranted by experience as a description of something $x$ observed. This may be described as a matter of *perceptual inference*, since it involves the use of language to describe the contents of experience. It is important to notice, however, that even perceptual inference does not guarantee the truth of a belief. What $x$ took to be a bottle of beer might turn out to be a new fruit drink that his daughter brought home from the corner store, a drink which comes in bottles that look like bottles for beer.

The conclusions of perceptual inferences depend upon language but are not warranted by language alone. Whether or not there is a bottle of beer in the refrigerator cannot be determined on the basis of the meaning of the words involved. However common an occurrence of an event of this kind may be, the truth of the belief that there is a bottle of beer in the refrigerator is not merely a matter of definition. The meaning of this sentence is compatible with its falsity as well as with its truth. If it should happen to be true, therefore, its truth or falsity depends upon how things are in the world and not merely on the meaning of words. Its truth is not "analytic."

Other beliefs, of course, might be warranted by *deductive inference* or by *inductive inference* from things already known. Inductive reasoning can be applied to draw inferences from the past to the future, from samples to populations, and from the observed to the unobserved—including inference to the best explanation, of course, as a special case. Deductive reasoning can be applied to derive what must be true if something else is true, where that reasoning may or may not be purely hypothetical. Both forms of reasoning are appropriately understood as assuming the form of arguments—where *arguments* are sets of sentences divided into two parts, premises and conclusions, where premises offer warrants for conclusions.

Thus understood, the concept of knowledge has a recursive character, since the premises that warrant deductive or inductive conclusions may require warrants in turn, which might be deductive, inductive, or perceptual in kind. The process of warranting thus continues until premises requiring no further warrant are encountered, such as analytic sentences, warranted by their own meaning, or descriptive sentences, warranted by perception—where the former, unlike the latter, cannot possibly be false. Knowledge that is neither analytic nor warranted by deductive reasoning applied to analytic premises is nonanalytic and is said to be "synthetic."[16]

*D. Conclusive versus inconclusive reasoning*

The differences between deductive and inductive reasoning are of very great import. Deductive reasoning is *conclusive*, but nevertheless displays two aspects that must be separated. There is an important difference between (deductive) arguments that are *valid* and arguments that are *sound*. An argument is valid when, if its premises were true, then its conclusion could not be false. An argument is sound when it is not only valid but its premises are true. The conclusion of every sound argument, therefore, has to be true and could not possibly be false. An argument with false premises, however, can have a false conclusion, even when it happens to be valid.

Inductive reasoning, by contrast, is *inconclusive*—and once again two aspects must be separated here. There is an important difference between (inductive) arguments that are *proper* and arguments that are *correct*. An argument is proper when, if its premises were true, its conclusion would acquire a degree of evidential support corresponding to the strength of the premises. An argument is correct when it is not only proper but its premises are true. The conclusion of a correct argument, therefore, has acquired a degree of evidential support, but its conclusion may still be false. Thus, inductive arguments remain inconclusive, even when they are as strong as they can be.

[16] The origins of distinctions between analytic and synthetic knowledge can be traced back to the work of eighteenth and nineteenth century philosophers, especially David Hume (1711–1776) and Immanuel Kant (1724–1804). Hume drew a distinction between knowledge of relations between ideas and knowledge of matters of fact, while Kant distinguished between knowledge of conceptual connections and knowledge of the world. While it would not be appropriate to review the history of the distinction here, it should be observed that it has enormous importance in many philosophical contexts. For further discussion, see Robert Ackermann, *Theories of Knowledge* (New York: McGraw-Hill, 1965); Scheffler, *Conditions of Knowledge*; and Fetzer and Almeder, *Glossary*. For a recent defense of the distinction, see Fetzer, *Artificial Intelligence*, pp. 106–9; and especially James H. Fetzer, *Philosophy of Science* (New York: Paragon House, 1993), chs. 1 and 3.

Suitable examples can be used as illustrations. The sentences "All senators are honest" and "Jones is a senator" can serve as the premises of a deductive argument that provides conclusive support for the conclusion "Jones is honest"—an argument which is valid and would be sound if its premises were true. The sentences "Many senators are honest" and "Jones is a senator," by contrast, can serve as the premises of an inductive argument that provides inconclusive support for the conclusion "Jones is honest"—an argument which is proper and would be correct if its premises were true. It thus provides a degree of evidential support relative to the strength of those premises.[17]

The development of a suitable measure of the degree of evidential support that inductive arguments confer upon their conclusions has proven to be a difficult task, which remains imperfectly understood. Nevertheless, at least two results have emerged. The first is that every argument has to satisfy the requirement of a *uniform interpretation*, according to which the words that occur in an argument must have the same meaning throughout. The second is that every inductive argument must satisfy the requirement of *total evidence*, according to which their premises must reflect all of the available relevant evidence. These conditions inhibit fallacious reasoning.[18]

Fallacies of ambiguity occur when words have more than one meaning. They may then appear in premises that are true (under one interpretation) and in conclusions that are false (under another interpretation). A person can be *mad* (in the sense of being angry), for example, without also being *mad* (in the sense of being insane). To forestall inferences from premises that describe someone as angry to conclusions describing him as insane, therefore, the requirement of a uniform interpretation has to be satisfied. This condition must also be imposed on models and theories as syntactic structures to ensure that they sustain systematic semantic interpretation.

Other fallacies occur when inductive arguments do not consider all of the relevant evidence that happens to be available. When coins are bent (dice are loaded, decks are stacked), that makes a difference to the probability with which various outcomes tend to occur. If we know that a coin is bent (that the dice are loaded, that the deck is stacked), then we would commit a fallacy were we to ignore that information. Information that is relevant is not always available, of course, and information that is available is not always relevant. The requirement of total evidence thus simply

[17] Thus, if the "many" who are honest were a large proportion of all the senators, then that degree of support should be high; if it were only a modest proportion, then it should be low; and so on. If the percentage were, say, $m/n$, then the support conferred upon the conclusion by those premises would presumably equal $m/n$. See, for example, Fetzer, *Scientific Knowledge*, Part III; Fetzer, *Philosophy of Science*, chs. 4–6; and note 34 below.

[18] On the total-evidence condition, see Carl G. Hempel, *Aspects of Scientific Explanation* (New York: The Free Press, 1965), pp. 53–79.

insists that whenever relevant evidence happens to be available, it has to be taken into account for inductive reasoning to be proper.[19]

### E. Formal science versus empirical science

Perhaps the most important ramification of these considerations within the present context arises from their relations to different kinds of knowledge. A distinction is commonly drawn between the *formal sciences*, such as set theory, various branches of logic (such as sentential, predicate, and modal logic), and various branches of mathematics (such as algebra, geometry, and calculus), on the one hand, and the *empirical sciences* (such as physics [classical mechanics, statistical mechanics, quantum mechanics], chemistry, and biology), on the other—where the empirical sciences aim at the discovery of laws of nature (of physics, of chemistry, of biology).[20]

The disciplines thus classified appear to differ with respect to their content and with respect to their methods. The formal sciences, for example, are typically pursued employing exclusively deductive reasoning, where the consequences of adopting various assumptions are developed into formal theories. These theories tend to assume the form of abstract calculi that might sustain various interpretations, which make them true or false of various—abstract or physical—domains. The empirical sciences, by contrast, are pursued using methods that are deductive and inductive, methods which rely heavily upon focused observation and controlled experiments.

Because the formal sciences are distinguished by methods that do not require data or information from the world around us and can be pursued independently of experience, they may properly be described as "*a priori*" disciplines. Because the empirical sciences are distinguished by methods that do require data or information from the world around us and cannot be pursued independently of experience, they can analogously be described as "*a posteriori*" disciplines. When abstract calculi are provided with abstract interpretations, they are (purely) "formal theories," yet when they are provided with empirical interpretations, they qualify as "empirical theories."[21]

The development of formal theories or of empirical theories presumes the availability of a language consisting of a vocabulary and of a grammar, where the vocabulary can be treated as primitive marks which pos-

[19] This is a pragmatic requirement that governs inductive reasoning.

[20] For further discussion, see, for example, Fetzer, *Philosophy of Science*, ch. 1.

[21] See, for example, Carl G. Hempel, "On the Nature of Mathematical Truth" and "Geometry and Empirical Science," both of which are reprinted in Herbert Feigl and Wilfrid Sellars, eds., *Readings in Philosophical Analysis* (New York: Appleton-Century-Crofts, 1949), pp. 222–37 and 238–49.

| | A PRIORI METHODS (formal proofs, etc.) | A POSTERIORI METHODS (experimentation, etc.) |
|---|---|---|
| ANALYTIC CONTENT | FORMAL SCIENCES | ——— |
| SYNTHETIC CONTENT | ——— | EMPIRICAL SCIENCES |

FIGURE 2. Formal versus empirical sciences.

sess no semantic significance. The development of a formal theory thus involves elaboration of the syntactical relations that obtain between the primitives that are postulated by the theory, where the deductive consequences that follow from its primitive assumptions are derived using exclusively formal methods. When these theories are interpreted in relation to abstract domains, therefore, they must be viewed as possessing strictly analytic content.

The situation with respect to the empirical sciences, however, assumes a very different character, since these theories, in relation to the physical world, have to be viewed as possessing synthetic content. Thus, the formal sciences represent the application of *a priori* methods to analytic content, while the empirical sciences represent the application of *a posteriori* methods to synthetic content, as Figure 2 suggests. Moreover, since the methods of formal science are exclusively deductive and their content wholly analytic, these disciplines can acquire a degree of certainty of knowledge about their subjects to which the empirical sciences cannot possibly aspire.[22]

### F. Implications for computer science

The most obvious implication for computer science concerns the kind of knowledge that expert systems require. An expert system for blood disease depends upon scientific knowledge of causal relations and statistical correlations between the occurrence of infections and diseases and the occurrence of various symptoms, as elements of its knowledge base. Such knowledge is clearly the synthetic product of observations and ex-

[22] Thus, as Einstein observed, to the extent to which the laws of mathematics refer to reality, they are not certain; and to the extent to which they are certain, they do not refer to reality—a point I shall pursue.

periments that provide evidence for inductive and deductive reasoning, where conclusions may be false even when all of their premises are true.

Because scientific knowledge is synthetic and can never be known with certainty, it always remains possible that, no matter how strongly it may be supported by the available evidence, what we take to be true may be false. If we define "knowledge" as warranted true belief, we can never be sure that what we take to be scientific knowledge qualifies as "knowledge." Consequently, we must either *redefine* "scientific knowledge" as warranted belief or *concede* that what we take to be "scientific knowledge" can be false.[23] Either way, even the perfect transmission and the flawless translation of expert knowledge cannot overcome its inherently fallible character.

There are intriguing cases that are more difficult to classify relative to these distinctions. The study of language through empirical inquiries, for example, appears to yield *a posteriori* knowledge that is based upon observations and experiments, but which supplies information about the meaning of words that is analytic. This should really come as no surprise, however, when properly understood, because analytic sentences are those whose truth is guaranteed by their meaning. What specific words mean and which sentences are analytic are matters which depend upon the syntax and semantics of that language. For ordinary languages, those relations must be learned.

This implies that our knowledge of *ordinary language* is synthetic, which means that, in relation to languages in use (English, French, Russian, and so on), the word meanings and analytic sentences that occur in those specific languages have to be discovered. Once we know the dictionary definitions that apply within a specific language, we can derive the conditional consequences that follow from the adoption of that language as a framework, as in the case of "If John is a bachelor, then John is unmarried" within English. That our knowledge of ordinary languages must be synthetic does not destroy the existence of *a priori* knowledge within those specific frameworks. But it does imply that what we take to be analytic within an ordinary language is not a matter about which we can possess knowledge that is certain.

Sometimes circumstances permit a language to be made up as a set of marks and a set of rules for their manipulation—that is, as an *artificial language*, without regard for whether anyone has used the language before. The discoveries of various non-Euclidean geometries qualify as relevant examples. While Euclid codified *axioms* (as unproven assumptions) and *theorems* (that were deducible from them) that were thought to be properties of physical space, Georg Riemann and Nikolai Lobachevski subsequently codified different axioms and derived different theorems as alternative geometries of abstract spaces. What we take to be analytic

[23] For further discussion, see, for example, Fetzer, *Scientific Knowledge*, pp. 14–15.

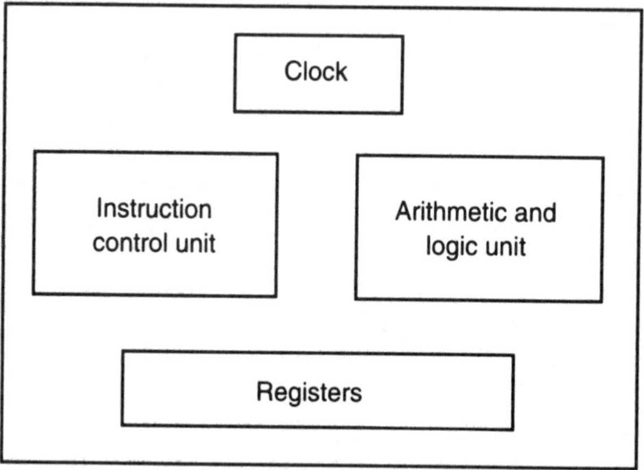


FIGURE 3. The components of a processor.

within an artificial language turns out to be a matter about which we can possess knowledge that is certain, because the definitions which appear in its dictionary are matters of stipulation. The assumptions upon which these definitions are based need no empirical support.[24]

## G. The arithmetic and logic unit

Another implication of the analytic-synthetic distinction is somewhat more subtle than its consequences for expert systems. This implication arises from the incorporation of hardware for processing logical and arithmetic operations. Apart from its memory, the most basic component of a computer is its *processor*, which contains the following four important elements: a clock, an instruction control unit, an arithmetic and logic unit, and a set of registers. The function of the registers is to record the operations and the operands that are being operated upon under control of the program. These four components are represented by the diagram provided as Figure 3.[25]

Since knowledge of arithmetic and of logical relations is paradigmatic of analytic knowledge, the arithmetic and logic unit represents analytic knowledge in the form of hardware. Thus, even the construction of the hardware of a computer appears to be "knowledge based" in a broad sense. It may be tempting to assume that knowledge of elementary arithmetic (addition, subtraction, multiplication, division) are matters about which everyone is his or her own "expert." But even when such an assumption is warranted, that knowledge still has to be translated into

[24] The differences between stipulative truths and empirical truths are crucial for understanding computer programming.

[25] Davis, *Fundamental Computer Concepts*, p. 20. It should be observed, however, that some consider the clock to be convenient for but not essential to computer operations.

the numerals and registers, voltages and circuits that are the physical embodiment of even elementary mathematics.

The physical limitations that are imposed by the resources available for implementing knowledge of this kind by means of arithmetic and logic units are by no means trivial. The first is that the size of the numerals which can be directly operated upon within a computer is determined by the size of its registers. Computers that operate on the basis of words that are 16 bits in length can represent numbers by 16 zeros and ones in binary arithmetic, of which the largest is 32,767 in decimal—or, in the case of 32-bit processors, by 32 zeros and ones, of which the largest is 2,147,483,647 in decimal. Larger numbers, which exceed register size, may be partially represented by approximations using, for example, what is called "floating-point" notation.[26]

The problems imposed by register size are obvious for infinite numbers, such as pi. The continuum of real numbers must therefore be "replaced" by a finite subset of the rational numbers, whose representations are not uniformly dense and many of whose members are only finite approximations: "The pseudo-arithmetic operations performed by real digital computers do not obey the laws of arithmetic. . . . In fact, each concrete computer is known to violate these laws, even for the integers."[27] As a consequence, algorithms with variables that assume real-number values may be impossible to program correctly, even when those algorithms are demonstrable.

Even more disturbing is the prospect that the hardware itself might not behave in accordance with the principles of arithmetic within the bounds of its own registers. A dramatic illustration has recently occurred in the case of Intel's Pentium microprocessor, whose arithmetic and logic unit has turned out to be flawed with an error whose magnitude can be many times larger than those of comparable microprocessors.[28] Intel executives sought to minimize the seriousness of the error by suggesting that it was a problem that should be encountered only rarely. As one observer remarked, however, "these kinds of statistics are based upon the probability

[26] *Ibid.*, p. 189. There are languages and machines that permit the representation of numbers of arbitrary size through the concatenation of 32-bit words, where limitations are imposed by memory resources.

[27] David Nelson, "Deductive Program Verification (A Practitioner's Commentary)," *Minds and Machines*, vol. 2, no. 3 (August 1992), pp. 283–307; the quote is from p. 289. On this and other grounds, Nelson denies that computers are properly described as "mathematical machines" and asserts that they are better described as "logic machines."

[28] Up to ten billion times as large, according to John Markoff, "Flaw Undermines Accuracy of Pentium Chips," *New York Times*, November 24, 1994, pp. C1–C2. As Markoff illustrates, the difficulty involves division:

*Problem:*
4,195,835 – [(*4,195,835* ÷ *3,145,727*) × 3,145,727] = ?
*Correct Calculation:*
4,195,835 – [(*1.3338204*) × 3,145,727] = 0
*Pentium's Calculation:*
4,195,835 – [(*1.3337391*) × 3,145,727] = 256

of events whose probability we don't know."[29] Depending upon the operation, it could run as high as 100 percent.

*H. The question of reliability*

The problem with Intel's Pentium is not unique. Intel's chip-models 386 and 486 both had different mathematical errors, and other problems have arisen with other microprocessors.[30] The public response to the Pentium chip, however, appears to have exceeded past concerns by several orders of magnitude. Commentaries have ranged from describing the situation as one involving a "crisis of faith," to describing it as merely "an obscure flaw," and then to humorous asides:[31] Sample question: Why didn't Intel call the Pentium the 586? Answer: Because they added 486 and 100 on the first Pentium and got 585.999983605.

The reasons for concern, moreover, are not difficult to discern. Intel is the leading manufacturer of microprocessors in the world. Thus, it would be expected to implement the highest standards of quality. The flaw in the Pentium involves elementary mathematics—a simple matter of inaccurate division—governed by principles that are familiar and easy to understand. This problem has not been generated by limitations imposed by register size or by difficulties in the operation of "floating-point" notation. If the leading manufacturer could nevertheless produce a product with a flaw of this magnitude, then the prospect of reliable computers seems remote.

The deepest felt concerns were articulated in a commentary that appeared on the op-ed page of the *New York Times*, by an author who plaintively inquired, "On the eve of the 21st century, what basis do we have for knowing if anything on our computer screen is error-free?" His answer is *faith*:

> The complexity of today's machines is far beyond our ability to check them by hand. All the fine points are floating; the only orthodox solution is to have more faith. We must accept on faith that

[29] The remark is attributed to William Kahan of the University of California at Berkeley by Markoff, "Flaw Undermines Accuracy," p. C1. A number of articles discussing the problem have since appeared, including John Markoff, "Error in Chip Still Dogging Intel Officials," *New York Times*, December 6, 1994, p. C4; Laurie Flynn, "A New York Banker Sees Pentium Problems," *New York Times*, December 19, 1994, pp. C1–C2; John Markoff, "In About-Face, Intel Will Swap Flawed Pentium Chip for Buyers," *New York Times*, December 21, 1994, pp. A1 and C6; and John Markoff, "Intel's Crash Course on Consumers," *New York Times*, December 21, 1994, p. C1.

[30] Including a security loophole with Sun Microsystems that was acknowledged in 1991, as Markoff observes in "Flaw Undermines Accuracy," p. C2.

[31] John Hockenberry, "Pentium and Our Crisis of Faith," *New York Times*, December 28, 1994, p. A11; Peter H. Lewis, "From a Tiny Flaw, a Major Lesson," *New York Times*, December 27, 1994, p. B10; and "Cyberscope," *Newsweek*, December 12, 1994. Another example of humor at Intel's expense: Question: What's another name for the "Intel Inside" sticker they put on Pentiums? Answer: A warning label.

> our telephone bills are absolutely error-free just as we must accept the integrity inside a microprocessor (even a free replacement chip).[32]

The question, no doubt, is well posed, but the answer leaves something to be desired. Articles of faith, after all, are things we believe, not because they are well supported, but in the absence of evidence or even in spite of it. The question the author raises appears to be rational, but his answer quite clearly is not.

Indeed, there are ample indications that the question is appropriate. We have discovered several grounds for disputing the reliability of our expert-system software: (1) The source of information upon which the system was constructed might be inaccurate or incomplete because the source was not an expert in the domain. (2) The transmission of that information may have introduced distortions or omissions because the "knowledge engineer" was not sufficiently competent. (3) The programmer who translated the information into a program using a programming language may have committed numerous programming errors. Because programmers are almost never experts with regard to the problem, they usually must depend on authorities for the information they program.[33]

Even when the source of information is an authority, the transmission of the knowledge introduces no distortions, and the programmer commits no mistakes—a case in which problems of kinds (1) through (3) do not occur—the inherent uncertainty of scientific knowledge would still remain because (4) even warranted scientific knowledge is still fallible and possibly false. We cannot know which among those warranted beliefs that we accept as true are *true* and which among those warranted beliefs that we accept as true are *false*. If we had direct access to the truth, after all, we would not depend on warrants. The risk of error is the price of scientific knowledge.[34]

Moreover, even leaving these sources of possible error to one side, there appear to be other problems that arise, not with respect to the software, but with regard to hardware components that no computer can function

[32] Hockenberry, "Pentium and Our Crisis of Faith," p. A11.

[33] As M. M. Lehman has observed, another—often more basic—problem can arise when changes in the world affect the truth of assumptions on which programs are based—which leads him to separate (what he calls) S-type and E-type systems, where the latter but not the former are subject to revision under the control of feedback. See, for example, M. M. Lehman, "Feedback, Evolution, and Software Technology," *IEEE Software Process Newsletter*, April 1995, for more discussion.

[34] Fetzer, *Scientific Knowledge*, p. 15. Other problems not discussed in the text include determining the precise conditions that must be satisfied for something to properly qualify as "scientific knowledge" (by arbitrating among inductivist, deductivist, and abductivist models, for example), and the appropriate measures that should be employed in determining degrees of evidential support (by accounting for the proper relations between subjective, frequency, and propensity interpretations of probability), a precondition for the proper appraisal of "certainty factors" (CFs), for example. These issues are pursued in Fetzer, *Scientific Knowledge*, and Fetzer, *Philosophy of Science*.

without: (5) every physical machine has inherent limitations with respect to its ability to process binary numbers imposed by the characteristics of its registers; (6) every physical machine has an arithmetic and logic unit that may introduce arbitrary errors, even if it was produced by the leading manufacturer. These difficulties appear to be even more disturbing than those encountered in the construction of knowledge-based software. The fallibility of synthetic knowledge, after all, unlike that of analytic knowledge, comes as no surprise.

## IV. Programming Languages, Models, and the World

### A. *Programming languages and virtual machines*

The distinction between natural and artificial languages has important ramifications for understanding computers and their reliability. Ordinary computers, as physical machines, operate on the basis of binary languages consisting of sequences of zeroes and ones. Programming by means of sequences of this kind is not merely extremely tedious but practically impossible. Different levels of programming languages have been developed, the lowest level of which is *assembly language*, where there is (more or less) a one-to-one relationship between computer commands and computer operations. In *higher-level languages*, such as Pascal, Prolog, and so forth, there is a one-to-many relationship between computer commands and operations (that is, a single command can cause the computer to perform a number of operations).

As a consequence, it becomes far easier to program using a higher-level language than it is using assembly language, much less using machine language itself. In effect, students are taught to program in languages that correspond, not to the *target machines* on which their programs are intended to run, but to *virtual machines*—hypothetical computers controlled by those languages. The connection between these higher-level languages and the language of the machine is thus effected by means of compilers or interpreters, which translate programs in higher-level (source) code into machine-level (target) code. *Compilers* translate whole programs into machine code and then execute them, while *interpreters* translate and execute programs line-by-line.[35]

For some programming languages, a compiler or interpreter for translating from source code to target code may not even exist. The language CORE, for example, has been introduced as a pedagogical device to familiarize students with basic principles of programming without confronting them with the necessity to master every detail. CORE thus exemplifies the possibility that there can be source languages for which

[35] See, for example, Davis, *Fundamental Computer Concepts*, pp. 110–13.

there are no target machines.[36] It functions as a model of a virtual machine for which there exists no physical counterpart. And it serves as a reminder that there can be differences between programming languages and the machines that execute programs.

The most important difference is that between virtual computers and physical machines. Because virtual computers are hypothetical machines, they exist as abstract entities that are not in space-time. Any connection between (the commands of) programming languages for virtual machines and (the commands of) machine languages for physical machines must be effected by compilers or interpreters, in the absence of which the programs cannot exert causal influence over any physical machine. Indeed, in the absence of a corresponding compiler or interpreter, a programming language has a standing that corresponds to that of an artificial language, for which the axioms and theorems that define machines of this kind are true merely by stipulation. The axioms that define CORE are true as matters of definition.

When virtual computers have physical counterparts in the form of target machines, including the existence of compilers and of interpreters, however, then programs that are written in their source code may exert causal influence upon the performance of those machines. The precise character of that influence depends upon the extent to which operations that are causal counterparts of commands written in those languages have been successfully implemented in the corresponding compilers or interpreters and in machine hardware, such as the arithmetic and logic units, in addition to the presence or absence of other causal factors that influence machine performance.

### *B. Programming languages and physical machines*

The difference between virtual machines and physical machines reflects an *ontological* (or "ontic") difference in the kinds of things that they happen to be, but it is one with significant *epistemological* (or "epistemic") implications for what can be known about them. When a program is written in a programming language for which there exists no physical (target) machine, that programming language may be properly viewed as defining a virtual machine whose behavior corresponds to that of the language as a matter of definition. The programming language defines the corresponding machine as an abstract entity whose behavior necessarily conforms to that language.

In cases of this kind, therefore, the type of knowledge that we can acquire about the performance of that virtual machine is analytic and therefore certain. However, when a program is written in a programming

[36] Michael Marcotty and Henry E. Ledgard, *Programming Language Landscape*, 2d ed. (Chicago, IL: Science Research Associates, 1986), ch. 2.

language for which there exists a physical (target) machine, that programming language may no longer be properly viewed as defining a virtual machine whose behavior corresponds to that of the language simply as a matter of definition. For the possibility now presents itself that the behavior of the physical (target) machine might deviate arbitrarily from that of the virtual (source) machine. We cannot merely stipulate that they in fact correspond.

There is an important similarity and an important difference in comparison with alternative geometries. Euclidean and non-Euclidean geometries alike may be viewed as axioms and theorems that are true of corresponding abstract domains of entities and relations that satisfy them as matters of stipulation. Thus, the sum of the interior angles of a triangle turns out to be *greater than* 180 degrees in Riemannian geometry (which is the geometry of the surface of a sphere), *less than* 180 degrees in hyperbolic geometry (the geometry of the surface of a saddle), and *equal to* 180 degrees in Euclidean geometry. And yet, as formal theories of abstract domains, all three geometries are equally analytic!

That certain axioms define an abstract domain and that certain theorems follow from them, however, does not determine whether or not those axioms are true of the physical world. We have already discovered that the study of formal systems for abstract domains can be pursued employing purely *a priori* methods. But when the elements of those systems are subjected to a physical interpretation—where *straight lines* are identified with rays of light and *points* with their intersections, for example—then their truth or falsity is no longer a matter of meaning alone but depends upon the properties of the world. And that is an empirical question that may only be settled by *a posteriori* methods appropriate to claims that are synthetic.

Indeed, while Euclid may have assumed that the axioms of his geometry were those of physical space and did not merely define an abstract domain, the mathematical structure of space within contemporary theories of physics is regarded as non-Euclidean. Thus, when programmers in turn presume that the axioms and theorems of a programming language control the performance of a physical machine, they are making assumptions that are synthetic, that are not determined by stipulation. A program written in a language for which there exists some physical machine has causal capabilities that purely formal systems (as abstract calculi) or even scientific theories (as interpreted formal systems) do not possess.[37]

### C. *Programs as causal models of algorithms*

While programs are constructed on the basis of algorithms when an appropriate step-by-step solution for a problem happens to exist, there is

[37] See James H. Fetzer, "Philosophical Aspects of Program Verification," *Minds and Machines*, vol. 1, no. 2 (May 1991), pp. 197–216.

an important difference between algorithms and programs. An algorithm can be implemented in different programs by different programmers who utilize different languages. The result is a causal model of that algorithm, by means of which that program can exert an influence on the performance of a physical machine that could not be exerted by the original algorithm.[38] Thus, the problem of determining whether integer *n* happens to be even or odd can be solved by means of a rather simple algorithm in two steps as follows:

> Step 1: Divide *n* by two.
> Step 2: If the remainder is zero then *n* is even; otherwise, *n* is odd.

This algorithm, as it stands, can exert no influence on any physical machine because it is formulated in English rather than in some programming language.

When that algorithm is implemented in the form of a program in a programming language for which there exist physical machines, such as Pascal, however, then the situation is completely different:

```
program even_or_odd(input, output);
var n: integer;
begin
  write('Enter an integer: ');
  readln(n);
  if (n mod 2) = 0 then
    writeln('The number is even')
  else
    writeln('The number is odd')
end.
```

This program, **even_or_odd**, takes an integer **n** and calculates whether the result after division by 2 (**mod**) is 0 or not. If the result equals 0, **writeln** ("write line") directs that a message be sent to the screen, "**The number is even**"; otherwise, "**The number is odd**."

The **writeln** command is among the simplest directions that computers can execute. In Microsoft BASIC, for example, there are commands such as **BEEP** which beeps the speaker; **CIRCLE(x,y)r** which draws a circle with its center at point **x,y** and its radius **r**; **COLORb,p** which sets background color and palette of foreground colors when in graphics mode; **LOCATErow,col** which positions the cursor; and **PLAYstring**, which plays music as specified by **string**.[39] Thus, in all of these cases, the commands that occur in a program possess a causal capability that goes far beyond

[38] See *ibid.*, p. 202.
[39] See James H. Fetzer, "Program Verification: The Very Idea," *Communications of the ACM*, vol. 31, no. 9 (September 1988), p. 1057.

that of ordinary formal systems, even when such systems are provided with empirical interpretations.

Precisely which causal capabilities a specific program may possess, however, clearly depends on several different kinds of factors. One is the programming language in which it is written. A program, like **even_or_odd**, that is written in Pascal, for example, might be executed by any computer equipped with a Pascal compiler or interpreter. In contrast, the same algorithm incorporated into a program written in CORE might properly qualify as a set of instructions for a virtual machine, but since there is no interpreter or compiler for CORE, it would not possess any causal capabilities with regard to a physical counterpart. It could not control any actual machine.

### *D. Smith's analysis of the role of models*

Other students of the foundations of computer science have noted that it appears to be heavily dependent on the use of models. As Brian Smith, for example, has observed, the construction of a program usually depends upon a presupposed model of the problem that is to be solved, where that model is supposed to represent some aspect of the real world. Techniques drawn from the field known as "model theory" can then be applied within computer science to determine whether or not our program corresponds to our model of the problem. As Smith remarks, alas, there is a hidden problem: "Unfortunately, model theory does not address the model-world relationship at all. Rather, what model theory does is to tell you how your descriptions, representations, and programs *correspond to your model*."[40] Thus, during the course of his discussion, Smith advances the diagram represented in Figure 4. He then invites us to think of computer systems, programs, descriptions or even thoughts as occupying the left-hand box, which is marked "COMPUTER," while "the very real world," marked "REAL WORLD," is on the right.[41]

Smith's discussion drives home the important point that "models" mediate the relationship between computer systems (computers, programs, and so on) and the world. Smith also emphasizes that models depend upon the essential use of *abstraction and idealization*, at least in the sense that they represent only some but not all of the properties of what they model. He acknowledges that model theory provides for the systematic investigation of the "left-hand" relationship (between models and computers), but asks: "What about the relationship on the right? The answer,

[40] Brian C. Smith, "Limits of Correctness in Computers," Center for the Study of Language and Information, Stanford University, Report No. CSLI-85-35 (1985); reprinted in Charles Dunlop and Rob Kling, eds., *Computerization and Controversy* (San Diego, CA: Academic Press, 1991), pp. 632–46. The passage quoted here is found on p. 638 (emphasis in original).

[41] Smith, "Limits," p. 639. As Smith also observes, computers and models themselves are "embedded within the real world," which is why the symbol for "REAL WORLD" is open in relation to the box, which surrounds the elements marked "COMPUTER" and "MODEL."

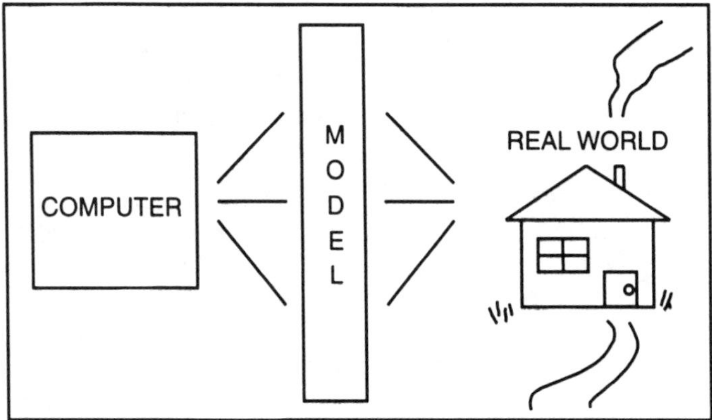


FIGURE 4. Computers, models, and the embedding world.

and one of the main points I hope you will take away from this discussion, is that, at this point in intellectual history, *we have no theory of this right-hand side relationship.*"[42]

At this juncture, however, a distinction needs to be drawn between the the model-world relation, on the one hand, and formulating solutions to specific problems, on the other. It is certainly correct to contend that the the construction of computers, the composition of programs, and the like, depend essentially upon the use of abstract and idealized models. And it is certainly correct to maintain that "model theory" provides resources for investigating the relationship between models of various kinds. But it is a mistake to suggest that, at this point in intellectual history, we do not have a theory of the model-world relationship or the resources to investigate it.

The relationship between models and the world, after all, is the domain of *empirical science*. The goal of empirical science can even be defined as that of constructing *a model of the world*, while the philosophy of science can be defined as having the goal of constructing *a model of science*.[43] The models that scientists construct are usually called "theories," and those that philosophers construct are also called "explications," but they are models in every sense that makes a difference here. The various sciences thus represent a division of labor in the pursuit of knowledge, where physicists seek to develop models of physical phenomena, chemists of chemical phenomena, and so forth. And philosophers of science try to model how this can be done.

Smith's apparent lapse regarding the model-world relation is even more surprising insofar as he explicitly considers the case of physics. He remarks:

[42] Smith, "Limits," p. 638 (emphasis added).
[43] See Fetzer, *Philosophy of Science*, pp. xii–xiii.

> How apparently pure mathematical structures could be used to model the material substrate of the universe is a question that has exercised the physical scientists for centuries. But the point is that . . . formal techniques don't themselves address the question of adequacy.[44]

This passage itself appears to suggest where his argument has gone wrong. For the fact that the relations that may obtain between different models can be investigated by purely formal methods does not imply that the relations that obtain between models of the world and the world cannot be investigated by methods that are not purely formal. That the relations between two models are deductively checkable does not preclude the prospect that the relations between models and the world may be inductively checkable.[45]

### *E. The model-world relationship*

The models that are objects of scientific inquiry may be "abstractions" or "idealizations" in the sense that they represent only some but not all of the properties of the phenomena they model, but they are not necessarily therefore either *inaccurate* or *incomplete* with respect to the properties of the phenomena that are causally (as opposed to statistically) relevant to an outcome or attribute of interest. Every instantiation of a physical system $x$ at a specific moment of time $t$ exemplifies an infinite number of properties $F1$, $F2$, . . . with respect to its spatial and temporal relations to other events. Yet that does not mean that each of those properties makes a difference to an outcome or attribute of interest. Most of them turn out to be irrelevant.

Consider diseases of the blood, for example. The expert system MYCIN depends upon laws relating diseases to symptoms and causes, yet many properties of persons who have diseases are not causally relevant to having those diseases or to manifesting specific symptoms. Properties such as *place of birth*, *level of education*, and *sense of humor*, for example, are properties whose presence or absence ordinarily does not contribute to bringing about the presence or absence of *leukemia*. When *being born near*

[44] Smith, "Limits," p. 639.

[45] Indeed, on the deductivist model of scientific inquiry, which has been advocated especially by Karl R. Popper, even the adequacy of scientific theories is deductively checkable by comparing deduced consequences with descriptions of the results of observations and experiments, which are warranted by perceptual inference. This process is not a symmetrical decision procedure, since it can lead to the rejection of theories in science but not to their acceptance. The failure to reject on the basis of severe tests, however, counts in favor of a theory. See Karl R. Popper, *Conjectures and Refutations* (New York: Harper and Row, 1968). On the deductivist model, see Fetzer, *Philosophy of Science*. The construction of proofs in formal sciences, incidentally, is also an asymmetrical procedure, since the failure to discover a proof does not establish that it does not exist.

*a toxic waste dump, having a Ph.D.*, and so on, make a difference to the propensity of members of a reference class (such as *adult white females*) to acquire an attribute such as *leukemia*, then they qualify as causally relevant to that attribute, but otherwise not.[46]

The use of the term "propensity" is crucial within this context, however, since it refers to the *strength of the causal tendency* for an outcome of kind *K* (such as leukemia) to be brought about under conditions of kind *C1* through *Cn* (such as adult white female born near a toxic waste dump). The criterion of *causal relevance* must therefore be separated from a counterpart criterion of *statistical relevance*, according to which any property whose presence or absence makes a difference to the frequency with which an attribute is manifested by the members of a reference class is statistically relevant to that attribute, but otherwise not.[47] The distinction is one between causation and correlation. Causal relations imply statistical correlations, but not conversely.[48]

That the difference between causal relations and statistical correlations is enormously important is widely acknowledged but is not therefore necessarily well understood. Virtually any two properties—shapes and sizes, or colors and textures, or heights and weights—stand in relations of statistical correlation, whether or not they are causally connected. The isolation and identification of properties that are not merely statistically correlated but causally related, by comparison, tends to depend upon systematic observation and controlled experimentation. The truth of a causal law requires that its formulation take into account the presence or absence of every property whose presence or absence makes a difference to its outcome.

This condition, which applies to laws themselves and is known as *the requirement of maximal specificity*, has a counterpart which applies to the application of laws for the purpose of explanation known as *the requirement of strict maximal specificity*.[49] While the former demands that every

[46] The use of the term "propensity" is crucial here, since it refers to the strength of the causal tendency. The general standard being employed may be referred to as the *propensity criterion of causal relevance*. See, for example, Fetzer, *Scientific Knowledge*, and Fetzer, *Philosophy of Science*, for technical elaboration.

[47] The use of the term "frequency" is crucial here, since it refers to the relative frequency of an attribute. The general standard being employed may be referred to as *the frequency criterion of statistical relevance*. See, for example, Wesley C. Salmon, *Statistical Explanation and Statistical Relevance* (Pittsburgh, PA: University of Pittsburgh Press, 1971). But Salmon mistakes statistical relevance for explanatory relevance.

[48] Strictly speaking, in the case of propensities, causal relations and relative frequencies are related probabilistically. See, for example, Fetzer, *Scientific Knowledge*, and Fetzer, *Philosophy of Science*.

[49] Even when the chemical composition, the manner of striking, and the dryness of a match are causally relevant to its lighting, that outcome may be predicted with deductive certainty (when the relationship is deterministic) or with probabilistic confidence (when the relationship is indeterministic) *only if* no other relevant properties, such as the presence or absence of oxygen, have been overlooked. For discussion, see, for example, James H. Fetzer, "The Frame Problem: Artificial Intelligence Meets David Hume," *International Journal of*

relevant property be included in the formulation of a law, the latter demands that every irrelevant property be excluded from a properly formulated explanation. When the laws of nature or relative frequencies that obtain within a problem domain are known, they can function as *natural algorithms* or as *heuristic guidelines* in formulating possible solutions to problems as distinct kinds of models of the domain.[50]

### F. The importance of specifications

Thus, in the case of an expert system such as MYCIN, for example, we have discovered that information about causal connections and statistical correlations between the occurrence of infections and diseases and the occurrence of various symptoms represents the kind of knowledge that science can provide. An expert system for predicting the behavior of a certain person, moreover, would presumably apply scientific knowledge concerning (normal or abnormal) human behavior to the features of that specific case. An expert system for income-tax preparation, of course, might not require scientific knowledge, but it certainly does not appear to pose any problems for modeling that could not be overcome by fashioning suitable algorithms.

While he is wrong to overlook the role of science with respect to right-hand relations between models and the world, Smith is right to sense that the *conception* of possible solutions to problems and their *formalization* as "specifications" appears to be a creative process controlled by imagination and conjecture—an art rather than a science.[51] He thus distinguishes between *specifications* as formal descriptions—typically in some canonical language—in which the behavior that is desired of the system is described (where the specifications are normally motivated by a model of the world), and *programs* as sets of instructions to govern the behavior of that system. The specification thus describes what proper behavior should be, while the program is a step-by-step characterization of exactly how that behavior would be achieved by such a system.[52]

Other authors have introduced a somewhat different conception of specifications. In a work on the management of software projects, for example, Neil Whitten advances a definition of "product specifications"

*Expert Systems*, vol. 3, no. 3 (1990), pp. 219–32; and James H. Fetzer, "Artificial Intelligence Meets David Hume: A Response to Pat Hayes," *International Journal of Expert Systems*, vol. 3, no. 3 (1990), pp. 239–47.

[50] Laws of nature are nature's algorithms. See Fetzer, "Artificial Intelligence Meets David Hume," p. 239. A complete theory of the relations between models of the world and the world would include a defense of the abductivist model of science as "inference to the best explanation."

[51] Smith thus appears to have committed a fallacy of equivocation by his ambiguous use of the phrase "theory of the model-world relationship."

[52] Smith, "Limits," p. 640.

as a detailed description of *the externals of the product*, in the sense of a description of every feature accessible to system users: "Every function, command, screen, prompt, and so on must be documented here so that all the participants involved in the product development cycle will know the product they are to build, test, document, and support."[53] The appearance of tension between their views on specifications, however, can be resolved by observing that Whitten's specifications are external-model "counterparts" to Smith's internal-model specifications.

An expansive interpretation of this "external model" would encompass the manner in which the system should interact with its users in the real world. Thus, it should not be limited to such outcomes as, say, a series of warning alarms appearing on the screen in response to commands sent by the program to the system; it would also include the behavioral response that the system users would be expected to display in turn as measures to cope with the situation thus encountered. The kinds of situations and the kinds of responses that may be required of system users, therefore, ought to be inventoried or catalogued with suitable explanations and notation in a *user's manual* that enables users to operate the system in the real world.

The failure to find problems with computer systems has sometimes had deadly consequences. For example, the Therac-25 was a computer-controlled radiation machine manufactured by Atomic Energy of Canada, Ltd., that was used during the 1980s for the treatment of cancer. The system allowed radiation to be applied at two levels—an X-ray diagnostic mode and a mild treatment mode—where the intensity of exposure in the X-ray mode could be one hundred times as great as in the treatment mode. If an operator happened to select the X-ray mode by mistake *and then corrected it using the proper controls within an eight second interval*, a patient would be exposed to the full dosage without protection. The result was three deaths due to software.[54]

### *G. The models used in computer science*

The Therac-25 therapy fiasco was further compounded by inadequate specifications in relation to the user's manual and the conditions encountered in the real world. Different warnings were flashed on its control screen identifying malfunctions by number (such as "Malfunction 54"), but they did not indicate the seriousness of the problems they represented. Whether its beam intensity was off merely a little or a lot, the warning looked the same. Moreover, the staff was so confident that their computerized system could not possibly harm their patients that they

[53] Whitten, *Managing Software Development Projects*, p. 13.

[54] Jonathan Jacky, "Safety-Critical Computing: Hazards, Practices, Standards, and Regulations," *The Sciences*, September/October 1989; reprinted in Dunlop and Kling, *Computerization and Controversy*, pp. 612–31.

ignored their complaints. When one patient objected, "You burned me!," the operator replied, "I'm sorry, but that's not possible, it's just not possible." The patient was severely injured.[55]

These considerations suggest that at least three kinds of models may be involved in the design, development, and utilization of reliable computerized products. The first is the *specification* itself as a model of the problem to be solved. When the problem is abstract or an algorithm exists that can solve it, the specification may have a deductive warrant; when it concerns causal relations and statistical correlations that have been subjected to scientific investigation, the specification may have an inductive warrant; but when warrants of neither kind happen to be available, a specification may have no more status than that of a conjecture regarding a possible solution.[56]

The second is the *program* itself as a model of the solution to that problem within a programming language. This component involves "modeling" of two different kinds. The more obvious of the two is that the program is the implementation of a solution to a problem, where that solution is represented by the specification. In this sense, a program is a model intended to satisfy another model, namely, a model of the problem solution in the form of its specification, which may have been proposed or imposed by another source. The less obvious sense in which the program involves modeling is that it is written in a programming language, which itself functions as a model for a virtual or physical machine. The adequacy of that model requires a warrant of its own.

The third kind of model is a model of the *computer system* consisting of a computer and its associated equipment situated in the world. Even in the case of a simple program such as **even_or_odd**, there is the presumption that the program software that implements an algorithmic solution to the problem is an integrated component of a larger system that includes, for example, an arithmetic and logic unit and a screen to which messages may be sent. In Microsoft BASIC, the system presumably includes speakers that can be beeped, background and foreground colors that can be set, and music that can be played. In the case of the Therac-25, the system includes radiation equipment with diagnostic and treatment capacities, a user-interface, etc.

These three kinds of models are obviously not independent. External specifications, for example, are presumably derived from a model of the system that is intended to employ them, and internal specifications are presumably derived from a model of external specifications. The program, in turn, is designed as an implementation of those internal speci-

[55] *Ibid.*, p. 617.

[56] As M. M. Lehman has observed (in personal communication with the author), specifications are frequently merely *partial* models of the problem to be solved.

fications by providing a set of instructions which, if it were executed by the hardware component of a computer system, would bring about behavior of that system in conformity with the original system model. Given our discoveries about many ways in which these systems can go wrong, the problem becomes whether computer system reliability can be assured. To what extent, if any, can we know when we can depend on the performance of a system?

## V. The Reliability of Computer Systems

### *A. The limits of formal methods*

From the perspective of the theory of knowledge, there appear to be three access routes toward the acquisition of knowledge of computer system reliability: deductive reasoning, inductive reasoning, and perceptual inference. The use of formal methods has been directed toward establishing that programs satisfy their specifications, where proofs of program correctness in this sense are known as *program verifications*. Among the foremost proponents of these formal methods is C. A. R. Hoare, who claims:

> Computer programming is an exact science in that all the properties of a program and all the consequences of executing it in any given environment can, in principle, be found out from the text of the program itself by means of purely deductive reasoning.[57]

This implies that certainty of knowledge about the performance of a computer might be obtainable, after all, by employing purely formal methods.

However, as Smith has remarked, a formal proof that the text of a program satisfies its specification has the character of a *relative consistency proof*, which might establish that the program would perform as desired on the assumption that the specification successfully defines the desired performance.[58] Thus, a distinction is commonly drawn between securing suitable specifications ("Getting the right system!") and writing a program which satisfies those specifications ("Getting the system right!").[59]

[57] C. A. R. Hoare, "An Axiomatic Basis for Computer Programming," *Communications of the ACM*, vol. 12, no. 10 (October 1969), pp. 576–80 and 583; the quotation may be found on p. 576.

[58] Smith, "Limits," pp. 639–43. Other authors have concurred. See, for example, Alan Borning, "Computer System Reliability and Nuclear War," *Communications of the ACM*, vol. 30, no. 2 (February 1987), pp. 112–31; reprinted in Dunlop and Kling, *Computerization and Controversy*.

[59] For further discussion, see, for example, B. W. Boehm, *Software Engineering Economics* (New York: Prentice-Hall, 1981).

Even the successful construction of a formal proof that a program satisfies its specifications could have limited import for securing the right outcome, because the specification model might actually be hopelessly inadequate.

However, the situation seems to be even more problematic than Smith suggests, because there are no built-in guarantees that a computer will properly execute a program, even when that program has been proven to satisfy its specifications—unless that computer is a virtual machine rather than a physical one.[60] The function of a program verification is therefore relatively restricted in relation to ultimate computer system performance, because the program itself is only one factor that contributes toward the behavior of a complex causal system. A proof of correctness can establish that a program conforms to its specifications, but cannot demonstrate that those specifications are suitable, or tell us what would happen were it executed.[61]

Hoare has sought to defend the use of formal methods by encompassing proofs of compiler and even hardware correctness within their scope:

> When the correctness of a program, its compiler, and the hardware of the computer have all been established with mathematical certainty, it will be possible to place great reliance on the results of the program and predict their properties with a confidence limited only by the reliability of the electronics.[62]

The problem now, however, has simply been compounded: the performance of compilers and hardware is no more amenable to formal proof in the case of physical machines than is the performance of programs. The situation that Hoare describes—in which the correctness of the program, its compiler, and its hardware have all been proven correct—can provide no guarantee that the execution of that software by means of that hardware would produce the performance desired using a physical machine.

The possibility that the model-world relationship may be the wrong one means that a proof that a program is valid does not establish that it is also sound. Its specifications might be mistaken because the model it represents does not conform to the world. In that case, getting the program right would not guarantee getting the right program. But there is a deeper problem because, *even if its specifications were correct*, a proof that a program is sound still could not guarantee computer performance. Getting the program right and getting the right program can insure what

[60] See Fetzer, "Program Verification," pp. 1056–57.

[61] See James H. Fetzer, "Author's Response," *Communications of the ACM*, vol. 32, no. 4 (April 1989), p. 512.

[62] Hoare, "An Axiomatic Basis for Computer Programming," p. 579.

would happen if that program were executed only on the assumption that the hardware, the software, and everything else behaves as expected.

*B. The limits of empirical methods*

The success of program verification as a generally applicable and completely reliable method to guarantee the performance of a computer when a program is executed is not even a theoretical possibility.[63] As Avra Cohn, one of the leading proponents of formal methods, has now acknowledged,

> neither an actual *device* nor an *intention* is an object to which logical reasoning can be applied. . . . In short, verification involves a pair of *models* that bear an uncheckable and possibly imperfect relation to the intended design and to the actual device.[64]

Formal methods applied to the text of a program cannot possibly guarantee the performance of a computer when it executes that program, because the causal capabilities of a program cannot be ascertained by purely deductive reasoning. Hoare's claim to possess certain knowledge of program performance on the basis of formal methods alone thus appears to be rooted in a misconception. It could only exist as a form of synthetic *a priori* knowledge.

The methods available for evaluating the reliability of computer systems, however, are not confined to purely formal methods. *Program testing*, for example, involves running a program, observing its behavior, and removing bugs as they are discovered. As Bev Littlewood and Lorenzo Strigini have observed, however, fixing a program or a device by attempting to remove its bugs runs the risk of introducing new ones: "Because nothing would be known about the new bug, its effects on the reliability of the system would be unbounded. In particular, the system might not even be as reliable as it was before the bug was found."[65] Debugging thus supplies no guarantees.

The three remedies that Littlewood and Strigini recommend, moreover, appear inadequate to the task. The first is to treat design failures as "nonquantifiable" and thereby avoid specifying performance requirements, an approach that they report is "now in fairly wide use." (We might call this "the ostrich policy.") The second, which they prefer over the first, is to impose limitations upon system requirements "so the role

[63] See Fetzer, "Program Verification."

[64] Avra Cohn, "The Notion of Proof in Hardware Verification," *Journal of Automated Reasoning*, vol. 5, no. 2 (June 1989), p. 132.

[65] Bev Littlewood and Lorenzo Strigini, "The Risks of Software," *Scientific American*, November 1992, p. 65.

of software is not too critical." (Call this "the reduced-role policy.") The third is to passively accept the risks involved in relying upon these systems. After all, "[s]ociety sometimes demands extremely high safety for what may be irrational reasons. Medical systems are a good example." (Call this "the blind policy.")[66]

*Hardware testing*, if anything, fares even worse. As David Shepherd and Greg Wilson have observed, a powerful microprocessor, such as the Inmos T800, which integrates a central processing unit with four communications links and four kilobytes of memory in a single device, turns out to have more possible combinations of input, memory, and output states than there are particles in the universe.[67] Exhaustive testing of an Inmos T800 is not even remotely a practical possibility. As a consequence, it must be tested using a modest subset of possible cases that the chip's designers hope qualifies as a representative sample that would support an inductive inference.

In fact, because the device has not yet been produced, its designers use programs running on other computers to simulate the T800's behavior. It turns out that the number of test results is so large that it is impossible to review each of them individually. As a consequence, designers compare a sample of the output of this new device against the output of a computer simulation or of an existing device already on the market. The problem that still remains, however, is that they cannot tell whether the standard of comparison they are employing might itself turn out to be incorrect.[68] It is not very reassuring when Shepherd and Wilson conclude: "The formal methods that Inmos is developing replace this design-and-test method with [formal] techniques guaranteeing that the final chip will behave correctly."[69]

### C. *The uncertainty of reliability*

If the choice among the three policies proposed by Littlewood and Strigini (the ostrich policy, the reduced-role policy, and the blind policy) is "rather disappointing," as they themselves concede,[70] then how should we proceed? At first blush, the situation would not seem to have to be this disappointing. The same methods of observation and experimentation that apply in the empirical sciences in general ought to apply here, where the laws of computer science are counterparts of the laws of physics, chemistry, and biology. We may even assume that these laws concern the

[66] *Ibid.*, pp. 65–66 and 75.
[67] David Shepherd and Greg Wilson, "Making Chips That Work," *New Scientist*, May 13, 1989, pp. 61–64.
[68] *Ibid.*, p. 62.
[69] *Ibid.*
[70] Littlewood and Strigini, "The Risks of Software," p. 75.

behavior displayed by computer systems under various conditions, given maximally specific descriptions.

At least two problems arise with this conception, however plausible it might initially appear. The first problem is that of specifying the complete sets of causally relevant factors involved here. As Hoare observes:

> I find digital computers of the present day to be very complicated and rather poorly defined. As a result, it is usually impractical to reason logically about their behavior. Sometimes, the only way of finding out what they will do is by experiment. Such experiments are certainly not mathematics. Unfortunately, they are not even science, beause it is impossible to generalize from their results or to publish them for the benefit of other scientists.[71]

The complexity of computer systems that combine software, hardware, and associated equipment to operate aircraft, treat cancer, and the like may be such that maximally specific descriptions are practically impossible to secure. Those laws no doubt exist, but they remain largely unknown.

The second problem is that software systems appear to be extremely sensitive to initial conditions, so that even small changes in system software can produce large changes in performance. As David Parnas once remarked, "[t]he thing that makes software so difficult is that we're dealing with highly irregular, discontinuous systems with many states and few, if any, exploitable regularities."[72] Indeed, the sensitivity of these systems is so acute that a single misplaced comma in the specification of a control program for an Atlas rocket carrying Mariner 1, the first U.S. interplanetary spacecraft, caused the vehicle to veer off course and have to be destroyed, perhaps the most costly grammatical error in history.[73]

These considerations raise the possibility that computer systems may be *chaotic systems*, in which the least change in initial conditions can cause enormous and unexpected changes in outcome performance.[74] Chaotic systems are not indeterministic systems, in which one or another outcome within a fixed class of outcomes occurs, not in every case but with a specific probability—but rather are deterministic systems, in which the same outcome occurs in every case under the same conditions. What makes chaotic systems difficult to understand and practically impossible

[71] C. A. R. Hoare, "Mathematics of Programming," *BYTE*, August 1986, p. 116.

[72] David Parnas, quoted in William E. Suydam, "Approaches to Software Testing Embroiled in Debate," *Computer Design*, vol. 24, no. 21 (November 15, 1986), p. 50.

[73] Littlewood and Strigini, "The Risks of Software," p. 63.

[74] For an introduction to chaos theory, see James Gleick, *Chaos: Making a New Science* (New York: Penguin Books, 1988).

to predict is that the minuteness of the changes to which these systems are sensitive makes them very hard to replicate and investigate.

If computer systems are sufficiently complex that it is practically impossible to provide them with maximally specific descriptions, and if they are immensely sensitive to initial conditions (as chaotic systems are), then the prospects for the formulation of laws of behavior for these systems are not encouraging. In the absence of knowledge of the laws of systems of these kinds, it appears altogether likely that the best we may be able to discover are statistical correlations that relate partial and incomplete descriptions of the causal factors that affect system performance to system performance. Given ignorance of system laws, information about correlations may have to serve as a fallible warrant for statistical predictions.[75]

## VI. Implications for Public Policy

Strictly speaking, the reliability of a computer system should be understood as the propensity of that system to produce the effects that its users expect. A system's specifications may not be the best evidence of what users should expect.[76] If those systems could be given maximally specific descriptions and be subjected to controlled experiments across large numbers of trial repetitions, then it would be possible, in principle, to draw inferences from the relative frequencies of system success and failure to the reliability of those systems—characterized as system propensities.[77] The difficulties that confront this conception, however, are rather imposing.

The conclusion that emerges from these considerations has been expressed by M. M. Lehman, who has advanced the following formulation as (what he calls) the "Uncertainty Principle for Computer Application": "*In the real world, the outcome of software system operation is inherently uncertain with the precise area of uncertainty also not knowable.*"[78] Provided we embrace a conception of morality that emphasizes respect for persons and their rights, this principle supports the inference that computer systems ought to be employed for safety-critical purposes where human lives are placed in jeopardy only when appropriate attention is devoted to an assessment of dangers and risks.

[75] See Fetzer, "The Frame Problem," pp. 228–29. Predictions based upon partial and incomplete descriptions of chaotic systems are obviously fallible—their reliability would appear to be unknowable.

[76] Sometimes unverifiable or incorrect programs can even be preferred; see Stephen Savitzky, "Technical Correspondence," *Communications of the ACM*, vol. 32, no. 3 (March 1989), p. 377. These include cases where a verifiably incorrect program yields a better performance than a verifiably correct program as a solution to a problem—where the most important features of a successful solution may involve properties that are difficult or impossible to formalize—and other kinds of situations.

[77] For further discussion, see Fetzer, *Scientific Knowledge*, and Fetzer, *Philosophy of Science*.

[78] M. M. Lehman, "Uncertainty in Computer Application," *Communications of the ACM*, vol. 33, no. 5 (May 1990), p. 585 (emphasis added).

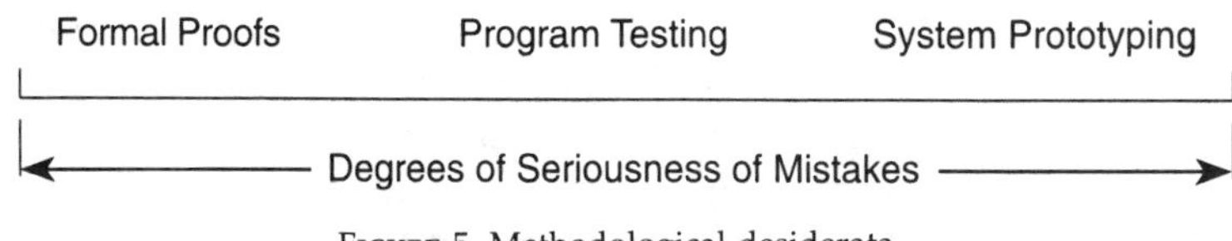


FIGURE 5. Methodological desiderata.

The most promising approach toward promoting health and safety arises from *system prototyping,* which involves testing entire computer systems within the environments for which they are intended. If the Therac-25 radiation machine had been subjected to severe tests deliberately designed to reveal potential inadequacies, that might have made a difference, but there are no guarantees. As David Nelson observes, system prototyping supports a different paradigm for computer science than that supported by the use of formal methods, since formal methods emphasize elegance and economy in programming, while prototyping and reliability testing emphasize safety-system redundancy and explanatory documentation.[79]

These results imply that statistical measures of the reliability of computer system performance should be employed as procedures intended to improve quality control. The use of formal proofs might even be statistically justifiable as a process that can contribute to improving the performance of computer systems when their performance is subjected to reliability tests.[80] In safety-critical situations, the point is not whether formal proofs may be useful but that prototype testing is indispensable.[81]

Other methods that can contribute toward the development of more reliable computer systems include the adoption of *software engineering standards,* which require programming projects to be conducted in specific stages with evaluations at each stage, and of a process of *certification and regulation* of competence in programming, enforced by requirements and periodic examinations.[82] Moreover, when systems fail, which they almost inevitably will, victims and survivors ought to be entitled to legal compensation by way of *liability protection,* which may take many forms, depending upon whether software is viewed as a service or as a product.[83]

[79] Nelson, "Deductive Program Verification" (*supra* note 27), p. 292.

[80] Donald Gillies has informed me that Hoare now advocates this position.

[81] The prospect of having to conduct statistical tests of nuclear weapons, space shuttle launches, etc., suggests the dimensions of the problem.

[82] See, for example, Jacky, "Safety-Critical Computing," pp. 622–27.

[83] *Ibid.*, p. 627. An excellent and accessible discussion of problems involving computer systems that affect many important areas of life is Ivars Peterson, *Fatal Defect: Chasing Killer Computer Bugs* (New York: Random House/Times Books, 1995).

Ultimately, the methods that should be employed for evaluating the reliability of computer systems tend to depend upon and vary with the seriousness of the consequences of making mistakes, as shown in Figure 5. Thus, no matter what solutions a society might adopt to enable its citizens to better cope with computer systems, such as software standards and liability protection, the full dimensions of the problem must be understood. Our confidence in this technology should not be merely an article of faith.

*Philosophy, University of Minnesota, Duluth*

# RESPONSIBILITY AND DECISION MAKING IN THE ERA OF NEURAL NETWORKS*

By William Bechtel

## I. Introduction

Many of the mathematicians and scientists who guided the development of digital computers in the late 1940s, such as Alan Turing and John von Neumann, saw these new devices not just as tools for calculation but as devices that might employ the same principles as are exhibited in rational human thought. Thus, a subfield of what came to be called *computer science* assumed the label *artificial intelligence* (AI).[1] The idea of building artificial systems which could exhibit intelligent behavior comparable to that of humans (which could, e.g., recognize objects, solve problems, formulate and implement plans, etc.) was a heady prospect, and the claims made on behalf of AI during the 1950s and 1960s were impossibly ambitious (e.g., having a computer capture the world chess championship within a decade). Despite some theoretical and applied successes within the field, serious problems soon became evident (of which the most notorious is the frame problem, which involves the difficulty in determining which information about the environment must be changed and which must be kept constant in the face of new information).[2] Instead of fulfilling the goal of quickly producing artificial intelligent agents which could compete with or outperform human beings, by the 1970s and 1980s AI had settled into a pattern of slower but real progress in modeling or simulating aspects of human intelligence. (Examples of the advances made during this period were the development of higher-level structures for encoding information, such as frames or scripts, which were superior to

* This essay was partly prepared while I was a visiting scholar of the Experimenteel-psychologische Onderzoekschool and affiliated with the Theoretical Psychology Faculty in the Department of Psychonomics at the Vrije Universiteit, Amsterdam. I am very grateful for the support I received there, especially conversations relevant to this essay with Huib Looren de Jong. I also thank Andy Clark, Larry May, and the editor of this volume, Ellen Paul, for their comments and suggestions on previous drafts of this essay.

[1] The term "artificial intelligence" was apparently invented by John McCarthy in the context of a seminal conference at Dartmouth College in 1956. For accounts of the early history of AI, see Pamela McCorduck, *Machines Who Think* (San Francisco: W. H. Freeman, 1979); and Howard Gardner, *The Mind's New Science: A History of the Cognitive Revolution* (New York: Basic Books, 1985).

[2] John McCarthy and Patrick J. Hayes, "Some Philosophical Problems from the Standpoint of Artificial Intelligence," in *Machine Intelligence*, ed. B. Meltzer and D. Michie (Edinburgh: Edinburgh University Press, 1969), pp. 463–502. For a fairly recent review of work on the frame problem, see K. M. Ford and P. J. Hayes, eds., *Reasoning Agents in a Dynamic World: The Frame Problem* (London: JAI Press, 1991).

simple propositional encodings in supporting reasoning or the understanding of natural [as opposed to computer or other artificial] language texts,[3] and the development of procedures for storing information about previously encountered cases and invoking these cases in solving new problems.)[4]

Since its inception, AI has embodied an ambiguity: Is the goal to design systems that are purely artificial and of interest only insofar as they serve human ends, or is it to develop systems that illuminate how we perform our mental activities? In some cases the goals coalesce and the best way to develop artificial systems to serve our ends is to employ information that has been gleaned in cognitive psychology, for example, about how humans reason. But in other cases the goals diverge. For example, successful chess-playing computers in the last two decades have generally not tried to model what is known about the reasoning of human chess players but to take advantage of the raw computational power of the computer to evaluate many more options than humans can. The divergence is manifest in an area such as the design of expert systems to aid or supplant human decision makers in such fields as medical diagnosis.[5] While designers of such systems often begin by incorporating the knowledge of human experts (often procured through interviews), since the real concern is with successful performance, designers often do not constrain themselves to having their systems employ the same reasoning procedures as humans.

At the theoretical edge of AI, though, the concern is to design systems that embody what is known about human cognition and to extend that knowledge by developing running computational models which can be tested against human agents. A common way of thinking about the relationship of AI to human mental activity is to view the AI program as a representation of a theory of human cognition. Such a representation of a theory has an advantage in that it can be tested not only by whether it can predict the data points produced by behavioral studies in psychology, but also by whether it can actually perform the task whose performance by humans the theory is to explain. A successful AI program is often viewed as an existence proof that a system operating according to this theory could in fact carry out the activity in question. In practice, most programs initially fail to accomplish what they were designed to do, thereby showing that the theories they embody are inadequate and require modification.

[3] Roger C. Schank and Robert P. Abelson, *Scripts, Plans, Goals, and Understanding* (Hillsdale, NJ: Lawrence Erlbaum, 1977); and Marvin Minsky, "A Framework for Representing Knowledge," in *The Psychology of Human Vision*, ed. P. H. Winston (New York: McGraw-Hill, 1975).

[4] Roger C. Schank and Christopher K. Reisbeck, *Inside Case-based Reasoning* (Hillsdale, NJ: Lawrence Erlbaum, 1989).

[5] Bruce G. Buchanan and Edward H. Shortliffe, eds., *Rule-based Expert Systems: The MYCIN Experiments of the Stanford Heuristic Programming Project* (Reading, MA: Addison-Wesley, 1984).

In what follows, my focus will be on cases in which the two objectives of AI come together, cases in which AI seeks to use knowledge about human cognition to design systems to carry out tasks that require intelligence when performed by humans and to employ these systems in decision-making contexts. I will be focusing on a highly speculative question, which I will motivate shortly: Will it make sense to hold some future AI systems themselves, and not their designers, morally responsible when they are employed in decision-making tasks? To hold the AI system morally responsible for its decision would, minimally, mean construing an AI system as a decision-making agent in the same sense in which a human person is thought to be. Any moral judgments that would be made of the human agent would also be directed at the AI system, and not attributed back to the designers or employers of that system. (Of course, in cases in which we might hold the employer of a human responsible for the employee's decisions, we might also hold the employer of the AI system responsible.) My primary goal is not to argue for the conclusion that we should hold certain AI systems of the future morally responsible, but to counter reasons that might be advanced for denying that such systems could be agents that are morally responsible for what they do. One thing I will try to show is that, given the degree to which these systems resemble us in their mental processing, the same reasons for not attributing moral responsibility to AI systems would support denying such responsibility to us. Accordingly, my title refers to the *era of neural networks* (neural networks are a particular kind of AI system to be discussed below), not simply to neural networks themselves. Even if one rejects the idea of holding an AI system morally responsible for its actions, answers to these objections raised against assigning responsibility to neural network systems are required if we are to defend our practice of holding humans morally responsible for their decisions. I will try to show, though, that these objections can be answered for both humans and AI systems.

As I noted above, AI systems have been designed to make recommendations as to decisions human agents might make (e.g., in the context of medical diagnosis). This brought to the fore the possibility of such systems making decisions on their own, not merely making recommendations to human agents. This practice is what raises the issue of whether AI systems should be held responsible, morally or legally, for their decisions, or whether the responsibility should be placed solely on the humans who have designed or employed the systems. (The practical aspects of holding AI systems legally responsible for decisions are complicated, but presumably one could allow such systems to earn money and pay fines or pay for particularly egregious actions by being shut down.[6] Since my concern is

[6] One may question whether turning off an AI system really constitutes punishment. This depends in part upon whether it makes sense to construe AI systems as having interests. Designing systems that have something recognizable as interests is now an active area of AI research, especially in the field of artificial life. Exploring this topic, however, is beyond the scope of this essay. For now I will simply assume that AI research will continue to be

with the features of the agents which justify attributing responsibility, not with the legal systems which may enforce such responsibility, I will restrict my focus to moral responsibility.)

The primary reason for exploring this option of localizing moral responsibility in the AI system, an option which most people would judge fanciful at present, is that to the degree that AI researchers build these systems by utilizing the best information available concerning the internal processes of humans engaged in reasoning and decision making, and to the degree that they are successful in building systems that resemble human agents in their behavior, these AI researchers will be building systems that reach decisions in the same manner as human agents. Whatever justification we have for assigning moral responsibility to humans should then carry over to these artificial agents. (There are aspects of human reasoning and decision making which I will not be able to discuss in detail in this essay. These are the affective and conative components. When I assume that systems are built using the best information we have about the internal processes in humans, however, I am assuming that these too are included. It is true that AI, and cognitive science more generally, began by assuming that cognition could be abstracted and modeled independently of these other dimensions. Nevertheless, the contemporary efforts to develop autonomous agents, often through a process of simulated evolution which not only provides the systems with innate knowledge but also sets goals for them, does not draw such principled distinctions. Whether the biological processes underlying affective and conative processes can themselves be modeled in artificial systems and blended into the models of cognitive processes, or whether one can only simulate their effects by solving whatever equations are discovered to characterize the behavior of the human affective and conative systems and then supplying appropriate inputs to models of cognitive processes, is not yet known. For purposes of this essay, I am simply assuming that the AI systems that I am considering will have affective and conative dimensions, and thus will exhibit whatever guilt, shame, remorse, or regret that is expected in human agents who would be held morally responsible for their actions.)

One common argument for not assigning moral responsibility to AI systems is to insist that these systems are built by humans and simply execute the directions set forth by the human designer in the program. But there are increasingly powerful reasons for rejecting this argument for not attributing responsibility to AI systems. First, realistic AI systems are extremely complex, and it is frequently not possible for the human designer to determine how the system will behave in the myriad of possible

successful in developing artificial agents that resemble humans in their decision making, including possession of motivational states.

situations in which it might be employed. In systems that employ conditional rules of the form "If symbols *A*, *B*, *C*, and *D* are active in working memory, construct a new symbol of form *E*, and store it in memory register *X*," for example, the number of possible interactions between rules and memory states can easily be intractable, so that humans could not go through all such interactions and make sure that the consequences were appropriate.[7] (For a discussion of some of the difficulties in testing ordinary computer programs, see James Fetzer's essay in this volume.) Second, many of these systems are provided with learning capacities so that the programs they implement are changed over time as a result of the consequences of their use. A simple example of such a learning system is a chess-playing computer that reevaluates its strategies depending upon whether it won or lost after applying them. More complex systems actually construct new rules and evaluate them in much the same manner as variation and selective retention is claimed to operate in biological evolution.[8] As a result of learning, these systems become as much a product of their learning history as they are of the designer. The combination of behaving in ways that are nontractable to begin with, and changing these ways of behaving as a result of experience, seems to render these systems autonomous mental agents and not comparable to simpler artifacts that do not exhibit these features. In these respects, sophisticated AI systems are comparable to human children, who also start off with complex innate desires and ways of processing information and who learn new desires and ways of processing this information through time. Insofar as we attribute moral responsibility to individual humans and do not insist on passing all responsibility back to their parents, so we should attribute moral responsibility to these AI systems.

During the 1970s and 1980s, most of the AI systems that were developed were what we can now call *classical*. What distinguishes them is that they function by representing information in language-like structures and applying rules to these representations to reach decisions. While classical AI systems initially seemed to hold great promise and attracted much

[7] Larry May, in personal discussion, has proposed an alternative perspective. When a human agent becomes intoxicated and begins to behave in irresponsible ways that are difficult to predict, we do not absolve the agent, but hold him or her responsible for becoming intoxicated. Perhaps we should hold AI designers who devise agents which they know will behave in ways they cannot foresee, similarly responsible. The context of constructing AI systems is, I think, significantly different from the context of becoming intoxicated. The systems are created because it is anticipated that they will generate many good outcomes (solving problems better than humans, etc.). The better analogy, I contend, is with giving birth to children. One hopes that one's children will be agents of good, even if, in ways that are currently unpredictable, some will cause great harm. We do not hold parents morally responsible for the actions of their (adult) offspring if they have done their best to provide an appropriate upbringing; neither should we hold AI designers responsible for the artificial agents they create if they have taken due precautions.

[8] See John H. Holland, Keith J. Holyoak, Richard E. Nisbett, and Paul R. Thagard, *Induction: Processes of Inference, Learning, and Discovery* (Cambridge, MA: MIT Press, 1986).

attention, some of the enthusiasm for them began to wane during the 1980s. One factor that helped to account for the lessened interest in classical AI was the reemergence of an alternative to the classical approach.[9] These systems are known variously as *neural networks* or *connectionist networks*; they are distinguished from classical systems in not using language-like structures to store information and, accordingly, not operating by applying rules to such representations.[10] (The basic principles of the operation of neural networks will be explained below.) Initially connectionist or neural networks, while affording a number of exciting properties for modeling cognition (e.g., the ability to work with degraded and novel inputs, to be sensitive to features of local contexts, and to employ multiple soft-constraint satisfaction in situations in which all constraints could not be simultaneously satisfied), were limited to rather exploratory applications. Increasingly, however, they are being applied in a number of real-life contexts (e.g., detecting enemy weapons or judging loan worthiness). Thus, the prospect of allowing such networks to make decisions on their own emerges; and accordingly, the question of whether they can be held accountable for their decisions is likely to arise for them as well as for more classical systems.

Twelve years ago, with neural networks explicitly in mind, I argued that it was, in principle, possible to design computer systems which could sensibly be held morally responsible for their decisions.[11] I argued, though, that the sorts of systems that could be held responsible would have to be considerably different from those now being used. Specifically, they would have to be systems that genuinely counted as *intentional systems*. The notion of an intentional system comes from Daniel Dennett, who proposed that some systems in nature could be usefully characterized from

[9] During the 1950s and 1960s, a number of researchers actively pursued the alternative connectionist or neural network strategy for creating artificial intelligent agents. See Frank Rosenblatt, *The Principles of Neurodynamics* (New York: Spartan, 1962); and Oliver G. Selfridge and Ulric Neisser, "Pattern Recognition by Machine," *Scientific American*, vol. 203 (August 1960), pp. 60–68. A critical analysis of the limitations of such systems by Marvin Minsky and Seymour Papert, *Perceptrons* (Cambridge, MA: MIT Press, 1969), helped to reduce interest in this approach. For a humorous recounting of the fall and reemergence of the neural network alternative, see Seymour Papert, "One AI or Many?" *Daedalus*, vol. 117 (1988), pp. 1–14.

[10] Perhaps the seminal event in the reemergence of such models was the publication of David E. Rumelhart, James L. McClelland, and the PDP Research Group, *Parallel Distributed Processing: Explorations in the Microstructure of Cognition*, vol. 1: *Foundations* (Cambridge, MA: MIT Press, 1986); and James L. McClelland, David E. Rumelhart, and the PDP Research Group, *Parallel Distributed Processing: Explorations in the Microstructure of Cognition*, vol. 2: *Psychological and Biological Models* (Cambridge, MA: MIT Press, 1986). As their titles indicate, Rumelhart and McClelland's preferred term for these models is *parallel distributed processing models*. For an elementary exposition of these models and their application to modeling cognition, see William Bechtel and Adele A. Abrahamsen, *Connectionism and the Mind: An Introduction to Parallel Processing in Networks* (Oxford: Basil Blackwell, 1991).

[11] William Bechtel, "Attributing Responsibility to Computer Systems," *Metaphilosophy*, vol. 16 (1984), pp. 296–306.

what he terms "the intentional stance."[12] From the intentional stance, one attributes mental states such as beliefs and desires to humans or possibly other systems. In philosophy of mind, these states are commonly referred to as *propositional attitudes*, since they seem to involve an agent having an attitude (believing, doubting, hoping, desiring, etc.) toward a proposition (which presents the content of the state). Thus, believing that Rembrandt's *Night Watch* is at the Rijksmuseum in Amsterdam involves two components, the attitude and the proposition. The characterization of mental states in terms of two components, an attitude and a proposition, it is argued, is often useful since we can compare people in terms of the attitudes they adopt toward certain propositions or we can explain people's actions in terms of the practical reasoning that connects different attitudes. Thus, if in addition to believing that the *Night Watch* is at the Rijksmuseum, I desired to see the *Night Watch*, I would (depending upon other beliefs and desires) make plans to go to the Rijksmuseum. Dennett construes this framework of describing people in terms of beliefs and desires as *intentional*, since these states relate agents to other states of the world.[13]

Dennett refers to the intentional stance as a *stance* in part because he maintains an instrumentalist position toward it. It is useful and informative, he contends, to characterize people or other systems in terms of beliefs and desires, but these terms do not pick out real features of people or systems. Dennett's instrumentalism is largely a rejection of the sort of realism toward propositional attitudes defended by Jerry Fodor, who proposes that in our heads there are actual encodings of language-like structures and that the ways the cognitive system employs these encodings determine whether a particular proposition is believed, desired, etc.[14] While agreeing with Dennett in rejecting this interpretation of propositional attitudes as corresponding to specific states inside the head, I nonetheless maintained that we should take a realist perspective on intentional attributions. The means to doing this is to construe propositional attitudes as characterizing the relations between the mental activities of people or other systems (taken as wholes) and their environment. Such attitudes specify, for example, what information about that environment people take account of and the goals for action they seek to realize. Thus, in intentional terms we describe how the mental activities of a person or

[12] Daniel C. Dennett, "Intentional Systems," *Journal of Philosophy*, vol. 68 (1971), pp. 87-106.

[13] Franz Brentano introduced the use of the term "intentionality" to refer to the fact that mental states are *about* things. He emphasized that this relation was unlike ordinary extensional relations since one could have mental states whose content did not exist. See Franz Brentano, *Psychology from an Empirical Standpoint* [1874], trans. A. C. Rancurello, D. B. Terrell, and L. L. McAlister (New York: Humanities Press, 1973).

[14] See Jerry A. Fodor, *The Language of Thought* (New York: Crowell, 1975), and *Psychosemantics: The Problem of Meaning in the Philosophy of Mind* (Cambridge, MA: MIT Press, 1987).

other system are adapted to an environment. (This view is developed further in Section II below.) In adopting an intentional account, we recognize that the mental activities of most such systems are not perfectly adapted to their environments; accordingly, we often must attribute some false beliefs and inappropriate desires to these systems.

My contention is that AI systems, as well as people, might be so adapted to their environments in terms of their mental processes that they are properly characterized as intentional systems. This proposal is directly opposed to John Searle's claim that computer systems could only enjoy "as if" intentionality, not intrinsic intentionality.[15] In my earlier essay, I contended that representational states of computational systems would enjoy intrinsic intentionality if these states were properly connected to the entities they represented. These states could acquire the appropriate kind of connectivity if the system in question was an adaptive system which developed its representational states as part of the activity of adapting to its environment. Learning systems, such as neural networks, I suggested then, exhibited this feature, and had the potential to be true intentional systems. The problem with contemporary neural networks is that most are not so connected to any actual environment to which they might adapt; rather, their activities all begin and end with symbolic representations constructed by humans, and hence any intentionality they seem to exhibit in response to their symbolic representations is all mediated by humans for whom these symbolic representations do have content. If this limitation is overcome and neural networks actually use their mental capacities to control interactions with an environment, and in the process adapt (always imperfectly) to their environment, they will be genuine intentional systems.

The reason for pressing for the connection between intentionality and moral responsibility is that in assessing whether agents are morally responsible for their actions in any given case, we appeal to intentional characterizations of them in terms of propositional attitudes. Thus, we inquire as to whether they knew what they were doing, what goals they were seeking to satisfy, what beliefs they had about the context of their action, and whether they arrived at their decision to act in a rational way

[15] John R. Searle, "Minds, Brains, and Programs," *Behavioral and Brain Sciences*, vol. 3 (1980) pp. 417–24. I have argued elsewhere that Searle's argument that we, and not AI systems (even those with robotic bodies that seem to satisfy the conditions I set out below), enjoy intrinsic intentionality rests on an illusion stemming from our use of language: with language we acquire the possibility of meta-representations that allow us to characterize the content of our mental states. This makes it seem as if, whenever we are in a mental state, its contents are directly presented to us and we know directly what they are about (part of Searle's argument that we and not AI systems have intrinsic intentionality). I contend, rather, that we have more than one representational system, and are able to use one to specify the contents of the other. See William Bechtel and Adele A. Abrahamsen, "Connectionism and the Future of Folk Psychology," in *Natural and Artificial Minds*, ed. Robert G. Burton (Albany, NY: SUNY Press, 1993), pp. 69–100.

on the basis of their beliefs and desires. Generally, if we can ascertain what people's beliefs and desires were, that their beliefs were not the product of delusion or deception, and that their decision to act was a rational consequence of their beliefs and desires, we hold them responsible for their actions. That is, we hold people responsible for the actions generated by their intentional states. By parity of reasoning, if we determine that AI systems act as a result of their own intentional states, we should hold them responsible for the decisions they make regarding their activities in their environments.

It is important to note, however, that recent philosophical theorizing about neural networks, the very AI systems which I contended were most likely to meet the conditions for being held morally responsible for their actions, threatens to undercut my argument for attributing intentional states to these systems and thus holding them responsible. Moreover, since the philosophers who advance these views also contend that neural networks provide the best account of our cognitive systems, they claim that attributing propositional attitudes to us is equally misguided; accordingly, if our attribution of moral responsibility to human agents depends upon ascribing propositional attitudes to them, attribution of moral responsibility to humans will be equally undermined. These philosophers adopt the label "eliminative materialism" for their position, and their contention is simply that intentional accounts of people in terms of propositional attitudes are the product of what we will come to recognize as a false account of how people operate, and hence that these accounts must be eliminated in favor of a truer way of describing the mental activities of humans.[16] In Section II, I will argue that this objection of the eliminative materialists is not successful in undermining our ability to characterize humans or AI systems in terms of propositional attitudes, and therefore does not pose the dire consequences for attributions of moral responsibility that it seems to pose.

The advent of neural network models, however, raises a second concern about attributing moral responsibility, either to them or to us. Part of the basis for attributing moral responsibility to agents is that, through the use of propositional attitudes, we can understand how agents arrive at whatever decisions to act that they do. This is particularly important when people make incorrect decisions for which we want to hold them

[16] The origins of eliminative materialism are found in the work of philosophers such as Paul K. Feyerabend, "Materialism and the Mind-Body Problem," *Review of Metaphysics*, vol. 17 (1963), pp. 49–67; and Richard Rorty, "Mind-Body Identity, Privacy, and Categories," *Review of Metaphysics*, vol. 19 (1965), pp. 24–54. The most vociferous contemporary statements of eliminative materialism are by Patricia S. Churchland, *Neurophilosophy: Towards a Unified Science of the Mind-Brain* (Cambridge, MA: MIT Press, 1986); and Paul M. Churchland, *A Neurocomputational Perspective: The Nature of Mind and the Structure of Science* (Cambridge, MA: MIT Press, 1989). A variant of the eliminative materialist position is found in Stephen P. Stich, *From Folk Psychology to Cognitive Science* (Cambridge, MA: MIT Press, 1983).

responsible. In such cases, we want to know if they failed to take account of, or misinterpreted, relevant information, or if they acted to achieve malicious goals. If we ascertain, for example, that people acted to achieve malicious goals, or that they did not show due care in seeking information, we may hold them responsible. If we discover, however, that people had benevolent goals and acted because of misinformation that even with due care they could not have detected, we are likely to absolve them of moral responsibility. If we cannot identify where in the process of arriving at a decision a person or an AI system went astray, it is difficult if not impossible to determine whether we should hold that person or system responsible. The problem with neural networks is that it is often difficult or impossible to analyze or decompose the way they arrive at decisions in such a manner (on decomposition, see Section III below). Thus, once again there seems to be a serious problem in holding AI systems morally responsible and, if we turn out to be neural networks, also a problem in holding humans morally responsible for their decisions. My proposal, advanced in Section II, for maintaining the use of propositional-attitude discourse with neural networks in fact seems to exacerbate this problem. In Section III, however, I will try to show that this objection too can be overcome.

## II. Eliminative Materialism and Connectionist Networks

Eliminative materialism, as noted above, contends that intentional characterizations of people in terms of propositional attitudes are simply false. For the most part, proponents and opponents of eliminative materialism have assumed that the alternative to it is a position that treats beliefs and desires as real entities *in the heads* of agents. Those who have held this alternative position, such as Fodor, have held that there is a state in the head that constitutes an agent having a certain desire, another that constitutes having a particular belief, and that these interact causally with each other (and with other beliefs and desires) to generate a reason for an action. What is crucial to this view is that propositional-attitude states be, in some significant sense, discrete states (e.g., that one such state could be replaced by another without affecting the remaining propositional attitudes). If this were not the case, then the ability to attribute responsibility for any given action to one belief that an agent had rather than another would seem to be undermined.

Over time it has seemed increasingly unlikely that such a view of how the mind works is correct. For one thing, as neuroscience develops, it is not finding specific brain regions that correspond to particular propositional attitudes (e.g., regions which, when active, correspond to an occurrent belief or desire). Defenders of the view that there are discrete propositional attitudes, though, often deny that their view is committed to *physical* discreteness in the brain; they contend instead that it is sufficient that the states be *functionally* discrete. This distinction between being physically and functionally discrete rests, in turn, on the account of the mind-body problem known as "functionalism." Proponents of functionalism contended that the identity of a particular mental state does not depend on the brain state that realizes it (they claim that the same mental state could be realized by a very large range of physical brain states), but on the interactions between it and other mental states.[17] The relation between mental states and the brain is construed as being much like the relation between software commands and a computer: the same software command can be realized in very different ways in different computers, but what makes it the particular command that it is are the relations between it and other software commands. Proponents of functionalism thus saw cognitive psychology, not neuroscience, as crucial to fixing the discreteness of intentional states. But the functional theories of how the mind works that have been developed in cognitive psychology have also not posited states corresponding to beliefs and desires.[18] The goal in most psychological research has been to explain performance in specific tasks, and the sorts of information structures and procedures operating on these structures that are posited do not correspond to the propositions that we might expect persons to believe or the sorts of reasoning that we might expect them to carry out consciously.

While neuroscience and cognitive psychology have not provided much comfort to those who want to construe propositional attitudes as inner mental states, some forms of classical AI have seemed to offer greater comfort. In some models, there is discrete storage of information as data structures, and this stored information might be thought to correspond to beliefs of the system.[19] In other computational models, fixed data structures are eliminated, and are replaced by sets of rules which direct the system's responses to the contents of working memory. These rules are known as *productions* (accordingly, the systems are known as *production systems*); they are applied (fire) when their antecedents are satisfied by the contents of working memory (a temporary buffer for storage of propositions), with the result that the actions specified in their consequent (frequently, a change in the contents of working memory) are performed. Even in these models, working memory constitutes a buffer in which both goal-states and currently relevant information are encoded in a proposi-

[17] For a review of the philosophical arguments for and against functionalism, see William Bechtel, *Philosophy of Mind: An Overview for Cognitive Science* (Hillsdale, NJ: Lawrence Erlbaum, 1988).

[18] For contemporary reviews of cognitive psychology, see Lawrence Barsalou, *Cognitive Psychology* (Hillsdale, NJ: Lawrence Erlbaum, 1994); and John R. Anderson, *Cognitive Psychology and Its Applications*, 3d ed. (San Francisco: Freeman, 1990).

[19] Zenon W. Pylyshyn, *Computation and Cognition: Toward a Foundation for Cognitive Science* (Cambridge, MA: MIT Press, 1984).

tional format. When these systems are designed to perform mental tasks, such as solving puzzles[20] or engaging in scientific reasoning,[21] it does seem plausible to take these encoded propositional structures as comparable to the system's current beliefs and desires.

With connectionist networks, however, the kind of discrete encoding of information which makes it possible to interpret the system as having beliefs and desires and responding in terms of these propositional attitudes, found in some classical AI systems, is lost. Connectionist networks operate on numerical principles through which units (simple processing devices conceived by analogy to biological neurons) take on levels of activations and, via pathways called *connections*, causally affect the activations of other units. A number of such units linked by connections constitutes a neural network. Generally one distinguishes a set of units as input units, another as output units; the network may contain other units residing between the input and output units known as *hidden units*. The specific behavior of a neural network is determined by which units are connected to which others, and by the weights on the connections, which determine how much influence a unit has on the behavior of another. For simplification, I will describe feed-forward networks; these are networks in which activation is conducted in only one direction from input units through one or more layers of hidden units to output units. Processing begins by assigning an activation to each input unit. That value (or the output of a function of that value) is sent along each connection leading from that unit and is scaled (multiplied by) the weights on those connections. To determine the activation of a given unit in the next layer, the network sums the products of activations of input units with connections to it and the weights on the connections, to arrive at the netinput. The actual activation of the unit is then determined from the netinput using a specified (usually nonlinear) function (see Figure 1). Such processing continues through successive layers until activations are produced on each output unit.

The pattern of activation presented to the input units of a network can be construed as a problem presented to the network, and the pattern of activation on the output units can be construed as the network's response. I will not go into them here, but there are a variety of learning procedures that can be employed with these networks which set the weights on the connections in ways that insure appropriate responses. Neural networks can be interpreted as functioning by recognizing patterns in the inputs. Their capacities at pattern recognition are, moreover, quite remarkable. Given a layer of hidden units, networks can acquire weights which enable

[20] Allen Newell and Herbert A. Simon, *Human Problem Solving* (Englewood Cliffs, NJ: Prentice-Hall, 1972).

[21] Patrick Langley, Herbert A. Simon, Gary L. Bradshaw, and J. M. Zytkow, *Scientific Discovery: Computational Explorations of the Creative Processes* (Cambridge, MA: MIT Press, 1987).

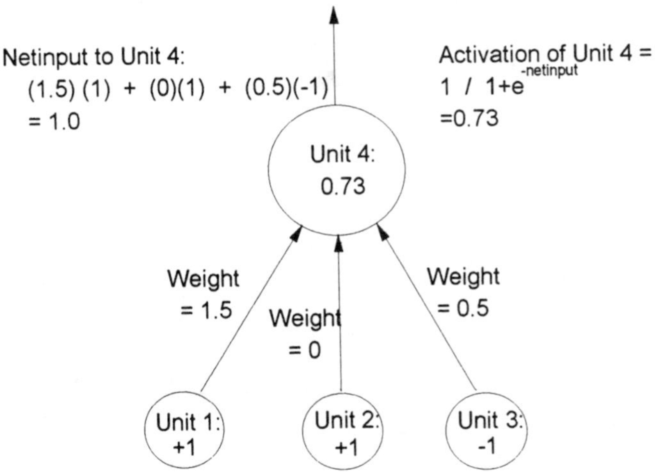


FIGURE 1. An illustration of processing in a connectionist network. The activation levels of the four units are shown beneath their labels. The weights on the three connections leading to Unit 4 are also shown. The netinput to Unit 4 is determined by multiplying the activation of each feeding unit by the weight on the connection and summing across the three feeding units. The activation of Unit 4 is then determined according to the logistic activation function shown in the upper right.

them to group together input patterns which are quite different but which we choose to classify together, and to differentiate input patterns that are quite similar but which we choose to distinguish. Basic cognitive tasks can be construed as determining an appropriate response as a result of recognizing a pattern;[22] hence, networks seem to be plausible devices in which to model such tasks. Networks, moreover, will respond even to inputs to which they have not been explicitly trained to respond, since this simply requires them to carry out their normal processing. What is interesting is that in a well-trained network, these responses are in fact generally quite reasonable. An example of a cognitive task which one might try to perform with a network is constructing derivations in propositional logic, since this involves recognizing the current state of a derivation and the goal state, and supplying the next step. Figure 2 portrays a network I have developed which can construct a number of simple derivations in propositional logic, including ones on which it was not trained.[23]

There are a variety of features about networks which make it difficult

[22] For a detailed development of this claim that does not itself invoke neural networks, see Howard Margolis, *Patterns, Thinking, and Cognition* (Chicago: University of Chicago Press, 1987).

[23] This network is described more fully in William Bechtel, "Natural Deduction in Connectionist Systems," *Synthese*, vol. 101, no. 3 (1994), pp. 433–63.

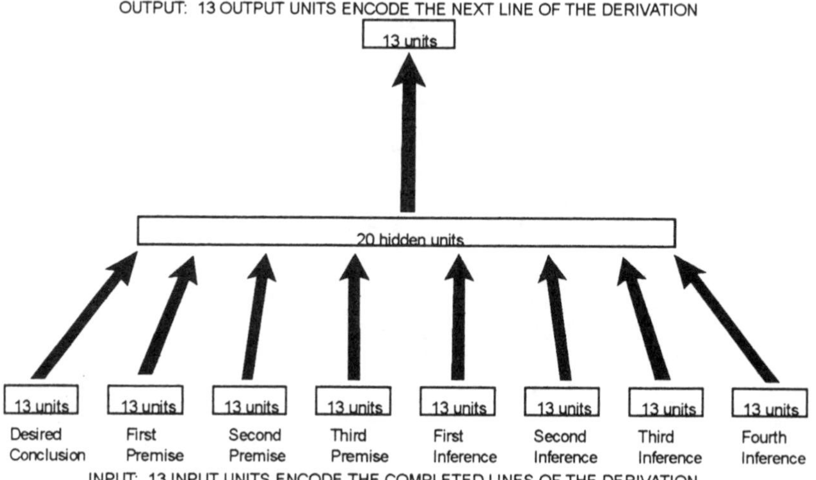


FIGURE 2. Network trained to construct natural deductions from three premises. The desired conclusion, three premises, and whatever inferences have already been completed are encoded on the appropriate sets of input units. After an inference is made, it is copied onto the appropriate input units, and the cycle is repeated. Units for inferences not yet completed are left blank. Each arrow represents 260 connections (e.g., one from each input unit to each of the twenty hidden units).

to interpret their performance in terms of propositional attitudes and which, when they are treated as models of human cognition, make them seem to support eliminative materialism. First, it is in terms of the weights on connections that a network stores any long-term knowledge it has. This knowledge is not stored in the form of propositions; a network seems to be a model of *knowing how* rather than *knowing that*.[24] Even more problematically, this knowledge is not discrete. In any task performance, it is the weights on many if not all connections in a network that are responsible for generating the output. (The only weights that will not figure are those on which the sending unit has 0 activation.) In learning to generate any given output from a given input, the network will tend to change the weights on all of the connections. The result is that it is not generally possible to explain the network's performance in terms of specific information it has acquired.[25] Second, while one will generally interpret the patterns of activations on at least the input and output units as representations, these representations are frequently distributed; that is, a given item is represented by activation values on many units, and any unit in that group is invoked to encode multiple other pieces of informa-

[24] This distinction is due to Gilbert Ryle, *The Concept of Mind* (New York: Barnes and Noble, 1949).

[25] William Ramsey, Stephen P. Stich, and J. Garon, "Connectionism, Eliminativism, and the Future of Folk Psychology," *Philosophical Perspectives*, vol. 4 (1990), pp. 499–533.

tion. Even in the situation in which individual input and output units are assigned discrete representational functions (an approach known as *localist encoding*), the activations on the hidden units are distributed.[26]

There is a way in which we might try to explain the activity of a network in propositional-attitude terms: we might construe the network's behavior in responding to the training inputs as applying rules that are defined in the training set. If the training inputs and target outputs can be characterized in propositional terms, then we could characterize the rules controlling the network's behavior in propositional terms, and characterize the network as reasoning from one proposition to another. However, the fact noted above that networks can respond not just to the specific input patterns of the training set to produce the intended target outputs, but also to any other input pattern that might be supplied, undercuts this attempt to supply a propositional interpretation of a network's behavior. If the input is similar to one on which the network was trained, it will generally provide an output very similar to the target training output. But the network might be given an input very different from any in the training set—for example, an input that combines features of two training inputs. In such a case, the network might respond with an output which combines elements of both target outputs or with an interpolation between the two target outputs.

The capacity of a network to generate responses to a much broader class of cases than those on which it is trained makes any propositional description of the relationship between inputs and outputs inadequate; the network's response capacities exceed those that can be specified propositionally. Philosopher Paul Churchland argues accordingly that networks are better understood as reasoning by application of prototypes than as reasoning with propositions.[27] This notion of a prototype stems from research on human concepts and categorization which has shown that humans do not categorize items under concepts in terms of necessary and sufficient conditions but in terms of comparison with idealized members of a category, which constitute the prototype of the category.[28] Church-

[26] Geoffrey E. Hinton, "Learning Distributed Representations of Concepts," *Proceedings of the Eighth Annual Conference of the Cognitive Science Society* (Hillsdale, NJ: Lawrence Erlbaum, 1986), pp. 1–12; and Timothy van Gelder, "What is the 'D' in 'PDP'? A Survey of the Concept of Distribution," in *Philosophy and Connectionist Theory*, ed. William Ramsey, Stephen P. Stich, and David E. Rumelhart (Hillsdale, NJ: Lawrence Erlbaum, 1991), pp. 33–59.

[27] Churchland, *A Neurocomputational Perspective (supra* note 16).

[28] For the initial challenge to the classical view of concepts, see Eleanor Rosch and Carolyn B. Mervis, "Family Resemblances: Studies in the Internal Structure of Categories," *Cognitive Psychology*, vol. 7 (1975), pp. 573–605. Rosch and Mervis focused primarily on establishing that categories had a "prototype structure" (that is, that members of a category were ranked from more prototypical to less prototypical), not on the mechanism by which people made assignments to categories. For a review of subsequent psychological research which has construed comparison to prototypes as the basis of categorization (as well as an alternative view which construes comparison to multiple exemplars or actual members of a category as the basis), see Barsalou, *Cognitive Psychology* (*supra* note 18); and Edward E. Smith, "Cat-

land's idea is that humans and networks can recall prototypes when presented with a wide variety of exemplars, but that no laws, stated in terms of presence or absence of features in those exemplars, can describe this ability. Churchland extends this idea by proposing that not just initial categorization but subsequent reasoning (for him, to be realized by subsequent processing in neural networks) is done in terms of these prototypes, not in terms of propositional representations.

The claim of eliminative materialists such as Churchland is that neural networks do not implement propositional attitudes, since there are no states within them that can be characterized in terms of beliefs and desires. If our mental capacities are realized by neural networks, according to the eliminative materialist, our cognition will consist not in reasoning based on propositional attitudes (i.e., inferring a new proposition to believe from others already believed), but in recognizing patterns and activating prototypes. If responsibility for decision making requires agents' having reasons characterized in terms of beliefs and desires, the consequence would be that *responsibility* too will be a notion apt for elimination. (While arguing for eliminative materialism, Churchland wants to preserve much of the purpose of moral philosophy. He contends that moral judgment rests largely on capacities for moral perception and that these capacities, like perceptual capacities more generally, can naturally be explained in connectionist terms. A moral individual is one who has developed capacities to recognize and act upon morally relevant aspects of the situations he or she confronts. Given this approach, Churchland may want to retain the notion of moral responsibility; moral responsibility will, however, be understood in more behavioral terms. Assessing moral responsibility will depend not upon determining the beliefs and desires of the agent, but upon determining the capacities of the person for moral perception and action.)[29]

The inference from neural networks to eliminative materialism can be blocked. This requires, however, adopting a different perspective on propositional attitudes. Most defenders and critics of propositional attitudes have assumed that if such attitudes exist, they must be discretely realized states inside of cognitive agents. Rather than interpreting propositional attitudes as states in an internal economy, one can construe them as states of a whole agent.[30] That is, instead of identifying the belief that neural networks give a correct account of human cognition as a particular state in a person's internal processing system, one can construe it as a characterization of the overall person. To characterize agents in terms of beliefs

egorization," in *Invitation to Cognitive Science*, vol. 3: *Thinking*, ed. Daniel N. Osherson and Howard Lasnik (Cambridge, MA: MIT Press, 1990), pp. 33–53.

[29] Paul M. Churchland, "The Neural Representation of the Social World," in *Minds and Morals*, ed. L. May, M. Friedman, and A. Clark (Cambridge, MA: MIT Press, 1995).

[30] See Bechtel and Abrahamsen, "Connectionism and the Future of Folk Psychology" (*supra* note 15).

and desires, on this construal, is to depict how they relate mentally to their environment; these characterizations specify what information about the environment the people have acquired and what goals they seek to fulfill by acting in that environment.

Such an account fits with how we attribute propositional attitudes to people or other systems. We attribute beliefs to agents on the basis of their behaviors and the information we know they have been exposed to; we do this without positing that particular states exist inside of them. Thus, we might attribute to an animal the belief that there is a predator in the area, on the basis of observing that the animal has access to information about the predator and seems to be employing that information in guiding its behavior. One of the ways in which human agents acquire information or indicate that they possess it is through the use of various symbol systems, such as language. Thus, the fact that an agent was told certain information (e.g., that the train would be late) and, in appropriate circumstances, would convey such information to others, would provide evidence that the person now believed this information. (The position I am advancing has certain affinities with logical behaviorism,[31] but it is distinct. Propositional attitudes are not being equated with behavioral evidence for them; rather, propositional-attitude states are construed as comparable to theoretical ascriptions for which there are typically multiple independent forms of evidence. The various propositional attitudes comprise a network of states of the agent which relate in complex ways. This will become clearer in the next section.)

According to this alternative position, propositional attitudes should never have been construed as states within the internal operation of an agent; rather, they apply to the agent viewed as a whole. As such, propositional-attitude discourse is not undermined by the failure to find corresponding states within an agent. This does not make propositional attitudes immune from elimination, for it may turn out that propositional attitudes do not provide the best way of characterizing agents' epistemic and motivational relations to their environment. (Given how much we, as humans, rely on language in negotiating our interactions with both our social and physical environments, it seems likely that attitudes toward linguistic representations will play a role in any account we give of humans. However, such attitudes may prove to be insufficient to characterize the relations of nonlinguistic creatures to their environments and may fail to characterize adequately more perceptual and motor aspects of our human interactions with our environment. Accordingly, we may find it fruitful to supplement our propositional-attitude framework with others.) However, if the propositional-attitude framework is to be replaced, it will be by a better way of characterizing the information agents have about

[31] For an explication of logical behaviorism, see Bechtel, *Philosophy of Mind* (*supra* note 17), ch. 2.

their environment and their objectives in acting in that environment. It will not be replaced because psychological or neuroscientific accounts of what happens within the heads of cognitive agents do not provide a place for propositional attitudes.

This does not mean that the propositional-attitude account of a person is totally dissociated from what goes on inside the head of the person. Our ability to have propositional attitudes depends to a significant degree on what happens inside our heads. The relationship between propositional attitudes and internal-processing activities, however, will be one of explanation, not identity. The internal-processing account must be able to explain how organisms stand in the relationships to their environments that we characterize in terms of propositional attitudes. If it turned out that the best account we have of what transpires in the heads of people cannot explain how they could have propositional attitudes, that would be a factor that would lead us to rethink our attributions of propositional attitudes. (There are occasions in the history of science when the attempts to explain a phenomenon have led to recharacterizing the phenomenon itself.[32] Such occasions, however, seem to be rare, and require strong alternative reasons to believe the new explanation, since its failure to account for the phenomenon which it was originally designed to account for constitutes a powerful piece of evidence against it. Thus, the failure of any account of internal processing to explain how we could have propositional attitudes would be fallible evidence against the account of internal processing.)

My contention, then, is that the fact that neural networks do not seem to have a place *in them* for propositional attitudes does not entail that the networks themselves cannot have propositional attitudes. If such networks stand in appropriate relations to their environments, they may have beliefs about their environments and desires with respect to future actions. Moreover, even if human beings' mental systems turn out to be neural networks, the eliminativist worries about whether we enjoy propositional attitudes can be answered: we as whole agents have beliefs and desires, even though there are no states in us that individually constitute particular beliefs and desires.

This does not mean that contemporary neural networks possess propositional attitudes. Most of them have not been designed to have the appropriate informational and appetitive relations to their environments. Instead, networks have been designed to carry out specific cognitive tasks assigned to them by their designers, such as producing the past tense of an English verb,[33] generating a phonological representation of words

[32] For an example, see William Bechtel and Robert C. Richardson, *Discovering Complexity: Decomposition and Localization as Strategies in Scientific Research* (Princeton, NJ: Princeton University Press, 1993), ch. 8.

[33] See David E. Rumelhart and James L. McClelland, "On Learning the Past Tense of English Verbs," in *Parallel Distributed Processing*, vol. 2 (*supra* note 10), ch. 18; and Kim

from morphological representations,[34] or even forming semantic representations of linguistic texts.[35] During their training sessions they become sensitive to the information in their input representations that is relevant to generating the proper output, but this connection does not extend out into the world in any interesting way. This limitation could in part be overcome by incorporating the network into a robot, so that it would receive inputs from sensors designed to pick up information from the environment and to produce outputs which would drive the machinery of the robot.[36] In such cases, the networks would actually be picking up information about the world and using it to control their behavior. Moreover, this would be a capacity that they would acquire through learning; it would not be something preengineered into them. In such cases, the networks could be characterized as knowing or believing things about their environment.

There may be another limitation that will have to be overcome before attributing intentional states to such networks that are as rich as those we attribute to human beings. At this point the representations created on output layers by networks cannot be used by the systems to perform other tasks. They are simply responses to particular aspects of the environment and, to use Charles Sanders Peirce's terms, constitute indices, not symbols.[37] Minimally, these representations need to figure in other processing by the network and, in the process, become integrated with one another. In training chimpanzees to use lexigrams (non-iconic symbols) symbolically, psychologist Sue Savage-Rumbaugh[38] found it neces-

Plunkett and Virginia Marchman, "U-shaped Learning and Frequency Effects in a Multi-layered Perceptron," *Cognition*, vol. 38 (1991), pp. 1–60.

[34] See Geoffrey E. Hinton and Timothy Shallice, "Lesioning an Attractor Network: Investigations of Acquired Dyslexia," *Psychological Review*, vol. 98 (1991), pp. 74–95.

[35] See Mark F. St. John and James L. McClelland, "Learning and Applying Contextual Constraints in Sentence Comprehension," *Artificial Intelligence*, vol. 46 (1990), pp. 217–57; and Risto Miikkulainen, *Subsymbolic Natural Language Processing: An Integrated Model of Scripts, Lexicon, and Memory* (Cambridge, MA: MIT Press, 1993).

[36] This approach of embodying neural networks in robots has been pursued by several researchers. In some of the most interesting work, it has been coupled with a procedure for evolving new network architectures through application of the genetic algorithm. (The genetic algorithm is a procedure for revising computer code by a process of random variation and selective retention of improved variants.) See S. Nolfi, Jeffrey L. Elman, and D. Parisi, "Learning and Evolution in Neural Networks," *Adaptive Behavior*, vol. 3, no. 1 (1994), pp. 5–28; and S. Nolfi, O. Miglino, and D. Parisi, "Phenotypic Plasticity in Evolving Neural Networks," *Proceedings of the First Conference from Perception to Action*, ed. D. P. Gaussier and J. D. Nicoud (Los Alamitos, CA: IEEE Press, 1994). I have argued for the importance of such approaches in creating networks with genuine intentionality in William Bechtel, "The Case for Connectionism," *Philosophical Studies*, vol. 71 (1993), pp. 119–54.

[37] See James Fetzer, *Artificial Intelligence: Its Scope and Limits* (Dordrecht: Kluwer, 1990); and Charles Sanders Peirce, "Speculative Grammar," in Charles Hartshorne and Paul Weiss, eds., *Collected Papers of Charles Sanders Peirce*, vol. 2, *Elements of Logic* (Cambridge: Harvard University Press, 1960).

[38] E. Sue Savage-Rumbaugh, *Ape Language: From Conditioned Response to Symbol* (New York: Columbia University Press, 1986).

sary to do two things: to teach the chimpanzees to recognize relationships between lexigrams, especially contrast relations,[39] and to dissociate the lexigrams from specific tasks in which they had learned to use the lexigrams. Only then could she establish that lexigrams for the chimpanzees were referential in the same way as words are for humans. Before we can attribute intentional states to networks, they may have to reach a similar state, in which their representations (i.e., patterns of activations on output units, which may in turn be inputs to yet other networks or other parts of the same network) exhibit internal relations and are used by the system flexibly in a variety of tasks. There is, however, no reason to think that this cannot be done by networks, and it is likely that if we decide it is useful to build networks that interact directly with their environments and yet interact with human agents (e.g., by reporting on what they have learned about their environment, or by responding to requests from humans), they will develop appropriate sorts of representations of the environment and of goals to be achieved. These networks will enjoy a rich set of propositional attitudes (especially if they are able to tell us what propositions they believe, etc., in language), and the eliminativist's worries about attributing responsibility to such networks will be discharged.

## III. Decomposing Decision Making in Neural Networks

In the previous section, I tried to defuse the argument of the eliminative materialist against attributing propositional attitudes, and consequently responsibility, either to humans or to neural networks. However, there is a second worry that arises when we contemplate assigning responsibility to neural networks (or to ourselves insofar as our minds turn out to be neural networks). This worry also concerns propositional attitudes, but in this case it concerns not the attribution of such attitudes but dynamic relations between them. In assigning responsibility to people, it is not generally enough to determine their beliefs and desires. We expect that propositional attitudes interact in generating actions and that this interaction is tractable. That is, we attempt to explain why the person acted as she did in prescribing a medication, for example, in terms of causal interactions between beliefs (such as that the medication would be effective in treating what afflicted the patient and that it would create minimal risk of bad side-effects) and desires (such as to assist in restoring the health of the patient). Often we characterize this interaction in terms of a practical syllogism that shows that certain actions follow from specifications of goal states and of beliefs about how those goals might be realized.

This expectation is manifest when someone behaves in a way we judge improper and we want to determine whether the person should be held

[39] The importance of these contrast relations is stressed by Terrence W. Deacon, *Symbolic Origins* (New York: W. W. Norton, forthcoming).

responsible for this improper action. If someone incorrectly treats a patient, for example, we question whether she made an incorrect diagnosis, had wrong beliefs about the safety or efficacy of a certain drug, reasoned improperly as to the effects of a proposed treatment, etc. We seek, in other words, to identify where in a dynamic of interactions of beliefs and desires, the failure arose. Sometimes we can identify the point of error in this dynamic by interviewing the caregiver. "Having ascertained that these conditions held, I thought (inferred) that it was safe to administer this drug," she might tell us, when in fact these conditions are not ones in which it is safe to administer the drug. Other times we might imaginatively project ourselves into her situation and consider what plausible false beliefs might have led to the unfortunate result. If we are not able to trace the reasoning of the agent, though, it seems difficult to judge the agent as rational, and hence to determine whether the error is something for which she is culpable.

In many classical symbolic AI devices, such as the expert systems that are employed in tasks like medical diagnosis, representations of information are explicitly stored and manipulated and it is possible to go back into the system and determine by what chain of reasoning the system arrived at its decision. If the output of the system is incorrect, we can then determine whether the error was due to the system being presented with incorrect information, lacking sufficient stored information, or applying inappropriate rules. (If we acknowledge that any reasoning agent is finite, and therefore must employ heuristics rather than algorithms that are guaranteed to promote success, we might judge that in fact the information the system drew upon and the rules it employed were appropriate, but that this just happened to be the sort of situation in which these heuristics would yield a bad result.) I would contend that a dynamic account of decision making in terms of propositional attitudes does not require that these states be discretely realized within the system. When trying to understand and explain people's actions in terms of propositional attitudes, we generally do not think of these as states within the system, but as states of the whole mental system that arise over time. Thus, we might say that someone has now reached the point of figuring out that a particular proposition is true, and is now evaluating whether that is a sufficient reason, together with what he or she had determined previously, to justify acting in a particular way. Many psychological studies of human problem solving, for example, ask people to talk out loud, describing all of their ideas and inferences as they solve a problem.[40] This provides the experimenter with information about the sequence of steps the person is going through. The problem with the neural networks I am focusing on here, then, is not that there are no states within them that are

[40] This process is known as *protocol analysis*. See K. Anders Ericsson and Herbert A. Simon, *Protocol Analysis: Verbal Reports as Data* (Cambridge, MA: MIT Press, 1984).

suitable candidates for propositional attitudes. Rather, it is that in producing their behavior, networks do not seem to go through stages of reasoning that can be characterized in terms of beliefs and desires.

One can, of course, always provide an explanation of why a neural network behaved as it did; its action was causally determined by the weights on each of its connections, and these in turn are the product of the application of its learning rules during its previous history. Such explanations tend not to be very informative when our concern is to explain action. Typically, when we seek to explain an activity, we attempt to show how the activity is the product of a relatively small number of other activities, each of which is described in a vocabulary which seems appropriately connected to the vocabulary in which we described the activity in question. For example, when we explain a physiological process, such as fermentation, we appeal to a number of chemical reactions, each of which transforms sugar or some intermediary substance into another substance until ultimately alcohol or lactic acid is produced. Explanation in such cases requires *decomposition* of an overall activity into a (reasonably small) series of steps, each of which we can *localize* in a responsible agent.[41] Often as such explanatory accounts develop, they become more complex, involving additional steps and agents, and often incorporating nonlinear pathways. Even so, the gap between the component processes and the overall process being explained remains quite small: the component processes perform intelligible steps in the overall transformation.

One problem with employing the model of mechanistic explanation that is applied in other sciences in the context of explaining behavior in propositional-attitude terms is that it assumes not just a decomposition of a larger process into steps, but the identification of those steps with component parts of the system. My contention that beliefs and desires are not to be identified with discrete components of the system entails rejecting the localization part of this approach. (This is not to deny that we might find ways of analyzing complex networks into parts and explaining the behavior of the overall network in terms of what the parts are doing. The application of techniques such as cluster analysis and principal-components analysis to determine how hidden units are re-representing information provided on input units so as to allow the connections later in the network to respond appropriately to each input is an example of a form of such decomposition.[42] But such analyses are not in terms of propositional attitudes.) Thus, a dynamic account of the behavior of a mental system in propositional-attitude terms cannot be developed in

[41] See Bechtel and Richardson, *Discovering Complexity* (*supra* note 32).

[42] For a discussion of the relative merits of cluster analysis and principal-components analysis, and a detailed example of using principal-components analysis to understand the behavior of a network, see Jeffrey L. Elman, "Distributed Representations, Simple Recurrent Networks, and Grammatical Structure," *Machine Learning*, vol. 7 (1991), pp. 195–225.

terms of the causal interactions of beliefs and desires as components within the system.

There is, though, a way to provide dynamic accounts of behavior in terms of beliefs and desires when these are not construed as component parts; but to present it, I need to provide a more elaborate account of propositional attitudes. Let us focus on the propositional attitudes of linguistic organisms. (We do attribute propositional attitudes to nonlinguistic organisms by invoking behavioral criteria to assign beliefs and desires. Such attributions suffer from a lack of specificity that, for example, leads philosopher Donald Davidson to reject such attributions.[43] But the degree of specificity that is possible is usually sufficient to explain animal action. The reason that I will not consider nonlinguistic organisms here is that they generally do not seem to exhibit the sort of complicated dynamics in reasoning about actions for which we advance accounts in terms of chains of reasoning in the case of humans. Thus, the need for a complicated decomposition of action into propositional attitudes and a dynamic interaction of such propositional attitudes, does not arise.) With linguistic organisms, we frequently rely on linguistic queries to determine beliefs and desires and the dynamic relations that develop between these. Of course, we do not generally simply ask people what they believe and desire, since there are too many such items, most of which the person is not aware of and can only become aware of by appropriate probing. But generally if one asks people whether they believe a specific proposition, they will answer, and many times they will respond to a more generic probe: "What do you believe (think) about X?" People do dissemble, but I will return to this difficulty below.

If we do not accept the view that in reporting beliefs, people are simply reporting on specific internal states, what are they doing? A natural way to characterize their reports of propositional attitudes is as expressing dispositions. (A disposition is a state of a system, and is due in large part to the internal composition of the system, but it need not map onto a specific component of a system. Thus, the disposition of a yeast cell to promote fermentation is due to the various enzymes and cofactors in it, and their interactions, not to a specific component which promotes fermentation. One way to appreciate this point is to observe that to explain a disposition one must generally switch into a different scientific vocabulary that is appropriate to the components of the system and then develop an account of how the interactions of those components generate the disposition.[44] The development of appropriate conceptual linkages between the two vocabularies is generally the result of the acceptance of these explanations.) Whatever the nature of the internal activities in them,

[43] Donald Davidson, "Rational Animals," *Dialectica*, vol. 36 (1982), pp. 318–27.

[44] See William Bechtel, "Biological and Social Constraints on Cognitive Processing: The Need for Dynamical Interactions between Levels of Inquiry," *Canadian Journal of Philosophy*, Supplementary Volume 20 (1994), pp. 133–64.

people are disposed to assent to particular sentences. A similar account can be given of reports of desires.

How does such a disposition to assent to a sentence relate to the behaviors which we seek to explain in terms of propositional attitudes? It seems reasonable, at least in most cases, to assume that dispositions to assent to propositions about desires are positively connected to dispositions to pursue particular goals, and that dispositions to assent to propositions about beliefs are positively connected to dispositions to employ the information in appropriate behaviors. There are cases in which this will not be true—cases, for example, in which someone assents to a proposition but in which the person's actions do not take that information into account. One such context involves cases in which the response has become automatic and is not under deliberative control. Then a person may act in a way that suggests a particular belief even as the person verbally denies that belief. In such cases, though, when attention is drawn to such information, people can generally, by consciously deliberating on how to act, alter their responses to accommodate the information. There is also no reason to think that the information available to a mental system is necessarily available to all activities of that system. We know that humans can believe contradictory propositions, but by appropriately restricting the context in which they employ each proposition, never recognize the conflict. Even though the connections between verbal dispositions to affirm beliefs and desires, and dispositions to act in other ways, are sometimes complex, there is ample reason to think that they are related in normal humans. If we found a person in whom the connections were regularly absent (that is, the person regularly acted in ways that conflicted with his or her stated beliefs and desires), we would take that as evidence for pathology.

One further reason to think that there is a positive correlation between affirmations of beliefs and desires and action is that, on the view espoused here, affirmations of belief and desire are simply actions generated in the manner of other actions. Much of the underlying perceptual and mental processes that figure into other actions also figure into the generation of linguistic responses. Due to the important role linguistic communication plays in human society, we tend to privilege it and think it offers direct and incontrovertible access to a person's mental states. This view of privileged access to our mental states is one relic of the Cartesian account of mind, and it coheres with the claim of Fodor and others that sentential representations are stored within cognitive agents. There is, however, no empirical evidence to support either the privileged position of verbal reports or the claim that the mental system contains a store of linguistic representations. According to contemporary models in cognitive psychology, we construct linguistic representations when we communicate or when we think to ourselves in language, and we respond to linguistic input from ourselves or others by extracting information that can be used for other activities. Hence, our linguistic productions ought to be able to utilize much of the information that is available in the system for directing other motor activities, even though they do not provide privileged access to this information.

One reason not to treat linguistic reports as direct reports of inner mental states is that humans do occasionally use language to deceive. One way we detect such deception is to compare linguistic responses with other behaviors; if people do not act upon information which they attest to believing, we may accuse them of deception. It is also the case that people often cannot report the information which guided their actions. In some cases they will even report reasons for action which can be demonstrated to be confabulations, not accurate reports.[45] One context in which people will confabulate rather than give accurate reports is when the action itself was not under deliberative control, and yet the person is required to give reasons for action. In these cases, other people may be able to offer alternative accounts that better fit the person's actions based on what they know of the person's access to information about the environment and the person's pattern of behavior. Accordingly, we should not treat linguistic reports as more than *fallible* indicators of the beliefs, desires, and patterns of reasoning an individual might go through, but we can treat them as such.

We are now in a position to return to the question which motivated this discussion: How, in dealing with neural networks, or with us if our mental systems are neural networks, is it possible to decompose the process by which decisions are made into propositional attitudes and reasoning based on them? It is possible if we construe occurrent propositional attitudes (propositional attitudes that an agent claims to be currently having) as states of the overall system, and if we construe reasoning in terms of propositional attitudes as changes in these overall states. Thus, beliefs are constituted by the information about the system's body and the broader world that is available to the action components of the system, including the speech generator, while desires are constituted by the information that is available to the action components about the goals the system is seeking to fulfill. (I am not concerned here to determine how the system develops particular goals. Clearly both biological evolution [or simulated evolution in the case of neural networks] and, in the case of social organisms like humans, social learning, play a large role. Such goals are realized in the neural processes. Only some of this information may be available to the speech-generating system.) The information that is available to the action components can change dynamically. Activity in the system that we count as reasoning may make new information available to the action components or lead to the formulation of subgoals. One especially im-

[45] Richard E. Nisbett and Timothy D. Wilson, "Telling More Than We Can Know: Verbal Reports on Mental Processes," *Psychological Review*, vol. 84 (1974), pp. 231–59.

portant way in which this information will change is through the system's initiating activities intended to yield new information, including exploration in the environment and formulation of queries that activate information latent in the system.

My contention is that there is good reason to think that the sort of dynamic account people do offer in propositional-attitude terms about their reasoning does characterize, albeit quite fallibly, the way their mental system goes about the process of arriving at a decision. It is not an account in terms of component activities, but an account in terms of state changes in an overall dynamic system. Such an account is explanatory, for it is by virtue of going through such state changes that a system reaches the decision it does. Moreover, it is an account that can support counterfactuals: had the system had this information available to it, or had it carried out such a self-query, it would have formed a different belief and reached a different decision. This is the sort of decomposition of reasoning that is required in making judgments about responsibility.

Why did it seem at first that connectionist networks could not be characterized in terms of dynamic interactions of propositional attitudes? The reason is likely to be that most networks designed to date have been designed to do relatively simple tasks in which we provide a problem on input units and record the proposed solution from the output units. In such simple tasks there is little potential for decomposition in terms of propositional attitudes, even when these tasks are performed by humans. In such simple tasks, we simply "see" the answer. A decomposition into propositional attitudes makes the most sense when the decision is the product of changes of the system over time (that is, when the system changes in time in the course of arriving at an action). Simple networks do not exhibit such temporal development in performing a single task, but recurrent networks do. (Recurrent networks have feedback as well as feed-forward connections. Inputs are supplied to the network one after another, but the processing of a subsequent input is influenced not only by that input but by the feedback from the processing of the previous input. See Figure 3 for a simple design of a recurrent network, due to cognitive scientist Jeffrey Elman, which has been used in numerous simulations of processing strings of linguistic text.) The potential for the system to go through stages characterizable in propositional-attitude terms, and for us to generate a dynamic account of processing in propositional-attitude terms, increases with such systems. As researchers continue to explore such systems, the appropriateness of invoking propositional-attitude accounts of the dynamics of the decision-making process will become more plausible.

In considering how sophisticated such systems might get, let me propose a possible design of a network. Consider a highly recurrent network that learns to perform a variety of tasks in the world (not by backprop-

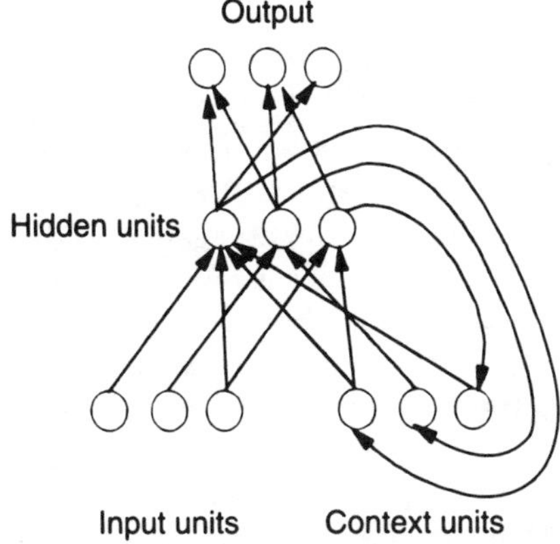


FIGURE 3. A simple recurrent network designed by Jeffrey Elman and used in many simulations of processing sequential material as in linguistic texts. Initially, an input is provided to the input units and processed as in a standard feed-forward network. Before the next input is provided, the activation patterns on the hidden units are copied onto a special set of units called "context units." On the next cycle, both the input units and the context units send signals over their connections to the hidden units. The use of recurrence through the context units provides a degrading memory of previous cycles of processing.

agation, which requires a teacher to specify the correct output in all cases, but by a procedure more like reinforcement learning, in which the network receives an error signal that only specifies how close or far from success its current performance is, and adjusts its behavior). Assume these tasks are related to long-term goals of the system. Among the tasks this system performs is the use of language to characterize aspects of the world in which it is acting and its own goals for action. Insofar as the network "lived" in a social environment of language users, developing this capacity might provide it with useful ways to acquire information needed to perform its other tasks. Once it had acquired rudimentary language capacities, it might seize upon its own linguistic outputs as useful information to use as further inputs, thus creating a feedback loop much in the manner which the Russian psychologist Lev Vygotsky proposes for the development of inner speech in humans.[46] For the outsider, these reports might be extremely informative as to the dynamics of reasoning progressing within the system, and they might be used much in the manner in which AI researchers Allen Newell and Herbert Simon employed verbal protocols from humans as guides to stages of reasoning.[47] With such a system, an explanation of how the system reaches decisions in propositional-attitude terms may seem as plausible as it now does with human beings.

[46] Lev S. Vygotsky, *Thought and Language* (Cambridge, MA: MIT Press, 1934, 1962).
[47] Newell and Simon, *Human Problem Solving* (*supra* note 20). See also Ericsson and Simon, *Protocol Analysis (supra* note 40).

## IV. Moral Responsibility and Neural Network–like Devices

The development of neural networks and their application in modeling human cognition raises serious questions about moral responsibility. These systems are already being used and will increasingly be used to make decisions previously reserved for human agents. To the degree that these systems employ the same procedures as humans in arriving at decisions, and acquire these procedures not directly from human designers but in the same way humans acquire their procedures for making decisions, by a process of learning, the question of whether to lodge moral responsibility in these networks becomes pressing. My contention has been that there is no less reason to hold such systems responsible than to hold human agents responsible for their decisions. My primary goal, however, has not been to argue directly for this thesis, but to respond to a challenge that stems from some philosophers who have been the most enamored with neural networks as models of human cognition. These philosophers have construed these networks, and the claim that our minds operate in the same manner as these networks, as evidence for eliminative materialism and the repudiation of propositional attitudes. Since attributing responsibility to people seems to require that they have propositional attitudes and that they reach their decisions on the basis of dynamic interactions of these attitudes, the eliminative materialist's challenge affects not just neural networks but humans as well.

I have argued, however, that this worry is misconceived. Having propositional attitudes does not depend directly on the inner nature of the mental processing system. Rather, it depends upon the system's being sensitive to information about its environment and using that information in determining actions in its environment. Decomposing the system does not require finding discrete components within the system, but requires being able to identify, in terms of dispositions of the system, what information it is applying and what goals it is pursuing. In a system whose decisions develop over time, we can potentially trace out in propositional-attitude terms the dynamics leading up to the decision. Although contemporary neural networks have not been developed to interact directly with the world and to use information derived from the world in guiding actions in the world, they are the sorts of systems that could do so. If, or more likely when, we design such relatively autonomous agents, they will be characterizable in propositional-attitude terms, and this sort of objection to holding them morally responsible for their actions will be avoided.

Since my primary goal has been to answer objections to attributing responsibility to us or to neural networks, I have not said very much about why one would want to do so. My only line of argument on this question has been to assume that neural networks (or robots that utilize them) will make decisions much in the manner of human agents, and that, especially since the behavior of such agents will be determined more by their learning history than by what is supplied by their designer, it is not reasonable to assign responsibility for their behavior back to their designer (unless that designer was malicious or negligent in that design). Rather, I suggested that the proper model is that of human offspring: as we hold the offspring, not their parents, responsible for the decisions of the offspring, so we should hold the network, and not the designer, responsible for the decisions of the network.

There is, of course, another option. We might absolve the designer of moral responsibility for the decisions of the network and also reject the applicability of moral responsibility to the network. In answering this, it is important that I have been assuming throughout that the networks we are discussing would be fully comparable to humans in the way they make decisions. If there are significant differences (if, for example, networks are not able to incorporate affect and thus fail to exhibit behavior associated with guilt and remorse), then that might provide grounds for not treating neural networks as moral agents. However, if there are no such shortcomings, then the only plausible grounds for not assigning moral responsibility to neural networks would seem to be chauvinism.

There is, though, also a positive reason for treating neural networks of the sort I have envisioned as responsible moral agents. Holding people morally responsible for their decisions serves, in part, to include them in the community of moral agents, a community whose members, in part, make their decisions on the basis of their moral habits and moral deliberations. To fail to hold children responsible for their actions is to keep them out of the moral community; not surprisingly, children treated in this way are likely not to develop moral habits or to engage in moral deliberation in making decisions. To the degree that neural networks begin to use language both to interact with others and to guide their own actions, it would seem likely that moral habits could be cultivated in them and that they could learn to engage in moral discourse and apply that moral discourse in their own decision making. If we are to empower neural networks to make decisions of significance to human beings, it would seem quite sensible to develop agents whose behavior is, in this way, brought under the scope of our moral discourse. Developing such artificial neural networks probably lies in the relatively remote future. But the idea of holding such systems morally responsible for their behavior does not seem to involve the sort of conceptual confusions that eliminative materialists or others might lead us to believe.

*Philosophy, Neuroscience, and Psychology,*
*Washington University in St. Louis*

# PREPOSTERISM AND ITS CONSEQUENCES*

By Susan Haack

> That is preposterous which puts the last first and the first last. . . . Valuing knowledge, we *preposterize* the idea and say . . . everybody shall produce written research in order to live, and it shall be decreed a knowledge explosion.
>
> — Jacques Barzun[1]

## I. Introduction

What I have to offer here are some thoughts about the "research ethic," and the ethics of research, in philosophy. There won't be any exciting stuff about the political wisdom or otherwise of research into racial differences in intelligence, or the ethics of scientists' treatment of laboratory animals, or moral issues concerning genetic engineering or nuclear technology, or anything of that kind. There will be only, besides some rather dry analysis of what constitutes genuine inquiry and how the real thing can come to be corrupted, some rather uncomfortable reflections about the present condition of philosophy, its causes and its consequences.

You are probably beginning to suspect already that I don't think philosophy is at present in a particularly desirable condition. You are correct; at any rate, when I read C. S. Peirce's wry complaints about philosophers "whom any discovery that brought quietus to a vexed question would evidently vex because it would end the fun of arguing around it and about it and over it"—and his descriptions of metaphysics as "a puny,

* This essay is dedicated to the late David Stove, with whom I would dearly have loved to discuss all this, and to whose matchlessly candid diagnosis of the state of the philosophy department at the University of Sydney, "A Farewell to Arts," *Quadrant*, May 1986, pp. 8–11, I am much indebted.

I have also been helped by Michael Dummett's candor about the effects of inappropriate conceptions of efficiency on the condition of graduate work in philosophy at Oxford, in Dummett, *Frege: Philosophy of Mathematics* (Cambridge, MA, and London: Harvard University Press, 1991), pp. viii–x; and by comments from Paul Gross, John Kearns, Mark Migotti, Louis Pojman, Sidney Ratner, Louise Rosenblatt, Israel Scheffler, Thomas Short, and Jenny Teichman. W. V. Quine, "Paradoxes of Plenty," in *Theories and Things* (Cambridge, MA, and London: Harvard University Press, 1981), pp. 194–99, is also apropos.

I have drawn on an earlier paper of mine, "The First Rule of Reason," written for a conference on "New Topics in the Philosophy of C. S. Peirce," to be published in *The Rule of Reason: The Philosophy of C. S. Peirce*, ed. Jacqueline Brunning and Paul Forster (Toronto: Toronto University Press, 1995); this paper focuses on Peirce's observation that the "first, and in a sense [the] sole, rule of reason," is that "in order to learn you must desire to learn."

[1] Jacques Barzun, *The American University* (New York, Evanston, IL, and London: Harper and Row, 1968), p. 221.

 

rickety and scrofulous science," and of philosophy as in "a lamentably crude condition,"[2]—I don't feel moved to protest, "Yes, but that was then, whereas now . . ."

My quotations from Peirce were not chosen only for vividness, nor are they incidental to what I shall have to say, which has much in common, epistemologically, with Peirce's diagnosis of the condition of philosophy in his day. "In order to reason well," he wrote, "it is absolutely necessary to possess such virtues as intellectual honesty and a real love of truth"; and the lamentable condition of philosophy, he went on, was due in large part to the lack of that real love of truth, the "scientific attitude," as he sometimes called it, the "craving to know how things really [are]," the "Will to Learn."[3]

The chief reason why philosophy was *not* being undertaken with the scientific attitude, according to Peirce, was that it was largely in the hands of theologians, who were motivated less by a real love of truth than by the desire to devise a philosophical system to support theological principles their commitment to which was fixed and determined in advance of inquiry. Or rather, in advance of "inquiry"; for, as Peirce observed, such persons are not really engaged in genuine inquiry at all, but in "sham reasoning."[4]

Peirce's observations about the importance of the motive with which intellectual work is undertaken are no less pertinent now than they were when he wrote them. But philosophy is no longer largely in the hands of theologians, so his account of the cause of the prevalence of sham reasoning in the philosophy of his time hasn't the same relevance. At least a significant part of the explanation of the present lamentable condition of philosophy is, rather, the "preposterism" of which Barzun complains, which has been an influence quite as "deplorably corrupt" as Peirce thought the domination of philosophy by theologians had been.[5]

I take it that philosophy is a kind of inquiry, that is, that philosophical questions are genuine questions to which there are true and false answers. This is not to deny that not a few of the questions with which philosophers have concerned themselves have turned out to be, and others may turn out to be, misconceived—for example, to rest on false pre-

[2] C. S. Peirce, *Collected Papers*, ed. Charles Hartshorne, Paul Weiss, and Arthur Burks (Cambridge, MA: Harvard University Press, 1931–1958), 5.520 (c. 1905), 6.6 (c. 1903), 1.128 (c. 1905). References are given by volume and paragraph number; parenthetical dates refer to dates of individual essays or fragments.

[3] *Ibid.*, 2.82 (1902) (the "real love of truth"); 1.43ff. (c. 1896) (the "scientific attitude"); 1.34 (1869) (the "craving to know how things really are"); 5.583 (1898) (the "Will to Learn"—William James's *The Will to Believe*, dedicated to Peirce, was first published in 1897).

What I have to say also has a good deal in common with Plato's account of "false philosophers" in Book VI of the *Republic*; not, however, his conception of knowledge as exclusively of the Forms, nor of philosophers as the only real lovers of truth—which is why it is Peirce, rather than Plato, who will be my guide here.

[4] Peirce, *Collected Papers*, 1.57 (c. 1896).

[5] *Ibid.*, 6.3 (1898).

suppositions. It is to affirm that this is not in the nature of philosophical questions as such. If this is false, if philosophy is not a kind of inquiry, then there could be no such thing as research in philosophy, and most of the questions I shall be discussing would themselves be misconceived.[6]

Let me begin, though, before turning my attention to philosophical inquiry specifically, with some reflections about inquiry generally.

## II. Pseudo-Inquiry, and the Real Thing

Inquiry aims at the truth. This is a tautology (*Webster's*: "**inquiry**: search for truth, information or knowledge; research, investigation"). If you aren't trying to find out the truth about whatever-it-is, you aren't really inquiring. There is, however, a lot of pseudo-inquiry about; that is why, when the government institutes an Official Inquiry into this or that, some of us reach for our scare quotes. Genuine inquiry seeks the truth with respect to some question or topic ("regardless of what the color of that truth may be," as Peirce shrewdly put it);[7] pseudo-inquiry seeks to make a case for the truth of some proposition or propositions determined in advance.

There are two kinds of pseudo-inquirer. The *sham* reasoner is not primarily concerned to find out how things really are, but to make a case for some immovably held preconceived belief. The *fake* reasoner is not primarily concerned to find out how things really are, but to advance himself by making a case for some proposition to the truth-value of which he is indifferent.

Though the term "fake reasoning" is mine, Peirce's remarks about the corrupting effect of "vanity"[8] indicate that he was aware of the dangers of fake reasoning as well as of sham reasoning—as does this biting comment on a contemporary of his: "real power . . . is not *born* in a man; it has to be worked out; and the first condition is that the man's soul should be filled with the desire to make out the truth . . . ; but —— is full of himself, and it stands immovably in the way of a thorough devotion to truth. He ought not to try to combine two aims so disparate and incompatible."[9]

Sham or fake inquiry is not genuine inquiry, true—tautologically so; but why do I refer to the "dangers" of sham and fake reasoning? Peirce exaggerated when he suggested, writing of "this first, and in one sense this sole, rule of reason, that in order to learn you must desire to learn,"[10] that the disinterested truth-seeking attitude is both necessary and sufficient for the discovery of truth. But he exaggerated something true and

[6] Mark Migotti reminds me that Aristotle observes that philosophy is unavoidable because to reject it intelligently demands that one engage in it, in order to defend one's rejection of it.

[7] Peirce, *Collected Papers*, 7.605 (1903).

[8] *Ibid.*, 1.34 (1869).

[9] Peirce, in Carolyn Eisele, ed., *The New Elements of Mathematics* (The Hague: Mouton, 1976), vol. 4, p. 977; Peirce is referring to Paul Carus.

[10] Peirce, *Collected Papers*, 1.135 (c. 1899).

important: that, in the long run and on the whole, disinterested truth-seeking tends to advance inquiry, while sham and fake inquiry tend to impede it.

The sham inquirer tries to make a case for the truth of a proposition his commitment to which is evidence- and argument-proof. The fake inquirer tries to make a case for the truth of some proposition advancing which he believes will benefit himself, but to the truth-value of which he is indifferent. (Such indifference, Harry Frankfurt observes, is the defining characteristic of the bull-shitter.)[11] Both the fake and the sham reasoner, but especially the sham reasoner, are motivated to avoid examining any apparently contrary evidence or argument too closely, to play down its importance or impugn its relevance, to contort themselves explaining it away. Both, but especially the fake reasoner, are motivated to obfuscate, to indulge in that "affected obscurity" which Locke, whose phrase I just borrowed,[12] recognized as a chief occupational hazard of philosophy.

The genuine, disinterested inquirer wants to get to the truth of the matter that concerns him, whether or not that truth comports with what he believed at the outset of his investigation, and whether or not his acknowledgment of that truth is likely to get him tenure, or to make him rich, famous, or popular. He is motivated, therefore, to seek out and assess the worth of evidence and arguments thoroughly and impartially—his work will manifest what Peirce once charmingly described as "peirce-istence" and "peirceverance."[13] (This doesn't just mean that he will be hardworking; it is a matter, rather, of willingness to rethink, to reappraise, to spend as long as it takes on the picky detail that just might be fatal, to give as much thought to the final 1 percent as to the rest. I am tempted to rephrase Edison: "genius is 1 percent inspiration and 99 percent peirce-piration.") The genuine inquirer will be ready to acknowledge, to himself as well as others, where his evidence and arguments seem shakiest and his articulation of problem or solution vaguest. He will be willing to go with the evidence even to unpopular conclusions, and to welcome someone else's having found the truth he was seeking. And, far from having a motive to obfuscate, he will try to see, and explain, things as clearly as he can.

Sham and fake reasoners may hit upon the truth, and, when they do, may come up with good evidence and arguments. Commitment to a cause and desire for reputation are powerfully motivating forces which can prompt energetic intellectual effort. But the intelligence and ingenuity that will help a genuine inquirer to figure things out, will help a sham or fake inquirer to suppress unfavorable evidence or awkward arguments more effectively, or to devise more impressively obscure formulations.

[11] Harry Frankfurt, "On Bullshit," in *The Importance of What We Care About* (Cambridge: Cambridge University Press, 1989), pp. 117–33.

[12] John Locke, *An Essay Concerning Human Understanding* [1690], III.x.6.

[13] Joseph Brent, *Charles Sanders Peirce: A Life* (Bloomington and Indianapolis: Indiana University Press, 1991), p. 16.

Genuine, disinterested inquirers may come to false conclusions or be led astray by misleading evidence or arguments. But an honest inquirer will not suppress unfavorable evidence or awkward arguments, or disguise his failure with affected obscurity; so, even when he fails, he will not impede others' efforts.

Of course, real human beings do not conform neatly to my three types; their motives are generally pretty mixed, and they are capable of many degrees and kinds of self-deception. The bona fide Will to Learn is both rare and fragile. "Few," as Samuel Butler observes, "care two straws about the truth, or have any confidence that it is righter or better to believe what is true than what is untrue."[14] The love of truth is, as A. E. Housman writes, "the faintest passion."[15]

But the environment in which it is conducted may be more or less hospitable to good intellectual work, in at least two relevant ways. A good environment will encourage genuine inquiry and discourage sham and fake inquiry; and the worst damage of sham and fake inquiry will be mitigated, and the contributions to knowledge that sham and fake reasoners sometimes make despite their dubious motivation will get sifted from the dross, if the environment enables mutual scrutiny among workers in a field. Honest scrutiny is best; but scrutiny even by other sham or fake reasoners with different axes to grind may be effective as a way of exposing error, confusion, and obfuscation. The environment is inhospitable to good intellectual work, conversely, if it encourages sham and fake inquiry, or impedes mutual scrutiny.

An environment will be hospitable to good intellectual work insofar as incentives and rewards favor those who work on significant issues, and whose work is creative, careful, honest, and thorough; insofar as journals, conferences, etc., make the best and most significant work in a field readily available to others working in the area; insofar as channels of mutual scrutiny and criticism are open, and successful building on others' work is encouraged. The environment will be inhospitable insofar as incentives and rewards encourage people to choose trivial issues where results are more easily obtained, to disguise rather than tackle problems with their chosen approach, to go for the flashy, the fashionable, and the impressively obscure over the deep, the difficult, and the painfully clear; insofar as the effective availability of the best and most significant work is hindered rather than enabled by journals and conferences bloated with the trivial, the faddy, and the carelessly or deliberately unclear; insofar as

[14] Samuel Butler, *The Way of All Flesh* (1903; New York: Signet Books, The New American Library of World Classics, 1960), p. 259; Butler continues: "Yet it is only those few who can be said to believe anything at all; the rest are simply unbelievers in disguise," revealing that, unlike some contemporary philosophers, he realizes that there is an internal connection between the concepts of belief and truth.

[15] A. E. Housman, *M. Manilii, Astronomicon I* (London, 1903), p. xliii; see Harry Frankfurt, "The Faintest Passion," *Proceedings and Addresses of the American Philosophical Association*, vol. 66, no. 3 (1992), pp. 5-16.

mutual scrutiny is impeded by fad, fashion, obfuscation, and fear of offending the influential.

Looking at this list, I don't see how the conclusion can be avoided that the environment in which academic work is presently conducted is an inhospitable one. I think this is true for all disciplines; but I shall focus, henceforth, primarily on philosophy.

## III. A Preposterous Environment

"[E]verybody shall produce written research in order to live"; Barzun exaggerates, but not much. Everybody aspiring to the tenure track, tenure, promotion, a raise, a better job, or, of course, academic stardom—increasingly, even everybody aspiring to a visiting position as a step toward the tenure track—had better produce written, published, research. "[A]nd it shall be decreed a knowledge explosion"; again, Barzun exaggerates, but, again, not much. It *is* pretty much taken for granted that this explosion of publications represents a significant contribution to knowledge.

Yet a good deal of what is published is, at best, trivial stuff, putting me in mind of that observation: "Rubbish is rubbish, but the history of rubbish is scholarship."[16] Seriously, though: few if any of us will have a truly original idea every few years, let alone every few months; genuinely important philosophical work usually takes years of frustration and failure, and a great philosopher may not produce his best work until middle age or later. Nevertheless, we not only half-pretend that this written research that everybody must produce in order to live is, nearly all of it, worthwhile; we breathe an atmosphere of puffery, of announcements in paper after paper, book after book, that all previous work in the area is hopelessly misconceived, and here is a radically new approach which will revolutionize the whole field. How did this atmosphere of preposterous exaggeration come about? Let me try to disentangle one strand of the explanation.

It is no longer possible to do important scientific work with a candle and a piece of string; ever more complex and sophisticated equipment is needed to make ever more *recherché* observations. Research in the sciences has become very expensive; a culture of grants-and-research-projects has grown up; and science has become, *inter alia*, big business. The consequences for science are not altogether healthy: think of the time spent "writing grants," not to mention attending seminars on "grant writing," of the temptation to shade the truth about the success or importance of one's project, of the cost to the progress of science when a condition of

[16] When I heard it, this observation was attributed to Burton Dreben. Israel Scheffler, however, tells me that his recollection is that the original source was Talmudic scholar Saul Lieberman, and the original observation, "Nonsense is nonsense, but the history of nonsense is science."

some body's supporting the research is that the results be withheld from the rest of the scientific community, etc. (Though "science is, upon the whole, at present in a very healthy condition," Peirce wrote in 1901, "it would not remain so if the motives of scientific men were lowered." And the worst threat, he continued, was that there were too many "whose chief interest in science is as means of gaining money.")[17] But when disciplines like philosophy, where serious work requires, not fancy equipment, but only (only!) time and peace of mind, mimic the organization of the sciences, when the whole apparatus of grants-and-research-projects becomes so ordinary that we scarcely notice how extraordinary it is, when we adapt to a business ethos, the consequences are still worse.

Why worse? In part because in philosophy the circumpressure of facts, of evidence, is less direct; in part because the kind of routine, competent, unexciting work that gets all the scientific details filled in has no real analogue in philosophy; in part because in philosophy the mechanisms of mutual scrutiny are perhaps more clogged and probably more corrupted.

How did this adaptation of philosophy to forms and organizational structures more appropriate to the sciences come about? In part because it is so intellectually impressive, in part because it is so useful, and in part, no doubt, because it is so expensive, science enjoys enormous prestige—prestige in which the rest of us would dearly like to share. Inevitably perhaps, in consequence of universities' having become such big businesses, many university administrators have become enamored of a business-management ethos which values "entrepreneurial skills," that is, the ability to obtain large sums of money to undertake large research projects, above originality or depth, and which encourages conceptions of "efficiency" and "productivity" more appropriate to a manufacturing plant than to the pursuit of truth.

Headlines in the official newsletter of the University of Warwick, I recall, announced "Major Research Success for Physics at Warwick"; the text informed us, not of some breakthrough achieved by our physicists, but of their landing major research funding. The application form for University of Miami stipends for summer research opens with a statement that preference will be given to "proposals that appear to best attract subsequent external funding," and on the next page advises that senior faculty "should emphasize career enhancement aspects of their project." I don't suppose either is atypical.

In disciplines like philosophy, feeling ourselves the poor relations in such a culture, we have adapted as best we could. At the extreme, this adaptation has encouraged such absurdities as the request for a letter of reference I last year received from a British university: though the job was described as a lectureship, I was told very plainly that teaching ability was not important, that the main qualification for the position was that

[17] Peirce, *Collected Papers*, 8.142 (1900).

the person appointed should publish, during the three years of his or her appointment, a sufficient number of papers in sufficiently prestigious journals to raise the standing of the department concerned in the government's "research rankings," so would I please be sure to say what papers my former student would publish in which journals over that period. Though the brazenness of this request was unusual, the attitude it so brazenly revealed was not. Reporting on the state of the university, the president of the University of Miami mentions budget balancing, student numbers, faculty recruitment—and adds that our library's ranking in the Association for Research Libraries has gone up for "volumes added," for "serial subscriptions," for "materials expenditures," and that "our faculty is publishing at an unprecedented rate." No mention is made, in his twelve-page letter, of what anyone *found out*. I don't suppose this is atypical either.

Our adaptation to this culture has also encouraged a kind of philosophical entrepreneurship, which often diverts time and effort from real work, and is sometimes, to speak plainly, nothing more than philosophical hucksterism: centers for this and that, new journals for the legitimation and promotion of the latest fad, projects requiring secretaries, research assistants, or, better yet, more expensive and powerful computers or, best of all, a laboratory. At the extreme, this mimicking of forms more appropriate to the sciences has encouraged such absurdities as the blurb put out by the journal *Social Epistemology*, informing potential contributors that jointly written papers are as a matter of principle preferred over papers by only one author.[18] The model is the jointly authored scientific paper; yet it is hard to think of any really major work of philosophy written jointly.[19]

Our adaptation to the culture of grants-and-research-projects has been a poor one, which has tended to lower the motive with which philosophical work is done; it has fostered an environment hospitable to sham and fake inquiry, inhospitable to the fragile intellectual integrity demanded by the genuine desire to find out. It is part of the meaning of the word "research" *that you don't know how things will turn out*. The culture of grants-and-research-projects, and the conception of productivity and ef-

[18] From the "statement of purpose" supplied by the editor, Steve Fuller: "The journal is committed to both examining and exhibiting the social structure of knowledge; thus, its policy is to publish 'collaborations' which are the collective product of several authors" (*Directory of American Philosophers, 1994–95* [Bowling Green, OH: Philosophy Documentation Center, 1994], p. 228).

[19] Thanks to Louise Rosenblatt and Sidney Ratner for suggesting *Principia Mathematica* as a possible candidate; I would think this better described, however, as combining Russell's philosophical work with Whitehead's mathematical work. The joint work of John Dewey and Arthur Bentley might be suggested as another possibility; none of this, though, seems to me as important as, say, Dewey's *The Quest for Certainty*, or his *Logic: The Theory of Inquiry*. Rosenblatt and Ratner also drew to my attention an observation of Max Fisch's likening the *Library of Living Philosophers* volumes to cooperative scientific work; but I find the likeness remote at best.

ficiency which that culture fosters, discourage candid acknowledgment that one may work for years at what turns out to be a dead end, and constitute standing encouragement to exaggeration, half-truth, and outright dishonesty about what one has achieved. In principle, you might fill out the application explaining what important breakthroughs your work is going to achieve, and fill out the report, later, explaining what important breakthroughs your work actually did achieve, without your private estimation of the worth of your work being affected. In practice, this is seldom exactly what happens; inevitably, intellectual honesty is eroded.

It has been a poor adaptation which significantly affects what kind of work gets done. True efficiency would have effort going into those questions most susceptible of solution at a given stage of inquiry; the present environment tends to channel effort into those questions most susceptible of attracting funding. In a philosophy department of which I was once a member, the argument was heard—and heeded—that we should "go into" postmodernism and literary theory, "because we can get Euromoney to do that." (I didn't stick around long enough to know whether any Euro-dollars were in fact forthcoming.) This attitude of "that's where the money is" is surely part of the explanation of the popularity of interdisciplinary work, especially work which allies philosophy with more prestigious disciplines such as cognitive psychology or artificial intelligence or medicine, etc.

And I don't think it is unduly cynical to suspect that our adaptation to the culture of grants-and-research-projects also significantly affects what kinds of conclusions are reached. When effort is directed by the hope of large grants into, say, the border territory of epistemology with cognitive science, the probability rises significantly that the conclusion that will be reached is to the effect that long-standing epistemological questions can be quickly resolved or dissolved by appeal to work in cognitive science. When effort is directed by the hope of large grants into, say, the relevance of feminism to philosophy of science, the probability rises significantly that the conclusion that will be reached is to the effect that feminism requires us, as Sandra Harding preposterously puts it, to "reinvent science and theorizing."[20] (Challenged, nearly a decade later, by skeptics wanting to know what breakthroughs feminist science had achieved, Harding replied that, thanks to feminist scientists, we now know that menstruation, pregnancy, and menopause aren't diseases.[21] Gosh.) No one is so naive as to imagine that large grants might be forthcoming to show that cognitive science *has no* bearing on those long-standing epistemological questions, or even that its bearing is (as I believe) though real

[20] Sandra Harding, *The Science Question in Feminism* (Ithaca, NY: Cornell University Press, 1986), p. 251.

[21] *Chronicle of Higher Education*, April 27, 1994, p. A15.

enough, oblique and undramatic[22]—or to show that (as I believe) feminism *has no* relevance to the theory of scientific knowledge.[23]

The psychological mechanisms here are quite subtle. Simple dishonesty is the exception; some degree of *self*-deception is the rule. Conor Cruise O'Brien gets the psychological tone about right:

> Young scholars . . . are likely to believe that if they write with excessive candor about certain realities . . . doors will close to them; certain grants will be out of reach, participation in certain organized research programs denied, influential people alienated, the view propagated that the young man is unbalanced or unsound. These fears may be exaggerated . . . but they are not without foundation. . . . [I]nevitably some . . . will adapt . . . with such concessions as they believe are necessary. And the scholars who adapt successfully are likely to be highly influential in their fields in the next generation.[24]

The adaptation of which O'Brien writes is likely, naturally, to leave a residue of ambivalence, such as one can hear in this plea for the psychologization of epistemology: "[a] return [to a psychologistic conception of epistemology] is especially timely now, when cognitive psychology has renewed prestige and promises to improve our understanding of cognitive processing."[25] The relevance or irrelevance of psychology to epistemology is a hard meta-epistemological question—on which, needless to say, the prestige of cognitive psychology has no bearing.

Increasingly, supposedly academic decisions have turned into intensely politicized competition for resources; questions of curricular requirements, for example, are only too obviously really small skirmishes in larger turf wars.[26] Still, all the puffery, the attempts to promote oneself or one's area, approach, or line—what I have begun to think of as academic boosterism—might be *only* a waste of time if, eventually, it came out in the wash of mutual scrutiny and criticism. Instead of efficient mechanisms of communication and mutual scrutiny, however, what we have is a mind-numbing clamor of publications, conferences, meetings, of "empty

[22] See my *Evidence and Inquiry: Towards Reconstruction in Epistemology* (Oxford: Blackwell, 1993), chs. 6, 7, and 8.

[23] See my "Science as Social?—Yes and No," in *A Dialogue on Feminism, Science, and Philosophy of Science*, ed. Jack Nelson and Lynn Hankinson Nelson (The Netherlands: Kluwer, forthcoming).

[24] Conor Cruise O'Brien, "Politics and the Morality of Scholarship," in *Morality and Scholarship*, ed. Max Black (Ithaca, NY: Cornell University Press, 1967), p. 73.

[25] Alvin Goldman, "Epistemics: The Regulative Theory of Cognition," *Journal of Philosophy*, vol. 75, no. 10 (1978), p. 523.

[26] Daniel Bonevac, "Leviathan U.," in Howard Dickman, ed., *The Imperiled Academy* (New Brunswick, NJ, and London: Transaction Press, 1993), pp. 1–26, is illuminating on these matters.

books and embarrassing assumptions,"[27] a clamor which makes it close to impossible to hear what is worthwhile.

The waste of time, talent, and energy, is significant; what real work might have been done by those who feel obliged, instead, to devote themselves to pointing out the absurdities of the latest fad? Also significant is the fact—almost, but not quite, too indecent to mention—that some who can make a better career of criticizing these absurdities than they could of constructive work, have an interest, consciously recognized or not, in the survival of what they criticize.

Occasionally someone is candid about this. The director of Rutgers University Press writes that "[w]e are . . . part of the university personnel system and . . . often publish books whose primary reason for existence is the author's academic advancement, not the advancement of knowledge."[28] The new editor of the *American Philosophical Quarterly*, Gary Gutting, writes that publishing in the journals has become less a way to communicate significant ideas than a form of professional certification, and that being adequately informed in one's field no longer requires that one actually *read* all that stuff.[29] Even more startling than the candor of his observations about the real role of the journals, is the blandness of his assumption that publication-as-professional-certification is perfectly okay. But it *isn't* perfectly okay; it gets in the way of—what is more than ever urgently necessary in a culture that encourages sham and fake reasoning—the mutual scrutiny that might mitigate the worst damage and separate the worthwhile from the dross.

Between 1900 and 1960, about forty-five new philosophy journals were founded in the U.S., Canada, and Britain, fifteen of them in the decade between 1950 and 1960; between 1960 and 1970, about forty-four, i.e., almost as many in a decade as in the previous sixty years; between 1970 and 1980, about sixty-five; between 1980 and 1990, about fifty-five.[30] Inevitably, it has become impossible, except by sheer luck, to find the good

[27] Peirce, *Collected Papers*, 1.645 (1898).

[28] Kenneth Arnold, "University Presses Could Still Become the Cultural Force for Change and Enlightenment They Were Meant to Be," *Chronicle of Higher Education*, July 29, 1987; cited in Charles Sykes, *Profscam* (Washington, DC: Regnery Gateway, 1988), p. 129.

[29] Gary Gutting, "The Editor's Page," *American Philosophical Quarterly*, vol. 31, no. 1 (1994), p. 87:

> Learned journals are ostensibly dedicated to presenting essential new discoveries to a community of scholars. This purpose alone, however, cannot explain the immense volume of contemporary journal publications. . . . [N]one of us can hope to read more than a very small percentage. . . . The obvious implication is that most articles published in journals are not essential scholarly contributions. . . . One common, if seldom explicitly noted, reason [for publication] is to certify the academic competence of their authors. . . .

[30] My estimates are based on the *Directory of American Philosophers* and the *International Directory of Philosophy*; they can be only estimates, because the information there is incomplete, and, in particular, does not include data about journals that folded.

But aren't there, after all, many more philosophers now, as well as many more journals, than in 1900 (a challenge pressed by Louis Pojman)? Indeed, there are. But—if I sound

stuff; inevitably, championship of a simple, startling idea—even, or perhaps especially, an egregiously false or an impressively obscure idea—has become a good route to reputation and money, as has the self-serving variation on a fashionable party line. Inevitably, too, the task of finding referees with the necessary expertise, time, patience, and integrity has become harder, the power of editors to make or ruin careers has grown, and once-idealistic young philosophers begin to say to themselves, "They're bound to ask for revisions anyway, so there's no point polishing it first," or, "They like controversy in their journal, so why bother spelling out all the qualifications?," etc., etc.

And, of course, inevitably, as it becomes harder to make oneself heard in the journals, one has to publish a book; and, as that book-published-by-a-reputable-academic-press becomes a requisite for tenure, we face the ever more bloated publishers' catalogues filled with ever more exaggerated descriptions and endorsements. And, inevitably, once again, it becomes impossible, except by sheer luck, to find the good stuff, and—but I won't bore you by writing the previous paragraph all over again!

It is not unheard of to find that a book of which a review has just appeared, having sold the few hundred copies which, these days, philosophy books typically sell, is already, just a couple of years after publication, out of print. Better, then, from the point of view of sheer self-preservation—let alone of impressing deans, etc., with one's "scholarly productivity"—not to spend too long writing a book. How absurd, after all, to spend ten years writing a book which, if you are lucky, five hundred people might read,[31] and the life of which, if you are lucky, might be four or five years.

It used to be an important role of the academic presses to publish significant books too specialized to be economic. Increasingly, however, as subsidies from their universities have shrunk, university presses are under pressure to publish books they believe will make money.[32] One effect seems to have been that referees' reports, though important for supplying those blurbs and for convincing your dean of the legitimacy of your publication record, no longer determine academic publishing decisions. This too is discouraging, to put it mildly, to the investment

---

cynical, so be it—the idea that there are, in the U.S. alone, nine thousand or so people all capable of genuinely significant philosophical work, strikes me as itself preposterous.

[31] Not to mention that a large proportion of those few hundred sales will be to university libraries, not to people spending their own money, actually intending to read the book.

[32] In an article entitled "Seeking Profits, College Presses Publish Novels," *The Wall Street Journal*, September 20, 1994, pp. B1 and B8, Marj Charlier writes that for Luther Wilson, director of the University Press of Colorado, "even to mention profits indicates a shift in academic publishing," and continues, "[t]raditionally, universities subsidized their presses so they could publish definitive—and probably money-losing—treatises. . . . But now, universities are reducing their subsidies, and budget-strapped libraries are cutting back on their academic purchases," and university presses are having to seek money-making projects.

See also Robert S. Boynton, "Routledge Revolution," *Lingua Franca*, March/April 1995, pp. 25–32, on the present condition of a once highly respected academic press.

of effort in difficult problems. Better, from the point of view of making oneself heard, to write the kind of book that might interest a trade publisher, or at least the kind of book that will get reviewed in the nonacademic press. And this too, inevitably, favors the simple, startling idea, even, or perhaps especially, the startlingly false or impressively obscure idea—but I promised not to bore you by writing that paragraph all over again!

Like books and journals, conferences might be, and occasionally are, important channels of communication. But we are all familiar with the reality that your home institution will pay your expenses *if* you give a paper; with the conference announcements which discreetly let it be known that, so long as you pay the large registration fee, your paper will be accepted; with the stupefying programs of day after day of umpteen parallel sessions; with the twenty-minute, the twelve-minute, even, of late, the ten-minute presentation; with the extent to which conferences have become less a matter of communication than of "contacts," of "exposure," and, of course, of expenses-paid trips to agreeable places.

Here is William James declining an invitation to join the then newly formed American Philosophical Association: "I don't foresee much good from a philosophical society. Philosophy discussion proper only succeeds between intimates who have learned how to converse by months of weary trial and failure. The philosopher is a lone beast dwelling in his individual burrow. Count me *out*!"[33] He has, with his usual shrewdness, got something important exactly right. Philosophy is a lonely business. One may make progress as a result of that hard-earned, real discussion James describes, which, however, is as often as not more profitably engaged with some philosopher long-dead than with a contemporary. But we surely overrate the usefulness of what we like to call "stimulation," and underrate the need for time, peace of mind, mature reflection.[34]

Recall George Santayana's character sketch of Josiah Royce: an "overworked, standardised, academic engine, creaking and thumping on at the call of duty or of habit, with no thought of sparing itself or anyone else."[35] Preposterism can only too easily turn the best of us into just such over-

[33] My source is Bruce Wilshire, *The Moral Collapse of the University* (Albany, NY: SUNY Press, 1990), pp. 106–7.

[34] I owe to Mark Migotti the following splendid quotations from Nietzsche, *Human, All Too Human* [1878], trans. Marion Faber (Lincoln: University of Nebraska Press, 1984), section 284, "In favour of the idle": "One sign that the valuation of the contemplative life has declined is that scholars now compete with men of action in a kind of precipitate pleasure, so that they seem to value this kind of pleasure more highly than that to which they are really entitled and which is in fact much more pleasurable"; and section 285, "Modern Restlessness": ". . . agitatedness is growing so great that higher culture can no longer allow its fruits to mature; it is as though the seasons were following upon one another too quickly. From lack of repose our civilization is growing into a new barbarism."

[35] George Santayana, *Character and Opinion in the United States: With Reminiscences of William James and Josiah Royce and Academic Life in America* (New York, NY: Charles Scribner's Sons, 1920); my source is Morton G. White, *Science and Sentiment in America* (Oxford: Oxford University Press, 1972), p. 244.

worked, standardized, academic engines—and can only too easily turn the worst of us into purveyors of philosophical snake-oil.

## IV. The Perils of Preposterism

Thus far it may seem that the perils of preposterism are much the same for philosophy as for other humanities disciplines. This is not quite so. For philosophy is the discipline to which it falls to inquire into inquiry itself, its proper conduct and its necessary presuppositions; and that responsibility exposes us to a particular peril. Recent philosophy manifests two tendencies which, though on the face of it radically opposed to each other, both result in part from our adaptation to a "research ethic" more appropriate to the sciences than to the humanities: first, scienticism,[36] that is, linking philosophy too closely, or inappropriately, to the sciences; and second, neo-Romantic radical critique of the sciences as no more than ideology masked by rhetorical bullying in the form of appeals to "rationality," "objectivity," and so forth. The former might be described as the effect of envy, the latter as the effect of resentment, of the success of the sciences.

Given my characterization, it is trivially true that scienticism is mistaken, but it is a substantial question what views qualify as scientistic, as linking philosophy to science *too* closely, or in the *wrong* way. Unlike some, I see philosophy as a kind of inquiry, a kind of truth-seeking, and so in that sense like the sciences; I see it also as aspiring, as the sciences do, to as much precision and rigor as possible.[37] I don't believe, however, that philosophical questions are misconceived, and should be abandoned in favor of questions that the sciences can resolve; or that it is realistic to expect that philosophical questions can be handed over to the sciences to answer; or even that philosophical writing can or should be held to the same standards of mathematization and rigor as, say, theoretical physics. These are, by my lights, the three chief varieties of scienticism.

The last is in a way the most superficial, but not, for all that, insignificant. Mathematical or logical pseudo-rigor is one kind of affected obscurity. My point is not that recourse to the languages of mathematics or logic never helps to make a philosophical argument or thesis clearer; of course it does. ("In order to be deep it is requisite to be dull," Peirce observed,

[36] I have invented this neologism—by analogy with Peirce's coinage of "pragmaticism," for his specific version of pragmatism—because I want to disassociate myself from some of the things Hilary Putnam says when, in *Renewing Philosophy* (Cambridge, MA, and London: Harvard University Press, 1992), he repudiates scientism; specifically, unlike Putnam, I do *not* mean to deny the possibility of "one true description of the world." Apropos, see my "Reflections on Relativism: From Momentous Tautology to Seductive Contradiction," in *Philosophical Perspectives, 11: Metaphysics*, ed. James E. Tomberlin (Oxford: Blackwell, 1996).

[37] See my "Between the Scylla of Scientism and the Charybdis of Apriorism," in Lewis Hahn, ed., *The Philosophy of Sir Peter Strawson* (La Salle, IL: Open Court, forthcoming), for an articulation and defense of a conception of philosophy which I there describe as "scientific but not scientistic."

having in mind particularly the dry details of his logic of relatives, on which, *inter alia*, his critique of Kant's categories depended.)[38] My point is, rather, that recourse to the languages of mathematics or logic sometimes stands in the way of real clarity by disguising failure to think deeply or critically enough about the concepts being manipulated with impressive logical sophistication.

The application form for National Endowment for the Humanities summer stipends requires applicants to indicate what "methodology" they will be using—not, obviously, a question expecting the answer "I shall think about . . ." but a question calling for some acceptably technical answer, appropriate or not.

My point about the second kind of scienticism is not that it hasn't sometimes happened that problems that used to be the province of philosophy gradually came to be formulated in a way that made them susceptible of investigation by the sciences; of course it has—"What is the world made of?," for example. Nor is my point that there aren't border questions in which both philosophers and scientists may take an interest—"Is perception a direct relation to external objects or a process of inference from sense data?," for example.[39] My point is, rather, that appeals to the sciences are often made in a way that covertly changes the subject—e.g., from "Which predicates are such that inductions involving those predicates are correct?" to "Why do humans tend, by and large, to make the kinds of inductive inferences that are correct?"; or from "What processes of belief-formation are reliable?" to "In what circumstances do people tend to use reliable processes, and in what circumstances unreliable processes?"[40]

The most ambitious style of scienticism, which would abandon philosophical questions in favor of scientific ones, represents the purest and most bizarre form of "science envy." (Philosophers of this boldest scientistic stripe, one might say, don't so much want to be *like* scientists, as to *be* scientists.) My point about this revolutionary scienticism is not that it is impossible in principle that results from the sciences might show that this or that philosophical problem is misconceived; they might, by revealing some presupposition of the problem to be false. My point is, rather, that no amount of investigation in the sciences could reasonably be expected to answer such characteristically philosophical questions as: Is science epistemologically special, and if so, why? Is its yielding true predictions an indication of the truth of a theory, and if so, why? Etc., etc.

[38] Peirce, *Collected Papers*, 5.17 (1903).

[39] In "How the Critical Commonsensist Sees Things," *Histoire, Epistemologie, Langage*, vol. 16, no. 1 (1994), pp. 9–34, I try to relate Peirce's approach to this question to J. J. Gibson's and R. L. Gregory's.

[40] W. V. Quine—in whose work a plausible naturalism sits side by side with an implausible scienticism—makes the first of these diversionary maneuvers; Alvin Goldman makes the second. See my *Evidence and Inquiry*, pp. 130–35, on the former problem-shift, and pp. 152–57, on the latter.

And it is incomprehensible why, unless these were not only legitimate questions, but legitimate questions with less-than-skeptical answers, one could be justified in proposing to do science instead of philosophy.

Perhaps that is why the revolutionary scienticism encountered in contemporary philosophy often manifests a peculiar affinity with the anti-scientific attitudes which, as I conjecture, are prompted by resentment, as scienticism is prompted by envy, of the sciences.[41] One hears from Paul Churchland that, since truth is not the primary aim of the ceaseless cognitive activity of the ganglia of the sea-slug, it should maybe cease to be a primary aim of science, and even that talk of truth may make no sense; from Richard Rorty, that truth is just what can survive all conversational objections, and that the only sense in which science is exemplary is as a model of human solidarity. One hears from Patricia Churchland that "truth, whatever that is, definitely takes the hindmost"; from Sandra Harding, that "the truth—whatever that is!—will not set you free." One hears from Stephen Stich that truth is neither intrinsically nor instrumentally valuable, and that a justified belief is one his holding which conduces to whatever the believer values; from Steve Fuller, that he sees no distinction "between 'good scholarship' and 'political relevance'."[42]

And now listen to Peirce on what will happen if sham reasoning becomes commonplace: "[M]en come to look upon reasoning as mainly decorative. . . . The result of this state of things is, of course, a rapid

[41] This peculiar affinity is strikingly manifested in the announcement of a conference organized by the Centre for Research in Philosophy and Literature at the University of Warwick in May 1995:

> VIRTUAL FUTURES 1995 is an interdisciplinary event that examines the role of cybernetic and specifically dissipative or non-linear models in the arts, sciences, and philosophy. The conference explores the relationship between postmodern philosophy and chaos theory, with topics ranging from: information technology, hypertext and multimedia applications, virtual reality and cyberspace, $C_3$, complexity theory, cyberfeminism, artificial life and intelligence, neural nets and nanotechnology. Literary themes such as apocalypse, narcotics, cyberpunk science fiction, and annihilation are all welcome. Philosophically, the conference emphasizes materialist schools of Continental philosophy and neurophilosophy. . . .

(My thanks to Jenny Teichman for sending me this announcement.)

David Stove: "[W]ill someone please tell me that the Logical Positivists were on the wrong track . . . and that the human race is not mad?" ("What Is Wrong with Our Thoughts?" in *The Plato Cult* [Oxford: Blackwell, 1991], pp. 179–205, quotation from p. 204).

[42] Paul M. Churchland, "The Ontological Status of Observables" [1982], in his *A Neurocomputational Perspective: The Nature of Mind and the Structure of Science* (Cambridge, MA, and London: Bradford Books, MIT Press, 1989), pp. 150–51; Richard Rorty, *Consequences of Pragmatism* (Hassocks, Sussex: Harvester Press, 1982), p. 165, and Rorty, "Science as Solidarity," in John S. Nelson, Allan Megill, and Donald McCloskey, eds., *The Rhetoric of the Human Sciences* (Madison: University of Wisconsin Press, 1987), p. 46; Patricia Smith Churchland, "Epistemology in the Age of Neuroscience," *Journal of Philosophy*, vol. 75, no. 10 (1987), p. 549; Sandra Harding, *Whose Science? Whose Knowledge?* (Ithaca, NY: Cornell University Press, 1991), p. xi; Stephen P. Stich, *The Fragmentation of Reason* (Cambridge, MA, and London: Bradford Books, MIT Press, 1992), pp. 118ff.; Steve ("yours in discourse") Fuller, E-mail message, May 4, 1994.

deterioration of intellectual vigor. . . . [M]an loses his conceptions of truth and of reason. If he sees one man assert what another denies, he will, if he is concerned, choose his side and set to work . . . to silence his adversaries. The truth for him is that for which he fights."[43]

I can match neither Peirce's prescience nor his eloquence. But perhaps I can add a little circumstantial detail to his diagnosis. Preposterism is a direct encouragement to sham and fake reasoning. Where philosophy is concerned, it is also an encouragement to envy of science, thus to scientism and to a certain kind of irrationalism, and to resentment of science and to an only-slightly-different kind of irrationalism. Within philosophy, furthermore, as the discipline to which the task of articulating the nature and goals of inquiry falls, the ubiquity of sham and fake reasoning has induced a factitious despair of the possibility of attaining truth by investigation—the despair revealed in the astonishing outbreak of sneer quotes with which so much recent philosophical writing expresses its distrust of "truth," "reality," "facts," "reason," "objectivity," etc.

But why is it to be expected, as Peirce maintained, that if pseudo-inquiry becomes commonplace, man will "lose his conceptions of truth and of reason"? When sham and fake reasoning are ubiquitous, people become uncomfortably aware, or half-aware, that reputations are made, acclaim achieved, as often by clever championship of the indefensible or the incomprehensible as by serious intellectual work, as often by mutual promotion among influential cliques as by merit. Knowing, or half-knowing, this, they become increasingly skeptical of what they hear and read. Their confidence in what passes for true declines, and with it their willingness to use the words "truth," "evidence," etc., without the precaution of scare quotes. And as those scare quotes become ubiquitous, so people's confidence in the concepts of truth and reason falters, and one begins to hear (from Richard Rorty): "I do not have much use for notions like . . . 'objective truth'," "'true' [is] a word which applies to those beliefs upon which we are able to agree";[44] or (from Bruno Latour and Steve Woolgar): "a fact is nothing but a statement with no modality . . . and no trace of authorship";[45] or (from Steve Fuller): "I am quite happy to talk to anyone about standards of scholarship, once you tell me who[m] you are trying to impress."[46] (And this in turn, naturally, encourages the idea that there is, after all, nothing wrong with sham or fake reasoning . . . and so on.)

The inference from the (true) premise that what passes for truth, objective fact, rational argument, etc., is often no such thing, to the (false)

[43] Peirce, *Collected Papers*, 1.57–59 (c. 1896).

[44] Richard Rorty, "Trotsky and the Wild Orchids," *Common Knowledge*, vol. 1, no. 3 (1992), p. 141, and Rorty, "Science as Solidarity," p. 45.

[45] Bruno Latour and Steve Woolgar, *Laboratory Life: The Social Construction of Scientific Facts* (Beverly Hills, CA, and London: Sage Library of Social Research, 1979), p. 82.

[46] Fuller, E-mail message, May 4, 1994.

conclusion that the notions of truth, objective fact, rationality, etc., are humbug, though manifestly invalid, has become ubiquitous. I call it "the 'passes for' fallacy."[47] The "passes for" fallacy is not only fallacious, but self-defeating; for if the conclusion were true, one could never have grounds for accepting the premise from which it is supposedly derived. It should come as no surprise, therefore, to read (in Stephen Cole): "Given that facts can easily become errors, what sense does it make to see what is at Time 1 a 'fact' and at Time 2 an 'error' as being *determined* by nature?"; and then, a few pages later, "the most important evidence in favor of my position is the fact that . . .";[48] or (in Ruth Bleier): "[I criticized various studies] for their sloppy methods, inconclusive findings, and unwarranted interpretations"; and then, a few pages later, "there must be an irreducible . . . distortion or biasing of knowledge production simply because science is a social activity performed by human beings in a specific cultural . . . context."[49]

Sad to say, this last quotation is quite typical of much recent feminist scholarship (or "feminist scholarship"). The vast recent literature of feminist approaches to ethics, epistemology, philosophy of science, philosophy of language, and lately even logic,[50] is a striking manifestation of some consequences of preposterism. Reading in this vast literature, one can hardly fail to notice how endlessly it is repeated that feminism has radical consequences for this or that area, and how frequently those radical consequences turn out to be trivial, or obviously derivative from some male philosopher, or manifestly false; how determinedly practitioners avert their attention from serious criticisms, and how lavishly they praise the work of others of their own persuasion.[51] Pondering on how this came about, one can hardly fail to think of how many reputations and careers, how many centers, programs, conferences, and journals, depend on the legitimacy of appealing to the feminist perspective on this or that. And one's darkest suspicions are confirmed when, in a moment of re-

[47] This is a term I first introduced in "Knowledge and Propaganda: Reflections of an Old Feminist," *Partisan Review*, Fall 1993, pp. 556–64; reprinted in *Our Country, Our Culture*, ed. Edith Kurzweil and William Phillips (Boston: Partisan Review Press, 1995), pp. 56–65.

[48] Stephen Cole, *Making Science: Between Nature and Society* (Cambridge, MA, and London: Harvard University Press, 1990), pp. 12, 21.

[49] Ruth Bleier, "*Science* and the Construction of Meanings in the Neurosciences," in Sue V. Rosser, ed., *Feminism within the Science and Health Care Professions: Overcoming Resistance* (Oxford and New York: Pergamon Press, 1988), pp. 92, 101.

[50] The relevance of feminism to social philosophy is clear enough; but more recent feminism is marked by an insistence on extending its relevance to all areas of philosophy, including the most central. This is manifestly the agenda in, for example, Sandra Harding and Merrill Hintikka, eds., *Discovering Reality: Feminist Perspectives on Epistemology, Metaphysics, Methodology, and Philosophy of Science* (Dordrecht, The Netherlands: Reidel, 1983). See also my review of this book in *Philosophy*, vol. 60, no. 232 (1985), pp. 265–70.

[51] This tendency to mutual admiration in recent academic feminist writing is shrewdly observed by Margarita Levin in "Caring New World: Feminism and Science," *American Scholar*, vol. 57 (Winter 1988), pp. 100–106.

markable candor, Sandra Harding acknowledges that yes, there can be such a person as a male feminist, and tells us that "[m]en who want to be 'in feminism' can advance the understandings produced by women feminists. They can teach and write about women's thought, writings, accomplishments. . . . They can criticize their male colleagues. They can move material resources to women and feminists."[52]

I hope I haven't given the impression that my point is that the feminist-philosophy bandwagon is peculiarly awful; I don't know that it is *peculiarly* awful, and in any case it is two quite other points that interest me here. The first is that the perception among these radical feminist philosophers that their profession is profoundly corrupt is, at worst, exaggerated; their profession *is* rife with pseudo-inquiry, and publication, promotion, stardom, etc., *are* cut loose from merit. I emphatically do *not* share the feminists' view that the best way to deal with this is to develop a shadow profession that is no less corrupt, but in which the corruption favors them. But leave that aside. The second point is that it is this perception of the ubiquity of pseudo-inquiry which has induced despair of the possibility of honest inquiry, now an almost obligatory theme in feminist philosophy.

It is an obligatory theme in much other contemporary philosophy too; to repeat, the point is not to pick on the feminists, but to articulate how the epidemic of sham and fake reasoning encouraged by preposterism threatens to loosen our grip on the concepts of truth and inquiry. (Though, I confess, I am struck by the irony of Peirce's writing, "*man* loses his conceptions of truth and of reason," as of O'Brien's unselfconscious assumption that the "young scholars" of whom he writes are "young *men*"; for women, certainly, as contemporary feminist philosophy reveals, are no less susceptible to the consequences of preposterism.)

Thus far, though I have talked at length about the "research ethic" in philosophy, I have said nothing explicit about the ethics of research. Implicit in what I have been saying is the conviction that the "factitious despair" of the possibility of honest inquiry which has begun to be heard in so many quarters of contemporary philosophy will, as Bacon eloquently put it long ago, "cut the sinews and spurs of industry"—and, as Bacon continued, "all for the miserable vainglory of having it believed that whatever has not yet been discovered and comprehended can never be discovered and comprehended hereafter."[53] More strictly ethical is a thought which follows on the heels of this: that it is *indecent* to make one's living as an academic if one does not—as those who despair of the possibility of honest inquiry *can* not—acknowledge what C. I. Lewis once described as our "tacit professional oath never to subordinate the motive

[52] Sandra Harding, "Who Knows? Identities and Feminist Epistemology," in Joan E. Hartman and Ellen Messer-Davidow, eds., *(En)gendering Knowledge* (Knoxville: University of Tennessee Press, 1991), p. 109.

[53] Francis Bacon, *The New Organon* (1620), Book I, aphorism LXXXVIII.

of objective truth-seeking to any subjective preference or inclination or any expediency or opportunistic consideration."[54]

Since this has been in the nature of a lay sermon—and in defiance of the certainty that Rorty will classify me as one of those "old-fashioned prigs" who will "solemnly tell you that they are seeking the truth"[55]—perhaps it is appropriate to end, as sermons do, with a text. Mine is the motto of chapter 11 of George Eliot's *Felix Holt the Radical*:

> Truth is the precious harvest of the earth.
> But once, when harvest waved upon a land,
> The noisome cankerworm and caterpillar,
> Locusts, and all the swarming foul-born broods,
> Fastened upon it with swift, greedy jaws,
> And turned the harvest into pestilence,
> Until men said, What profits it to sow?

*Philosophy, University of Miami*

[54] C. I. Lewis, *The Ground and Nature of the Right* (New York: Columbia University Press, 1955), p. 34.

[55] Richard Rorty, *Essays on Heidegger and Others* (Cambridge: Cambridge University Press, 1991), p. 86.

# INDEX